ECOTOURISM
Principles and Practices

ECOTOURISM
Principles and Practices

Ralf Buckley
International Centre for Ecotourism Research
Griffith University
Gold Coast, Australia

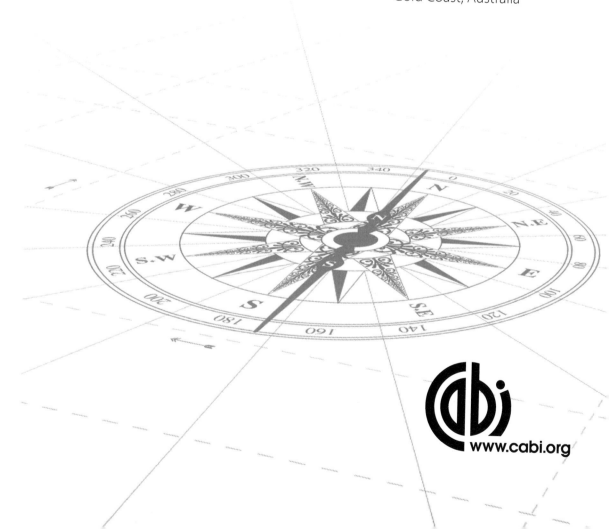

www.cabi.org

CABI is a trading name of CAB International

CABI Head Office
Nosworthy Way
Wallingford
Oxfordshire OX10 8DE
UK
Tel: +44 (0)1491 832111
Fax: +44 (0)1491 833508
E-mail: cabi@cabi.org
Website: www.cabi.org

CABI North American Office
875 Massachusetts Avenue
7th Floor
Cambridge, MA 02139
USA
Tel: +1 617 395 4056
Fax: +1 617 354 6875
E-mail: cabi-nao@cabi.org

A catalogue record for this book is available from the British Library, London, UK.

Library of Congress Cataloging-in-Publication Data

Buckley, Ralf.
  Ecotourism : principles and practices / Ralf Buckley.
    p. cm.
  Includes bibliographical references and index.
  ISBN 978-1-84593-457-6 (alk. paper)
  1. Ecotourism. I. Title.

  G156.5.E26B838 2009
  910.68--dc22

                        2008015475

ISBN: 978 1 84593 457 6

Typeset by SPi, Pondicherry, India.
Printed and bound in the UK by Cambridge University Press, Cambridge.

CONTENTS

ABOUT THE AUTHOR

Ralf Buckley is Professor and Director of the International Centre for Ecotourism Research, established in 1993 at Griffith University, Australia. He has published over 200 journal articles and ten books, including six on ecotourism and related topics. He has several decades' experience in various forms of adventure recreation, and used to work as a tour guide for a US-based international natural history tour company. His research focuses on the various interactions between the tourism industry and the natural environment.

LIST OF TABLES

LIST OF READINGS

PREFACE

The structure adopted for this volume is intended to make it both broadly accessible and easy to update. I hope it will prove useful for practitioners as well as researchers and students; for readers in developing as well as developed nations; and for those with backgrounds either in business or science, tourism or ecology, outdoor education or development studies. In addition, by focusing on fundamentals rather than current controversies, I hope that it can remain relevant for many years.

With these goals in mind, each chapter contains up to five components as follows:

Review	a general overview of the chapter topic in non-technical language
Research	summaries of recent research literature tabulated by topic and geographic region
Revision	lists of major issues in bullet-point format
Reflections	some questions to provoke further consideration
Readings	supplementary materials on specific sub-topics

For some chapter topics, relevant research is sparse, and previous literature is incorporated into the main Review section. For others, however, it is extensive and detailed and is therefore summarized separately in the Research section. Readings are drawn largely from previous work by the author, and are provided only for some chapters, to illustrate particular issues addressed in the Review sections. The balance between information and detail provided in the various sections thus differs between chapters.

This volume is not intended as a self-contained training text for ecotourism operators or tourism analysts. It focuses solely on those components of the tourism sector which are considered under the rubric of ecotourism. It is designed to be studied in conjunction with basic textbooks on tourism more generally, or on environmental or parks management, depending on the reader's particular interests.

In addition, any one author can only bring a single perspective to a topic so broad as ecotourism. There are several other excellent ecotourism textbooks in print, many of them referenced extensively in these chapters. This volume complements their ideas and approaches rather than replacing or encompassing them. That is, I encourage students to read my colleagues' books as well as my own; and I encourage lecturers in ecotourism to prescribe several textbooks simultaneously, not only this one!

This volume is one of a series of ecotourism and related texts by the same publisher, and can best be read in conjunction with those other volumes. Case studies in ecotourism were provided by Buckley (2003a), and in the broader outdoor and adventure sector by Buckley (2006). The environmental impacts of ecotourism were examined in detail in Buckley (2004a), and ecotourism in parks and reserves by Eagles and McCool (2002) and Buckley *et al.* (2003a). This volume updates and summarizes all these issues, but does not duplicate the detail available in those companion volumes, all of which are recommended to the reader.

chapter 1

CONCEPTS
AND DEFINITIONS

Living area of a private wildlife ecolodge in a semi-desert area in Namibia. Note open design for low-energy light and ventilation, ceiling fan, and rustic design and décor. Spherical ornaments mimic the shape of a characteristic local plant.

REVIEW

Introduction

Ecotourism is a useful concept, but not a very well defined one. Various people and organizations have put forward a range of different definitions, from precise to vague, concise to extended. This chapter outlines the history and components of these concepts and definitions, considering related terms and different perspectives, and setting the scene for the later chapters.

History

The earliest known use of the term 'ecotour', undefined, seems to have been by Parks Canada in the 1960s (Fennell, 1999). One heavily promoted though rather verbose definition was put forward by Ceballos-Lascurain (1992). An official international definition was adopted during the UN International Year of Ecotourism in 2002 (UNEP and WTO, 2002). The major components, as analysed by Buckley (1994a) do not seem to have changed: nature-based product, minimal-impact management, environmental education, contribution to conservation. An alternative but congruent analytical concept suggested by Buckley (2003a) namely 'geotourism with a positive triple bottom line' (see Reading 14.1), seems to have received little attention. An analysis of published literature by Donohoe and Needham (2006) identified these same four aspects but also added benefit-sharing and ethics. An analysis of ecotourism literature by Weaver and Lawton (2007) indicated that debates over definition have remained a significant theme.

Purpose

Whether a word needs a precise definition depends on the context in which it is used. If the term 'ecotourism' is being used for marketing, for example, it does not need to be defined at all, as long as it persuades people to buy products. There are, however, several circumstances where a precise definition becomes important.

The first is where any kind of legal or financial decision depends on whether a particular tourism product is considered ecotourism. For example, some protected area management agencies grant preferential access rights or concession conditions to ecotourism operators, relative to tour operators more generally, so they need precise criteria to decide when to apply their own policy. Similarly, government tourism agencies have sometimes provided small-business grant programmes, or subsidized marketing, specifically for ecotourism operators, and once again they then require precise criteria to determine whether particular companies are eligible to apply for such assistance. In both of these instances, the agency concerned has the authority to make its own judgement in relation to any particular operator or product, and will commonly retain the discretion to do so. Where such decisions are based on criteria published in government documents, however, any decision on eligibility may be subject to legal challenge, so a precise definition becomes important.

A precise definition may also be important in the collection of statistics. To compile data on the economics of commercial ecotourism in any country, for example, that country must have a precise and workable definition to decide which companies and products should be included. In addition, if these statistics are to be aggregated at a regional or global scale, or disaggregated into subsidiary jurisdictions, then the same definition needs to be used throughout. Finally, a precise definition can be important in academic analysis, though this depends on the particular question addressed.

Critical criterion

The critical issue distinguishing ecotourism from tourism more generally is the potential positive contribution to conservation of the natural environment. It is this aspect that potentially merits the prefix 'eco', and this is why that prefix is used in the tourism industry but not in other sectors such as mining or manufacturing, forestry or farming. Even if a triple-bottom-line accounting approach is used, it is the environmental bottom line that distinguishes ecotourism from its closest analogues in other sectors. A positive financial bottom line is essential for any self-contained private enterprise to survive and thrive. A positive social bottom line is equally achievable in almost any industry sector, and is also the goal of development aid projects and development non-governmental organizations (NGOs). Improving the bottom line for the natural environment, however, is generally perceived as the province of public-sector protected-area management agencies, multilateral environmental aid and environmental NGOs. Private landowners may indeed contribute to conservation, but they do not generally see this as a core business goal, unless they are paid for it by government agencies. The key feature of ecotourism, therefore, is that private enterprises could potentially generate a positive net contribution to the natural environment, a bottom line with a positive environmental, as well as social and financial, component.

Significance

In practice, it appears that ecotourism enterprises that do in reality make a net positive contribution to conservation are extremely rare, as outlined later. A significant number of enterprises lay claim to some kind of direct or indirect contribution, but with no attempt to account for the net overall effects once direct and indirect costs and impacts are also considered. A much larger number of enterprises lay some claim to reducing overall environmental impacts through some form of environmental management or technology, but with no suggestion of any active positive contribution to conservation. And a still larger number of enterprises, indeed the majority of those that refer to themselves as ecotourism, mean only that they take advantage of the natural environment as a key part of the tourism product, with no suggestion that they help to conserve that natural environment through any of the mechanisms envisaged in the UN definition of ecotourism and considered in more detail in this book. There are even companies that use the term 'ecotour' to sell products that have no connection to nature. On Australia's Gold Coast, for example, there is a minibus shuttle company specializing in airport transfers, which uses the word 'ecotour' in the company name. If challenged, they claim that the term refers only to an economical price.

Despite the endless debate over definitions of ecotourism and the many uses and misuses to which the term is put, the concept remains valuable in a number of contexts. Perhaps most importantly, there are cases, albeit few, where ecotourism does indeed fund conservation in developing countries. There are cases where the concept may perhaps help the commercial tourism industry to promote low-impact rather than high-impact activities in public protected areas, though there is rather little evidence that it actually does achieve this successfully. There is the often-mentioned possibility that ecotourism operators could lead the way to improve environmental management throughout the mainstream tourism industry, through a kind of demonstration effect. This does seem to have happened to some degree.

Even if ecotourism has not yet lived up to its full potential in any of these arenas, it is none the less a significant social phenomenon in the sense that many travellers claim to be ecotourists and many travel companies claim to practice ecotourism. In addition, ecotourism has become a significant component in the lexicon of international development policy and assistance, referred to routinely as a potential new source of income for any area with a scenic landscape, whether natural or cultural. The UN International Year of Ecotourism in 2002 was itself an indicator of the importance that multilateral agencies attach to ecotourism (Weaver and Lawton, 2007).

Perspectives

There are several different perspectives from which ecotourism can usefully be analysed. The majority of the academic research literature in this field takes a normative approach, i.e. it starts with a concept of how ecotourism ought to operate or what it should be able to achieve, and then compares actual tourism products and enterprises against these norms. A second approach is to focus on marketing, the kinds of claim that enterprises make about their own operations under the heading of ecotourism. A third approach, arguably most important but least often adopted, is to analyse and quantify what tourism enterprises actually do in relation to the natural environment: how they actually incorporate it into tourism products, what actual steps they take to reduce environmental impacts and what actual impacts they have.

A wide variety of terms have been adopted by different authors, both academic and otherwise, to promote concepts allied to ecotourism. Most of these terms remain rather vague and undefined. Some came into vogue for a short period but no longer seem to be in use. Some are common in current use, but have a different meaning from the term 'ecotourism' itself. There are also various terms that have been used to indicate subdivisions or different types of ecotourism. A short glossary of such terms is given in Table 1.1.

Product terms

Most of the various definitions of ecotourism, and related concepts as outlined in Table 1.2, refer to various operational aspects as well as the primary product or attraction. There is also a suite of more straightforward terms, which are based purely on that product or attraction. Thus, 'wildlife tourism' (Newsome *et al.*, 2005) simply means tourism where the primary attraction is watching wildlife. This can include marine as well as terrestrial wildlife (Cater and Cater, 2007), and it can also include captive as well as free-ranging animals. It can also include consumptive activities such as hunting and fishing, as well as non-consumptive wildlife watching,

Table 1.1. Terms related to ecotourism.

Term	Meaning
Green tourism	An early term essentially synonymous with ecotourism, but never very well defined.
Alternative tourism	A term used in the academic tourism literature to draw a distinction from mainstream or mass tourism; effectively, therefore, it means any kind of tourism with a small or specialist market, or any product that cannot normally be booked through a mainstream travel agent.
Endemic tourism	A little-used phrase, derived from a term used in biology, and intended to indicate any type of tourism product where the primary attraction occurs only in a particular localized area.
Geotourism (geological version)	Tourism where the primary attraction is a geological feature, including spectacular scenery (Dowling and Newsome, 2006); little-used.
Geotourism (geographic version)	Usage proposed by *National Geographic*, closely similar to ecotourism; not taken up widely, confusion over meaning.
Responsible tourism	Little-used term, presumably derived by analogy with the 'Responsible Care' initiative by the chemical industry; focus on social considerations.
Sustainable tourism	Heavily used but poorly defined term, indicating tourism that complies with the principles of sustainable development, which is itself a very vague and much contested expression; refers broadly to environmental management in the mainstream tourism industry, not restricted to ecotourism; adopted in the UNWTO Tour Operators Initiative for Sustainable Tourism, TOIST.

whalewatching, birdwatching, photo safaris, game lodges, etc. Not all forms of wildlife tourism, therefore, would necessarily qualify as ecotourism.

'Nature tourism' or 'nature-based tourism' (Newsome *et al.*, 2002a; Buckley *et al.*, 2003a) is a somewhat broader term, covering all types of tourism that rely on relatively undisturbed natural environments or natural features. Nature-based tourism thus includes wildlife tourism, but it also includes tourism based on plants or vegetation and on natural scenery, as long as the principal activity is essentially observation or contemplation.

If the natural environment is used principally as a setting for adrenalin-based or outdoor sporting activities, it would be considered adventure tourism (Buckley, 2006) rather than nature-based tourism. There are fine distinctions between sport, recreation and adventure tourism;

Table 1.2. Related product terms.

Term	Meaning
Nature or nature-based	Any kind of tourism where features of the natural environment provide the primary attraction
Wildlife	Tourism where the main attraction is the opportunity to watch wild animals
Adventure	Tourism where the main attraction is an outdoor activity with an excitement-based component
Cultural	Tourism that focuses on exposing or introducing tourists to different local cultures
ACE	Aggregate term: Adventure–Culture–Ecotourism
NEAT	Aggregate term: Nature, Eco- and Adventure Tourism
Outdoor	All forms of tourism that take place outdoors: essentially the same as NEAT, but including high-impact and consumptive tourism such as motorized vehicles, hunting, etc.

adventure can include urban activities as well as those in a natural setting. There is no clear dividing line between adventure tourism and nature-based tourism, since different participants on the same tour may perceive the same experiences in different ways. The term 'outdoor tourism' has sometimes been used to include nature-based and adventure tourism in a single term. Both nature-based tours and adventure tours may potentially qualify as ecotourism, but neither need necessarily do so.

In contrast to nature and adventure tourism, cultural tourism emphasizes human rather than natural environments. Specifically, it refers to tourism products where the primary attraction is the opportunity for tourists to experience a culture different from their own. This difference may be relatively small, as for example when tourists travel between regions or countries within Europe, Asia, Latin America or North America, or it may be quite considerable, as for example when wealthy urban tourists from developed nations travel to remote rural areas in developing nations. The degree of cross-cultural interaction between tourists and host community may also differ greatly between tours. The defining feature, however, is that the culture of the host community becomes part of the tourism product. The term 'cultural tourism' does not in itself indicate whether the host culture is authentic or commodified, or whether any cross-cultural interactions are mutually educational and respectful. These are issues that are incorporated in some conceptual approaches to ecotourism, but they refer to social impacts, not product packaging.

In practice, many real-life retail tourist products contain both natural and cultural attractions, and may also contain adventurous elements or activities. At least two authors have suggested composite terms that reflect this overlap. Fennell (1999) suggested the term 'ACE' (Adventure–

Culture–Ecotourism), where ecotourism may be interpreted to include nature tourism more broadly. Buckley (2000a) suggested the term 'NEAT', standing for Nature, Eco- and Adventure Tourism, with no reference to culture. The general term 'outdoor tourism' has also been used with essentially the same meaning as NEAT (Buckley, 2006).

A somewhat different conceptual approach was proposed by Buckley (2003b), who drew a distinction between inputs from the natural environment to commercial ecotourism products, and outputs from those products to the natural environment. The inputs may include aspects of the setting, the activity, the attraction and marketing. The outputs may include both environmental impacts, which represent a cost to conservation of the natural environment, and potentially at least, various possible positive contributions, which ecotourism could make towards conservation of the natural environment. Environmental management measures, environmental education programmes and mechanisms to contribute to conservation may be seen as tools to increase positive and reduce negative outputs. The success of these tools can then be measured using a triple-bottom-line accounting approach (Chapter 14).

Conclusions

This volume examines the principles and practices of ecotourism from an analytical rather than a normative perspective, i.e. it attempts to summarize, analyse and present the various links between tourism and environment as they actually operate in the real world, rather than how they might ideally operate in a conceptual sense.

Chapter 2 outlines the commercial context for ecotourism, considering tourism subsectors that are closely related to ecotourism but distinguishable on various criteria. Chapters 3–5 examine the basics of ecotourism business operations, products and marketing, leading to a broader review of the economics of the ecotourism subsector in Chapter 6.

Chapters 7, 8 and 9 consider environmental management, impacts and contributions to conservation, leading on to guiding and interpretation in Chapter 10, social and community issues in Chapter 11 and access to operating areas in Chapter 12. This in turn leads to broader-scale planning aspects in Chapter 13, and triple-bottom-line accounting aspects in Chapter 14. The concluding chapter then evaluates practical progress in ecotourism to date, against all of these criteria.

RESEARCH

In the early days of ecotourism, environmental organizations generally insisted that only tourism that is nature-based, sustainably managed, conservation-supporting and environmentally educated should be described as ecotourism (Ziffer, 1986; Boo, 1990; Ceballos-Lascurain, 1992; Eber, 1992; Swanson, 1992; Figgiss, 1993; Young and Wearing, 1993). Industry and government, however, focused more on the product aspect, often treating ecotourism as effectively synonymous with nature-based tourism. Environmental management aspects were often considered under rubrics such as 'sustainable' or 'responsible tourism' (Ashworth and Goodall, 1990; Pigram, 1990; Buckley, 1991a; Butler and Waldbrook, 1991; Farrell and Runyan, 1991).

Definitions of ecotourism have subsequently been devised, dissected, deconstructed and reconstructed at enormous length. Much of the relevant literature is rather repetitive. As some indication of the degree of attention devoted to this issue, it has been discussed in over 30 different publications since 1990. These include Fennell and Eagles (1990); Boo (1990); Farrell and Runyon (1991); Whelan (1991); Buckley (1994a); Cater and Lowman (1994); Hvenegaard (1994); Nelson (1994); Stewart and Sekartjakrarini (1994); Bottrill and Pearce (1995); Markwell (1995); Orams (1995); Brandon (1996); Goodwin (1996); Blamey (1997, 2001); Jaakson (1997); Lindberg and McKercher (1997); Burton (1998); Fennell (1998, 1999); Lew (1998); McLaren (1998); Diamantis (1999); Ross and Wall (1999a); Bjork (2000); Ryan *et al.* (2000); Mader (2002); Nyaupane and Thapa (2004); Cater (2006); Donohoe and Needham (2006); Cousins (2007); and Weaver and Lawton (2007).

In addition to these general discussions about defining ecotourism as a sector, several authors have focused on defining ecotourists as a category of tourists. These include, for example, Kretchman and Eagles (1990); Ballantine and Eagles (1994); Crossley and Lee (1994); Eagles and Cascagnette (1995); Diamantis (1998); Woods and Moscardo (1998); and Young (1999). Crossley and Lee (1994), MacKay *et al.* (1996), and Hvenegaard and Dearden (1998) set out specifically to differentiate ecotourists from mass tourists, each in a different geographical region. Amador (1997) distinguished ecotourists from cultural tourists, and de los Monteros (2002) distinguished them from nature-based tourists. Various authors have subdivided or segmented ecotourism in different ways, including Palacio and McCool (1997), Acott *et al.* (1998), Malloy and Fennell (1998), Weaver (2005), and Zografos and Allcroft (2007).

The concept of ecotourism has also come in for criticism from several authors, including Pleumarom (1993, 1994, 1995), Munt (1994), Wheeller (1994a,b, 1997), Mowforth and Munt (2003) and Stern *et al.* (2003).

REVISION

Disputed definitions

- Ecotourism means different things to different people
- Principles not always met in practice
- Many definitions proposed

History of definitions

- First use: Parks Canada in 1960s
- Heavily quoted: Ceballos-Lascurain (1992)
- Analysis of components: Buckley (1994a)

- Internationally accepted: World Ecotourism Summit (2002)
- Also cited: The International Ecotourism Society (2007)

Key components

- Nature-based product
- Minimal-impact management
- Environmental education
- Contribution to conservation

Input–output framework

- Environment as input to ecotourism products
- Ecotourism impacts as outputs to environment
- Triple-bottom-line accounting approach
- Impact management, environmental education, conservation contributions as tools
- Net bottom line needs measurement

Definition or concept?

- For most purposes a general concept is enough
- Precise definition needed only for statistical or legal reasons
- For example, if ecotourism operators get preferential parks permits
- Or if they get access to particular government funds
- Or inclusion in particular marketing programme

Critical issue

- Net benefit for environment
- That is, contribution to conservation outweighs impacts
- Contributions may be direct or indirect

Why does ecotourism matter?

- Can fund conservation in developing countries
- Can reduce tourism impacts in protected areas
- Might improve environmental management in mainstream tourism
- It is a significant social phenomenon
- It is used as a development policy instrument
- UN International Year of Ecotourism 2002

Ecotourism theory and practice

- Normative – how it 'ought to be'
- Descriptive – how it is
- Marketing – using it to sell tours

Related terms

- Sustainable tourism
- Responsible tourism
- Alternative tourism
- Geotourism
- And more!

Related sectors

- Nature-based tourism
- Adventure tourism
- Wildlife tourism
- Cultural tourism

Aggregate terms

- ACE (Fennell, 1999)
- NEAT (Buckley, 2002a)
- Outdoor tourism

REFLECTIONS

1. Search the World Wide Web for ecotourism definitions. Are they all similar, or different? Are there common components and, if so, what are they? Do the different definitions reflect the interests of the people or organizations who put them forward and, if so, how?

2. Select one particular tourism operator that advertises an ecotourism product: one you have experienced yourself; one that is reported in a relevant publication; or one described in detail on a website. Compare the product against the defining criteria for ecotourism as outlined in this chapter. How well does it satisfy those criteria and how can you tell?

3. Which do you think is a more useful term, 'ecotourism' or 'sustainable tourism'? How do they differ and how does each contribute to: (i) the tourism industry and (ii) the natural environment?

4. Many countries have their own ecotourism associations or societies. Find the official websites of several such groups and compare their activities. Are they involved in marketing, information exchange, training, certification or what?

chapter 2

RELATED SECTORS

Whitewater rapid on a first commercial descent of a Himalayan river in far north-eastern India, an area only recently opened for tourism. The tour used both rafts and kayaks, with guides and clients of many different nationalities.

REVIEW

Introduction

Real-life retail tourism products and tour operators cannot always be parcelled up into cleanly divided categories. As noted in Chapter 1, different people use different definitions for ecotourism itself, and hence draw different boundaries between ecotourism and related subsectors. Some concepts of ecotourism, for example, include cultural components, whereas others do not. Some concepts effectively include the entire range of nature-based tourism products, whereas others are much more restricted because of environmental management, interpretation and conservation criteria. This chapter examines subsectors of the tourism industry that are closely related to ecotourism but none the less distinct.

Types of outdoor tourism

In broad terms, it seems useful to distinguish five types of outdoor tourism that are closely related to ecotourism: nature, wildlife, adventure, cultural and farm tourism. Note that these subsectors are defined purely with reference to the product or principal attraction, and do not include the operational or outcome criteria applied specifically in ecotourism. In addition, there are marine components both to ecotourism as strictly defined, and to the related nature, wildlife and adventure tourism subsectors, and these marine components are largely distinct, in functional terms, from their terrestrial counterparts (Cater and Cater, 2007).

Nature tourism, also known as nature-based tourism, is a broad term that covers all types of tourism where features of the natural environment are the principal attraction. Thus, it includes low-key scenic sightseeing, as well as more specialist product subsectors such as wildlife tourism, and more tightly defined subsectors such as ecotourism. Nature tourism is a term used more by analysts than practitioners. It is not a phrase commonly used in corporate marketing materials. Tour operators would be more likely to use terms such as natural history, scenery or wildlife, or ecotourism. From an analytical perspective, however, it is a useful term, since it describes the product aspect of ecotourism without reference to the more contested management aspects. Much of this volume, to the extent that it describes nature-based products, business, management and marketing, refers as much to nature as to ecotourism.

The wildlife tourism subsector is a large and well-defined component of the nature tourism sector more generally. It is often treated as a distinct subsector in its own right. There are at least three books specifically on wildlife tourism: Shackley (1996), Higginbottom *et al.* (2001) and, most recently, Newsome *et al.* (2005). Again, much of this volume applies as much to wildlife tourism as to nature tourism more broadly, and many of the examples used to illustrate particular aspects of ecotourism might equally well be classified as wildlife tourism. Wildlife watching, however, also involves a specialized set of management issues associated with animal behaviour, and most especially with the various interactions between humans and wildlife. These are considered in more detail in this chapter.

In a similar way, some tours marketed under an adventure label could equally be considered ecotours, but others could not. The distinction depends on the activity involved and on the design of the tour product and management of the tour clients. The majority of the adventure tourism subsector, however, involves relatively high-impact activities and is marketed to clients who are not necessarily concerned about conservation of the natural environment. At least two books have been written specifically on adventure tourism, by Swarbrooke *et al.* (2003) and Buckley (2006). An additional volume edited by Hudson (2002) focuses principally on fixed-site outdoor sports such as ski resorts, but also includes adventure tourism more broadly. There are also a number of volumes on outdoor recreation, the forerunner to commercial adventure tourism and still a very large sector in its own right (e.g. Manning, 1999; Pigram and Jenkins, 2006). In view of the recent review of the adventure tourism subsector (Buckley, 2006), adventure tourism is not addressed here in any detail.

Interactions with wildlife

There are many different types or categories of tourism based on wildlife, with corresponding variation in the degree of impact on the animal populations concerned. The most common perception of this subsector is of non-consumptive terrestrial wildlife tourism, which includes: safaris, off-road tours, guided rides and walks; game lodges and jungle lodges; and birdwatching tours and wildlife cruises. From an economic perspective, however, the largest subsector is consumptive terrestrial and wildlife tourism, which includes sport hunting and bow hunting, and recreational fishing and angling.

There are parallel patterns in marine wildlife tourism. Above-water, non-consumptive marine wildlife tourism includes tour products where the primary attraction involves watching whales or dolphins, seals or sea lions, or seabirds such as penguins, puffins or albatross. Below the water, most forms of recreational diving and snorkelling may be considered marine wildlife tourism. This includes tourism specifically to watch sharks, rays or whalesharks, and many of the more general diving and snorkelling tours on offer worldwide. There is also a consumptive marine wildlife tourism sector, which includes game-fishing and bill-fishing, recreational spearfishing, and shell and coral collecting. Since even catch-and-release fishing causes significant mortality, these types of tours are not considered ecotourism.

Tourism products based on wildlife differ enormously in the types of interaction between people and animals, and the consequent impacts on the animals. Broadly, there are four main types of interaction.

There are hunting and fishing trips where individual animals are caught and/or killed. At least some hunting safari operators in some countries, however, argue that their industry helps to conserve habitat and populations of the species concerned (Buckley, 2003a, pp. 208–215). It is worth remembering that the World Wide Fund for Nature, formerly the World Wildlife Fund, was originally established to maintain wildlife populations for recreational hunting.

There are not necessarily any conservation benefits from hunting tourism in general, however. For example, there are many instances where target species have been introduced to areas where are not native, specifically for recreational hunting, with major ecological impacts on native wildlife and vegetation. There are also cases, however, where non-native animal species introduced for commercial production have become feral, and recreational hunting may help to control populations. A number of fish species, notably various trout, have also been introduced to lakes and rivers where they are not native, specifically for recreational angling. Again, these introductions have had major ecological impacts on native fish species. For all these reasons, and despite a few arguments to the contrary, hunting and fishing tourism are not generally considered forms of ecotourism.

The second category of human–wildlife interaction in the wildlife tourism industry is with captive wildlife. There is enormous variation within this sector, from well-managed wildlife parks where the animals live in near-natural conditions and tourists travel through the same habitat area in order to see them; through a variety of zoos where the animals are held in cages or close enclosures and the tourists watch them through bars or fences; to cases where individual animals, commonly icon species, are tethered for tourists to watch or even touch. There are also so-called petting zoos, specifically for tourists to handle the animals, but these usually involve domestic livestock rather than native wildlife. For many zoos and wildlife reserves, the organization's principal aim is conservation of the animal species concerned, and tourism is a way to fund conservation programmes and to educate the public about conservation.

The third major form of interaction is between tourists and free-living but habituated wildlife. This is the principal form of interaction in the case of commercial wildlife tours and safaris, including those that would qualify as ecotourism. Habituation takes many different forms. For a wildlife-watching ecotour, the ideal is a so-called neutral interaction: the animals ignore human presence with no change to their behaviour. To achieve this generally takes a significant period of time, sometimes more than one generation of the wildlife concerned, so that the animals perceive humans neither as a threat, nor as a source of benefits, nor as potential prey or competitors; the humans learn to interpret the subtleties of animal behaviour and body language, and to keep a sufficient distance and behave in such a way as to avoid any disturbance to the wildlife. There are a number of commercial wildlife safari and ecotour operators who do seem to have achieved this goal, generally in private conservation reserves where nobody else has access to the animals concerned. These, however, are the minority.

At the other extreme, and far more commonplace, are individual animals that have become habituated to expect benefits from interacting with humans, typically in the form of food. Feeding wildlife has a range of actual and potential ecological impacts (Buckley, 2004b, pp. 216–217), but it typically provides tourists with a much closer, albeit less natural, interaction than would otherwise be the case. Examples of habituation due to routine feeding include a wide range of wildlife species: parrots and other birds, monkeys and marsupials, various species of dolphin, and a variety of both bony and cartilaginous fish.

There are also a number of instances where habituation has led animals to tolerate the negative consequences of interactions with tourists because it is too difficult or too costly to avoid such interactions, despite the disturbance they cause. Examples include: helicopter sightseeing of surfacing sperm whales off Kaikoura, New Zealand; coachloads of tourists watching fairy penguins come ashore on Phillip Island in Victoria, Australia; tourists watching adult marine turtles laying eggs on sandy beaches throughout the tropics and subtropics; spotlighting safaris and tours of nocturnal mammals in many sites worldwide; and tourists watching wildlife at regular watering holes or feeding spots, such as bears fishing for salmon on the cold temperate coastlines of north-east Asia and north-west North America. All of these animals are forced to tolerate human disturbance to a certain degree, because they need access to air, water, food and/or breeding sites simply for survival.

The fourth main category of human–wildlife interaction involves free-ranging and non-habituated animals encountered by accident, by skilled tracking or by knowledge of the animals' behaviour. Under these circumstances, most animals are likely to flee or attack rather than simply ignore the humans. To get a good view of non-habituated wildlife generally requires skilled stalking, so that the animals are not aware of the human presence. Since relatively few commercial ecotourism clients have the necessary stalking skills and experience, this approach is rarely used in commercial wildlife-watching tours. It is, however, used in many birdwatching tours, and also in a variety of boat-based tours where animals on shorelines or riverbanks can be approached quietly from the water.

Different types of wildlife tour involve different levels and types of interaction. From a product perspective, there is a trade-off between the chance that clients will get good views of a particular species, and the chance that the individual animals concerned will be behaving naturally. For a backcountry tour where icon wildlife species are significant in marketing but unlikely to be seen either often or closely, tour operators need to make sure they do not make promises they cannot keep. Thus, for example, a High Arctic seakayak tour may advertise searching for narwhal, rather than watching them (Buckley, 2005a, 2006). In countries with rather more lax trade practices legislation, tour operators may quite commonly advertise icon wildlife species as though there was a good chance to see them, even if in reality they are very rare and very rarely seen. Hiking tours in Ecuador, for example, may advertise tapir and cock-of-the-rock (Buckley, 2006, pp. 288–298). This approach, however, is not likely to bring much repeat business, unless clients enjoy other aspects of the tour enough to offset not seeing icon species.

Most of the more up-market and best-known wildlife tourism operations rely on animals that have been habituated very carefully over many years to achieve the essentially neutral interaction referred to above, so that a highly skilled guide can provide opportunities for completely unskilled clients to see icon wildlife species at close range with little or no behavioural modification. Some of the older private game reserves in southern Africa provide particularly well-known examples.

Even once the animals are well habituated, a considerable level of guiding skill is required to interpret the nuances of animal behaviour and also to exercise tight control over the behaviour of the clients. The former is needed because there are many circumstances, notably when protecting immobile offspring or when feeding during a seasonal energy deficit period, when animals may not flee from human disturbance even if they are significantly stressed. Guides need sufficiently detailed knowledge of the particular species, and sometimes particular individuals, to interpret whether they are relaxed, fearful or aggressive.

Equally, the way in which the animals react to human disturbance depends on how the humans behave. For example, animals habituated to seeing people in vehicles may react very differently to people on foot. Guides must therefore be able to persuade all their clients to follow predefined behavioural protocols without any breaches. Generally, such protocols are very simple, such as sitting still and making no noise, but it can be difficult to ensure that every one of the clients follows even a simple instruction at all times.

Interactions with other cultures

The opportunity to experience different human cultures is one of the earliest reasons for tourism, and interactions between tourists and local residents are a long-standing and heavily studied topic of tourism research. Many cultural tourism products have little or no relation to ecotourism: for example, urban tours to see art or architecture, foods or fashion. Likewise, many nature and adventure tours, or even those with an archaeological component, may involve very little interaction with locals or modern cultures.

Equally, however, there are many retail tour products, especially in developing nations, which combine natural and cultural attractions, and there are many academic analyses of ecotourism that emphasize a cultural component.

The types of cultural attraction and degree of cultural interaction differ greatly between individual tour products. At one extreme, there are tour operations where the local on-ground component is owned and led entirely by a local indigenous community, and the tour consists of an introduction to the natural environment through the eyes of an indigenous inhabitant living a traditional lifestyle. However, at the other extreme, there are many nature and adventure tours where the cultural component is limited to a few hours' local shopping, often advertised as 'retail therapy', before the international flight home.

Between these extremes, there is an enormous variety of different cultural attractions and interactions. A tourist visiting a wildlife lodge in sub-Saharan Africa principally to see wildlife, for example, is likely to meet: people from local communities working as game-drive guides and wildlife trackers; local staff working in lodges in positions up to and including senior management; staff and/or local residents who may put on dance performances or other events for the lodge's guests; and, if they wish, residents of local communities including schoolteachers and school children, health clinic workers, and people selling artefacts.

Many tourists seem to experience some confusion over the crossover between traditional and modern cultures in many regions of the world. They expect a clear contrast between developed and developing nations, between Western and traditional societies. They are surprised when they find, for example, that there are often enormous disparities in wealth between different members of the same indigenous community; or that traditional and Western religions have been blended into an eclectic amalgam, which is the basis for social codes of behaviour; or that local people will use modern weapons to hunt traditional prey for social status rather than subsistence; or that local staff of a tourist lodge will appear dressed in traditional costume but perform what appears to be an MTV dance routine. All these paradoxes, however, occur equally within Western societies; and local residents may be equally confused about the behaviour of Western tourists who deliberately choose to travel on foot or by seakayak while they themselves are travelling in four-wheel-drive vehicles or speedboats.

Farm tourism

With its origins in rural hospitality, bed-and-breakfast establishments and dude ranches, farm tourism now contributes a significant component of income streams for farm landholders in many parts of the world. These tourism products fall into two main categories: those actually based on farming activities and farm landscapes, and those based on scenery, terrain and natural environments, which happen to be on private farm landholdings. Generally, only the former is considered farm tourism; the latter is considered nature or adventure tourism as the case may be.

In various parts of the world, there are traditional farming landscapes that are sufficiently well-known to have become tourism attractions, either in their own right, e.g. as views from a tour bus, or packaged with local accommodation and food, in the form of a rural holiday. Examples of such landscapes include Mediterranean olive groves, French vineyards, dairy farms in the Swiss Alps, sheep farms in the English Lake District, rice paddies in South-east Asia, terrace cultivation in China and the Himalayas, and many more. Farm tourism operations in North America, Europe and elsewhere have been reviewed and compared recently by Ollenburg (2008).

Some types of farming, particularly broad-acre cattle ranching where the stock are driven on horseback, have developed a particular romantic attraction for some tourists, apparently driven by the 'cowboy' genre of literature, film and music. In addition to the cowboys on the dude and working ranches of the American West, this category of farm tourism also includes stockmen on cattle stations in the Australian outback, gauchos on the pampas of South America, and perhaps also the horse-based cultures of Central Asia. In practical product terms, any of these may be combined with nature and adventure attractions and activities in the same regions. There are also farms that have set up farm-related but entirely commodified attractions such as petting zoos and corn mazes, as a way to attract urban tourists for a day or overnight visit. These, needless to say, have little connection to nature or adventure tourism products.

Conclusions

Ecotourism as narrowly defined (Chapter 1) is part of a much broader tourism product sector, which includes the nature, wildlife, adventure, cultural and perhaps also farm or rural tourism. Considerations relating to business basics, products and marketing in ecotourism, covered in the next three chapters, also apply broadly across these related subsectors. It is only the environmental management, education and conservation components, considered later in this volume, that distinguish ecotourism.

RESEARCH

Research in tourism subsectors related to ecotourism has been reviewed recently in a number of books and need not be reiterated here. Nature-based tourism has been examined by Newsome *et al.* (2002a) and Buckley *et al.* (2003a), and wildlife tourism by Newsome *et al.* (2005). The particular case of tourism in parks, protected areas and wilderness areas has been examined extensively by, for example, Eagles and McCool (2002), Hendee and Dawson (2002), Lockwood *et al.* (2006) and Pigram and Jenkins (2006). Recent research on parks as tourism attractions in Sweden has been reported by McDonald *et al.* (2007). Marine ecotourism, including marine nature-based tourism, has been reviewed recently by Cater and Cater (2007). In the wildlife tourism subsector, Higham and Bejder (2008) examined questions of sustainability, and Coghlan and Prideaux (2008) found that most visitors to Cairns, Australia would rather visit a wildlife park than take a wildlife tour. The adventure tourism subsector has been reviewed recently by Buckley (2006) and previously, with a somewhat different emphasis, by Swarbrooke *et al.* (2003). Particular aspects of adventure tourism are also considered by Pomfret (2006) and Buckley (2007, 2008). Patterns and developments in farm and rural tourism have been described by, for example, Fennell and Weaver (1997) in Canada; Bryan and Whelan (1991), Gartner (2004) and McGehee (2007) in the USA; Ollenburg and Buckley (2007) in Australia; Busby and Rendle (2000) in the UK; Alsos and Carter (2006) in Norway; and Barke (2004) and Hall (2004a) in southern Europe. The particular case of volunteer farm tourism in New Zealand is reported by McIntosh and Bonneman (2006). The most recent global comparative review is provided by Ollenburg (2008).

REVISION

Main types

- Nature
- Wildlife
- Adventure
- Culture
- Farm

Nature tourism

- Broad term, refers to natural attractions
- Used by analysts more than industry
- Includes ecotourism
- But also all tourism based on natural attractions
- Irrespective of management, interpretation, or conservation
- Includes wildlife tourism but also tourism based principally on scenery

Wildlife tourism

- Consumptive cf. non-consumptive
- Terrestrial cf. marine
- Levels of habituation
- Types of interaction

Adventure tourism

- High-volume, low-skill, low-price, cf.
- Low-volume, high-skill, high-price
- Expanding edge of tourism industry
- Worldwide geography
- >20 activity subsectors
- Often combined with nature/ecotours

Cultural tourism

- Cultural immersion tours
- Language tours
- Art, music, dance
- Museums, heritage
- Traditional customs
- Artefacts and retail

Farm tourism

- Natural attractions on private rangeland
- Traditional farming practices as tourist attraction
- Cowboy, stockman, gaucho, baqueano
- Dairy cattle, sheep fells, olive groves, etc.
- Vineyards, orchards
- Farm-related activities:
  - Horse trails, sheep-shearing demonstrations
  - Children's farm activities

REFLECTIONS

1. Ecotourism, nature-based tourism, cultural tourism and adventure tourism are sometimes treated as separate sectors, and sometimes as a single combined sector under titles such as ACE or NEAT. Which approach do you think is more accurate or useful, under what circumstances, and why?

2. It has been suggested that the same individual tour can represent an adventure experience for one participant, but a nature-based or cultural experience for another participant on the same tour at the same time. Do you think that this would be commonplace or unusual, and why? Provide an example of a particular tour, real or imaginary, where this situation could arise, and explain how.

3. Choose any one kind of outdoor tourism activity that can be used as the basis for ecotourism, and trace its financial and social links to other industry sectors, including those outside the tourism industry itself. Which of these links are most important for the example you have chosen, and why?

READING 2.1. THE NEAT SECTOR

Introduction

This reading examines three interrelated trends as follows: (i) emergence of a recognizable industry subsector incorporating nature, eco- and adventure tourism (NEAT); (ii) recognition of its economic significance, and initial attempts to quantify its economic scale; (iii) growth of commercial tourism and private recreation in many protected areas to a scale where it jeopardizes conservation objectives, producing new economic opportunities for tourism in other public and private lands. Clearly, there are links between these. Until the boundaries of the sector are defined, its economic scale is not quantifiable and its economic significance not apparent, and once its scale is recognized, land management agencies see it as a potential source of revenue and a major management issue.

Recognizable NEAT sector

There has been endless debate over the precise meaning of terms such as 'ecotourism', 'nature-based tourism' and 'sustainable tourism' (Lindberg and McKercher, 1997; Stabler, 1997; Lindberg *et al.*, 1998; Hall and Lew, 1999). To date, however, this debate has not defined a recognizable market sector analogous to sectors such as MICE (Meetings, Incentives, Conventions and Events), or VFR (Visiting Friends and Relatives).

The reasons seem to be as follows. First, these terms confound criteria relating to product, as in nature-based tourism, with criteria relating to environmental management, as in sustainable tourism. Second, environmental management may indeed be an important component of the product, for some clients, so the distinction is not entirely straightforward. Third, many stakeholders consider two additional criteria in defining ecotourism, namely education about the environment and a contribution to conservation (Buckley, 1994a); different stakeholders use these criteria in different combinations.

Thus for tourism marketers, almost any form of nature-based tourism is advertised as ecotourism, irrespective of environmental management, education or conservation. Some community-based environmental groups would not classify tourism as ecotourism unless it incorporates all four of these components. Indeed, some such groups have coined terms such as 'eco-terrorism' to describe the growth of high-impact tourism in natural areas (Hanneberg, 1994; McLaren, 1998). Government agencies in developing nations or depressed rural and regional economies use the term to mean tourism growth that is based on local natural and cultural features and provides both local employment and a boost to the regional economy.

I suggest that there is now substantial coalescence, in markets, operators and concepts, between nature-based tourism, ecotourism, adventure travel and outdoor recreation, and that this coalescence is sufficient to recognize a distinct NEAT sector, as least as well defined as MICE or VFR.

Note that the NEAT sector does not include so-called 3,4,5-S tourism (sun, sand, surf, shopping and/or sex), because the latter is largely urban. In particular, the final S is commonly linked to built beachside attractions, whether cafes or casinos, surf clubs or nightclubs. Of course, there are overlaps. There are NEAT operators who offer tours to wilderness beaches, and any group activity may potentially offer new social opportunities. There are also tourists who buy products in both NEAT and 3S sectors, just as there are MICE travellers who buy a 3S or NEAT add-on, but the NEAT sector, where nature and adventure are the product's primary attraction, is quite well differentiated from 3S packages.

NEAT is a product sector. NEAT products do not necessarily incorporate best-practice environmental management, nor an educational component or a contribution to conservation. Some do, some do not. Those that do, may or may not be considered ecotourism, depending on definitions, but by any definition, ecotourism is part of the NEAT sector.

Economic size and significance

There has been considerable debate in many countries over the economic size and significance of the ecotourism subsector. On the one hand, some countries consider their entire tourism industry to be nature-based. On the other, academic analysts have suggested that only 1–2% of Canada or Australia's tourism products qualify as ecotourism in the strict sense of the word (McKercher, 1998).

The difficulty is that the more complex and stringent definitions of ecotourism are not easily translated into forms suitable for collecting economic statistics. From an environmental perspective, it may be useful to consider an ecotourism continuum, based on the aggregate degree to which a tour operator or activity complies with the various criteria for ecotourism.

From a marketing perspective, it may be useful to ask how significant each of the components of ecotourism are in influencing tourism product purchasing decisions by individual tourists.

However, from an economic perspective, it is more meaningful if the tourism sector can be partitioned into mutually exclusive and measurable subsectors with no gaps or overlaps. The NEAT concept makes this feasible.

The total value of the NEAT subsector in the USA, including equipment, was estimated a decade ago at US$220 billion per annum, or about half the size of the tourism industry as a whole. About half of this repres ents equipment, about one seventh is tours, and most of the remainder is fixed-site adventure attractions (Mallett, 1998). Preliminary estimates for Australia, assuming a similar structure to the USA, indicated that the NEAT sector was then worth US$7–15 billion per annum, or about a quarter to a third of the total tourism industry (Buckley, 1998a). This was a 1998 supply-side estimate. A 1995 demand-side estimate, calculated by questioning individual tourists, was slightly lower at US$6.6 billion (Blamey and Hatch, 1998). This, however, was only for international visitors and only for the nature tourism sector, i.e. excluding adventure tourism, equipment etc. A 1998 demand-side estimate (Tourism Queensland, 1999) indicated that about 27% of tourists in Australia were 'definite ecotourists' distinguished by multiple criteria such as taking vacations in natural locations, undertaking nature-based activities, and appreciating nature and wanting to learn about it. These estimates, derived from quite different approaches, were in surprisingly good agreement. Continuing supply-side surveys over the past decade (Buckley, unpublished) indicate that the NEAT sector still constitutes a similar proportion of the growing Australian tourism industry.

The economic significance of the NEAT sector to the tourism industry, regional and national economies and public land management has only recently begun to be recognized. This is due to a combination of factors, of which the growth of the sector is only one. From the tourism industry perspective, the most important factor is the increasing commercialization of outdoor recreation. Most of the activities concerned have a long history in private recreation, but because this did not involve commercial tour operators and agents, it was not counted as part of the tourism industry. Although it involved considerable expenditure per person per day, people used privately owned vehicles and equipment, and their expenditure was not distinguished from domestic and household activities.

The growth of outdoor recreation hence became apparent principally through booming sales of recreational equipment. As well as growing rapidly in sales volume, this equipment has become very much more high-tech, specialized and expensive. Outdoor recreation in the 1940s, 50s and 60s was carried out largely with inexpensive army surplus equipment (Mallett, 1998). Now, however, even the manufacture of water filters and camping stoves is a multi-billion dollar business worldwide, let alone skiing equipment, recreational boats and clothing. Because this equipment expenditure has not been counted as part of the tourism industry, the tourism industry has not recognized the economic significance of the NEAT sector.

Currently, a combination of social factors is leading to sudden and rapid growth in recognition of NEAT's importance. The continuing and increasing urbanization of Western societies has created a growing class of relatively well-off people who have some appreciation of the environment from TV programmes and magazine articles, but little or no contact with natural or even rural landscapes in their everyday lives, and have never acquired the basic skills to live and travel safely in such environments. They have relatively little leisure time in which to learn those skills and often do not possess the equipment with which to apply them. Increasingly, therefore, they rely on commercial guides and outfitters to provide packaged adventure and nature tours. The economic growth in NEAT is thus due at least in part to a shift from private outdoor recreation to commercial tourism.

NEAT in public parks and forests

As with private recreation, commercial NEAT occurs principally on public lands, especially national parks. The continuing and increasing growth in the number of visitors to national parks (Lockwood et al., 2006) is forcing park management agencies to spend more and more on visitor infrastructure, management and education, so that they have less and less to spend on management of their natural resources for conservation. Hence, they are in severe need of increased funding, either through increased government budget allocations, or by direct charges and levies on visitors and tour operators (Buckley, 2003e).

To lobby for government funding, they need to demonstrate the economic significance of the nature tourism industry, which is based largely on parks. To charge visitors and tour operators, they need to treat them as commercial clients, and themselves, at least for this purpose, as part of the commercial tourism industry. Hence they need information on the size and the geographical, competitive and price structures of the NEAT sector. Of course, they also need better information on management tools and indicators to ensure that the environmental impacts of private recreational visitors and commercial tours do not cause irretrievable damage to the primary conservation values of the parks concerned, since that is the reason for their existence. Either way, however, the economic scale and activities of the NEAT sector have become a key issue for national parks and heritage management agencies.

In many countries, large areas of public lands, including areas of high value for nature tourism, are controlled by state and national forestry agencies, and the NEAT sector is becoming increasingly important for these agencies. Controversies over the impacts of logging and woodchipping on forest biodiversity, and the relatively low economic returns to the public from commercial logging and chipping, have focused attention on the potential value of tourism as a major land use in public forests (Ward, 2003).

In countries such as the USA, the Forest Service has long since set aside major areas of the lands under its control as wilderness areas, managed for recreation; for many decades, it has operated a programme of trails, signs, rangers, maps, minimal-impact training, permitting systems, etc. In addition, many of the major ski resorts in the USA are on Forest Service land.

According to the Chief Executive of the US Forest Service almost a decade ago, the value of the Forest Service estate for tourism at that date was about 25 times greater than it was for logging, and this differential is likely to increase (Dombeck, 1998; Johansson, 1998).

In Australia, tourism in State forests is still in its infancy. While some States, notably Western Australia, Tasmania and more recently New South Wales, have encouraged commercial tour operators in State forests, others are only now beginning to contemplate this possibility. While increasing tourism in State forests would improve the economic return to the forest management agencies and increase economic inputs to regional economies, there are sectors of the forest industries that reap considerable economic benefits from current arrangements, and might well be reluctant to have these arrangements challenged by the growth of forest tourism. There was initial opposition to tourism from private-sector forestry employees both in Australia, as for example in the Wet Tropics of Queensland World Heritage Area, and in the USA (Forbes, 1998). In many areas, however, it would be possible for tourism and logging to coexist, over a long timescale, as long as sufficient areas of old-growth forests are left un-logged as core tourist attractions.

Nature tourism in public forests is clearly part of the NEAT sector. Whether it would constitute ecotourism depends on definition and implementation. Evidently, it is nature-based. It may or may not be managed for minimal impact, but in any event, its impacts will be less than those associated with logging, hence the argument to concentrate higher-impact nature tourism activities in state forests rather than national parks. There is no reason why it should not have an educational component, and this can address forest history and management practices as well as flora and fauna sighted and similar conventional interpretive materials.

Whether it contributes to conservation will depend on how it is done. It has the potential, however, to make a very large contribution, perhaps larger than any other form of tourism (Buckley, 1999a). One mechanism for this is to reduce the impacts on national parks, by syphoning off some of the visitor pressure. Whether this happens in practice will depend on park management policies and market conditions in the NEAT industry. The second and potentially more significant mechanism is that in the long run, forest tourism may assist in reducing impacts, including clearance, in forest areas of high conservation value. Even if tourism is initially introduced purely as an adjunct to current logging practices, if its greater economic significance becomes clear before a particular area is next due to be cut, tourism could catalyse a change in land management practices. Of course, this will be of little value for either conservation or tourism, if all remaining old-growth areas are logged before being made available for tourism.

The growth of forest tourism in areas managed by forestry agencies could potentially avoid a major conservation problem, which has been prevalent recently in countries such as Australia, to the detriment of the tourism industry: as soon as there is the slightest suggestion that the uses of any area of land might be restricted for conservation purposes, the landholders or land management agencies often move as quickly as possible to destroy its conservation value, to not lose any measure of control over its use. The foreshadowing of controls on clearing of native vegetation in South Australia in the early 1980s, for example, led to widespread clearance by farmers not only in South Australia but also in neighbouring Victoria. In New South Wales, any inkling that an area of State forest might be converted to national park has precipitated immediate and complete logging of the area concerned. This was demonstrated very clearly by large peaks in the annual volume of timber sold (Ward, 2000a).

Conclusions

There is a well-differentiated sector of the tourism industry that relies on outdoor natural environments. It may be referred to as NEAT. It also includes commercial outdoor recreation, education and sports. It is a large sector, at least a quarter of the total tourism industry in developed countries such as the USA and Australia, and more in developing nations. NEAT is a product sector; ecotourism is a subsidiary segment defined by management criteria.

The NEAT sector has considerable economic significance worldwide. Industry associations and governments have been slow to appreciate this, but recognition is increasing. Part of the economic growth of the NEAT sector is due to commercialization of private outdoor recreation, and part to the increasing sophistication and expense of equipment, as well as the increasing popularity of NEAT activities.

Most of the growth in NEAT is occurring in and around national parks. This is generating increasing interest in the economics and management of protected areas, the role of NEAT in contributing to operating costs for parks, and the role of NEAT as an alternative or adjunct to logging in public forests.

The growth of NEAT in national parks and protected areas is increasing pressure for land management agencies to adopt operator permitting systems, which encourage best-practice environmental management by the operators, and which raise funds for park operating costs. As the number of commercial tour operators in protected areas continues to grow, there is increasing interest in screening, audit and accreditation to ensure that their environmental management is adequate.

Since NEAT is increasing and remaining wilderness areas are shrinking, best-practice environmental management in NEAT is becoming increasingly significant. This includes minimal impact education and interpretation.

The profitability of NEAT, and its ability to provide income for rural communities is providing incentives for private farmlands and public forests to turn to NEAT as an alternative or additional land use.

In conclusion, therefore, it seems that while ecotourism, with its emphasis on minimal-impact management, environmental education and a contribution to conservation currently makes up only a small proportion of the large and economically significant NEAT sector, these characteristics are becoming increasingly significant for the NEAT sector as a whole. Ecotourism may yet catalyse change.

Acknowledgements

This is a revised, shortened and rewritten version of an article first published in the *International Journal of Tourism Research* (Buckley, 2000a).

READING 2.2. ADVENTURE TOURISM AND RELATED INDUSTRIES

Introduction

In its practical operations on the ground, adventure tourism is very closely allied to ecotourism, and under some definitions may even be considered part of the ecotourism sector; from a financial perspective, adventure tourism is also tightly tied to the clothing, fashion and entertainment industries. Particular clothing companies use sponsored athletes and specialist lifestyle entertainment media to sell clothing and accessories at both a high volume and a high mark-up to non-sporting but fashion-conscious urban consumers, and adventure tourism is one of the links in the marketing chain. The surfing industry provides a particularly good example, but the same process applies for skiing and snowboarding, rock-climbing and other outdoor adventure activities. The process is directly comparable to the sale of sports shoes and sports utility vehicles in cities and suburban markets. This reading examines these links.

Adventure travel is commonly considered part of or closely allied to the ecotourism sector, as recognized by terms such as ACE (Fennell, 1999) or NEAT (Buckley, 2000a). The Adventure Travel Society (2007) has run an annual World Congress of Adventure Travel and Ecotourism for over two decades.

From a financial perspective, however, adventure tourism might equally be considered part of the rag trade. There seem to be some strong links between the commercial adventure travel sector and the clothing, fashion and entertainment (CFE) industries. My aim here is to identify and explore such links, and examine how significant they might be for the ecotourism sector.

The link between adventure tourism and the CFE sectors does not seem to have been raised previously in the academic tourism literature, apart from a brief mention by Buckley (2000b). I am not sufficiently familiar with academic analysis of the fashion industry to identify whether it refers to adventure tourism. I argue here that commercial practice in the CFE sectors makes use of adventure activities, professionals and imagery, but it is perhaps unlikely that the CFE sectors have any specific interest in tourism, even adventure tourism.

What is adventure tourism?

The distinctions between nature tourism, ecotourism, adventure tourism, adventure travel, commercial expeditions, outdoor recreation and outdoor education are blurred (Weaver, 1998; Fennell, 1999; Manning, 1999; Buckley, 2000a, 2006; Newsome *et al.*, 2002a). Here I shall use the term 'adventure tourism' to mean guided commercial tours where the principal attraction is an outdoor activity that relies on features of the natural terrain, requires specialized sporting or similar equipment, and is exciting for the tour clients. This definition does not require that the clients themselves operate the equipment: they may simply be passengers, whether in a dogsled, a white-water raft or a tandem parachute harness.

As with most aspects of tourism, this is an artificial definition in the sense that it identifies one particular set of human behaviours from a broad multidimensional continuum, with no prior evidence that it corresponds to an empirically identified clumping within that continuum. Individual people have many different expectations and experiences from outdoor activities, and excitement is only one of these. The same tour can mean different things to different people. The distances people travel, and the times they spend in outdoor activities, are continuously variable. Levels of individual skill, self-sufficiency and equipment ownership, as compared with commercial support, also vary continuously. There is no definitive distinction between adventure and non-adventure, between commercial tourism and individual recreation, between remote and local sites, and so on. Such distinctions may or may not be significant from the various perspectives of, for example, an economic statistician, an outdoor equipment manufacturer, a tour operator and equipment rental agency, a protected area management agency, a public liability insurer or an individual person planning a holiday trip.

While the boundaries of adventure tourism are not well defined, its core activities are. An archetypal example, perhaps, would be a multi-day white-water rafting tour, where the tour operator provides all the equipment, the clients need no prior skills and the principal attraction is running rapids rather than riverside scenery. Climbing, abseiling, seakayaking and white-water kayaking, skiing and snowboarding, caving, ballooning, skydiving and parapenting, mountain biking, diving and snorkelling, surfing and sailboarding, snowmobiling and off-road driving, heliskiing, and many similar activities may also form the basis for adventure tourism.

Definitional issues

There are three commonly drawn distinctions that are particularly difficult to apply in the case of adventure tourism. The first is that for the purposes of economic statistics, a leisure activity only qualifies as tourism if it includes an overnight stay and/or travel away from the participant's place of residence. In Australia, the minimum threshold travel distance is set at 40 km, but this does not apply worldwide. Many commercial adventure activities are single-day tours. Most of their clients, however, are holidaymakers who are already far from home and so qualify as tourists. In addition, many single-day adventure tours travel more than 40 km from the pick-up point in the nearest gateway town, to the location of the day's activity itself. Hence it is reasonable to consider these 1-day activities as tours, which is indeed how they are marketed.

The second difficult distinction is between adventure tourism, where a client pays a tour operator to provide an adventure experience, and adventure recreation, where individual participants carry out the same activity on their own. From a legal perspective, for example, in regard to liability insurance or access and operating permits for a particular site, this distinction is clear and very significant. As noted earlier, however, in terms of practical logistics there is considerable overlap. A private recreational group, particularly non-profit groups such as schools, may be much larger than a small commercial tour. A commercial tour may provide all the equipment and specialized clothing that participants need, so they can arrive in street clothes with no prior skills. At the other extreme, the tour company may provide only a guide, with participants expected to arrive with all their own equipment and the skills to use it. So-called tag-a-long four-wheel-drive tours operate this way, for example, and so also do some hiking tours and mountaineering expeditions.

The distinction between a group of skilled and well-equipped people led by a paid guide, by a volunteer guide whose expenses are paid, by one of their own number who is particularly experienced, or by a process of consensus, is a rather fine one. To complicate matters even further, a private group with a private leader may contract an outfitter to provide equipment, guides and catering for a private trip. Again, the distinction between a private group, which charters a tour company to guide and outfit them, and a similar group, which makes a group booking on a scheduled but otherwise identical tour, is also a fine one, especially where the tour operator is the same in each case, and their tours are irregular and depart only if a large enough group signs up by a specified predeparture date. A dive tour company that runs 300-seater high-speed wave-piercing catamarans to the Great Barrier Reef every day is a very different operation from one that takes a single small group of highly experienced divers under the ice in the Arctic or Antarctic.

A third significant distinction is between fixed-site and mobile activities. Again, the dividing line is not clear. A ski resort, for example, has a fixed site, whereas a backcountry ski tour is mobile. However, heliskiing, for example, is a mobile activity with a fixed base. Similarly, a dive boat on the Great Barrier Reef is mobile, but it relies on a fixed wharf or marina to load passengers and supplies, and some boats journey routinely to elaborate pontoon facilities moored permanently on the outer reef. Some surf tours operate entirely from live-aboard boats; others operate from lodges or resorts near particular surf breaks. Skiing and snowboarding are certainly excitement-based outdoor leisure activities that require specialist skills and equipment and rely on features of the natural terrain, i.e. an adventure activity. Tourist expenditure at ski resorts makes up a large component of Mallett's (1998) estimate of the economic scale of adventure tourism in North America; the figure increases enormously if associated real-estate development is also included (Johnson and Borrie, 2003). Corresponding attractions for resort-residential development in subtropical areas, however, such as marinas and golf courses (Warnken and Buckley, 1997), are generally not considered adventure tourism, even if some of the boats based at the marinas do operate adventure tours.

Social trends and emerging markets

As societies in developed Western nations become increasingly urbanized, increasing numbers of people have lifestyles that lack any outdoor component, except during leisure activities.

Many of these people are relatively well off but have little leisure time: they are cash-rich, time-poor. They see wilderness environments and wildlife through television programmes and travel magazines, perhaps without appreciating just how much time, equipment and expertise is required to make a wildlife documentary film. They also see athletes engaging in a variety of outdoor sports and recreational activities, perhaps without appreciating that these are a select and sponsored few who have made a career in the outdoor sport concerned. These factors have created a cohort of people who have the desire, money and basic fitness for outdoor recreation in remote areas, but not the time, skills, equipment or experience. There is also an older cohort of people who have prior experience and skills, but no longer have the time to organize their own expeditions, no longer have their full former strength and skills, or simply prefer to pay for support services rather than organizing their own trips. It is these groups that provide the increasing market for commercial adventure tourism.

In the past, people interested in outdoor recreation would commonly buy their own equipment, and learn relevant skills gradually either from friends or through clubs. Both for social and financial reasons, therefore, this led them to focus on one particular activity. As equipment has become more sophisticated and expensive, the option of renting it as part of a commercial adventure tour product has become more attractive financially. If people no longer need to buy their own equipment, however, and if they can rely on guides for trip planning, leadership, safety and basic skills training, then they no longer need to focus on a single outdoor recreation activity.

It therefore appears that outdoor recreation is now treated much more as a purchasable short-term holiday experience than as a gradually acquired lifetime skill with its own set of social rewards and responsibilities.

Although commercial adventure recreation has absorbed a proportion of the outdoor recreation market, individual outdoor recreation has continued to grow at the same time. For most of these activities, individual adventure recreation is probably still many times larger than commercial adventure tourism, though there do not yet seem to be any published quantitative analyses either of the number of people involved, or patterns of expenditure. Of course, the same individual may take part in the same activity sometimes as an individual, sometimes as part of a private group, and sometimes as part of a commercial tour.

Links to clothing, fashion and entertainment

Over the past decade or so, quite strong and mutually reinforcing business links have arisen between adventure tour operators, clothing manufacturers and the entertainment industry. These business ties are essentially mediated by fashion, rather than any fundamental logistic links, so in the longer term they may well prove ephemeral. Currently, however, they are strong enough to have quite significant financial implications for the adventure tourism sector.

The way it works is similar for many different activities, but can be illustrated well by the surfing subsector as below. There are similar patterns for other types of adventure tourism.

Snowboarding, for example, is used to sell winter street clothing. Rock climbing provides adventure images used to advertise a wide range of lifestyle consumer goods, from mobile phones to chewing tobacco. Manufacturers of expensive recreational equipment, especially motorized equipment such as snowmobiles, personal watercraft (jet skis), off-road and all-terrain vehicles, and sport utility vehicles rely heavily on adventure imagery to maintain sales. Even ancient activities such as yoga have been adopted as fitness fashions with their own clothing brands.

Historically, the hunting and fishing industries have also promoted their own clothing styles, but these have not penetrated mass urban streetwear markets to the same degree as modern adventure-style clothing. The closest historical analogue is the highly successful use of sports athletes, such as professional basketballers, to market specialized sports shoes as mainstream urban streetwear, but this lacks the commercial tourism component.

Surfing industry case study

There are estimated to be about 10 million surfers worldwide, perhaps more, though not all of these are active (Buckley, 2002f). Most of them are young recreational surfers, and surfing is a very high priority for their disposable income and leisure time. A significant proportion is older, with established careers and families, very short of time but with greater financial resources. Currently, most active surfers are male, but the number of female surfers is increasing, particularly in younger age groups.

The number of full-time professional surfers is quite small. The peak professional international surfing competition, the World Championship Tour, is limited to the world's top 46 male and 18 female surfers. Some of these are fully sponsored, while some live on a combination of sponsorship and prize money. The Tour consists of a series of surfing competitions held at different locations worldwide during the course of the year, each contributing ranking points as well as prize money. There are separate Tour competitions and rankings for men and women. There are additional competitions, many of them by invitation only, which are not part of the Tour, but may carry considerable prize money or status, and a separate World Qualifying Series that feeds new members into the WCT. Many of the surfers in all these competitions are sponsored to some degree, but not all of them, and not necessarily with cash. In addition, there are a small number of individual surfers who are sponsored not for their competition rankings, but for their skills and reputation in big-wave riding or aerial manoeuvres, both useful in advertising.

Each of the major surf clothing and equipment manufacturers sponsors a team or stable of individual surfers, under arrangements that range from occasional free equipment, to an 11-year contract. Where the same companies also manufacturer clothing for other adventure sports such as snowboarding, they may also sponsor team riders in those activities. They sponsor major competitions, both within the World Championship Tour and independent events with different judging criteria, such as big-wave or aerial events. Critically for the surf tourism sector, they sponsor surf trips for their own pro teams, with world-class surf photographers, to remote locations with high-quality surf.

All this sponsorship is a marketing exercise, and a very effective one. It only works, however, if: (i) it reaches potential customers, and (ii) it persuades them to buy the sponsors' products. Such persuasive communication is achieved through high exposure in specialist magazines and dedicated websites, plus less frequent but broader exposure in generic lifestyle magazines and TV adventure shows, i.e. the lifestyle entertainment sector.

Historically, the main lifestyle marketing medium for specialist surf clothing companies has been specialist surf magazines, and these are still a key component. In recent years, however, both individual corporate websites and broader mass entertainment have become critical in expanding sales to customers who are not surfers themselves. Specialist surfing magazines aimed at recreational surfers have existed for decades, but were few in number and low in circulation. In recent years, new magazines have proliferated, and circulation has become much more mainstream, e.g. through city newsagents worldwide, as well as through specialist surf shops. The original surfing magazines have also spawned a series of specialist subsector magazines, e.g. for bodyboarders and longboarders. At least one of these is specifically aimed at surf travel, including commercial surf tourism.

There are three main components to these magazines. There is trade information on competitions, competitive rankings, recent sponsorship deals, personality profiles and so on. There are advertisements for surfboards, wetsuits, accessories, clothing, surf tours, videos and so on, and sometimes also for snowboards, skateboards, four-wheel-drive vehicles, etc. The main bulk of these magazines, however, consists of heavily illustrated articles, most of them featuring sponsored surfers at locations visited by surf tour operators, photographed by professional surf photographers. Video footage from the same trips is used to make surf videos and DVDs, which are advertised through the same magazines.

These magazines help to sell surfing equipment and surfing tours, and the equipment advertisements and surf tour stories help to sell the magazine. That works fine, but in financial terms, it is only a small part of the picture. The big money, as noted earlier, is in selling surf-branded clothing and accessories to non-surfers, few of whom are likely to read surfing magazines. Reaching these broader markets requires communications channels with a wider reach, which convey four messages: surf clothing is cool, particular brands are coolest, here's what you need, and here's how you get it.

This is very much a fashion message and, indeed, the big surfwear companies see themselves as being in the 'fashion apparel business' (Billabong, 2002). Note that while selling surfwear to actual surfers certainly involves an element of fashion, it does also require underlying functionality: boardshorts whose pockets are streamlined for paddling, wetsuits that keep you warm with minimum restriction, reef booties that save you from coral cuts but still let your feet feel the board, bags that let you carry your gear and your board on your bicycle or an airplane. For the urban streetwear market, none of this matters – clothing can be identical to no-name equivalents, and the brand alone makes for many times the mark-up.

On the basis of simple statistics rather than stereotypes, there are still relatively few female surfers. There seems to be no published information on actual numbers. My impression is that the proportion is increasing, but is still well below the proportion of women in other adventure sports, such as rock climbing, white-water kayaking or mountain biking. One of the main reasons why the major surfwear manufacturers have grown so fast over recent years, however, is that they have successfully created a fashion market for surf clothing and accessories as urban streetwear, for both women and men who do not surf, and who live far from the ocean. Indeed, both the degree of brand consciousness and the number of items purchased may well be higher for non-surfers than for actual surfers.

The growth, decline and social implications of such fashions are themselves an interesting topic in human behaviour, but beyond the scope of this contribution. The critical issue for surf tourism is that the major sponsors for the world's top surfers, the world's top-ranked competitions, and the world's most spectacular surfing trips and stories, are clothing manufacturers who make most of their money not from selling functional surfwear to surfers, but by selling surf-branded fashion clothing to non-surfers. The total economic scale of these surf clothing businesses was around US$6.3 billion per annum in 2002 (Buckley, 2003c). The scale and significance of the surf clothing industry is such that it was the subject of a cover article in *The Bulletin* magazine in 2002 (Gliddon and Syvret, 2002). The release of the mainstream feature movie *Blue Crush* (Universal Studios, 2002), with the lead characters clad ostentatiously in Billabong clothing, marked another step in surfwear marketing.

In 2002, the website for Voodoo Dolls®, ostensibly a women's surfwear manufacturer, incorporated a range of lifestyle images with little connection to surfing as such, and sold a range of fashion accessories as well as clothing. 'Young, free and single' was the tagline, and the top banner said 'ask your sex question here'. The website sold make-up packs and 'girlie stuff' (their words not mine!), with barely a surfboard in sight. A few years later, however, the website (Voodoo Dolls, 2005) became much more conservative, citing the company's associations with fashion designers, and offering snowboard gear as well as bikinis.

The mainstream surfwear companies all have girls' lines, and some have separate websites such as Roxy® and BillabongGirls®. Rip Curl® no longer seems to operate its former site RipCurlGirl®, but now includes women's clothing in the main site. They offer girls' street gear in demure pastels with flowers and butterflies and understated logos, as well as more lurid lines. There's even a second-hand Internet market for Mambo Goddess® clothing. In the early 2000s, the major surfwear manufacturers developed separate product lines for children in various age groups (Buckley, 2003c), though these now seem to receive less emphasis. Even more surprisingly, the surf industry seems to have successfully created surf fashion for male surfers and their street imitators, with rapidly changing style factors such as the precise length and pattern of boardshorts, tabs or cord loops on pockets, ankle strings or zips on cargo pants, and so on. This constant market repositioning has kept surfwear share prices on the rise for many years.

Perhaps equally important is cross-marketing between adventure sports. Companies such as Quiksilver® produce snowboarding clothing as well as surf clothing, and most recently, core snowboard manufacturers such as Burton® have also started to put their brand on running shoes and summer gear, and to use professional surfers to advertise them. Their 2005 product catalogue, self-described as a 'Rider's Journal' (Burton Inc., 2005) features famous surfers David Rastovich, Kalani Robb and Sanoe Lake, co-star of the movie *Blue Crush*. As well as snowboards, boots, bindings, bags and snow clothing, it also features a range of 'clothes you'll live in' (p. 125) and accessories such as the 'WMS hook-up kit', subtitled 'your walk of shame quick fix kit' (p. 129) – a very American phrase and reminiscent of the Voodoo Dolls® website in 2002. Hey, whatever works. With Burton® team riders such as Victoria Jealouse carving under a cornice at Mt Cook (p. 57), Kelly Clark airborne with Mike Wiegele Helicopter Skiing in Canada (p. 47) or JP Solberg in the Montana backcountry (p. 75), Burton® has more than enough credibility in its markets to sell lounge pants (p. 127), purses or anything else.

Conclusions

Surf fashion is not new: by the 1960s, 'surf chic was a cultural phenomenon' as the Quiksilver website says. What is new this decade is the growth in 'adventure' imagery: in lifestyles, clothing and accessories, and entertainment. Adventure is fashionable. Adventure tourism may have grown from outdoor recreation, but both have now become inseparable from the clothing, fashion and entertainment sector. This is not immediately apparent to consumers and tourists, but a glance at corporate financial figures tells the story loud and clear.

Acknowledgements

The bulk of this reading is a revised version of an article first published in the *Journal of Ecotourism* (Buckley, 2003c). The surf tourism case study is revised from Buckley (2006), pp. 452–454.

chapter 3

BUSINESS

Elephants are a key attraction both in Africa (as here) and India. Even though this one is close, its ears are folded back, its trunk is hanging loosely and its eye is not looking at the tourists, so the guide judges it to be relaxed and not dangerous.

REVIEW

Introduction

Ecotourism, like tourism in general, is an industry as well as a social phenomenon, and for a private-sector ecotourism operator, ecotourism is a business enterprise. This chapter introduces the components and considerations for assembling and operating a commercial ecotourism business. Since the majority of ecotourism operations are indeed private businesses, an understanding of commercial considerations is a core component in analysing the ecotourism sector, and this chapter aims to provide information at that level. It does not attempt to substitute for professional training in business practices. A more detailed text on the business aspects of ecotourism and other forms of nature-based tourism was provided by McKercher (1998). McKercher's text applies general small business principles, with particular reference to tourism, specifically to the nature-based tourism sector. It is a university teaching text, not an operating manual.

Books, videos, training courses, guidelines, checklists and advice to help entrepreneurs establish new businesses are legion. Most of the general principles apply as well for ecotourism businesses as any other. These are the basic staples of many undergraduate degrees in business or commerce, and of even more business self-help books. It is well beyond the scope of this text to duplicate, summarize or even comment on them. Rather, this section attempts to summarize some of the particular features of ecotourism that may influence an ecotourism business, focusing on lessons learnt by observing a series of small start-ups in recent years. These are not necessarily applicable, of course, to larger established tourism corporations, which are now turning to ecotourism.

Business models

Different tourists use commercial tourism services to different degrees, and this applies equally to ecotourists. A group of friends who drive in their own vehicle from their home town to a national park a few hours away for a multi-day backcountry hiking, camping and birdwatching trip, for example, would use relatively few commercial services along the way. A group of friends from the other side of the world who undertake the same trip by purchasing a fully packaged ecotour from their country of origin, however, would use a wide range of commercial services in the process. Typically, a fully packaged ecotour will include travel, accommodation, catering, activities and guiding, and each of these components may either be purchased from a supplier or subcontractor, or provided directly by the tour operator.

A large tour company may own its own aircraft, vehicles, ships, lodges and catering facilities, and employ a large number of permanent staff as guides, pilots, captains, lodge managers and hospitality staff. This, however, is relatively uncommon. Many ecotourism providers own nothing but a business name and a client data base: they purchase or subcontract all transport, accommodation, catering, activities and equipment rental, and they hire guides on a trip-by-trip individual basis. There are also many ecotourism businesses that offer only one component of an overall ecotourism trip. For example, a business may simply operate a single ecolodge, and leave it to other companies to assemble groups of clients, arrange their transport to the lodge, and plan and guide their activities once they are there.

Another common business model is to provide a single-day guided ecotourism activity where clients are collected from their accommodation in the morning and returned there in the evening. Some enterprises start by offering a single activity, move on to sell other companies' activities on commission, and then progress to offering a range of activities themselves, either by purchasing other operations or by setting up in competition. This model is most common at well-known ecotourism destinations where the same clients may want to take part in a range of different activities.

Where a company has an established client base and wants to promote repeat business by offering a range of different products in different places, a franchise-style model is often adopted. Under this approach, the primary tour operator is essentially a retail marketing arm, with actual on-ground or on-water operations carried out by local operators, but under the name of the primary tour operator. From the client perspective this approach provides quality control, and from the local operator's perspective it provides a supply of clients who might not have booked directly.

Fine-tuning

A tourist activity or attraction, no matter how amazing, is only the beginning of a commercial tourism product. To form the basis of a profitable business, an ecotourism activity or attraction must first be packaged into a purchasable product and then sold to a continuing supply of customers. Neither is straightforward. Most commercial ecotourism products undergo continual fine-tuning as to exactly what the product includes, what it lists as an optional extra but does not include in the initial package price, and what it leaves out. It is not uncommon to find that, despite the best efforts of the companies concerned, different clients on the same tour have actually purchased slightly different combinations of components, commonly because they have gone through different agents using slightly different versions of the on-ground product.

At one extreme, an ecotour operator may sell a minimalist core product to cut prices, and then charge clients for every additional feature or service. This business model is common in price-conscious markets such as the backpacker sector. It also applies, in a slightly different form, for upmarket tours and lodges where the operator wants to offer options such as which vintage wine to purchase with dinner, or whether to spend a day gamewatching, birdwatching, diving, walking on a deserted beach, or taking advantage of spa and massage facilities.

At the other extreme are all-inclusive packages where the initial price includes all the activities on offer, snacks and drinks as well as meals, and even the after-dinner liqueurs. This approach is generally more common for up-market tours where the tour structure focuses strongly on a single activity on each individual day, with relatively limited choice, and the degree of variation in costs between individual clients is rather small.

Even in those cases, however, closely competing operators may package their products differently as a means of market differentiation. The world's two best-known heliski tour operations, for example, are both based in nearby areas of the Canadian Rocky Mountains, and they both offer week-long package tours based out of their own lodges. They compete in very much the same marketplace and their products are very similar, but there are some differences none the less. One company, for example, provides both a lead and a tail guide for each ski group, whereas the other provides a lead guide only, with the clients taking turns to bring up the rear with a second set of safety equipment. One charges extra for vertical elevation skied above a predefined threshold, while the other includes unlimited vertical in the package price. Both include powder skis as part of the package, including tuning and waxing in the lodge gear shop; if clients bring their own skis or snowboards, one company includes tuning and waxing in the package price, whereas the other charges extra.

Similar comparisons may be drawn between closely competing tour operators in many other sectors and destinations. Some dive tour operators in Australia's Great Barrier Reef marine park, for example, include the park entrance fee in their tour package price, whereas others collect it separately. As fuel prices have risen worldwide in recent years, some tour operators have simply increased tour prices accordingly, whereas others have kept their base price unchanged and instead added a fuel levy, which is still a compulsory component of the total package price, but does not appear in initial marketing. Some overland bus tour operators also split their price into two components, a travel component payable in advance to company headquarters, and a so-called kitty for food and drink, payable in local currency when the tour actually starts.

As a broad pattern, there are many relatively small ecotourism products and few larger ones (Buckley, 1998a,b). Similar patterns were subsequently reported from tourism enterprises more generally (Smith, 2006). As outlined earlier, there are several different business models, which have enabled ecotourism and other outdoor tourism operations to grow to a very substantial financial scale, but relatively few of these rely on a single high-volume, high-revenue product as the sole mainstay (Buckley, 2003a, pp. 240–245). Similarly, there are relatively few large international tour operators who package NEAT tours worldwide, including international travel components. The majority of ecotourism products are local in operation and expect clients to make their own way to the local departure point, either independently or through another tour or travel agency. This applies both for ecotourism activities and for accommodation. For most ecolodges, game lodges and outdoor adventure lodges, for example, the marketing may be international, but the product only covers the period and place from local check-in to check-out, either at the lodge itself or at some nearby transfer point, shuttle station or gateway airport.

Occasionally, but not commonly, the commercial synergies between accommodation, activity and transport operators may be so great that they may purchase cross-shareholdings in each other, or one may buy up another completely. The game lodge operator Conservation Corporation Africa, for example, now has such arrangements with a light aircraft operator, which shuttles clients out to the lodges. The New Zealand heliski operator Harris Mountains Heliski, which was essentially an expert guiding company, at one time took a stake in The Helicopter Line (THL), the company supplying its helicopters. Subsequently, THL purchased HMH in its entirety. Neither of these arrangements, however, was immediately visible to clients.

At the opposite extreme from localized products such as those outlined above are the integrated international tour packages sold within the same ecotourism market by tour operators such as Aurora Expeditions, Natural Habitat Adventures or World Expeditions. The principal products offered by tour operators such as these are fully packaged and guided from a major international gateway airport, or sometimes from the participants' country of origin. They include accommodation at the principal destinations, whether in lodges, camping or live-aboard boats, and they include all the arrangements for local tours and activities, whether wildlife watching or cultural or adventure options.

In many cases, both the accommodation and activities are also marketed directly by the individual local operators concerned. Especially for international clients, however, there are several advantages in purchasing an integrated product, as for package tours in any sector of the industry. Perhaps most important is that the tour operator has prior experience in the destination area, so they should know how to get the best out of a visit. This might include the particular places to go to, the most comfortable and convenient places to stay, the best time of year to see icon wildlife species, or local guides with the community contacts to provide clients with a more authentic cultural experience. The second advantage is that the tour operator arranges and manages all the logistics efficiently. A third is that, in some cases, tour operators may be able to obtain discounted rates for local accommodation and activities, which may (though not necessarily!) be reflected in the package price.

These advantages apply only for reputable and well-established tour operators for whom repeat business and word-of-mouth client-to-client recommendations are an important part of their marketing strategy. There are other agents and packagers, certainly, who choose local accommodation and tour providers more on the basis of commissions received than client satisfaction. Marketing by the more reputable operators, therefore, considered in a later chapter, typically includes guarantees of quality for potential clients.

Business basics

Irrespective of the owner's intentions or motivations, a private-sector ecotourism enterprise is still a business, and subject to the same basic constraints as any other business. These may usefully be considered in six categories: money, markets, machines, land, labour and laws. Every business needs capital and cashflow, cost control and debt collection, accounting systems and auditors. Every business needs customers, including ways to identify them, ways to reach them and ways to convert enquiries into paid-up bookings. Every business needs equipment, whether it is simply hiking boots and binoculars, or an ice-strengthened expedition vessel, and equipment must be leased or purchased, maintained and replaced. Every business needs somewhere to operate, not just the booking office and the equipment shed, but access to the area of land or water where the tour actually takes place. Access includes both physical access, i.e. a way to get there, and legal access, i.e. the right to be there. Every business needs people, whether part-time involvement by a sole proprietor, or a staff of thousands, and the business has to make sure that they each have somewhere to work. Finally, every business is subject to a wide range of different laws, not only those for the licensing or registration of the business itself, but laws relating to taxation, currency transfers, employment, health and safety, transport, land access, equipment operations and more.

A good idea alone is not enough. A great deal of information, analysis and planning is needed to convert a potential prospect into a viable business opportunity. As noted by McKercher (1998) for nature-based tourism in general, when new businesses fail it is usually because of these business basics rather than any specific feature of the particular business concerned, or even of the tourism industry more generally. Many new ecotourism enterprises, for example, underestimate the costs of initial marketing: both the costs of marketing itself, and the costs of keeping the business going until it has generated a profitable cashflow. This may take not just months, but years.

Competition

Once a new ecotourism product is successful, the entrepreneur may well face a different but equally serious problem: cut-price copycat competitors who offer very similar products with confusingly similar names, taking free advantage of the time, effort and resources invested in marketing by the original entrepreneur. The copycat operators do not have to recover this initial investment, so just as the original entrepreneur has established sufficient demand to raise prices and improve profits, copycat competitors can undercut those prices and force a price war, imposing an additional capital drain on the originator.

There are various potential measures to combat this problem, but none of them is easy. It is difficult, for example, for a new start-up business to demand that its marketing and distribution agents sell its particular product exclusively and refuse to market competing products. It is rare that an ecotour involves new technology a tour operator can patent, and even if it does, a patent may mean little if the owner does not have the resources to enforce it. If a tour operates on private land, the tour operator may be able to negotiate exclusive access arrangements with the landowner, but this may be costly.

If a tour operates on public land or water, such as a national park, the management agency may operate under legislation that requires it to offer all commercial opportunities equitably, e.g. by open tender. This applies particularly if the activity concerned is also available to private recreational visitors and there are no specific safety or intellectual-property issues to be considered. In practice, despite any such requirements, many protected area management agencies do in fact grant operating licences for particular activities or sites only to a limited number of commercial operators, for a variety of reasons (see Chapter 12). For any new ecotourism business, this issue is certainly something worth considering carefully.

In developing nations, arrangements for operating commercial ecotours within protected areas or other public lands may be rather more flexible or laissez-faire – either for cultural or political reasons, or simply because of lack of resources. A new ecotourism business may work hard to design a quality product and establish a market, only to find itself undercut, or worse, by powerful locals. If the original entrepreneur happens to be an expatriate, they may even find that sharp practice by local copycat operators receives local political support, at least covertly. This may happen even if the expatriate operator has invested enormous personal time, effort and resources into establishing a business that provides local employment and benefits local communities.

Well-known examples include John Gray's Sea Canoe in Thailand (Buckley, 2003a) and David Allardice's Ultimate Descents in Nepal (Buckley, 2006). In Gray's case, businessmen from Bangkok copied his boats, his itineraries and his company name, ignored the minimal-impact measures adopted by Gray's own company and, eventually, shot and wounded his Thai manager. In Allardice's case, the local silent partner staged a hostile takeover of the company once it had become successful. Both Gray's and Allardice's businesses have in fact survived and prospered, but only after several years of difficult times. Even where no sharp practice is involved, new start-up ecotourism operations still need to consider the likelihood that their products will be copied. The first commercial rafting trip in Nepal, for example, seems to have been by World Expeditions on the Sun Khosi, but a number of other operators soon began to offer competing trips. In such circumstances the question of who started first soon becomes commercially irrelevant. What matters is the ability to reach customers, especially overseas; to establish and maintain a reputation for higher safety standards and a better quality of service; and to continue pioneering new trips and itineraries, or adding new features to existing trips, to offer something that competitors do not.

Legal issues

This volume cannot attempt to cover the entire range of legal issues facing any individual ecotourism or adventure tourism operator, just as it cannot cover all the other financial and business issues. It is, however, useful to consider legal issues in three major categories, all of them important. The first category essentially consists of permission to operate, from relevant regulatory authorities. This may include business licences, development approvals, boat and bus driving licences, and access and activity permits for the area where the tour takes place. For a sizeable operation running multiple trips in multiple places, just keeping all these permits up to date can require a dedicated full-time position.

The second major category consists of operating contractual arrangements with other private-sector organizations. These may include sales and marketing agreements of various kinds, franchise and subcontracting agreements, employment contracts, and so on.

The third category consists of legal arrangements intended to cope with any unforeseen incident, whether medical, financial or political. Essentially these consist of legal arrangements to avoid or transfer liability, e.g. through client disclaimers, and arrangements for compensation of unavoidable liabilities, i.e. through various types of insurance. These two aspects are closely interrelated. For example, one way of minimizing liability is to require clients to carry their own travel, equipment and medical insurances, including medical evacuation and repatriation insurance. At the same time, however, the tour operator also needs to carry comparable insurance, both for its staff and as a backup where clients have failed to take out their own cover. In addition, land management agencies may require commercial tour operators to carry significant third-party liability insurance, and to indemnify the agency against any claims from the tour operator's clients or staff.

Permits and licences

Before it can operate legally, a new ecotourism business will typically be required to obtain permits and operating licences from a range of regulatory bodies. These may be considered in three main categories:

- Those required for the operation of any business, such as business registration, auditors, planning and development approvals, etc.
- Those required for any tourism business, such as licences to operate commercial accommodation and transport of various kinds.
- Those required especially for ecotourism operations, such as licences to take commercial groups into national parks and other public lands.

The precise permits required will depend on the scale and type of the tourism operation, and the jurisdictions in which it operates. These vary greatly, but it would be a very rare operation that did not require permits of some type. Permits and licences are hence an important consideration in establishing any new ecotourism business.

Tourism businesses, like businesses in any other sector, are subject to a range of environmental legislation. In particular, new tourism developments in greenfields areas are commonly subject to environmental impact assessment as a condition of planning approval or development consent. Tour operators in national parks, conservation reserves or other public lands commonly require permits or licences, which may be subject to environmental conditions. The discharge of wastes is also subject to pollution control legislation. In the case of deliberate point-source discharges such as sewage and sullage, discharge licences may be required. Formal permits may not be needed in cases of diffuse and unquantified discharges, such as runoff and leachates from lawns and landscaping, but such discharges are still subject to legislation, e.g. in relation to fisheries and marine pollution.

Irrespective of local legislation, legal issues may also arise for international investments. Most businesses need investment capital and, because lenders may be liable for environmental offences by borrowers, many banks and other financial institutions undertake audits of potential environmental problems before approving loans. The scale and significance of such audits vary greatly from one country to another, depending on legal frameworks for lender liability. An American, European or Australian lender, for example, would look askance at a coastal resort development without adequate sewage treatment, no matter what country it might be built in. Similarly, any proposed tourism development that required formal environmental impact assessment, swaps of private and public land, or construction in the habitat of an endangered species, to name just three examples, would receive more intensive environmental scrutiny by a financial institution than would, say, an urban hotel.

Because of persistent breaches of environmental legislation, particularly pollution control legislation, by a number of industrial operations over recent decades, many governments have increased the penalties for such breaches quite considerably. Gaol terms and large fines for individual directors and executives, as well as penalties applied to corporations, are commonly within the remedies available to courts in many jurisdictions. In some cases, these penalties may be transferable to receivers, managers and lenders. Environmental legislation can no longer be breached with impunity, even by large corporations.

Green capital

There is now a substantial pool of so-called green money, funds deposited in ethical investment trusts and similar financial vehicles, and available as start-up capital for enterprises that meet environmental criteria established by trustees or reference panels. Since very few industrial developments can currently claim to be ecologically sustainable, the few that can substantiate such a claim currently have access to a relatively easy source of investment capital in the form of these trusts. With planning and in some cases a relatively small additional investment, many tourism developments can indeed make such a case, and the tourism sector has a significant advantage over most other industry sectors in this regard.

Management structures

Unless it consists of a single individual who does everything, any business needs a management structure, and this applies equally for ecotourism and related subsectors. Most aspects of the management structure for an ecotourism enterprise are much the same as for any other business, e.g. responsibilities for reaching customers, managing cash and operations, and ensuring compliance with applicable law.

In addition, many ecotourism businesses involve outdoor activities in relatively remote areas, so there are particular management issues related to equipment maintenance and to health and safety. Somebody needs to know where all the gear is at the beginning and end of every day, and to check it is still in good working order and organize repairs or replacement if it is not. Somebody needs to consider carefully what kinds of accidents could occur, who does what to avoid them, and who does what if they actually happen. The existence of a clearly defined risk management structure is in itself an important component of risk management, in a legal as well as a practical sense.

Finally, environmental management and interpretation, critical for any ecotourism operation, do not happen through good intentions alone. A comparative analysis of rafting tour operators, for example (Buckley, 2006), found that there were three essential prerequisites for good environmental management practice. First, the owner or manager of the company doing the retail marketing must have good environmental management as a strong and explicitly stated goal, communicated to clients as well as staff. Second, whoever supplies the operational equipment, whether in the same company or a subcontractor, must be aware of this goal and supply equipment needed to meet it. Thirdly, the lead guide on each individual trip must emphasize both to clients and to other staff what specific actions are required and why.

Staff skills

People who start up new ecotourism and adventure tourism businesses come from all walks of life. They do not necessarily have prior experience in tourism, in a service industry, or in business at all. Where they do have prior experience in outdoor tourism, it is often as a guide in someone else's business, i.e. a position where they do not deal with sales, budgets or legal issues except peripherally. Indeed, many people who start outdoor tourism businesses do not even have experience as a commercial guide. They may be skilled and experienced in a particular form of outdoor recreation, and see this as an opportunity to make a living. They may have expertise in biology rather than tourism, perhaps a particular knowledge of specific wildlife species. They may be experienced and successful business people who have moved to a new area for lifestyle reasons, and are looking for local commercial opportunities. They may be experienced independent travellers who are familiar with iconic nature, adventure and cultural tourism destinations in a particular continent, and with the logistics required to visit them.

All of these may be good reasons to start an ecotourism enterprise, but to be successful, such an enterprise needs a full range of business skills. The same applies in other specialist subsectors. A study of farm tourism in Australia, for example (Ollenburg, 2006), found that working long-term farmers who started to take in guests did not initially have a good appreciation for the standards of accommodation and service quality that urban tourists expected. Rural amenity migrants, who purchased small farms for lifestyle reasons and opened farm tourism businesses for cashflow, had a much better idea of what their clients would expect. They were also more likely to have drawn up a business plan and to have sought professional advice, e.g. in regard to marketing.

For a large ecotourism or adventure tourism company, staff skills are still critical but the issues are somewhat different. In this case, the critical issue is that the owners and managers have to make sure that employees have the staff and training required for their particular job. This is of particular concern for frontline operational staff such as field guides, and for anyone responsible for equipment maintenance or other aspects of safety, especially for tour operations involving potentially hazardous adventure activities. In some countries, there are legal requirements that commercial guides or instructors in particular activities must have professional qualifications both in the activity concerned and in first aid or emergency medicine. In other countries, there may be no formal requirement, but if it is common practice within the industry sector, then courts and insurers might consider it critical in the event of any legal argument over liability for injury. Equally critical for the commercial success of the company, guides must be good at communicating with clients and keeping them happy, and the company manager or lead guide needs to keep an eye on their skills and provide on-the-job training if needed.

The design and fine-tuning of staffing structures can be a critical component in the commercial success of any ecotourism or related business, particularly those with a seasonal product or strongly seasonal demand. Most operators, no matter how small and seasonal, will at least maintain a mechanism for taking bookings year-round, even if everything else closes down in the off season.

A typical model for a medium-sized operation may thus include four different categories of staff. First there are the core management and administration staff who maintain the bookings, the accounts, the client database and all the other essential mechanics of the business. Second are the sales staff, who may typically be paid on a commission basis so that costs are automatically curtailed in proportion to revenue. Third are specialist contract staff, such as auditors or tax accountants, who are paid for a short period to carry out a specific task. Fourth are the trip leaders, guides and field staff, who may be engaged through a range of different mechanisms. Key guides, who are well-known and identified with the company, and for whom there will be continuing work throughout the season year after year, may be placed on the payroll or on multi-year seasonal contracts. Other guides may be engaged by the season, or for individual trips. Many ecotourism operators maintain a stable of specialist natural history guides who have regular professional employment elsewhere, but lead one or two trips for the company each year.

The balance between these various approaches for the different categories of staff required depends on the type of products offered and the size of the company. Whether large or small, year-round or seasonal, the critical issue is to have skilled staff available when they are needed, but to avoid having to pay them when they are not. Since demand and availability can rarely be matched perfectly, an ecotourism enterprise has to find a compromise, a mixture of different staffing structures and strategies that can be adjusted to match changing circumstances as well as possible.

Conclusions

Most ecotourism enterprises are small or medium-scale businesses, and face similar start-up and operating constraints as any other business. No matter what the motivations may be in setting up such an enterprise, its staff and owners must be successful in the business aspects if it is to survive. Even the most well-intentioned ecotourism businesses, established with local communities and conservation in mind, still face competition from other operators who may not share the same scruples. They are still subject to local legislation and still need to attract, train and retain staff, and they still need to design, establish and sell actual ecotourism products. These issues are considered further in following chapters.

RESEARCH

There seems to be rather little published research on the basic business aspects of the commercial ecotourism sector. Reliable information on the business profiles and characteristics of commercial ecotour operators themselves is in remarkably short supply. Indeed, this applies for the entire outdoor tourism sector (Buckley, 2006). This contrasts with, for example, the hotel and hospitality sector, where business and management issues have received much more attention. The main reason for the shortage of research seems to be an attitude by academic tourism journals, that business aspects of tour operations have insufficient theoretical content to merit publication. This has generated a significant gap in academic appreciation of the outdoor tourism industry.

Lubeck (1991) described the general characteristics of safari operators in East Africa. Holden and Kealy (1996) surveyed 45 tour operators in the UK; Wallace and Pierce (1996) examined ecolodges in the Brazilian Amazon; and Weaver *et al.* (1996) surveyed 27 operators in Manitoba, Canada. In Australia, Burton (1998) and McKercher and Robbins (1998) surveyed and/or interviewed 31 and 53 tour operators, respectively. Sheppard (2002) detailed two case studies from Thailand. Silva and McDill (2004) interviewed 45 ecotourism stakeholders in two states of the USA, but only some of these were actual tour operators. The compendium of 170 case studies in ecotourism assembled by Buckley (2003a) included around 75 private tour operators, of which about half (38) had been audited in person. The later volume on adventure tourism (Buckley, 2006) included over 150 individual tour operations audited in person by the various contributing authors.

REVISION

Ecotourism business basics

- Ecotourism is still tourism
- Same basics as any other business
- Capital, cashflow, equipment, marketing, staffing
- Competition with other tourism products

Management structures and responsibilities

- Environmental management
- Guiding and interpretation
- Safety and risk management

- Logistics and equipment maintenance
- Sales, accounting, cash control

Key legal issues

- Land and water access and permits
- Sales, marketing and commission agreements
- Insurance and client disclaimers

Staff skills and training

- Sales, accounting, management
- Logistics: reliability, competence
- Guides: leadership, qualifications
- Guide training: hard and soft skills

Staffing structures, contracts

- Owners and working shareholders
- Core employees, e.g. sales manager, lead guides
- Contract staff, e.g. seasonal guides
- Ability to cut salary costs if sales fall
- Ability to add volume if sales rise

REFLECTIONS

1. Establish a conceptual design for a new ecotourism product, and identify and detail everything you would need to put in place before you could start to offer the product.

2. Draw up a proposal for a new ecotourism business and construct an outline business plan, identifying places, products, people.

3. Identify a specific medium-size outdoor tourism enterprise, either actual or conceptual, and draw up a staffing structure that lists each staff position, the skills it requires, the salary range appropriate and reporting relationships. Consider how difficult or easy it might be to obtain the staff required and how you would set about doing so.

chapter 4

PRODUCTS

View across part of a guest room in a wildlife lodge in Botswana. Note mosquito nets over guest bed, sunken lounge area, large sliding screen doors for natural ventilation, and both indoor and outdoor showers at far right.

REVIEW

Introduction

Commercial businesses need to sell products, and ecotourism enterprises are no exception. To stay in business, ecotourism operators must design and package up marketable tourism products, and persuade clients to purchase them at prices and volumes that provide ongoing operating profits. This chapter therefore outlines some of the components that a typical ecotourism product contains, and some of the key issues in designing such products. In particular, ecotourism and related industry sectors rely almost entirely on relatively undisturbed outdoor natural environments to provide the primary tourism product and attraction. The particular components that form the attraction, the ways in which they are used, and the ways in which they are packaged as tourism products can vary enormously.

The basic structure of tourism products, whether travel, accommodation, activities or additional components, or a package including all of these, is analysed in general tourism textbooks and in books on the business of nature-based tourism (McKercher, 1998). Any tourism product must include a well-defined set of goods and services, which can be sold as a single item under legally unambiguous terms, with clearly specified inclusions, exclusions and contractual conditions. In the case of tourism products particularly, each component is also tied to a specific date or dates. This chapter does not attempt to reiterate these basics.

Regional differences in products

Ecotourism and related sectors have developed in different ways in different countries. There are different outdoor traditions, different rights of access to land and water, and different types of terrain and climate. In east and southern Africa, for example, the dominant tradition is that of safari, originally meaning simply an extended cross-country journey. The term was adopted long ago first for hunting safaris, and then for photographic safaris, and more recently for any kind of multi-day journey. Thus in Africa, but not elsewhere, a multi-day horseback tour or even canoe tour would be sold as a horseback safari or canoe safari.

In North America, the term 'outfitter' is used to describe a commercial enterprise that rents out all the equipment necessary for a particular outdoor activity. The term originates from the pioneering days: pioneers crossing the country had to fit themselves out with equipment, commonly including riding and pack horses and sometimes also livestock, and the travelling ensemble came to be known as an outfit. Since travellers no longer needed their outfits once they had arrived, outfits came to be bought and sold in their entirety. People or companies dealing in such equipment, or brokering entire outfits, came to be known as outfitters. When wealthy individuals later took to recreational hunting and fishing trips, the term 'outfitter' was applied to the people who organized logistics for these trips. Many of these expeditions were, and indeed still are, in public lands such as national forests, and the term 'outfitter' was gradually applied to any concessionaire offering commercial outdoor recreation in these areas. Currently, even a company providing, say, canoes and camping equipment for a multi-day paddling trip, or running a guided hiking trip in a national park, might be referred to as an outfitter.

In Australia, in contrast, neither 'safari' nor 'outfitter' were terms in common use. When the term 'ecotourism' was introduced in the *National Ecotourism Strategy* in 1994, therefore, it was adopted much more readily than in Africa or North America, since it was a useful term to describe an industry sector for which no other general term existed. The same applied in a number of Latin American nations. Since the term 'ecotourism' includes criteria related to management as well as product, however, whereas outfitter and safari do not, this has led to many years of confusion, which are arguably still ongoing. Recent reports from Scandinavia (Gössling and Hultman, 2006) indicate that much the same difficulty has arisen there.

Irrespective of terminology, differences in history and geography between continents and countries have led to differences in the types of products offered. Not surprisingly, a tour where the primary attraction is diving on a coral reef is packaged somewhat differently from one where the primary attraction is to watch large and potentially dangerous wildlife from a safari vehicle, or to travel through the winter snows behind a dog sled. As a result, commercial ecotourism products in different parts of the world seem to have recognizable regional signatures (Buckley, 2003a). Ecotourism products in Scandinavia, for example (Gössling and Hultman, 2006) look rather different from those in Africa or Australia.

Within any one adventure activity subsector, however, regional patterns are rather less distinct (Buckley, 2006), though they do still exist. Indeed, each major activity subsector has its own geography, which depends largely on the physical environment, but also on access, convenience, cost, safety and indeed fashion. It has been suggested (Buckley, 2006) that each adventure activity has a global set of icon sites, and that this set changes over time for various reasons that are essentially human rather than physical.

Even for the ecotourism sector more narrowly defined, human factors are an important component of regional signatures. For example, language is an important consideration affecting which particular destinations are preferred by tourists from different countries of origin. In addition, people from different ethnic backgrounds tend to prefer different types of recreational activity, and to have different attitudes towards the natural environment and other cultures, whether in their own countries or overseas. The geography of tourism and recreation in general has been studied quite extensively (e.g. Hall and Page, 2006). The more detailed geography of ecotourism and related sectors, however, has received rather little attention to date.

Product packaging

The ecotourism industry includes many different types of tourist products, which appeal to different market segments and which may be packaged together into integrated tours or sold separately. Some products focus on the place, with a lodge or other accommodation as the key component, and local activities as add-ons. Others focus on an activity, with accommodation as secondary.

Factors such as the level of luxury and the degree of local community involvement can differ enormously between otherwise similar products. A wilderness lodge for watching wildlife, for example, may be a low-key dormitory-style bunkhouse, or a set of individual luxury villas with private spa baths in every room, a gourmet kitchen and thousand-dollar aromatherapy massages on offer. Similarly, a birdwatching tour may be a half-hour walk with a guide who points out the better-known species; or it may be a 6-week journey around an entire continent, with air transport and luxury accommodation, visiting highly specific sights to search for individual rare and localized species. In the former case, the participants may take the trip at a moment's notice, with no equipment other than their own eyeballs. In the latter, it may be a long-planned lifetime experience, where the participants are equipped with binoculars and cameras worth tens of thousands of dollars. There is a similar range of tour options in marine environments. Coral reef tours, for example, range from half-day snorkelling trips to multi-week dive charters on luxury live-aboard vessels with their own chefs and videographers. A trip to see seals may merely mean driving to a suitable piece of rocky coastline and walking a few hundred metres; or it may mean a 10-day expedition voyage to look for elephant seals on sub-Antarctic islands.

Even an organization such as Lonely Planet®, which established its reputation by providing information for backpackers and other low-budget independent travellers, has recently released an ecotourism-style guidebook called *Code Green* (Lorimer, 2006), which features some extremely upmarket establishments as well as backpacker and community enterprises.

The practical business of ecotourism involves not only identifying and marketing key attractions, but packaging together the logistics that allow clients to experience those attractions with ease, comfort and safety. This applies as much for ecotours as any other form of tourism. For all but the shortest tours, a tour will typically include transport and transfers, accommodation and food, equipment and activities, information and guides, and any necessary permits or access rights. One of the major reasons why tourists travel with a commercial tour operator rather than making each of these arrangements individually as they go along is to save time and worry through smooth and efficient logistic links. Even where the ultimate destination of a tour may be a remote backcountry area with minimal creature comforts, tour clients typically expect a smooth journey there and back, and will bring home bad memories if they did not receive the quality of service they had paid for.

Ecotourism products may operate on either public or private land. Irrespective of tenure, by far the majority of ecotourism products take advantage of relatively undisturbed natural rural settings, because it is features of these landscapes, or their plants and animals, which provide the primary attraction. While many ecotourism products operate on privately owned rural land or on public land allocated for multiple use, it is the relatively undisturbed portions of those tenures – those most similar to national parks – which are most valuable for ecotourism.

Contemplative cf. active tours

Broadly, nature-based outdoor tourism products may usefully be divided into two major categories: contemplative and active. In the former, the principal attraction for tourists is the opportunity to experience a particular natural environment, or specific components such as individual plant or animal species. These are generally described as nature-based tourism, including ecotourism. In the latter, the natural environment provides a necessary setting, but the principal tourist attraction is a sporting or similar activity that provides excitement rather than serenity. These are generally described as adventure tourism.

These categories are poles on a continuum, rather than clearly separated subsectors of the nature-based tourism industry. Similarly, the human technologies involved, and the degree of environmental impact, may vary widely within each of these categories. Some waterfalls can be viewed from a car park, others only after several days of bushwalking. Both downhill and telemark skiers need snow and mountains, but the former also need massive infrastructure developments, which the latter do not.

Contemplative nature-based recreational activities include all those where the principal aim is to observe particular plant or animal species, plant and animal communities, landscapes and scenery, or other specific features of natural environments such as rivers and lakes, beaches and waterfalls, cliffs and mountains, etc. Whether these involve motorization depends principally on the means of access. Whalewatchers may travel in seakayaks or high-speed wavepiercing catamarans; waterfall watchers may travel on foot or in helicopters. Many outdoor recreational activities, particularly safari-type tours and various types of non-motorized wilderness travel, involve both active and contemplative components. Equally, many contemplative recreational activities include cultural as well as nature-based components. Tourists in Kakadu or Carnarvon Gorge National Parks in Australia, for example, commonly expect to see Aboriginal rock art as well as scenery and flora and fauna.

Active outdoor or adventure tourism activities may be considered in two groups: those that require or involve motorized transport or other motorized mechanical support, and those that do not. The motorized category includes activities such as off-road vehicles and trailbikes; recreational powerboats, sportfishing, jetskis, etc.; downhill skiing and snowmobiles; recreational aircraft, helicopters and ultralights; vehicle-based hunting, etc. Those that do not require motorization except for transport to the site of the activity include: yachting, boardsailing and seakayaking, rowing and canoeing, white-water rafting and kayaking; gliding, ballooning and hang-gliding; rock-climbing, ice-climbing, mountaineering, canyoning and abseiling; telemark and cross-country skiing and backcountry snowboarding; horseriding, horsepacking, yak and llama packing, camel safaris, etc.; mountain biking; hunting and bowhunting; flyfishing; orienteering and rogaining; and hiking and bush walking.

Real tourism products

Commercial tour operators sell products, not definitions. They package tours that appeal to their target markets, and have largely ignored long-running debates as to what does and does not constitute ecotourism. A single commercial tour may commonly contain elements of ecotourism, elements of broader nature-based tourism, elements of adventure tourism and perhaps also elements of cultural tourism. Recognizing this, several academic authors have suggested aggregate terms that link these components together (see Chapter 2).

Viewed as a type of tourism product, ecotourism is closely allied to several other subsectors that incorporate similar tourism attractions and activities but without necessarily involving the environmental management, education and conservation components that distinguish ecotourism. These are thus similarities in the product, which may be distinguished from: similarities in environmental management, e.g. between ecotourism and sustainable mainstream urban tourism; similarities in environmental education, e.g. between ecotourism and the outdoor education sector; or similarities in conservation goals, e.g. between ecotourism and a number of private-sector conservation initiatives.

Some of these related product subsectors are financially very large, others smaller and more specialized. Recreational hunting and fishing in the USA alone, for example, are multi-billion dollar sectors (Outdoor Industry Association, 2005). The adventure tourism sector as a whole is apparently worth several hundred billion dollars annually, or over a trillion dollars if ski resorts and recreational boating marinas are included. The various forms of educational, cultural and ethical tourism, in contrast, are a great deal smaller in financial terms, though still very significant in social terms.

Most major industry sectors are interlinked in a wide variety of ways, and tourism is no exception. Links to sectors such as transport and construction, and through them to the manufacturing sector, are straightforward and immediately apparent. Of particular interest for ecotourism and related sectors, however, are links to other leisure and associated industries. There are many links, for example, between nature and adventure tourism, and nature and adventure entertainment in the shape of television programmes and movies. There are also significant links between tourism, entertainment and the fashion and clothing industries (Buckley, 2003c, 2006). Particular brands of clothing, while sold principally for streetwear, are linked through advertising to various outdoor adventure activities, which are themselves popularized through magazines, DVDs and tourism.

Safety and scenery

Most tourists, especially those with families, prefer safe destinations; and safety may include environmental considerations such as pollution and food poisoning as well as social considerations such as crime and armed conflict. Up to a threshold, poor air and water quality do not prevent tourists from visiting major cities; but high levels of pollution are certainly a deterrent, and clean air and water are an added attraction. Tourism advertising materials that refer to, for example, ocean breezes, mountain air, sparkling waters, crystal creeks, healthy holidays, healthy environment, etc., often with accompanying illustrations, indicate the significance of these considerations.

The significance of landscapes in tourism is so universal that if your room is not advertised with a view, you can be fairly sure it hasn't got one. Perhaps more than anything else, the main motive for tourism is to see new places, and natural landscapes are a fundamental part of this. It is not for nothing that we speak of picture-postcard views. Illustrations of scenery, landscapes and views are a central feature in advertising materials for all but the most urbanized tourism attractions. In some cases, well-known photographs have become icons for the destinations concerned. Indeed, such illustrations are often used to advertise products that have little or no real connection with the view depicted (Buckley and Vogt, 1996; Buckley and Araujo, 1997a). Characteristically, views used in advertising nature-based tourism select and emphasize the natural features of the landscape, cropping out human structures such as buildings, roads, power lines, etc.; it is the scenery that people want to see. Indeed, the value of a view can often be expressed in economic terms through its effect on land prices.

Wildlife

Like scenery, some animals, and to a lesser degree plants, have become icons of particular tourism destinations. In some cases, through their use in marketing campaigns, they have also become associated with particular tourism corporations. Kangaroos are associated with Australia, but also with Qantas. Some plant and animal species are an important part of visitor expectations, to the extent that tourists will feel short-changed if they don't see one. First-time international visitors to Australia, for example, are disappointed if they don't see a kangaroo, and visitors to Yellowstone National Park in the USA are disappointed if they don't see bears, bison and bighorn sheep.

Tours to see particular plants and animals have always been a large component of the nature-based tourism industry, from the 18th century onwards. The wildlife safari industry in east and southern Africa provides perhaps the classic example. Currently, there are many tourism products that are based entirely on particular plants and animals, often on a single species. Examples include wildflower tours in South Africa and southwest Western Australia; wildlife safaris in Africa and America; boat tours of the Galapagos Islands; the tourist industries based on the mountain gorillas of Rwanda, the polar bears of Churchill, the dolphins of Monkey Mia and the penguins of Phillip Island; and the continuing popularity of zoos, botanical gardens, and tourism attractions such as Currumbin Sanctuary on Australia's Gold Coast.

Tourist expectations vary considerably with regard to their interactions with flora and fauna they have paid to see. At one extreme are hunting, fishing and spearfishing trips where the aim is to kill the animals concerned. At the other extreme are walking tours that aim to observe plants and animals in their natural habitats without interfering with any of their day-to-day activities. A large proportion of nature tourists, however, want to approach animals as closely as possible, either to photograph them or in many cases to touch or hold them. Not surprisingly, this can involve considerable and in some cases lethal stress for the individual animals. The Australian manager of one very large Japanese tour company, for example, argues that the opportunity to touch, feed or otherwise interact closely with animals is one of the major reasons that Japanese tourists visit Australia and that if they are no longer permitted to do so they will go elsewhere.

It is clear that a significant proportion of the international tourism industry relies on particular plant and animal species for its continuing existence. Additionally, in recent years tour operators, and national and regional tourism promotion agencies, have begun to advertise biological diversity per se as a tourism attraction (Buckley and Clough, 1997), particularly in areas such as South and Central America, where many potential clients are not familiar with the individual species concerned. People are unlikely to visit Brazil, for example, in the specific expectation of seeing a jaguar in the wild, or with the specific desire to encounter a tree sloth, but they do expect to see a wide variety of plants and animals, from the colourful butterflies of the forest to the pink dolphins of the Amazon.

Conclusions

This chapter provides a brief overview of some specific features of ecotourism products, without reiterating the basic aspects of tourism product design and construction as described in standard tourism textbooks. The conception of an ecotourism product, however, is linked tightly both to the design of a business model, and to the marketing strategy used to sell the product. Marketing aspects are therefore considered in the following chapter.

RESEARCH

Several authors have designed general protocols to evaluate and compare opportunities and constraints for nature tourism at different sites (Anand and Herath, 2002; Deng et al., 2002; Arrowsmith, 2003; Nyaupane et al., 2004).

Opportunities for game and wildlife watching have been examined in general terms by Kock (1996) for Zimbabwe; Luzar et al. (1995, 1998) for Louisiana, USA; Mangun and Mangun (2002) for the western USA; and Herath (1997) for Australia. Jolly and Rasmussen (1991) suggested that islands should be used much more extensively for private conservation and tourism. Shackley (1995a) studied gorilla tourism in Rwanda, and Russell and Ankenman (1996) examined orang-utan tourism in Borneo. Rodger et al. (2007) described the characteristics of the wildlife tourism sector in Australia. Boyd and Butler (1999) looked at opportunities for wildlife tourism in northern Ontario, Canada; and Croft (2000) for western New South Wales, Australia. Shackley (1996) examined wildlife tourism more generally, and many of the case studies in Buckley (2003a) and Buckley (2006) refer specifically to wildlife tourism products.

The ecotourism potential of marine wildlife has also been examined in some detail (Cater and Cater, 2007). Whales and dolphins have received particular attention, e.g. by Berrow et al. (1996) for dolphins in Ireland; Hughes (2001) for dolphins in the UK; Karxzmarski et al. (1998) for dolphins in South Africa; Duffus (1996) for grey whales in Canada; Anderson et al. (1996) for humpback whales in Australia; Findlay (1997) for whales in South Africa; and Beach and Weinrich (1989), Hoyt (2000) and Higham and Lusseau

(2007) for whales worldwide. Other marine species that have been considered for tourism include: stingrays in the Cayman Islands (Shackley, 1998a) and Western Australia (Newsome *et al.*, 2004a); and fish and molluscs in Zanzibar (Gössling *et al.*, 2004). The diving subsector of the adventure industry has been reviewed more recently by Buckley (2006), who also provided case studies of whalewatching under the seakayaking and expedition cruising subsectors.

The most comprehensive collection of ecotourism case studies published to date is that compiled by Buckley (2003a). Previous collections include Baker and Holing (1996); Font and Tribe (2000) with particular reference to forests; and Hawkins *et al.* (1995) with particular reference to ecolodges. These are several dozen published examples of individual cases (Table 4.1).

REVISION

Tour components

- Travel and transfers
- Accommodation and meals
- Activities and equipment

Packaging and selling tour products

- Sell components separately or as package
- On-ground operators
- Packagers and retailers
- Inbound and outbound agents

Ecotourism products

- Most are local only – exclude long distance travel
- Ecotourism accommodation: ecolodges, camps, etc.
- Ecotourism activities: guided, low-impact
- Ecotours include local activities, travel and/or accommodation
- Single-day cf. multi-day products

Nature as tourism product

- As attraction or as setting
- Contemplation cf. action
- Scenery, wildlife, plants
- Marine cf. terrestrial
- Icon species cf. diversity

Table 4.1. Some published individual case studies in ecotourism.

Continent, country	Site, case or community	Author(s) and date
Africa		
Botswana	Okavango Delta	Mbaiwa (2005)
Ghana	South Tongu	Koku and Gustafsson (2003)
Mauritania	Banc d'Arguin	Crosby and Galan (1992)
South Africa	Addo Elephant Park	Kerley (1997)
South Africa	Lake St Lucia	Preston-Whyte (1996)
Zimbabwe	CAMPFIRE*	McIvor et al. (1997)
Americas		
Belize	Baboon Sanctuary*	Edington and Edington (1997)
Belize	Toledo Ecotourism Assoc.*	Beavers (1997)
Canada	Grasslands National Park	Saleh and Karwacki (1996)
Costa Rica	Monteverde Cloud Forest*	Wearing (1993); Aylward et al. (1996)
Costa Rica	Tortuguero	Place (1991); Lee and Snepenger (1992)
Guatemala	Maya Biosphere Reserve	Santiso (1993); Langholz (1999)
Honduras	Rio Platano	McCain (1997)
Mexico	Ruta Maya, Yucatan	Crosby (1992); Long (1992)
Europe and Asia		
Austria	Hohe Tauern NP	Mose (1993)
Belarus	Berezinsky Reserve	Blangy et al. (1996)
China	Xishuangbanna	Tisdell and Xiang (1996)
Cyprus	Akamas	Ioannides (1995)
India	Lakshadweep Islands	Kokkranikai et al. (2003)
India	Sundarbans	Tisdell (1997)
Indonesia	Tangkoko Dua Sudara	Kinnaird and O'Brien (1996)
Indonesia	North Sulawesi	Ross and Wall (1999b)
Japan	Iriomote Island	Tisdell and Takahashi (1992)
Romania		Hall and Kinnaird (1994)

Continued

Table 4.1. *Continued.*

Continent, country	Site, case or community	Author(s) and date
Sabah	Kinabatangan	Schulze (1998)
Saudi Arabia	Asir National Park	Paul and Rimmawi (1992)
Thailand	Kanchanaburi*	Pitamahaket (2002)
Oceania and Antarctica		
Antarctica	Continent	Stonehouse *et al.* (1994)
Australia	Seven Spirit Bay*	Buckley (1995)
New Zealand	Subantarctic islands	Sanson and Smith (1994)

*See also Buckley (2003a).

Types of landscape

- Any reasonably undisturbed natural environment
- National parks, private reserves, forests, rangelands, wilderness
- Generally not urban parks, farms, rural landscapes

Combining components

- Adventure + culture + eco
- Nature + eco + adventure
- Commercial outdoor recreation

Geography of ecotourism products

- Different histories: safaris, outfitters, etc.
- Regional signatures in modern products
- Dependence on physical geography
- Wildlife biogeography
- Cultural frameworks
- Expectations of tourists from different origins
- Preferences of different ethnic groups

Market sectors

- Backpacker, overlander
- Lonely Planet® *Code Green*
- Birdwatching, wildlife watching
- Wilderness lodges
- Commercial outdoor recreation

- Diving, marine
- Community, cultural
- Luxury, 'wellness'
- Most products mix attractions

Product packaging

- Access, transport, transfers
- Accommodation, meals, service
- Attractions
- Activities, guides

Related tourism subsectors

- Adventure tourism
- Hunting and fishing
- Those sectors worth hundreds of billions of US$ annually
- Cultural tourism
- Educational, museums
- These sectors much smaller

Links to other industries

- Fashion, clothing
- Advertising
- Entertainment, media
- Equipment
- Construction

REFLECTIONS

1. Is wildlife tourism necessarily ecotourism? How can you decide? Illustrate with some examples. Then consider: would the 'Big Five' wildlife tourism industry in eastern and southern Africa qualify as ecotourism? What about expedition cruises to watch penguins, seals and seabirds in Antarctica? What about trophy hunting for thar in the Himalayas?

2. Choose any particular type of ecotourism product, such as wildlife lodges, guided hiking trips, whalewatching tours, etc. In which parts of the world do such tours operate? Can you construct a world map of operations, for example, using web searches to identify products and sites? Would you say the geography of your chosen type depends only on terrain, climate and biology, or does it also depend on access, politics and population? How can you tell?

3. There are now several global series of guidebooks for independent travellers, including the well-known *Lonely Planet*® series and the *Rough Guides*®. Find any one such guidebook and analyse its content to address the following issue: if you were concerned to plan your travel to comply as far as possible with ecotourism principles, would your chosen guidebook give you enough information to do so?

4. Design and describe a new ecotourism product you could offer in your own local region. Present a SWOT (strengths, weaknesses, opportunities, threats) analysis for your proposed product, as a new business venture.

READING 4.1. ECOTOURISM LAND TENURE AND ENTERPRISE OWNERSHIP

Introduction

Ecotourism has been promoted widely as a potential tool in conservation and community development, in both developed and developing nations (Fennell, 1999; Weaver, 2001). In some instances at least, ecotourism has indeed contributed to conservation on private, community or public lands outside the protected area estate (WTO, 2002; Buckley, 2003a; TOISTD, 2003). Elsewhere, however, tourism industry promoters have used the term 'ecotourism' simply as an avenue to increase access to protected areas by commercial tourism operators, often under the guise of so-called partnerships (Buckley, 2002a, 2003b, 2004c). The outcomes of ecotourism hence depend not only on the ecotourism enterprise itself, but on the land or water where it operates. This aspect of the ecotourism sector, however, seems to have received rather little attention in the research literature. It has been particularly contentious since the 1990s because of political pressures to expand commercial tourism operations in protected areas (Buckley, 2003c), and efforts to improve conservation on private land. The degree to which existing ecotourism enterprises operate on various different types of land tenure is thus relevant worldwide. This reading describes a case study from the Australian continent.

Methods

Questionnaires were sent to every outdoor tour operator listed in telephone directories throughout Australia, asking *inter alia* what land tenures they used. The response categories for this question were: national park, state (public) forest, private land, Aboriginal (community) land, leasehold pastoral land and 'other'. National parks included World Heritage areas, and 'other' categories included land owned by local government agencies. Information on the types of land tenure used was provided by 217 respondents. Almost all these responses were from private-sector tourism operators, and only these are reported here.

Few respondents indicated what proportions of their operations took place on each of the different land tenure types they referred to, or the spatial extent of the areas concerned. For each completed questionnaire, therefore, the data available are simply a set of yes/no responses for each potential land tenure type. In analysing such data, the relative weightings attached to different responses are potentially critical. If one ecotourism enterprise operates only in national parks, whereas another operates in, say, three different land tenure types of which national parks are only one, should the two positive data points for the national park category be accorded equal weight, or should the latter receive only one-third weighting? If two enterprises both use pastoral lands but one has ten times the annual financial turnover of the other, should the two positive data points for pastoral lands be accorded equal weight, or should one receive ten times the weighting? To examine whether the results are sensitive to such weightings, responses were examined using three different approaches.

In the first 'raw' approach, all records were treated equally, so that (e.g.) a record of a company operating on private land only was treated the same as a record of a company operating on private land but also elsewhere. In the second, 'proportional' approach, each company was given equal weight, so that records for a company operating on private land, parks and pastoral leases would be scored at one-third each. In the third, 'weighted' approach, the proportional data were weighted according to the approximate annual turnover of the company concerned, in four categories: <US$10,000 per annum, US$10,000–US$100,000 per annum, US$100,000–US$1,000,000 per annum and US$1,000,000–US$10,000,000 per annum (1999 Australian dollars). Under this approach, records for a company in each turnover bracket received weightings of 1, 10, 100 and 1000, respectively.

Results

The response rate to the mail-out was only 10%, and responses may not necessarily have been representative. Based on these responses, results were as follows. By far the majority of Australian outdoor tour operators use more than one type of land tenure: only 18% use only a single type, and many use three, four or more. Fewer than 5% overall used pastoral leases, local government or other lands, and these are excluded from the analysis below. Raw responses indicate that 37% of outdoor tour operators in Australia use national parks, 26% use private lands, 24% use public forests and 13% use community lands (Buckley, 2004d). There were no significant differences between revenue categories. Dividing records proportionately between multiple land tenure types intensifies these differences slightly: 43% in national parks, 26% on private lands, 21% in public forests and 10% on community lands. Weighting by annual revenue suggests that ecotourism operations in national parks contribute 38% of total annual revenue, private lands 33%, public forests 16% and community lands 13%. For enterprises with annual turnover >US$1M, approximately three-quarters of their revenue derives from operations on parks or private lands and one-quarter from public forests and community lands. For businesses with annual turnover <US$1M, corresponding figures are approximately two-thirds cf. one-third.

The questionnaire responses also contained information on the geographic areas or regions where each tourism operation is based. Broadly, it seems that most businesses take advantage of all land tenures locally available. Aboriginal lands and pastoral leases are not uniformly distributed geographically, for example, so businesses are more likely to use these tenures in some regions than others. We did not ask respondents to estimate the spatial area of each land type they used. They may, for example, operate in a large national park plus a small private property nearby. Hence the figures above cannot be converted to area terms.

The principal conclusion from the data, therefore, and one which would appear to be reasonably robust, is that outdoor tourism operations in Australia are by no means restricted to a single land tenure such as protected areas. Rather, they use all available lands, with private land almost as popular as parks.

Acknowledgements

This reading is a revised and shortened version of an article by Buckley (2004d) originally published in the *Journal of Ecotourism*. Data and further discussion are available in the original article.

chapter 5

MARKETING

Two lions waking up from an afternoon nap, ready for the evening hunt. They caught a zebra shortly after night fell.

REVIEW

Introduction

Tourism marketing has undergone major changes in recent years. Most notable is the shift from printed brochures and travel agents to web sites and direct online bookings. In many respects, this shift was pioneered by specialist ecotourism and adventure travel operators. As the commercial outdoor tourism industry began to expand during the 1980s, new enterprises found their access to conventional tourism distribution channels was limited because of their low sales volume. They were simply too small and specialized for most travel agents to sell their tours. They relied on local referrals, or they found funds to send staff to international tourism trade shows, or they attempted to establish marketing syndicates. The advent of the Internet gave them a new avenue where they could reach a specialist clientele worldwide at low cost, and they were quick to adopt it.

While web sites and e-mail lists gave ecotour operators a new way to contact more potential clients, however, they also increased competition between operators as tourists found it easier to identify and compare an ever-increasing range of tour products. In addition, without the conventional chain of agents and wholesalers to provide quality control and legal recourse, purchasers became increasingly concerned to find mechanisms for quality assurance, both for financial payments and for the products purchased.

This provided an opportunity for certification schemes of various types. For ecotourism enterprises endeavouring to appeal specifically to environmentally concerned travellers, or to gain commercial access to public conservation reserves, ecocertification programmes provided a mechanism both for retail marketing and for political lobbying.

This chapter therefore examines ecotourism marketing approaches in general, and ecocertification schemes in particular. It does not attempt to review the details of traditional tourism distribution systems, and nor does it aim to provide instructions for high-visibility web sites or electronic marketing campaigns.

Ecotourism marketing basics

Ecotourism businesses need markets like any other. An ecotourism business that has to support equipment inventory, guides and office staff, and marketing expenses must have a reliable source of sufficiently well-heeled customers. These customers, or at least potential customers, need to be identified before the business starts.

Most new ecotourism businesses focus on a single activity in a single geographical area. To identify markets for such a venture, the entrepreneur needs to answer the following questions. First, who in this area would want to do this activity? Second, can they already do it on their own or with another company? Third, how many potential customers are there and how much would they pay? And, fourth, how can the new business identify the customers, contact them, get its marketing information to them, and sign them up?

There is no absolute minimum market size for a profitable business; it depends on what each client will pay, and how total revenue relates to total operating costs. A business that runs expedition-type tours to particularly remote areas, for example, might survive by running only a couple of trips a year with less than a dozen clients each time, if each client is prepared to pay US$5000 or US$10,000 per trip. At the other extreme, a company can operate profitably by charging only US$10 a client, if it has a guaranteed 20 clients every day and negligible operating costs apart from a single guide's salary, for example, someone who leads short walks for clients who arrive on-site in a larger company's coach tours.

Relatively few ecotourism operators have access to large-scale multi-component marketing strategies designed and executed by specialized marketing and advertising agencies. Generally, only large, well-established, nature-based and adventure travel operators, or specialized ecotourism operators that are subsidiaries of large tourism corporations, have sufficient funds. Other ecotourism operators use a variety of approaches.

In addition to electronic marketing, considered later in this chapter, a number of low-cost local advertising options are available for smaller ecotourism businesses. They can distribute printed leaflets and advertising materials through local tourist accommodation, eating and meeting places, chambers of commerce, travel agents, and advertising outlets at airports and tourist information centres. They may have access to free or low-cost advertising in local community newsletters, tourist newspapers, tourist guidebooks, conservation newsletters, government information material, newsletters of societies and associations, and local community radio and TV stations. They can take out targeted print advertisements in outdoor magazines, equipment magazines, and specialist sport and adventure magazines.

While advertising is one of the more conspicuous aspects of a marketing strategy, it is only one of the critical components. A successful marketing strategy must first identify a product that people will buy, and the people likely to buy that product. It must ensure that the potential buyers are aware of the product and are keen to buy it. It must make it easy for the buyer to place an order and transfer funds, and the seller to close the deal and deliver the product. Finally, an effective strategy needs to maintain feedback loops to provide continual improvement of the three steps above.

The process of identifying a product and market sector and matching the two is an interactive one, which typically involves ongoing changes to the product and the target market sector. Commonly this may involve pilot trials of different products and surveys of actual and potential customers to establish which features are desirable or otherwise. The process of matching product and market may start with either the product or the market segment. In the ecotourism sector both approaches are commonplace. Smaller ecotourism operations established from scratch commonly start with a product that they can offer, and attempt to identify a potential market. Larger tourism corporations that establish ecotourism subsidiaries, on the other hand, typically do so because they have identified an unmet market demand and set out to offer a product that can take advantage of that demand. Many companies make gradual adjustments in the individual tourism products they offer, and in their overall range of products, to take advantage of changing market demands.

Product packaging and price are central to any marketing strategy. In the tourism sector, where patent protection for new products is rarely feasible, any successful operator will soon attract copycat competitors. As in any business, an ecotour operator must develop a marketing strategy that delivers a sufficient market share for the business to remain economically viable despite such competitors.

As with any business, the effective strategies available in a stable, well-informed or over-supplied market are different from those available in a new, poorly informed or rapidly growing market. In the former, the principal means of competition are price and product quality, either real or perceived, and in packaging and presentation. This commonly applies, for example in the airline, coach travel and city hotel sectors, where companies jockey for competitive advantage through relatively small changes and differentials in pricing, services offered and packaging of aspects such as add-ons, options and restrictions. In the ecotourism and adventure travel sectors, in contrast, the overall market size is growing rapidly, and new products and indeed operators enter the market faster than individual tourists, or even agents, can obtain information about them.

Traditional tourism distribution systems

Traditional tourism distribution systems involve a chain of packagers and agents, each of which adds to the overall retail price. There are retail travel agents who maintain shopfronts, and sell airfares and hotel nights, but generally will only handle high-volume tours for which they have been supplied with brochures. There are domestic and outbound tour operators and packagers who put together all the components of a tour and sell it either through retail agents or through catalogue mailouts and direct marketing events. There are inbound operators and agents who will put together all the transport, accommodation, activities and other logistics for a tour in a particular country, and market that tour through outbound operators in a variety of other countries. Also, there are individual on-ground tour operators who, under this traditional system, compete to have their products included in packages assembled by the inbound agents.

This traditional system, however, with its series of cascaded commissions and its reliance on high volume, has never been very successful for specialist low-volume ecotourism products. Even for high-priced products that can support the commission structure, it is only one of many means used in a modern marketing mix. As a result, relatively few ecotourism products rely on traditional tourism distribution systems involving travel agents and trade shows. Instead, they have developed a range of marketing mechanisms, which are more cost-effective for relatively low-volume and specialized products or niche markets. Web sites, client lists, direct mailouts and word-of-mouth referrals are important tools for many operators, and relatively low-cost advertisements in specialized magazines that appeal to particular target markets are another commonly used approach.

Travel agents are an integral part of the traditional mainstream tourism industry. Perhaps more than any other industry except share trading or insurance, the tourism industry has historically relied on brokers to link buyers and sellers. Even where an individual consumer can buy a retail-level product direct from the primary seller, as in the case of airline tickets, many consumers will still choose to make their purchase through a travel agent, and for accommodation and package tours and holidays, purchases through a travel agent are the rule rather than the exception.

As with brokerages of all kinds, most individual retail travel agents are subsidiaries or franchises of larger corporations or chains. To conduct their businesses efficiently they prefer to offer the same general set of individual products through each individual store or agent. To do this they will generally only accept for sale products with relatively high volume, i.e. those where there are good prospects of selling a particular product to a large number of individual purchasers. Even if an individual agent is prepared to market a particular product through a single store, potential sales volume is still an important consideration. The addition of any new tourism product to an agent's sales range requires an investment in staff time to learn about the product and be able to market it effectively, and in space and display materials in order to advertise it within the store. To recoup this investment, an agent needs to be able to make a significant number of sales for the product concerned.

Small operators therefore face several problems. If they attempt to reach their potential clientele directly, rather than via travel agents, they face relatively large advertising costs to reach a relatively small sector of the overall tourism market, and they also face potential competition from travel agents. Many ecotourism operators do adopt this direct marketing approach none the less, trying to reach potential clients through a highly focused strategy that bypasses the mass marketing of larger tourism operators.

Alternatively, if small ecotour operators do market their products through travel agents, they must first invest sufficient funds in advertising materials to supply a large number of brochures to a large number of agents. Even this, however, is not enough to guarantee that agents will handle their products. If a small ecotour operator can only take a few dozen clients a year, for example, then any individual travel agent is unlikely to receive a commission on more than one or two individual sales. This is unlikely to justify the agent's investment in staff time to answer queries about the product, and staff time and communication costs in contacting the tour operator to determine whether places are available on specific dates, etc. In addition, if the agent is successful in promoting the product and demand increases, but the total client capacity of the operator remains unchanged, then the agent is likely to have unsatisfied customers who are unable to obtain a place on one of the operator's tours.

Finally, every additional operator an agent handles increases the agent's commercial risks and hence, at least potentially, their insurance premiums. Small operators may have fewer financial resources than larger ones, and hence be less able to survive a temporary downturn in business and more at risk of bankruptcy. In addition, ecotourism and adventure travel operators may be perceived as potentially facing relatively higher risks of liability claims, and this may be reflected in increased insurance premiums or deductibles. The overall effect of these factors is a general reluctance by mainstream travel agents to handle products offered by smaller ecotourism operators.

Syndicated marketing options

Syndicated marketing systems for small operators provide one potential avenue to overcome the marketing difficulties faced by low-volume tourism enterprises. Under this approach, a number of small operators, generally but not necessarily in the same geographic region and offering similar products, market their individual products jointly under a single banner, with a single set of advertising materials to be distributed through travel agents. Agents receive commissions if clients purchase products from any of the individual operators.

Any such syndication arrangements involve contractual arrangements between the operators involved. Many different variations are possible. In its loosest form, for example, syndicate members simply share a group product name in order to increase market exposure, but would still produce individual advertising materials using this name as well as their own, make individual arrangements with travel agents, and deal individually with potential clients. One such example is the 'Adventure Collection'. A slightly more coordinated approach involves joint contributions to the cost of a single set of group advertising materials, which list individual company contact points.

Both the arrangements outlined above are very loose forms of syndication. Alternatively, the individual tour operators may establish either an unincorporated joint venture, or a separate company or corporate body. Each operator would have a specified though not necessarily equal number of shares in the marketing corporation, and would subscribe capital in proportion to the number of shares held. Arrangements with travel agents would be made by the syndicated marketing corporation (SMC), rather than by the individual operators. The syndicate's advertising materials would show all the individual products offered by each of the operators in the syndicate, but only a single contact point and booking procedure. The SMC would employ a person authorized to make bookings on behalf of any of its members, and the referring travel agent would receive its commission on the basis of bookings by the SMC. If the specific product selected by the client was not available, as for example if one of the individual operator's trips was already full for the date concerned, then the SMC could, if its members chose to grant it this power, negotiate with the client in regard to purchasing one of the other products in the syndicate's joint marketing materials, even though the new product was in fact offered by a different member of the syndicate.

Where this approach has been tried in practice, a number of difficulties have arisen. None of these are insurmountable, but they do seem to have reduced the use of SMCs in practice. The first is that an SMC is likely to be most effective as a marketing tool if its members offer similar products in the same geographic area, since this effectively provides greater choice for potential clients and greater total sales volume available. Such similar operators, however, are likely to be each others' principal competitors. Those who consider themselves to be more successful, therefore, even if only marginally so, will be reluctant to contribute to an SMC that gives an equal advantage to competitors whom they might otherwise try to drive out of the marketplace altogether.

As a result, companies that have less to offer and more to gain are more likely to join than companies that have more to offer and less to gain. This is known as adverse selection. Less well-known members of marketing syndicates may effectively gain a free ride through the association with better-known syndicate members. As with most syndicates, individual companies will generally only join the syndicate if their expected marginal benefits outweigh their expected marginal costs. These marginal costs and benefits may depend on which other companies are already members of the syndicate, and vary as other syndicate members come and go.

This difficulty can be overcome by forming syndicates of small operators based in the same geographical area but offering different types of product. That, however, reduces the principal marketing advantage of an SMC, i.e. to increase the potential sales volume of similar products. Indeed, if operators with different types of products are to market them jointly, a more effective approach would probably be a package rather than an SMC, so that clients could purchase products from several of the operators simultaneously, in the form of modules from a single package. This benefits both the operators, who gain additional clients, and their customers, who gain greater value for time and money by combining several different tours in the same holiday package.

Another difficulty in the successful establishment of SMCs is that to be effective, they do need at least one permanent staff member with office and communication facilities to respond to queries and referrals from travel agents. Even though each of the syndicate members is only contributing a proportion of this cost, it still represents a substantial outlay for a small company, in addition to the production costs for the syndicate's advertising materials. Many small ecotour operators are unwilling or unable to make such a capital contribution at the outset of the SMC. Perhaps because of these and similar barriers, there appear to be rather few successful syndicated marketing schemes for small ecotour operators, although several have been tried.

There are, however, some successful analogues in the farm tourism sector. Indeed, one of the most effective examples of syndicated marketing is the New Zealand farm-stay industry. Individual farms, privately owned and still operated principally for agricultural production, offer short stays to small numbers of tourists in order to see New Zealand rural agricultural landscapes, meet local farmers, and see or indeed take part in the day-to-day operations of a working farm. New Zealand farms are generally relatively small in area, and family owned and operated. The visitors typically stay in the family farmhouse, eat meals with the family and travel round the farm in the farmer's own tractor or four-wheel-drive vehicle. Farm-stay tourism has proved such a valuable source of additional revenue for many farmers that they have built additional accommodation, but the number of people who can stay in any individual farm is still very small, and the ambience is of private house guests rather than commercial tourism accommodation.

Since the initial introduction of commercial farm-stays some decades ago, they have proved so successful and popular that a large number of individual farms have adopted this practice. In consequence, although each individual farm can only accommodate a very small number of people, the farm-stay sector as a whole is quite large. Farm-stays are generally short, usually only 1 or 2 days. It is hence quite feasible for a large proportion of tourists to New Zealand to include a farm-stay in their itinerary. Since the primary business of the hosts is farming rather than tourism, they do not compete strongly for clients, and indeed commonly refer clients to each other when their own accommodation is full on a particular night. Travel agents and national and regional tourism marketing associations promote farm-stays as a generic New Zealand tourism experience. The net outcome has been the establishment and growth of an industry segment that earns foreign exchange and assists New Zealand's farmers in maintaining their current rural lifestyles.

Marketing programmes operated through formally established associations, such as national ecotourism associations or smaller associations for individual activities, seem to survive longer than independent syndicates, perhaps because there is an organizational structure independent from any individual operators. There are also national, regional and local marketing programmes run and funded by government agencies, which list and represent individual operators in a given geographic area. Most of these, however, are restricted to relatively high-volume operators and may not be available to smaller specialist ecotourism and adventure operators.

Electronic marketing

A very wide range of adventure and ecotour operators now advertise through the Internet, often with linked e-mail addresses for enquiries, electronic booking forms, automatic currency converters for price information, and in some cases, provision for payment of deposits or fees by credit card. Web sites can contain maps, photo galleries, sound, video clips or animated photo sequences, and cartoon and other graphics as well as text. In addition to descriptive material, a web site may contain details of terms and conditions, updates of all itineraries, comments from past clients, and copies of past media coverage in any format.

A web browser is generally much quicker and more comprehensive than a travel agent, and can identify many more options worldwide for a potential tourist. There is less financial recourse against unscrupulous operators, however, and potential tourists must sift through potential providers themselves rather than relying on the expertise of travel agents to conduct a preliminary screening. In addition, the Internet can of course only link customers and operators who are both connected to it.

Over the past decade at least, perhaps the majority of smaller-scale eco and adventure operations have come to rely principally on their web sites to convey information to potential clients. The critical issue is thus how to make such potential clients aware that the company exists, and persuade them first to examine the web site and second to convert an enquiry into an actual booking. To draw attention to a web site there are three principal approaches. The first is electronic: paid or free advertisements and/or links from other web sites; e-mail campaigns to existing listservers, to databases of previous customers, to commercially purchased client lists, or to target e-mail addresses identified by automated web searching engines. The second is through traditional means, either on paper or in person: brochures; listings or advertisements in travel magazines and commercial directories and in specialist recreational magazines; and stalls and individual networking at travel trade shows.

The third approach is also traditional: inviting travel journalists and travel agents on familiarization trips, generally free of charge, in the hope that agents will market the tour product more energetically, and that journalists will write articles and editorials that promote the tour operator's products or at least mention its web site. Most ecotourism and other outdoor tourism operators use most or all of these approaches, track the number of paid bookings attributable to each, and adjust their strategy based on net returns relative to the cost of each approach. Some of the practicalities are reviewed by McKercher (1998).

Converting web site hits or e-mail or telephone enquiries into actual paid bookings is a sales task and requires sales skills. Larger ecotour operators maintain their own sales teams. Smaller operators must balance the cost of commissions, if they sell their product through agents or packagers, against the cost of time if they reply in person to every enquiry, knowing that many will lead to nothing. Different operators use different approaches.

With the advent of travel blogs and online travel recommendation and review sites, electronic marketing has gained an additional layer of complexity. It is no longer enough to maintain an attractive web site. Tourism operations must now monitor web sites worldwide to maximize the number of positive reports and recommendations, and minimize, remove or counteract any negative press or complaints. Successful ecotourism operations are typically cross-listed in the web sites of: regional and national tourism marketing organizations; activity-specific travel review agencies and magazines; specialist web sites for high-yield clients such as yoga retreats or honeymoon planners; and generalized electronic travel booking agencies such as Expedia®. They continually search for opportunities to have favourable reviews posted in online versions of travel magazines, and when they are successful, they also feature these links and reports in their own web sites. They submit their own comments to semi-formalized travel blog sites such as Lonely Planet's Thorn Tree® site. The aim is to generate continuing positive feedback: the more web sites contain favourable comment, the more likely that other web sites will also include favourable comments. Some specialist ecotourism operators have become highly skilled at this approach.

Ecolabels

Tour operators may label themselves as ecotourism for a number of different reasons, including personal convictions and political positioning. Most tour operators who use an ecotourism label, however, do so at least partly for retail commercial reasons. Theoretically, since ecotourism is a narrower term than tourism in general, an operator that adopts ecolabels anticipates that they will attract a greater proportion of a smaller market sector, with a net positive effect on overall profitability. Tour operators will use an ecotourism label as a retail marketing tool if they believe that they will get either more customers or higher-paying customers, by marketing a tour as an ecotour. That is, they are aiming their marketing efforts at tourists who: (i) want to see natural scenery or watch wildlife; (ii) want to be guided by someone who provides environmental interpretation as well as logistic assistance; and/or (iii) are personally concerned with minimizing the environmental impacts of their holiday experience or providing support for conservation.

For this marketing approach to succeed, the perceived value of such components or characteristics, by the potential purchaser, must exceed any perceived price or other differential between the advertised ecotour and any similar competing products lacking that label. It is in fact quite difficult for potential customers to obtain accurate information on any of these aspects, especially before taking a tour. There is thus a significant opportunity for marketing materials to play on people's perceptions and philosophies, even if a tour does not in fact deliver any significant environmental benefits relative to its competitors.

In practice, however, since it generally costs no more for a company to advertise as an (uncertified) ecotour, and since there is little or no indication that tourists draw any distinction between certified and uncertified products, tour operators do not need to assess the financial benefits of advertising as an ecotour with any degree of precision, because there is essentially no marginal cost to make such a claim. They can adopt an ecolabel in parallel with other marketing measures, without being concerned over potential conflicts.

This raises the issue of ethics in ecotourism, including ecotourism advertising. A number of academic authors, in particular, have argued that there is an ethical dimension to ecotourism (Fennell and Malloy, 1995, 1999; Fennell, 1999, 2006), though this can be difficult to apply in some circumstances (Buckley, 2005a). In practice, the ecotourism label is very often used to advertise tourism products that would not comply with accepted definitions of ecotourism such as that propounded by the United Nations. Tour products that have adopted an ecotourism label purely for marketing purposes in this way have been referred to as 'ecotourism lite' (Honey, 1999). Because this practice is so prevalent, the actual marketing value of the term ecotourism is greatly diminished, because potential purchasers do not believe it means anything. Ecotourism certification schemes, considered below, were intended to overcome this problem by providing a reliable and easily recognizable distinction between ecotourism lite and ecotourism that deserves the label. Since many tourism ecocertification schemes have such lax entry criteria that there is no real distinction between certified and uncertified products, however, the certification approach is still problematic.

In recent years, environmental issues have indeed assumed an increasingly important role in consumer choice: whether in regard to retail household goods, clothing, construction materials or leisure activities. The growth in nature-based and ecotourism is in itself a reflection of this growth in environmental awareness. Even urban tourism providers, notably large international hotel chains, now find that many of their clients are concerned about environmental management issues such as water, energy and resource conservation. Environmental performance, and environmental advertising, have thus become an important feature of establishing and maintaining markets. Ecocertification programmes have thus become a widespread component of green marketing strategies.

Ecocertification

Various forms of certification are available for ecotourism operators. To date, they are all voluntary and optional, and a new company must decide if the potential economic returns of certification are likely to outweigh the investment required to obtain it. Potential costs of certification include: the costs of time spent preparing application materials; the costs of any staff training required; the costs of any necessary modifications to equipment or operating practices; and the costs of fees paid to the certifying organization, including both application and annual fees.

There are several possible returns from ecocertification. Potentially at least, certification may yield more client enquiries, e.g. through access to or inclusion in syndicated or government marketing for certified operators. It may increase the proportion of enquiries yielding paying clients, if certification is a significant factor in clients' choice of operator. It may yield a higher price and profit per client, if clients are prepared to pay more for a certified product. In addition, ecocertification may potentially provide preferential or easier access to permits for particular areas or activities, if certification is a significant consideration for land management and licensing agencies. It can provide preferential or cheaper access to capital, if certification is treated as an indicator of financial security and stability by lenders, and it could provide easier or cheaper access to insurance, if brokers and underwriters treat certification as an indicator of low risk.

Ecocertification schemes in the tourism sector are still in their infancy. Parallels from other professional and industry sectors indicate that when certification schemes are constructed, they are initially cheap and easy to join. It takes time for such schemes to become influential, but if and when they do, it becomes more difficult and expensive to join them. Many certification schemes never do become influential, and effectively collapse. This has already happened for a number of tourism ecocertification programmes.

The nominal aim of any ecotourism certification process is to distinguish operators who are competent, to some pre-defined standard, from those who are not. In theory, the function of certification systems is to reduce the time, effort and expertise that potential clients, regulators and other operators need to invest in order to assess the competence of a particular operator, and to reduce the uncertainty in their assessments. Without such a system, any individual or organization dealing with a particular tour operator has to investigate its credentials from scratch, and since in most cases they will not have the time or resources to conduct such an investigation thoroughly, their judgements are likely to rely on reputation, advertising or chance.

In theory, therefore, a certification system is supposed to provide a reliable seal of quality for anyone dealing with the operator concerned, which encapsulates the results of detailed investigations conducted by the certifying agency. Clearly, this process is only useful if it is consistent and reliable, i.e. if the presence or absence of certification conveys a large amount of information with a low degree of uncertainty. In practice, this is rare.

Tourism ecocertification schemes commonly contain both substantive and procedural requirements. Substantive requirements are those that specify, for example, that in order to be certified, an operator must use a particular technology, have successfully completed a particular training course, be able to pass a specified examination, or have been accepted as a member of a relevant professional association, etc. Procedural requirements are those relating to the process itself, e.g. a requirement to be nominated by someone who is already certified, to submit an application in a particular form or with a particular fee, or to allow a defined period for comment from other interested parties, etc.

Experience from other sectors indicates that purely procedural certification schemes are largely ineffective when first introduced. They tend to lead to certification of existing operators whether they are competent or not, and in some cases to the formation of cliques by which established operators can use the certification system to erect barriers to market entry for new operators. From the perspective of a potential client, therefore, certification under such a scheme contains very little information. It is only if public complaints and public scrutiny of the scheme forces it to adopt consistent evaluation criteria, that a purely procedural system can function effectively, and this takes time, if it occurs at all.

A certification scheme with substantive requirements, in contrast, is likely to be effective much more rapidly. Potential disadvantages are first, that it may be difficult to reach agreement on substantive criteria in order to establish the scheme initially; second, that it may be cumbersome to update the criteria as best practices change. With regard to the former, it is arguable that if substantive criteria cannot be generally agreed, there is little point in having a certification scheme, since it will hardly be meaningful to potential clients. With regard to the latter, updating can be achieved simply by including a review mechanism in the scheme.

For an ecocertification scheme to be useful to consumers, they need to know that certification is granted only after a careful and informed evaluation of an operator's actual performance, and is not simply a marketing label assigned in response to the operator's own representations. A useful scheme, in other words, must conduct its own audits in addition to compiling information from applicants.

In addition, for a certification scheme to be useful to consumers, the criteria on which it is based must be made explicit and publicly available. Commonly, it may be useful to have subsidiary certification categories relating to different aspects of operator performance, e.g. customer service cf. environmental management. In the case of ecotourism, it may be useful to have separate rankings for environmental management, education, and equipment, and different criteria for ecolodges and ecotours.

Customer perspectives change through time. As the market for ecotourism products becomes increasingly more sophisticated and better informed, subsidiary categories of certification with higher information content and greater specificity may prove more useful.

Industry perspectives on ecocertification depend on the relative maturity of the industry, and on the competitive position of the individual operator. While the private sector is generally wary of any new form of government regulation, including government-administered certification schemes, established operators may often support such schemes if they effectively comprise a barrier to market entry for new operators, maintained at public expense. In addition, if some operators have expended considerable investment in establishing a high quality of customer service and environmental performance, and ensuring that their reputation is known among their potential clientele, then it will be in their interests to support a certification scheme, which helps to differentiate them in the market from competing operators who have not made such an investment.

Certification programmes may be run by either public or private agencies. Neither is necessarily better or worse, from either consumer or industry perspectives, but there are commonly differences in the way in which they operate in practice. In particular, if a certification programme is run by representatives of the industry to which it applies, there is the risk that it will either: (i) be used or abused as a competitive marketing technique; or (ii) be applied so indiscriminately that certification provides neither information for the consumer nor competitive advantage for the operator.

The current market context for tourism ecolabels suggests that, to be effective, a scheme should incorporate four essential components. It needs global brand recognition and audit procedures, but with customized local implementation. It needs different detailed criteria for various types and scales of tourism accommodation, transport, tours and activities. It needs at least two levels of labelling, with a broad basic mass-market easily obtainable label for above-average environmental management performance, and a much more detailed, restricted and hard-to-get specialist label restricted to top performers on a range of stringent environmental criteria. Furthermore, it needs transparent criteria and procedures, with detailed information readily available to the public as a backup for the labels themselves.

For an ecolabel scheme to provide something that can continue to satisfy consumers that they receive value for money, it must generally contain two critical features, which have been described (Buckley, 2002b) as guts and teeth. The guts are the substantive criteria that distinguish between products, professionals or corporations that have earned the ecolabel, and those that have not. For example, these might include specific differences in environmental impacts, management technologies or practices adopted, or skills possessed by an individual tour guide.

The teeth of a scheme are the procedures adopted to ensure that the label is only used where it has been earned, and that it is withdrawn if no longer applicable. These include application, assessment and audit procedures, and effective and appropriately enforced penalties for unauthorized use of the ecolabel (Buckley, 2001a).

One of the more recent developments in ecocertification is the supply-chain approach, first adopted in other industry sectors and currently under trial in tourism. As of 2008, there still seems to be only one such programme still operational, known as World Hotel-Link. This is essentially an online booking system with added customer commentary, rather than a third-party certification programme. Previous attempts at supply-chain certification, adopted by individual tourism corporations such as British Airways Holidays and the German Touristik Union International, do not seem to have survived. Since World Hotel-Link is in itself a marketing and booking system, and since it is not restricted to ecotourism, it will probably be difficult to determine the degree to which customer feedback related to ecotourism criteria may influence retail sales.

In summary, the context for any form of consumer quality labelling, including tourism schemes, includes: the level of interest, knowledge, and concern over the issues addressed by the label among customers, regulators, other stakeholders and the general public; market demand and willingness to pay or choose between alternative providers for ecolabelled products; and the evolution of procedures and criteria that satisfy customers that the ecolabel is meaningful and reliable, and satisfy providers that the market advantages of ecolabelled products outweigh the costs of obtaining the label.

Environmental awards

Ecolabels, ecocertification and environmental awards are conceptually quite different, but from an ecotourism marketing perspective, they serve much the same function and are commonly seen as substitutes for each other. An ecolabel is simply an environmental label of some kind applied to a product or a company (Font and Buckley, 2001a). This is a very broad term, since it includes self-applied unsubstantiated labels as well as externally certified and audited labels. Thus the term ecotour is itself an ecolabel, whether or not it is certified. These issues are considered in detail in Font and Buckley (2001), Buckley (2002b), Font (2002) and Font and Harris (2004).

From a marketing perspective, an externally granted third-party label is much more valuable than a self-applied one, not only because it is perceived as more reliable, but because the third party will promote the labelling scheme and thus also its recipients. The most valuable, and the most difficult to obtain, are competitive awards that are granted annually by a well-known international travel or environmental organization that already has an effective mechanism for promoting the awards to potential clients of the awardees (Font and Tribe, 2001). Best-known of these are the Condé Nast World Savers Award, and the World Travel and Tourism Council's Tourism for Tomorrow Awards. In 2004, a third such scheme started operations, the World

Legacy Awards operated by *National Geographic* magazine and Conservation International. These were highly coveted and contested, but the scheme appears only to have operated for a single year.

Condé Nast Traveler is a well-established, upmarket magazine with a large, literate, well-off and highly travelled readership. The Condé Nast awards thus have the advantage that they are promoted directly to a particularly significant market sector for many ecotourism businesses, namely rich, sophisticated, frequent travellers. Different subsectors of the travel industry are considered for awards in different years. The Tourism for Tomorrow awards were originated by British Airways, but are now operated by the World Travel and Tourism Council. While well-known within the tourism industry, these awards are not as well known or recognized by the general travelling public, and it is up to the award recipient to promote the award to potential clients, which reduces its value as a marketing tool.

Tourism portfolios and promotion agencies in several individual countries, and subsidiary states and provinces, also have their own annual award schemes, which may include an environmental or ecotourism award. These, however, have rather limited market range or persuasive power, though they may help a recipient to obtain a more valuable award or label in due course. Indeed, it is commonplace for the same operator to receive multiple awards, since that is easier for both the applicant and the award judges.

There are two main reasons why ecocertification schemes do not carry the same prestige as these environmental awards. The first of these is simply that far fewer potential clients care about environmental management than quality of experience. There may be many people who care about the environment impacts of tourism, but relatively few of these may be potential clients for the tourism operations concerned; and there may be many potential clients for the tourism operations concerned, but relatively few of these may care about environmental management. The second reason is that even among environmentally concerned clients, few pay much attention to ecocertification programmes. Essentially, even if they think that ecocertification is a good idea, they do not believe that existing ecocertification programmes mean very much, because most schemes suffer from significant shortcomings. Many do not publish their certification criteria. Most have very lax entry requirements. For those with multiple tiers, the distinctions between tiers are often useless. Few have any routine system for independent and transparent external audit, and in most cases, there seems to be little or no evidence that these schemes decertify operators or products that no longer comply, and certainly not in a public manner.

At the upmarket end of the ecotourism accommodation sector, there are two trade associations, which, strictly speaking, are simply marketing syndicates, but where entry is so competitive that from a marketing perspective they operate like highly prestigious awards. The two groups are called Relais et Chateaux, and SLH (Small Luxury Hotels of the World). As their names imply, they are based purely on the quality of the customer experience, not at all on environmental management or other aspects of ecotourism. Ecolodges are therefore competing directly, in an open field, with prestigious luxury accommodation of all types. Inclusion in either of these listings, which cross-market among themselves, is thus a major promotional opportunity. Several of the game lodges operated by Conservation Corporation Africa, for example, are members of one or both of these groups.

Conclusions

Ecotourism enterprises need effective marketing strategies, like any other form of commercial business. Especially for smaller and more specialized products, traditional travel distribution systems did not serve the ecotourism and adventure subsectors well. Modern marketing systems in these subsectors rely strongly on web sites and e-mail, but do still include printed brochures and mailouts.

Electronic marketing systems have increased the reach of ecotourism enterprises but have also increased competition. As a result, eco-awards and, to a lesser extent, ecocertification programmes have become significant components of many marketing strategies, even if this was not the original intention of these schemes.

RESEARCH

There was an early text on ecotourism marketing written by Ryel and Grasse (1991) and published by Island Press, but it is no longer listed on the publisher's website. The principal text on marketing of sustainable tourism is still that by Middleton and Hawkins (1998). Several authors have examined ecotourism marketing either from theoretical perspectives (Durst and Ingram, 1988; Kalafatis and Pollard, 1999) or from a more practical standpoint (Buckley and Clough, 1997; Malek-Zadeh, 1998; Christian, 2007). Individual case studies in ecotourism marketing are listed in Table 5.1.

The most comprehensive review of tourism ecocertification to date is the volume edited by Font and Buckley (2001). Discussions published since that analysis include: Font and Tribe (2001), Buckley (2002b), Font (2002), Honey (2002), Sasidharan *et al.* (2002), Font and Harris (2004), Medina (2005) and Black and Crabtree (2007). Ecocertification of tourist destinations in particular has been examined by Kozak and Nield (2004), and of tour guides in particular by Black and Weiler (2005) and Black and Ham (2006). Tourist responses to ecocertification and ecolabels have been examined by Fairweather and Maslin (2005).

Various authors have drawn attention to the use of ecotourism terms to market tourism products that do not conform to the principles in generally accepted definitions such as those put forward in the UN International Year of Ecotourism (UNEP + WTO, 2002). Examples include: Pleumarom (1993, 1994, 1995), Weiler (1993), Wheeller (1994a,b, 1997), Arlen (1995), Porritt (1996), Lawrence *et al.* (1997), Broad and Weiler (1998), Mowforth and Munt (1998), Honey (1999, 2002), Jamal *et al.* (2006) and Donohoe and Needham (2008). The issue

Table 5.1. Case studies in ecotourism marketing.

Continent and country	Site or topic	Reference
Americas		
Canada	National and outbound	Eagles and Wind (1994)
Canada	Northern Ontario	Twynam and Robinson (1997)
Canada	Misuse of ecotourism term	Donohoe and Needham (2008)
USA	South-east	Jamrozy et al. (1996)
USA	Market segmentation	Singh and Formica (2007)
North America	Regional	Wight (1996a, b)
Europe and Asia		
Finland	Eco-resorts	Bjork (1997)
Sweden	National parks	Reinius and Fredman (2007)
UK, Greece	Consumer intentions	Kalafatis and Pollard (1999)
Scotland	Market segmentation	Zografos and Allcroft (2007)
Bulgaria	Competitive clusters	Hawkins (2004)
Mongolia	Cultural landscape	Buckley et al. (2007)
Oceania		
Australia	Resorts	Polonsky et al. (1994)
Australia	Earthwatch clients	Weiler and Richins (1995)
Australia	National	Blamey and Braithwaite (1997)
Australia	Gold Coast accommodation	Buckley and Araujo (1997a)
Australia	National	Lang and O'Leary (1997)
Australia	World Heritage	Trauer and McIntyre (1998)
Australia	Marine wildlife	Moscardo (2000)
Australia	Gold Coast hinterland	Weaver and Lawton (2002)
New Zealand	Adventure	Christian (2007)
Global		
World	Developing countries	Durst and Ingram (1988)
World	Adventure and ecotourism	Buckley and Clough (1997)

was expressed by Lawrence *et al.* (1997) in terms of 'legitimacy'. This approach underpins the various attempts at ecocertification. Just as the ecotourism label was co-opted purely for marketing, however, tourism ecocertification schemes may equally lose legitimacy in their quest for financial survival and profit.

Recent research in the electronic marketing of ecotourism and related sectors has revealed some interesting results. Singh and Formica (2007) found that tourism destination marketing organizations in the north-eastern USA generally use different images on their web sites from those in their printed brochures. Govers *et al.* (2007) found that tourist perceptions of particular destinations are, in any event, not based on promotion by the tourism industry. Po-Hsi and Scott (2006) examined Internet-based marketing by selected ecolodges in Latin America, and Pan *et al.* (2007) suggested that tourist perceptions of destinations can be derived from travel blogs.

REVISION

Ecocertification schemes

- Labels
- Awards
- Membership of supply-chain
- Checklists cf. quantitative criteria
- Audits and penalties

Marketing

- Mainstream tourism distribution system
- Alternative marketing: web sites, referrals, associations
- Syndicated marketing for ecotourism SMEs

Ecotourism as a marketing label

- Is there an ecotourism market segment?
- What makes people purchase ecotours?
- Attraction, activity, guide, ethics?
- 'Ecotourism lite' and 'greenwash': dilution and disbelief

Ecolabels, awards and ecocertification

- Independent awards, e.g. Condé Nast, Tourism for Tomorrow
- Competitive-entry associations, e.g. Relais et Chateaux, SLH
- Membership-based certification, e.g. Ecotourism Australia scheme
- Supply-chain systems, e.g. World Hotel-Link

REFLECTIONS

1. Identify a specific ecotourism product, either actual or conceptual, and construct a strategic marketing plan for that product, which takes into account countries of origin, seasonality, competition and costs.

2. Would you, yourself, take any ecolabels, awards or certification into account in purchasing a holiday or tourism product? If so, what aspects would you consider important, and why? If not, why not?

3. Draw up a table of tourism ecocertification systems operating in your area, including strengths and weaknesses of each. Select an actual ecotourism product currently on offer in your area and prepare a report and recommendation on which, if any, of these schemes you would suggest they join, and why.

4. What are the purposes and/or potential benefits of tourism ecocertification programmes, from the perspectives of tour operators, government tourism agencies, landholders and land management agencies, and individual tour clients? Choose any two actual tourism ecocertification programmes and compare their structures, funding arrangements, eligibility and certification criteria, audit procedures and penalties, and public transparency. How well does each of these schemes deliver its expected benefits to each of the stakeholder groups as above?

READING 5.1. GREEN ADVERTISING IN MAINSTREAM COASTAL TOURISM

Images of the natural environment have long been commonplace in advertising by many sectors of the tourism industry. Various sectors also depend on the natural environment in different ways and degrees. Buckley and Araujo (1997a) examined how the tourism industry in the Gold Coast, Australia's principal tourism region, used environmental images and text references in their advertising brochures.

They found that around 100 tourism enterprises distributed printed brochures and that, of these, two-thirds used the environment in some way. For 34%, the environment was the mainstay of the product offered, e.g. in rainforest tours. For 18%, it provided a setting but not the principal attraction per se, e.g. for rural horseback riding, golf or resorts. For 15%, the environment was exploited for an excitement-based product with little or no concern for damage, e.g. in four-wheel-drive follow-the-leader bush-bashes. The remaining brochures did not mention the natural environment at all. These proportions differed considerably between different types of business: 80% of four-wheel-drive tours, for example, used the environment as a product; 89% of resorts use it as a setting. Overall, tours tended to use the environment as a product or something to exploit, whereas fixed-site attractions used it more as a setting or not at all.

Almost all the brochures were illustrated, most in colour. There were over a thousand individual images. Overall, one-third of these images featured the natural environment in some way. The proportion of images showing landscapes, plants or animals was highest (72%) in brochures for four-wheel-drive tours. Brochures for four-wheel-drive tours also contained proportionately more text references to the natural environment and wildlife than other types of business. Only five of the brochures, all of them theme parks, advertised that the operator makes some material contribution to conservation of the natural environment. Not a single brochure mentioned the operator's environmental management practices, and only three were printed on recycled paper.

Buckley and Araujo (1997a) concluded that for about a third of Gold Coast tourism businesses that advertised through brochures, the natural environment was peripheral to their operations and not mentioned in the brochures. For the majority that did use the natural environment in their advertising, it was overwhelmingly as part of the product: either as the principal focus, or as a setting. The proportions that advertised environmental education, contributions to conservation or low-impact operating procedures were very low. Overwhelmingly, the impression from these brochures was of firms that advertised how they used the natural environment for current clients' gratification, but not what they do to conserve those environments for the enjoyment of further clients in future.

chapter 6

ECONOMICS

Ecotourism student group dressed in traditional Gurung costumes on the trek to Annapurna Base Camp, Nepal. Photo courtesy of Chelsea Northrope.

REVIEW

Introduction

This chapter outlines the economics of the ecotourism sector, focusing on its scale, valuation, contributions to communities and conservation, fees and charges, and economic equity issues. All of these issues are at a micro or meso scale in economic terms. Smaller-scale financial factors affecting the profitability of individual enterprises are considered in Chapter 3. There are relatively few countries where the ecotourism sector is large enough to affect other sectors of the economy, the balance of trade or payments, the value of the currency or similar macroeconomic considerations. Examples include some of the smaller island and developing nations, which depend strongly on tourism. Even for these nations, however, macroeconomic linkages remain unstudied.

Overall economic scale

The economic scale of ecotourism depends on what is included: ecotourism in the strict sense, nature tourism broadly defined, or the entire NEAT sector. Rather few tourism operations comply with the strict definitions of ecotourism, which require a contribution to conservation as well as a nature-based product, minimal-impact management, and environmental interpretation. Ecotourism in the strict sense is thus rather small globally, perhaps as low as a few hundred millions of dollars annually.

If nature tourism more broadly is considered to include all visits to national parks and other protected areas, however, then the social economic value of such visits can be estimated using time, travel and equipment costs as well as direct fees and charges. Using this approach, the total economic scale would be in the order of tens or hundreds of billions of dollars, depending on how such values are calculated. If the entire NEAT or outdoor tourism sector is included, then estimates of total economic scale range up to US$1 trillion per annum, again depending on what is included. The main factors involved in these estimates are outlined below.

Outdoor tourism or NEAT is a substantial sector. In countries such as New Zealand and Costa Rica, it appears that nearly the entire tourism industry is in the outdoor sector. In Australia, outdoor tourism, largely in the adventure sector, seems to make up about one-quarter to one-third of the tourism industry overall (Buckley, 1998b), i.e. currently around US$20 billion annually. In the USA, the figure is currently believed to be around US$730 billion per annum (Outdoor Industry Association, 2007).

The outdoor tourism sector has shown unprecedented growth during the past decade. This seems to be due at least in part to the increasing commercialization of outdoor recreation (Buckley, 2006). This in turn seems likely to be due to increasing urbanization in both developed and newly industrialized nations, producing a cohort of relatively well-off people with outdoor interests but no outdoor skills. It may also be driven by the increasing cost of outdoor recreational equipment, and by the increasing cross-linkages between the outdoor recreation, clothing and entertainment industries (Buckley, 2003c).

Components

The precise economic scale of the NEAT sector worldwide depends on which activities are included, what cost components are considered and how the value of equipment is accounted for. Most estimates of the economic scale of tourism include travel for private purposes in addition to packaged tours. For example, the VFR subsector, people travelling to visit friends and relatives, is a recognized component of the tourism industry. Under this definition, therefore, expenditure by people travelling to visit national parks or undertake private outdoor recreation, as well as people purchasing nature or adventure travel packages, should be accounted as part of the NEAT sector. Likewise, the equipment they buy or hire for such activities, from hiking boots to helicopters, should be included.

This is straightforward for items that are used only for recreational purposes. Many items, however, may be used for work as well as play, and data are rarely available to partition the relevant expenditure between uses. Four-wheel-drive vehicles are one commonly cited example, but there are many others.

There are two particular issues in determining which activity subsectors should be included. Wildlife watching, for example, though clearly nature-based, can also be highly adrenalin-charged and adventurous in some circumstances. Adventure activities such as rafting and mountaineering, however, while classified as adventure, also provide opportunities for contemplation of nature. If the outdoor tourism sector is considered as a whole, this distinction becomes unimportant.

The second issue applies to large-scale outdoor tourism activities that use a fixed site or at least a fixed base, and which may be integrated with retail and real estate sales and property development. The principal examples are ski resorts and boating marinas. These are highly significant in economic terms, because of the high property values and construction costs. Much of the marine NEAT industry, including diving and whalewatching tours, operates out of recreational marinas rather than industrial ports. The main clientele for most marinas, however, is the local residential population. Economic parameters related to these large-scale, fixed-site developments therefore need to be partitioned between tourism and residential use. This is far from straightforward.

Estimation approaches

In practice, there are several different ways to estimate for the economic scale of various components of the outdoor tourism industry. The first approach, most precise but also most limited, is based on estimating the retail value of commercial tours offering a particular activity in a particular geographic region. These are essentially just aggregate sales figures for a specified set of individual tour operators: for example, dive tours in the Caribbean (Green and Donnelly, 2003) or whalewatching worldwide (Hoyt, 2000). Such estimates, however, do not capture the costs of domestic and international travel to get to the tour's starting point; or expenditure on private individual recreation involving the same activity in the same area; or any of the associated components such as equipment manufacturing, clothing, entertainment and property development, except inasmuch as these are incorporated in package tour prices.

In addition, these bottom-up approaches that rely on identifying all the individual operators and asking them to provide financial information are likely to underestimate the total size of the sector, for two main reasons. The first is that some operators may not be identified, may not respond, or may provide incomplete or inaccurate information. The second is that if the sector is growing more rapidly than the tourism industry as a whole, the lag in compiling data will lead to a greater proportional underestimate of total size than for national statistics in the tourism industry as a whole or other industry sectors.

The second type of estimate attempts to aggregate all components of the adventure tourism sector for a particular geographic region, by adding together the various individual activities and expenditures involved. The third type of information derives from the sales of outdoor adventure equipment and clothing, either from individual companies or for manufacturing associations in individual countries.

A fourth type of information is derived from a somewhat different approach, a demand-side rather than a supply-side measure. Essentially, it involves asking people how they spend their time and why, and partitioning their total expenditure accordingly. A fifth approach is to disaggregate national tourism statistics from the top down. Since no statistics are kept on environmental management performance, environmental education or contributions to conservation in the tourism sector, a top-down approach cannot currently be used to estimate the size of the ecotourism sector in its most restrictive sense. It is, however, a useful way to estimate the scale of nature-based tourism in its broad sense. The principal difficulty is that many tourists visit both nature-based and urban attractions in a single trip. Indeed, many tourism packages incorporate both nature-based and urban components. To establish what proportion of overall tourism expenditure is nature-based would therefore require analysis of all such packages, apportioning expenditure between nature-based and other components and multiplying by the number of clients for the package concerned, and surveys of free and independent travellers (FITs) to obtain corresponding information. This does not yet seem to have been attempted.

To test the reliability of these estimates, we can compare measures derived from supply-side or bottom-up, and demand-side or top-down approaches. In Australia, for example, both of these approaches indicate that outdoor tourism makes up about one-third of the tourism industry as a whole.

One of the difficulties in top-down estimation approaches is that the size of the tourism industry as a whole is also imprecise, depending on how it is defined and how it is measured. For example, a broad distinction may be made between holiday travel and business travel, but many people combine work and play in a single trip. Similarly, tourism is generally interpreted to include domestic recreation by families and individuals as well as international holiday travel, but at what threshold should day-to-day entertainment and leisure be distinguished from recreation as a separate activity? To overcome these difficulties for statistical analysis at a macro level, tourism and travel are generally considered a single aggregated sector; domestic recreation is counted as tourism if it involves an overnight stay away from the normal place of residence, whether in commercial accommodation or visiting friends or relatives.

Economic statistics quoted for the global tourism industry by the UN World Tourism Organization (UNWTO, 2007), for example, seem to be quite different from those quoted by the World Travel and Tourism Council (WTTC, 2007). The WTTC figures, which include a broader bundle of components associated with travel and tourism, suggest a global total approaching US$7 trillion for 2006. This would be about 11% of higher end estimates of global GNP.

There are apparently no global estimates as to what proportion of this constitutes outdoor tourism. For some countries, nearly the entire tourism industry is outdoors, but these tend to be the smaller countries. In Australia, the proportion may be about one-third, as noted above. In North America, it may be similar, especially if hunting and shooting are included. In Europe, it is probably smaller, though the ski and boating industries are certainly significant. In Asia, it is small at present, but growing rapidly. Even if the proportion at a global scale were less than one fifth, however, this would still indicate that the global outdoor tourism industry is worth over US$1 trillion annually.

Because these estimates are so incomplete, they are not sufficiently reliable to indicate trends in economic scale over time. More reliable indications of trends can be derived from repeated and retrospective surveys of participation and expenditure in particular areas. Figures released by the Outdoor Industry Association (2005) in the USA, for example, found that two-thirds of the US population had taken part in some form of outdoor recreation, principally hiking, during 2003.

Product prices

Retail prices for commercial ecotourism products vary enormously. Top-end luxury game lodges, diving retreats or expedition vessels may charge over US$1000 per person per day, and some adventure tourism products charge even more. The majority of high-volume family-orientated products, however, cost less than US$100 a day, and some products aimed at the backpacker market cost only tens of dollars a day. Likewise, some low-key community ecotourism products priced for local markets charge less than US$10 per person per day, generally not including accommodation. However, some equally low-key community ecotourism products that have successfully attracted international attention and clientele may charge hundreds of dollars per person per day despite a very rudimentary level of service. Where product prices include fees charged by parks or other landowners or land management agencies, these fees may range from nothing to over US$100 per person per day, depending on the country, the particular place and the activity concerned.

Contributions to local communities

The economic and social impacts of any industry depend not only on its overall profitability, but also on its financial structure at various scales. The tourism industry has been described as renting out local environments to visiting strangers, and the issue is not only whether the rent covers the maintenance cost, but who receives the rent and who pays the cost. A backpacker staying in a local bed-and-breakfast establishment will generally pay less for a night's accommodation than an international package tourist staying in an upmarket hotel, but the former pays cash to the locals who actually live in the bed-and-breakfast house, whereas the latter will typically pay an overseas travel agent, which pays a hotel booking agency, which pays the company that owns the hotel chain, which pays the operating costs of the individual hotel. Alternatively, the money may go first to the operating hotel, but the hotel may have to pay commissions, franchise fees, shareholders' dividends, etc.

The hotel also has to pay its immediate operating costs, notably labour, utilities, maintenance and consumables, and it may purchase these goods and services locally or import them. It may hire on the local job market, or if it has foreign ownership and caters largely to tourists from overseas, it may hire a significant proportion of its staff from the country concerned, e.g. on working holiday visas or other arrangements. Even if it hires staff from within the country where it is built, they may be skilled workers from cities or itinerant construction workers, rather than members of local communities.

During construction, the hotel may buy all construction materials and all items of plant and equipment from manufacturers and suppliers in the country where it is built, or it may import them from manufacturers and suppliers elsewhere. In some cases, imports are inevitable since the items concerned are simply not manufactured or available locally. A new resort development on a small Pacific island, for example, would generally have to bring in everything it needed, and a new development in a remote coastal area of a large country might well find it cheaper to import items by boat from overseas than to transport them by road from a distant city within that country.

For urban hotels, water and electricity will generally be purchased from the local municipal supply or utility. In greenfields sites where a resort has to install its own generators, water supply and waste treatment systems, these become additional items of plant, which could be purchased anywhere. The same applies to smaller items of equipment for routine operations, such as computing and telecommunications, hardware, white-goods and electrical appliances, furniture, crockery and cutlery, and disposables. Even food may be supplied from overseas in preserved or frozen form, particularly for higher-value items used if a hotel is supplying the cuisine of an overseas nation to meet the expectations of international visitors.

Overall, therefore, it is clear that while the construction and operation of a hotel could yield a significant economic input for a local community, it could also contribute little or nothing. In consequence, even though the cost of a night's accommodation at a hotel will generally be higher than at a bed-and-breakfast establishment, the economic return to the local community may be either higher or lower, depending on a wide range of variables in the way the hotel is owned and operated.

Similar considerations apply for transport, tour operators and tourist activities and entertainment at all scales from airlines, international coach companies and major theme parks, to small-scale tours and local attractions. Note that while environmental, social and cultural issues are often mentioned together, there is not necessarily any connection between them. A small specialist ecotour operator in a developing nation, for example, may well import rafts, mountain bikes or backpacks from overseas, and employ overseas nationals as guides, irrespective of its policy, practice and performance in relation to minimal-impact and environmental equipment and management. Conversely, a locally owned company using local transport and equipment may show little or no concern for environmental protection.

A distinction also needs to be made between nationals, in the sense of people resident in the country concerned, and locals, in the sense of people who were already resident close enough to the tourist activity to be within easy commuting distance by the usual local means of transport. There are instances in many countries, at all stages of development, where wealthy and powerful individuals from the cities have established tourist operations in rural and regional areas without employing any locals, and indeed, often in competition with local enterprises.

Overall, therefore, the question of direct financial return to local communities by hiring local people or buying local products can be quite a complex issue. Indirect returns are more complex still. For example, a new greenfields tourist development may provide potential business opportunities and market for local enterprises, even if it did not hire locals and buy their products initially. It may provide infrastructure such as improved roads, electricity, docks or airstrips, which can provide new opportunities for locals, unrelated to tourism. It may provide community services in the form of schools or medical facilities.

Of course, the opposite may also occur. It may cause congestion and speeding on existing roads. It may bring children with an inner-city background of school violence to formerly peaceful local schools. It may increase levels of petty or organized crime. There is no simple or universal pattern.

National legislation

These patterns also differ between countries, depending on local policies and legislation. Many countries have legal, financial and taxation mechanisms designed to trap foreign exchange. These range from the relatively subtle to the extremely crude. For example, if a country makes it difficult for foreign nationals to obtain work permits, that essentially forces foreign-owned companies to hire locals, even if this requires extensive training at the company's expense. Of course, such a policy can backfire if it makes it difficult for tour operators to provide a level of service that will satisfy their customers, so that the customers go to another country and the operator goes out of business. On the other hand, if there is in fact a supply of adequately skilled nationals in search of employment, this policy can be an effective mechanism to ensure they are not discriminated against.

Many countries also have restrictions on foreign ownership of corporations. For example, special government permission may be required for a company to have a majority overseas shareholding. Again, such requirements may be two-edged swords. On the one hand, they may prevent a foreign-owned company making a profit at the expense of locals, and then repatriating that profit to shareholders overseas. On the other hand, it may restrict the access of local entrepreneurs to investment and development capital, if it increases the risk that international investors may lose control over their investment.

Government policies and legal mechanisms such as the above affect all industry sectors, not only tourism. Some countries, however, have adopted financial mechanisms that discriminate blatantly between nationals and overseas visitors. Some countries insist that all foreign visitors pay for travel and accommodation in foreign exchange, typically US dollars or euros, rather than in local currency. Some require that foreign visitors must spend a minimum average daily amount, in foreign exchange, while in the country. Some have different price schedules for airline, train, bus and taxi fares, and different accommodation tariffs, for foreigners as compared to nationals. Some charge different entrance and activity fees for national parks and other public lands, and for some tourist attractions. Perhaps the extreme example, as used by China during the 1980s, is to have an entirely separate currency for foreign visitors, with separate fares, separate accommodation and even separate shops.

Depending on their precise structure, discriminatory measures such as these may be contrary to the provisions of the World Trade Organization. Many developing nations, however, have been slow in bringing their laws, policies and practices in line with WTO rules, and a number of discriminatory practices still exist.

Irrespective of compliance with international rules, whether a particular provision is equitable in a broader social sense depends heavily on the economic status of the country concerned. For example, if foreign visitors have far higher real earnings than nationals, it seems reasonable that they pay more for access to parks or facilities. An entry fee of a few dollars may have little effect on foreign visitors, but could exclude local access from a national park completely.

Contributions to conservation

There are many different mechanisms by which the tourism industry may, or could, contribute directly or indirectly to conservation of the natural environment. At the broadest level are company, sales and personal income tax contributions to general government revenue, of which a part is used to fund parks management agencies. These contributions are proportionately larger in countries with a heavy economic dependence on nature-based tourism. At a somewhat smaller scale are government levies on tourist operators in a particular area or sector, earmarked for conservation projects or environmental science research. Marine tour operators in Australia's Great Barrier Reef Marine Park, for example, pay such a contribution. Governments may also charge licence fees, lease payments or headworks charges for tourism developments on public lands in or adjacent to national parks. It is now commonplace for parks agencies to charge entrance, permit, licence or user fees for individual tourists or commercial operators in national parks and other conservation reserves and public lands, though these are not necessarily spent on conservation.

In addition to compulsory payments as above, some tour operators make voluntary contributions to park management, conservation projects, ranger salaries, etc., or play a formal or informal role in policing conservation areas against wildlife poaching, tree cutting, etc. Some tour packages also include contributions to conservation organizations as one component in the package price. In addition, financial contributions to local economies provide incentives for local conservation efforts and a competitive alternative to other industry sectors causing greater environmental damage.

Should parks keep fees?

One particularly contentious issue is the degree to which funds raised from tourism by park managers, e.g. through entrance fees, should be earmarked or 'hypothecated' for use by the park concerned. If such funds are returned to general government revenue, then they involve parks staff in additional work collecting fees, when their time could better be spent on conservation activities, ranger duties and public education. The fees make a very small proportional contribution to total government revenues, and cause considerable resentment as they are levied very conspicuously. In addition, such fees may be perceived as double dipping by governments, since national parks are public lands, and the public has already paid for management through income taxes.

There are several additional indirect risks to conservation if parks agencies are permitted and expected to keep all the funds raised from visitors and the tourism industry. The first is the risk that funding for park management from general government revenue will be reduced by the amount raised in entrance fees, giving park managers an extra workload in fee collection, but no additional operating funds overall. The second is pressure on parks agencies to raise funds for routine conservation activities through commercial enterprises, leading to severe conflicts of interest. Third is the risk that national parks and conservation reserves will come to be perceived as lands where recreation and tourism are the primary purpose, rather than lands where conservation is the primary purpose and recreation secondary. Indeed, in some national parks it has already proved necessary to restate the primary conservation functions explicitly in management plans, in response to public concern over a shift in management policies.

There are a few instances where visitor entrance fees cover the entire operating costs of privately owned or privately run reserves, but most of these are relatively small areas. There are also examples of large public reserves where the total private revenues from nature-based tourism greatly exceed the total public management costs, but where there is no direct financial link between the two. The Great Barrier Reef Marine Park and the Wet Tropics of Queensland World Heritage Area provide good examples (Driml, 1997).

Tourism cf. other land uses

One of the most significant economic features of ecotourism is that it can potentially generate an economic return from areas of relatively undisturbed natural environment, with a much lower level of environmental damage than other types of industry. To assess the practical significance of this role requires quantitative data on the economic return from various types of tourism-related land use in comparison to other potential industrial activities (Ward, 2003).

There are many instances where a shift in regional economies and land use towards tourism has indeed occurred. The principal example is perhaps the growth of wilderness recreation and commercial ecotourism in many areas managed as public forests. This includes: designated Wilderness Areas in national forests managed by the United States Forest Service; the Wet Tropics of Queensland World Heritage Area; and areas still within active logging cycles in British Columbia and Tasmania. In marine environments there has been a parallel growth of recreational fishing and commercial fishing tours in areas previously used only for large-scale commercial fish harvesting, e.g. in Alaska, USA and the Great Barrier Reef, Australia. At a more localized scale, there are a number of places where individual recreation and commercial tourism have taken over as the main land use in areas previously used principally or partly for mining, e.g. the Flinders Ranges and Kakadu National Park, Australia. In many rural regions worldwide, nature-based and farmstay tourism have become established as major land uses in areas previously used only for large-scale agricultural production.

There are also many instances where the economic potential of the current and future tourism industry is at risk from development in other industry sectors. Well-known examples include water-supply and hydroelectric dams in countries such as China, Chile and Australia. In some of these cases, the tourism industry has survived despite the dams; in others, it has been closed down completely.

Equity and revenue distributions

From a public policy perspective, overall profitability is not the only concern in determining whether particular public lands should be allocated preferentially to tourism or to some other land use. Questions of equity are also important. At the most basic, a public agency needs to consider: who gains and who loses; how many people there are in each category; and whether there is any mechanism for those who gain to compensate those who lose. In practice, such agencies also consider whether the people and companies involved are domestic or overseas citizens; if the former, whether they are local residents or distant company owners and shareholders. Even within a single local community, they may consider whether revenues are distributed to make a significant if small material improvement to a large number of people, or concentrated in the hands of a few individuals who may already be wealthy. The degree of importance that governments assign to these goals varies considerably from one country to another, and from one political party to another, but most of them are incorporated in government policy in one form or another.

At a larger scale, a number of structural economic factors contribute to the relative evenness or otherwise of revenue distribution in any particular industry sector, including tourism. For example, the commercial activity concerned may be conducted principally by a few very large corporations, or distributed across a larger number of small to medium-sized enterprises (SMEs).

The companies concerned may be limited-liability publicly listed corporations with a large number of shareholders, or they may be privately owned proprietary companies. The distribution of revenue also depends on: how much of a company's income is spent on salaries, how much in directors' fees, and how much is paid to shareholders as dividends; the employment conditions and pay rates for employees; and the proportions of company income spent on purchasing goods and contract services, and the proportions of these supplied by local businesses.

Conclusions

The overall economic scale of the ecotourism sector depends on how the sector is defined and how its economic impacts and significance are measured and valued. Outdoor tourism as a whole may be a trillion-dollar industry worldwide, but ecotourism more narrowly defined is far smaller. Key economic issues in ecotourism policy include contributions to local communities and to conservation, and neither of these is straightforward. The former, for example, involves significant issues of community equity, considered further in Chapter 11. The latter includes perennially thorny questions related to parks fees.

RESEARCH

Research on the economics of ecotourism can usefully be considered in three main categories. The first addresses the value of natural attractions attributable to ecotourism and outdoor recreation. The second records actual expenditure of ecotourists at particular sites, occasionally with estimates of regional economic impact. The third studies the use, effectiveness and economic significance of fees charged by landowners or land management agencies for ecotourists and other visitors to enter a particular area and carry out particular activities.

In each of these categories there are established reference books and methodological analyses as well as numerous case studies. Valuation methods, for example, have been reviewed or analysed by Aylward (1992), Clawson (1992), Carson (1993), Holmes *et al.* (1998), Hearne and Salinas (2002), Haab and McConnell (2002), Stoeckl (2003), Douglas and Johnson (2004), Stevens (2004), Baumgartner *et al.* (2006), Azqueta and Sotelsek (2007), and Bebbington *et al.* (2007). Estimates for protected areas worldwide were calculated by Bagri *et al.* (1998) and Font (2000), for tropical forests by Gössling (1999), and for coral reefs by Brander *et al.* (2007). Methods for estimating economic impact were addressed by Smith (2000), Dwyer *et al.* (2004), Alpizar (2006), Frechtling (2006), Loomis (2006), Stynes and White (2006), Lindsey *et al.* (2007) and Mehmetoglu (2007). Economic impacts may also include increases in property values adjacent to heavily visited protected areas (Johnson *et al.*, 2003; McDonald *et al.*, 2007). Tourist expenditure and economic impacts may fall when the natural resource is degraded (Andersson, 2007). Fee systems have been considered by Dixon and Sherman (1991), Lindberg (1991, 1993), Laarman and Gregersen (1996), Barker (1997), Beal and Harrison (1998), Dharmaratne *et al.* (2000) and Buckley *et al.* (2003b). Case studies are listed in Tables 6.1, 6.2 and 6.3. One particular case study that was well ahead of its time is that by Alderman (1990, 1994) who examined the economics of 93 private reserves in the Americas, including reference to ecotourism.

Table 6.1. Case studies, economic valuation of ecotourism.

Continent and country	Area, region or subject	Reference
Africa		
Kenya	NPs	Moran (1994)
Kenya	Lake Nakuru, flamingos	Navrud and Mungatana (1994)
Madagascar	NPs	Maille and Mendelsoln (1993)
Madagascar	NPs	Mercer et al. (1995)
South Africa	Clean beaches	Ballance et al. (2000)
South Africa	Eastern Cape	Kerley et al. (1995)
Botswana	Moremi NP	Mmopelwa et al. (2007)
Americas		
Canada	Point Pelee NP, birds	Butler et al. (1994)
Canada	Jasper NP, forests	Englin et al. (2006)
USA	Vermont, whitewater	NNRC (1997)
USA	Pennsylvania, outdoors	Shafer et al. (1993)
USA	Moab, Utah, biking	Fix and Loomis (1997)
USA	Trinity River, California	Douglas and Taylor (1998)
USA	McNeil River, Alaska, bears	Clayton and Mendelsohn (1993)
Costa Rica	Monteverde Cloud Forest	Echeverria et al. (1995)
Costa Rica	Forests	Menkhaus and Lober (1996)
Colombia, Bolivia	Forests	Broekhoven (1996)
Peru	Amazon rainforest	Peters et al. (1989)
Europe		
Scotland	Orkneys, etc., wildlife	Crabtree et al. (1994)
Ireland	Forest nature reserves	Scarpa et al. (2000)
England	Southwest, grey seals	Bosetti and Pearce (2003)
Italy	Section of Alps	Gios et al. (2006)
Asia		
Sri Lanka	Asian elephant	Bandara and Tisdell (2004)
Sri Lanka	Coral reefs	Berg et al. (1998)

Continued

Table 6.1. *Continued.*

Continent and country	Area, region or subject	Reference
India	Kerala, angling	Korakandy (1998)
Sikkim	Lake Khecheopalri	Maharana *et al.* (2000)
South Korea	Mt Minju	Lee (1997); Lee *et al.* (1998)
South Korea	Five NPs	Lee and Han (2002)
Thailand	NPs	Mercer *et al.* (1995)
Indonesia	Lesuer NP, Sumatra	Van Beukering *et al.* (2002)
Malaysia	Selangar, fireflies	Othman and Othman (1998)
Oceania		
Australia	Ningaloo, Western Australia, whalesharks	Davis and Tisdell (1999)
Australia	Wet tropics, WHA	Driml (2002)
Australia	Fraser Island, WHA	Ward (2000b)

NP, national park; WHA, World Heritage Area.

Table 6.2. Case studies, ecotourism expenditure and economic impact.

Continent and country	Site or region	Reference
Africa		
Central African Republic	Dzanga-Sangha Park	Blom (2000, 2004)
Uganda	Mgahinga, Bwindi	Archabald and Naughton-Treves (2001)
Tanzania	Maasai lands	Goodman (2002)
Seychelles	National	Archer and Fletcher (1996)
Botswana	Northern	Borge *et al.* (1991)
Botswana	Wildlife tourism	Barnes *et al.* (1992); Barnes (1996)
South Africa	Kruger NP	Saayman and Saayman (2006)
Americas		
USA	Montana	Yuan and Christensen (1994)
USA	SE Arizona, birds	Leones *et al.* (1998)
USA	Apalachicola NP	Shrestha *et al.* (2007)
USA	Chattooga River	Siderelis and Moore (2006)
USA	Montana	Wilton and Nickerson (2006)

Continued

Table 6.2. *Continued.*

Continent and country	Site or region	Reference
Mexico	Islands, NW	Tershy *et al.* (1999)
Caribbean	Marine parks	Dixon and van't Hof (1997)
Belize	Possum Point	Kangas *et al.* (1995)
Belize	National	Lindberg and Enriquez (1994); Lindberg *et al.* (1996)
Costa Rica	Parks	Burnie (1994)
Costa Rica	Monteverde Cloud Forest	Tobias and Mendelsohn (1991)
Asia		
Nepal	Parks	Wells (1993)
Nepal	Chitwan NP	Bookbinder *et al.* (1998)
Indonesia	Komodo NP	Walpole and Goodwin (2000)
Oceania		
Australia	5 WHAs	Driml and Common (1995)
Australia	Great Barrier Reef and Wet Tropics WHA	Driml and Common (1996)
Australia	Koalas	Hundloe and Hamilton (1997)
Australia	Backpackers	Loker-Murphy and Pearce (1995)
Australia	Monkey Mia, Hervey Bay	Stoeckl *et al.* (2005)
World		
Global	Whales	Hoyt (2000)

NP, national park; WHA, World Heritage Area.

Table 6.3. Case studies, fees and economic instruments.

Continent and country	Site or region	Reference
Americas		
Canada	Parks	Eagles (2002)
USA	Wilderness	Richer and Christensen (1999)
USA	Recreation sites	Schroeder and Louviere (1999)
USA	RFDP	Watson and Herath (1999)
USA	RFDP implementation	Martin (1999)

Continued

Table 6.3. *Continued.*

Continent and country	Site or region	Reference
USA	RFDP, low-income effects	More and Stevens (2000)
USA	RFDP	Ostergren *et al.* (2005)
USA	Hawaii, Hanauma Bay	Mak and Moncur (1998)
Costa Rica	3 parks	Lindberg and Aylward (1999)
Costa Rica	National	Chase (1997); Chase *et al.* (1998)
Caribbean	Marine parks	Dixon *et al.* (1993)
Europe		
Sweden	Snowmobiles	Vail and Heldt (2004)
Sweden	Hunting	Gunnarsdotter (2006)
Oceania		
Indonesia	Komodo NP	Walpole *et al.* (2001)
Australia	Great Barrier Reef NP	Green and Lal (1991)

RFDP, Recreation fee demonstration programme; NP, national park.

REVISION

Measuring economic scale

- Size of sector depends on what is included
- Strictly defined ecotourism very small
- National park visitation intermediate
- Overall outdoor tourism very large

Ecotourism strictly defined: specific tour operators

- Measure aggregate turnover of ecotourism operations
- Define on most limiting criterion
- That is, net contribution to conservation
- Screen and sample actual case studies
- Very few satisfy this criterion
- So total economic scale very small

Nature tourism broadly defined: visiting parks

- Broad definition uses product criterion only: nature-based attraction
- Largest component is visitation to national parks

- Parks run as public good not commercial operation
- So estimating economic value requires indirect measures
- For example, travel cost and time value as well as fees and direct costs
- Park entry and activity fees vary enormously between countries and parks
- Fees often differ between locals and long-distance visitors
- Fees are set more by political than economic factors
- Fees are small cf. economic value

Valuing park visits

- Minimum value of park visit measured by expenditure to experience it
- Four components: fees, travel, time, gear
- Fees = direct charges by park
- Includes entry, camping, activity
- Travel = costs to get there
- For example, tour package, plane or bus, private vehicle costs
- Includes accommodation, etc. as part of travel
- Time cost = value of time lost during travel and visit
- For example, as measured by income foregone
- Fraction of time depends on precise economic issue addressed
- Gear = recreational equipment
- Specialist equipment value in full
- Divided over years of use
- For example, birdwatching binoculars, tents, sleeping bags, etc.
- Non-specialist gear partitioned by use, e.g. four-wheel-drive vehicles

Outdoor tourism industry or NEAT sector

- Ecotourism and nature tourism are part of outdoor tourism industry
- Outdoor tourism also includes a large adventure tourism subsector
- With associated equipment and clothing subsectors
- Much of equipment is mechanized and hence expensive
- Sector also includes fixed-site activities
- Notably ski resorts and boating marinas
- These include residential real estate components
- Adventure recreation also triggers amenity migration
- Total scale of outdoor industry is hence US$ trillions per annum

Some statistics

- US outdoor industry = US$730 billion in 2006 (Outdoor Industry Association, 2007)
- Includes ski resorts

- Outdoor tourism ranges from <20% to >90% of total tourism in different countries
- Global estimate is at least 20% of overall tourism sector
- Total global tourism approx US$7 trillion (WTTC, 2007)
- That is, global outdoor tourism >US$1 trillion
- Possibly up to US$1.5–2 trillion

High-priced adventure tours

- Highest prices are in adventure tourism
- For example, US$20 million space tourism
- Also various aircraft and helicopter options >US$1000 per day
- Few if any would be considered ecotourism
- Some expedition wildlife cruises also >US$1000 per day
- Generally would be considered ecotourism
- Prices for various adventure activities US$50-500 per person per day
- Prices for luxury ecolodges and guided ecotours up to US$4000 per person per day
- But most around US$200 per day
- High-volume and family nature tours commonly <US$100 per person per day

Parks and community ecotours

- Direct costs to visit national parks typically <US$20 per person per day
- But may be up to US$100 in particular parks
- Short low-key community ecotours in developing countries may cost <US$10
- Community ecolodges and guest houses typically <US$20 per person per day
- Generally, high-volume products are low-priced and vice versa
- But many mid-priced high-volume adventure tourism products (e.g. rafting)
- And some low-priced low-volume community ecotourism products

Fees and charges

- Big differences between public and private land
- Private landowners negotiate individual contracts
- May include fixed rental or revenue sharing
- And/or use fees per day or per person
- Can have different charges for different operators
- Can offer exclusive access at premium price
- Or can operate own tourism business
- Commercial arrangements, driven by profit

Recreation fees in public parks

- Many parks charge visitor entrance and activity fees
- Fees generally do not cover cost of recreational infrastructure management

- But most parks are expected to provide recreation as well as conservation
- Therefore, these fees help to offset recreation costs
- And hence, indirectly, maintain more of public funding for conservation
- No estimates yet available of total global cashflow
- In developed countries, fees are typically only a few per cent of total budget
- In developing countries, however, visitor fees may be major source of operating cash

Tour operator fees in public lands

- Operations subject to laws and policies on equity, procedure, etc.
- May be one-off negotiations for large tourism operations
- But, typically, standardized arrangements for many small operators
- May include qualification, registration or certification requirements
- Fees typically in two major components
- Annual commercial activity permit
- Plus recurrent entry, camping, activity fees
- Commonly similar to fees for private individual visitors
- But may be either higher or lower depending on park policy
- Fees for international visitors may be different from locals

Community contributions

- High retail price does not necessarily mean large local income
- Most of package price may go to airfares, retailer, agents, packagers
- Ecotourism generally aims to increase local expenditure
- For example, park fees, community lease payments
- Local employment, contractors
- And local purchasing, food, supplies, etc.
- Different degrees of localness
- For example, neighbouring village cf. national capital
- Particular issue for countries with tribal structure

Conservation contributions

- Contributions to conservation are key feature of ecotourism
- Political contributions possible but unproven
- Principal contributions are financial and economic
- Financial contributions include direct cash income for private reserves
- Also cash revenue for public parks, minus costs
- Broader economic contributions include regional employment from park-based tourism

Funding private conservation

- Wide range of models
- Some set up specifically for conservation

- Funded by upmarket game lodges and wildlife tours
- Some involve partial conservation management of rangeland
- Tourism may provide one of several income streams

Private reserves

- Funded principally through philanthropy
- Increasing number funded through ecotourism
- Main examples are in Africa and Latin America
- A few examples elsewhere in Asia, Australia, etc.
- Strong reliance on charismatic wildlife as key attraction
- Many are adjacent to public parks

Indirect economic contributions

- Employment and opportunities for local residents
- Derived from tourism based on conservation attractions
- Maintains support for conservation cf. other land uses
- For example, in developed nations, conversion from logging to parks
- In developing nations, protects parks from subsistence farming
- Limited data on global scale of park-based tourism
- Relatively few comparative analyses

Comparative case studies

- Economic scale of tourism cf. logging
- Queensland Wet Tropics World Heritage Area
- Tourism value = 7 × logging immediately
- Continuing strong economic growth subsequently
- Ward (2003) parks cf. forests, eastern Australia
- Tourism up to 100 times more valuable than logging in some areas
- On average about ten times larger

REFLECTIONS

1. Why is the economic scale of the ecotourism sector so imprecise? Distinguish factors relating to data from those relating to definitions. What different techniques and approaches are available to estimate its size at local, national or global levels?

2. What are the principal practical and policy issues relating to fees charged to commercial tour operators by protected area management agencies? Distinguish issues relating to setting and collecting fees from those relating to the use of funds collected. Do the same issues apply for all types of fees and charges, or can fee structures be devised to overcome any difficulties?

3. How would you set about estimating the total net economic contribution of outdoor tourism to conservation of the natural environment at different scales from a single local enterprise to globally? What are the various mechanisms, either direct or indirect? What data might be available, and how could you obtain and compile such data?

4. Identify 10–20 tourism products in your own country that are marketed as ecotourism. Who owns or manages the land they use? Does their website or advertising material mention how much, if anything, they pay to use that land? Is there any other way to find out? If you can discover the price, would you say it is fair, and why?

READING 6.1. POLICY PERSPECTIVE ON VISITOR FEES

Introduction

Many public protected areas worldwide charge fees for entrance, overnight camping and commercial tour permits. These visitor or user fees raise revenue and may influence visitor behaviour. Many protected areas are forced to charge fees because government funding is inadequate for conservation and visitor management in the face of rapidly rising visitor numbers and demands. Acceptance and effects of fees, however, depend on the historical, political, legal, economic and social context. Two issues are particularly significant: (i) equity between various social groups; and (ii) control and use of funds raised.

Visitor fees and other user charges for recreation in national parks and other public lands are widespread and contentious. This reading examines major practical and public-policy issues associated with different types of visitor fees under various types of land tenure and other circumstances. It refers principally to publicly owned and managed protected areas corresponding to World Conservation Union (IUCN) Category II reserves. These are commonly known as national parks (Lawton, 2001). The term 'parks' as used in this review, unless otherwise qualified, refers to IUCN Category II reserves. In some federated nations, they include protected areas under subnational jurisdiction. They may also include areas designated as nature reserves. Comparisons are also drawn from other land tenures where relevant, notably privately owned protected area and publicly owned forests.

Many of the issues reviewed here were considered in an American context by Harris *et al.* (1987), and more recently in joint special issues of the *Journal of Park and Recreation Administration* (especially Bowker *et al.*, 1999; Krannich *et al.*, 1999; Martin, 1999; Trainor and Norgaard, 1999; Watson, 1999) and the *Journal of Leisure Research* (Watson and Herath, 1999). Watson and Herath (1999) identified seven key themes: tradeoffs between collective and consumer perspectives; roles of visitor and agency; when to charge fees and what to do with the revenues raised; public support for fees; who is most affected by fees; how managers can assess effects of policy on visitors; and how to integrate science into policy formulation.

Practices and policies in developed and developing nations in other continents may be widely different. For example, international differences in access to land under different types of tenure were considered in 2001 in a special issue of the *Journal of Sustainable Tourism* (e.g. Kaltenborn *et al.*, 2001; McCool and Stankey, 2001; Willams, 2001). International reviews of relevant issues are also available in Lindberg (2001a,b), Munasinghe and McNeely (1994) and World Commission on Protected Areas (2000), and a Canadian perspective in van Sickle and Eagles (1998).

Most national parks are used for recreation as well as conservation, and recreation often includes commercial tourism. Generally, the toolkit that parks agencies use to manage visitor impacts may include both measures to harden the environment, and regulations, education programmes, and economic incentives to influence visitor behaviour (Buckley, 1998c, 1999b; Newsome *et al.*, 2002a).

Management costs money. Parks need money to protect, monitor and restore natural environments, endangered species and heritage items, which are subject to impacts from land uses both within and outside their boundaries. This includes managing increasing numbers of increasingly demanding visitors to minimize their impacts on the environment and each other, and maximize their safety and enjoyment (Watson and Herath, 1999; Newsome *et al.*, 2002a; Watson and Borrie, 2003).

For historical and political reasons, government funding allocations for park agencies in many countries are commonly small relative to both: (i) the needs of the park agencies for good management; and (ii) the relative economic significance of parks. Parks agencies and conservation groups therefore lobby governments for improved allocations from central treasuries, but commonly with little success. Currently, therefore, many parks agencies are compelled to raise operating funds by charging fees for park users. In some countries and jurisdictions, governments deliberately require or encourage them to charge such fees.

Visitor fees raise funds and influence visitor behaviour simultaneously – no fee can do one without the other. The current low levels of fees charged in most parks both in Australia (Buckley *et al.*, 2001) and worldwide (Lindberg, 2001a, b) do not affect visitor numbers greatly; larger fees generally raise more money and also change behaviour more, but different people respond differently to fees of different sizes and structures.

Visitor fees may be viewed as taxes to raise revenue, as economic instruments of public policy, as visitor management tools, or as prices charged for goods and services in a competitive market. Each of these perspectives is valuable and none is complete.

What do visitor fees include?

A visitor fee is in itself a rather broad and ill-defined term. Parks agencies and other land managers may charge private visitors for entry into the park, admission to particular areas, camping and other overnight stays, and specific activities such as climbing, rafting or diving. They may set up permit systems for commercial tour operators and charge them application, licence and renewal fees, as well as per capita fees for their clients, which may or may not be the same as those charged to private recreational visitors for the same activities. They may charge for additional services such as ranger-guided walks and talks. They may rent out equipment and operate transport and accommodation facilities and retail shops within their parks, or they may grant leases or concessions for private corporations to offer any of these services.

In some jurisdictions and land tenures, land management agencies may also contract with private companies to construct and operate visitor infrastructure of various types, and charge visitors directly. In the broadest sense, any of these might be considered visitor fees. Some public land management agencies, of protected as well as production and multiple-use areas, may also grant commercial rights for activities such as filming, bee-keeping, fishing and grazing.

Commonly, however, visitor fees are understood to refer to charges imposed by landowners and land management agencies on either independent visitors or commercial tour operators and their clients, for entry, admission, overnight stays, recreational activities and tours, educational walks and talks or use of recreational and/or educational facilities.

In many countries, visitor fees are most contentious for private recreational use of public lands, especially protected areas. People using private land on a regular basis would generally expect to pay the landowner for the privilege, especially if the use is commercial. Different countries have different social frameworks for public access to private, commercial and public lands. England, for example, has a complex historical network of rights of way, though these are not always respected by landholders. Scandinavian nations have a social tradition, effectively enshrined in modern law, under which members of the public have a 'right to roam' on uncultivated private land, including limited rights to harvest wild produce for personal consumption (Kaltenborn *et al.*, 2001). This 'allemansrätt', however, is being tested at present by the growth of outdoor recreation and its conflicts with farming (Kaltenborn *et al.*, 2001; Gössling and Hultman, 2006).

In most of the tourism industry worldwide, facilities are indeed on private land, and tourists and tour operators pay to use them. This applies, for example, to most hotels and motels, campgrounds and caravan parks, golf courses and marinas, arcades and amusement parks. Similarly, other commercial users of public lands and resources would expect to pay royalties or lease fees, though in some instances the costs of public infrastructure provided to such users exceeds the royalties or fees collected.

Visitor fees for recreational use of public protected areas exclude: costs for actual transport and accommodation services provided at near-market rates, such as buses and hotels within a park, whether these are operated by the park agency itself or by private concessionaires; prices or royalties charged for hire of equipment or sale of food and beverages, clothing, souvenirs and other retail goods within a park, whether by the park agency or concessionaires; prices paid by commercial tour clients to commercial tour operators for tours operating at least partly within a park; and payments made under special leases and contracts for large-scale infrastructure within the park, including cost-, revenue- and profit-sharing arrangements between land managers and private construction and operating companies. Also excluded is revenue from economic activity outside the park, driven by tourism and recreation within it, e.g. from gateway service businesses, tourist travel and accommodation, recreational equipment and real-estate transactions.

This distinction is convenient but somewhat arbitrary, depending on the perspective from which it is viewed. The similarities and differences between different types of fees, for example, will appear more or less significant to land managers, tour operators and individual visitors. Similarly, fees that act identically in an economic sense may be readily distinguishable in a legal sense or vice versa.

As one example, a visitor who has already entered a park and wants a guided walk may not care, or even know, whether they are paying for a tour led by a member of park staff, by a private guide contracted to the park, by a volunteer, or by a private guide charging visitors directly – especially since many private guides wear uniforms that imitate those of park rangers. If they pay the same price and get the same service and the tour goes smoothly, then from the visitor's perspective these four options will be identical. From the land manager's or tour operator's perspective, however, the options are different in economic terms because the fees received and costs incurred are distributed differently for each option.

The options are also different from a legal perspective, in terms of liabilities and duties of care. If a visitor is dissatisfied or injured, and wants to demand a refund or compensation, then the legal circumstances will prove rather different for each of these options. From a legal perspective, a person carrying out a particular activity in a park as an individual private visitor will always be distinguishable from a person carrying out an identical activity in the same park as a commercial tour client or a member of an organized non-commercial group.

The significance of user fees differs between stakeholders and depends on the size and types of fees, how they are set and collected, and how the funds raised are controlled and applied. For the director of a private park, for example, user fees may be the basis of a business. For the director of a public national park, user fees may be a useful addition to operating funds, an effective tool for managing visitor numbers and activities, or a costly administrative inconvenience forced upon them by agency headquarters or central government, which annoys visitors without affecting numbers or behaviour.

For a wealthy tourist making a one-off visit, a user fee may be an insignificant imposition or a small contribution to conservation, which they are glad to make. For more impoverished visitors or local residents, user fees may change where they go, what they do or how often they visit.

Similar considerations may apply to commercial tour operators, depending on the business structure and competitive position. For an operator with a strong competitive position and profit margin, a user fee that is small relative to tour costs may be insignificant. Even a park fee that is large relative to other costs may not affect a tour operator's business if the park contains an attraction for which demand exceeds supply, and competing tour operators have to pay the same fees. If there are competing operators with low profit margins and differential access to areas with different user fees, however, then fees may affect some operators significantly.

Political context

The size and structure of user fees, and the ways in which they affect land managers, visitors and tour operators, all depend on context. For convenience, this context may be divided broadly into political, legal, economic and social factors, but the distinctions between these categories are by no means clear-cut.

The practical ability of land managers to charge user fees depends heavily on the political system in which they live. In areas without stable and effective political systems and law enforcement, land managers may charge whatever fees they can get people to pay, with little accountability. In East Africa in the 1970s, for example, it was commonplace for rangers to supplement their very meagre salaries with gate takings (author, personal observation, 1974–75). Perhaps it still is. In many developing nations, local villagers may erect road barriers policed with machetes, and exact a road toll from visitors who look as though they could pay. In China, provincial government officials sometimes charge large fees – thousands of dollars or more – to allow visitors to access particular areas (author, personal observation, 1994, 2007).

The opposite can also happen: visitors may refuse to pay even legally constituted user fees if there is no means of enforcement, particularly if the legal basis for the fees is uncertain. For example, a government agency in the Mentawai Islands of West Sumatra, Indonesia established a daily per capita user fee of US$5 for surf tours in the region, but some tour operators did not recognize its legitimacy and refused to pay, and the fees remained in abeyance for a number of years while the issue was disputed in court (R. Cameron, personal communication, 2001, 2008). A similar fee charged for tour boats in Australia's Great Barrier Reef Marine Park, however, is collected routinely by all tour operators and passed to the management authority (author, personal observation 2001, 2002). The same applies for a daily per capita user fee charged by the Western Australian State Government for commercial whaleshark tours in the Ningaloo area.

In areas with powerful central governments that have strong enforcement capabilities and do not depend on a popular vote, public land management agencies can charge visitor fees with little regard to social equity, economic efficiency or market conditions, unless they are concerned about international competition in the tourist trade. This applies irrespective of political colour, to dictatorships or revolutionary oligarchies alike.

In countries with stable democratic political systems and well-established legal structures including enabling legislation for public land management agencies, visitor fees are subject to a wide range of political constraints, many with a strong historical element. If people have been able to visit protected area in the past without paying visitor fees, or carry out particular activities there, then they may raise strong objections to newly introduced fees, to the point of political action. If habitual park visitors hold strong principles in regard to the function and management of public lands, then they may take such action even if the fees are small. For example, people may decide to go elsewhere, they may take the fees into account in deciding how to vote, or they may form political associations and lobby groups.

Even if fees are accepted both in practice and in principle, government agencies may avoid them because of potential political consequences. The current (2008) State Government of Queensland, Australia, for example, has a longstanding electoral promise not to charge entrance fees for individual visitors to parks, even though the parks agency itself does already charge camping fees and would like to be able to charge entrance fees, and even though parks agencies in other states do charge entrance fees.

Legal constraints

In many jurisdictions, visitor fees imposed by parks and other public land management agencies are subject to legal as well as political constraints. These may include: general requirements applying to all government agencies, e.g. in relation to social equity; specific statutes controlling the establishment and operation of the agency concerned; duties under common law; and contractual obligations. In addition, in countries with federal systems of government, there may be constitutional constraints on the ability of different levels of government to impose taxes and charges of different types (Buckley, 1991b).

For example, establishing legislation may specify whether the agency concerned has the legal power to charge visitor fees and, if so, within what limitations. Statutes or subsidiary instruments such as regulations and legally adopted management plans may define what categories of fees may be charged, maximum fee rates and who has authority to set and collect visitor fees. They may also set other management conditions, such as the powers of the parks agency to restrict access, numbers, activities or length of stay, which will change the context in which visitor fees operate.

In some jurisdictions, charging a visitor fee may create additional obligations and liabilities for the land management agency. Note that such obligations may be altered by many other factors as well as fees; these may include, for instance, infrastructure, signage and advertising. Very broadly, wherever an agency charges a fee, particularly if it is similar in magnitude to fees charged by private landholders for similar services, then the agency is likely to have greater obligations towards fee-paying users. This might include, for example, an obligation to improve facilities at public campsites or an increased liability for public safety (McDonald, 2001).

Similarly, where an agency charges permit fees to commercial users such as tour operators, this may also create additional responsibilities and liabilities as well as additional expectations – particularly if the revenues raised exceed collection and administration costs for the permit fee system.

Economic policy

User fees are an economic instrument, and their economic context is especially critical to their effectiveness. For example, the strength of a country's economy and currency may influence whether it charges fees for visitors to enter its national parks and whether it charges a differentially higher fee for foreign nationals. Similarly, currency exchange rates will influence the ability and willingness of foreign visitors to pay such fees.

Even considering only domestic visitors within a relatively strong economy, government economic policy may have a strong influence on user fees. The economic policies of specific governments commonly depend on their political power bases. Governments that treat conservation and recreation in parks as part of their electoral mandate may provide sufficient central funding to park agencies that visitor fees are unnecessary. Governments with a political power base in rural regions may try to use protected areas as a means to promote regional economic growth in rural regions. Governments with a power base in large-scale industry sectors such as mining, forestry and agriculture are likely to give these sectors subsidized access to public land, sometimes including national parks. In many countries, for example, logging companies are granted rights to cut timber in publicly owned forests at royalties that do not even cover public infrastructure costs, even though the economic value of recreation in those forests may be orders of magnitude higher (Ward, 2000a).

In addition to the political base of the government in power, its economic planning and budget processes and priorities also influence visitor fees. For example, governments in most democratic nations allocate some of their budgets to assisting particular geographic regions and industry sectors. They do not necessarily expect to receive a financial return on such investment through increased tax revenues, since governments trade in votes as well as money. In such circumstances they are dealing with a social rather than a strictly financial measure of economic value, i.e. they base their decisions on the perceived economic value of the outcome to a part of the society that they were elected to govern. This social economic value may include not only the financial scale of economic activity and the cash income received by the individuals concerned, but the value placed by the citizens concerned on factors such as their time, their investment in a particular form of employment, and the opportunity to continue a particular lifestyle in a particular place as part of a particular social group.

While a government may consider social economic value to justify some decisions, however, for other decisions it may consider only actual cash revenue received by one of its agencies. For example, in both Australia and the USA it has now been demonstrated repeatedly that the economic activity associated with recreation and tourism in public forests is at least an order of magnitude greater than that associated with logging (Driml, 1997; USDAFS, 2000; Ward, 2003). In addition, the environmental impacts – and hence current and future on- and off-site restoration costs – are at least an order of magnitude lower for recreation than for logging. If the rationale were economic rather than political, these governments would treat tourism and recreation as the priority land use for public forests, with timber production as a secondary use, i.e. the opposite of the current priority.

In Australia, public forests are held under state rather than federal jurisdiction, and state forestry agencies argue that the relative social economic value of tourism and timber in their forests is irrelevant to them, since they receive cash revenue from timber royalties but not from tourism and recreation. Even if the economic activity associated with forest-based tourism generates greater tax revenue than that associated with timber production, this will not necessarily change the behaviour of Australian forestry agencies, for three main reasons. First, in Australia income taxes are collected by the federal government and reallocated to the state governments, not necessarily pro rata; second, forestry agencies receive their funds from state government treasuries, not directly from users; and third, timber towns may be of more value to governments as sources of votes than sources of money.

This would therefore seem to be a prime opportunity for the imposition of user fees. If Australian public forestry agencies were able to charge directly for any type of use, whether for timber production, water supply or recreational access, and also to keep the revenues raised, this could lead quite rapidly to significant changes in land use practices. In the few cases where Australian public forest agencies have deliberately constructed tourist attractions such as canopy walkways, these have been highly successful financially (Dowell-Hentall, 2001).

For parks, their highest value to the human economy is conservation of biodiversity and air and water quality, to maintain a global ecosystem capable of supporting a human economy at all (Costanza *et al.*, 1997). This is true whether from a legal perspective a park was established primarily for conservation, primarily for recreation or for both equally. Except where a water supply utility buys water from a park catchment, however, or a pharmaceutical corporation buys the rights to biodiversity prospecting, these benefits are public rather than private, so park agencies cannot raise operating funds from them directly but only via government budget allocations. Government budget allocations rarely reflect the value of conservation, because conservation benefits generally accrue at larger scales, in both time and space, than those at which election processes operate. Unless a government's political power base assigns high value to conservation benefits at a worldwide scale over periods of decades, therefore, governments will always underfund park agencies for their primary conservation function.

Recreation in parks, including commercial tourism, is always secondary to conservation in its ultimate value to the human economy, but it can provide benefits that can be captured quickly and locally, and, therefore, have more political significance. Private recreation, in parks as elsewhere, provides benefits to human health and wellbeing, and income and employment for equipment manufacturers, transport and accommodation providers, and all their suppliers. Commercial tourism provides all of these benefits, though not necessarily to the same degree as private recreation, and it also provides income and employment for tour operators and guides. All of these influence political processes, so it is not surprising that governments focus on the recreational uses of parks. Increasing recreational use, however, increases park operating and management costs, and failing any other options, this forces parks agencies to recover these increased costs from users (Watson, 1999).

In both Australia and the USA, therefore, and perhaps also in Canada and other countries, current federal governments encourage logging in preference to recreation in public forests even though recreation is worth more to the electorate and the economy in both the short and long term, and even though revenue from the higher-value use could be captured by the public land management agency through recreational user fees (Ward, 2000a). They encourage recreation in preference to conservation in public parks even though conservation is worth more to the economy in the long term, and expect the land management agency to capture revenue from the lower-value use through recreational user fees (Buckley *et al.*, 2001). This is political sense but economic nonsense.

Visitor fees in national parks, forests and other public lands, therefore, are not the same as prices charged by private landholders. They are set in a context of political strategy, not business planning.

Social context

Visitor fees also operate within a social context. The political, legal and economic issues outlined previously are of course all part of an overall social context. In addition, however, many people simply object to paying to enter or use public lands. Some of the most common objections are based on the following arguments:

- strong social tradition of a general right of access even on private land, as in Scandinavian nations (e.g. Kaltenborn *et al.*, 2001);
- historical public rights of way, as in the UK;
- philosophical objection to double taxation – taxpayers have already paid for protected areas;
- economic inefficiency – it is a wasteful way of funding a public good;
- free access historically – why should fees be introduced now?
- local residents' expectations – continuation of access even if tenure changes to protected area.

Perhaps the most widespread of these objections is the issue of double taxation. For individuals who rank environmental conservation as a high priority for public spending, it rankles strongly that governments will devote public funds to industrial subsidies in preference to park management. As noted earlier, however, there are political reasons why this happens. A related objection is that collecting park operating funds from individual users has a high administrative cost compared to collecting park operating funds within the general taxation system. To illustrate this, imagine if all road construction and maintenance were funded by road tolls. Many longstanding low-impact private users of parks and wilderness areas also have strong objections both: (i) to the growth of high-impact uses, especially motorized uses; and (ii) to the use of parks by commercial tour operators, for profit rather than personal recreation.

Commonly, the degree of acceptance or objection to fees by users depends on the purpose to which the fees are put, and the visitors' confidence that the fees will be well used (Vogt and Williams, 1999). In general, visitors seem to be more willing to pay fees if they are confident that the fees will be used for management in the park in which they are paid. Of course, this issue may be somewhat moot if visitor fees are offset by a corresponding reduction in government budget allocations.

Control and use of funds

Visitor fees for public protected areas and other public lands are set by a wide variety of mechanisms and influenced by a wide range of factors, of which the commercial balance between demand and supply, i.e. 'what the market will pay', is typically only a minor consideration. In Australia, for example, fees may depend on historical precedent, level of facilities, cost recovery and so on (Buckley *et al.*, 2001, 2003b).

Even though visitor fees are not set in the same way as business prices, they are still subject to many of the same market forces and economic considerations. From the perspective of visitors who pay the fees, they are part of the price to enjoy a particular experience, and other competing experiences are available at competing prices. From the perspective of commercial tour operators, they are a cost paid to a supplier and recovered, as far as market conditions allow, from clients. From the perspective of the land manager, they are a source of income and sometimes also a management tool.

Perhaps the single most important issue in raising funds for park management from visitor fees is who controls the funds once they are raised. This is important not only for land managers, but also for environmentally concerned visitors who want to see their fees spent on conservation management and tour operators who want to see the fees spent on visitor infrastructure. Some of the options (Buckley *et al.*, 2001) are:

- fees retained to manage the specific activity from which they were raised;
- fees retained in the park where they were raised and used for visitor infrastructure;
- fees retained in the park where they were raised and used for conservation management;
- fees retained in the region where they were raised, but not necessarily the same park;
- fees retained by the parks service, but not necessarily in any particular region;
- fees retained for park management but in a trust account not managed directly by the parks service;
- fees retained by the government environment portfolio, but not necessarily the parks service; and
- fees paid into general revenue for the government concerned.

In each of these cases, the impacts of the initial fund allocation and control also depend on any offsetting mechanism adopted by a higher level of government. For example:

- the park manager allows a particular activity to keep fees but allocates less from the park budget;
- the regional park director allows an individual park to keep fees but allocates less from the regional budget;

- the parks service allows a region to keep fees but allocates less from the central agency budget; and
- the government treasury allows the parks agency to keep fees but allocates less from overall government budget.

Many different hybrid options are also possible. Higher levels of the parks service or the government may take a portion of the fees and allow the lower levels to retain the remainder. Or they may take the entire amount but give part back. Or conceivably, they might provide an additional allocation proportional to the fees raised, in the form of a pro rata matching grant. This last, however, does not seem to be common, at least in Australia (Buckley *et al.*, 2001).

Different stakeholders may have strong views on how funds raised from visitor fees should be allocated. Typically, for example, tour operators think fees should only be used to upgrade visitor infrastructure. Of course, the primary tourist attraction in protected area is generally the natural environment, not built infrastructure, so this argument may not be very logical. True, the natural environment is enjoyed by individual visitors as well as tour clients, but in most cases individual visitors also have to pay visitor fees (Watson, 1999; Buckley *et al.*, 2001; USDI and USDA, 2001). Again, some protected areas receive many more individual visitors than tour clients, but for others the reverse is true; and some commercial tour clients may have lower per capita impacts on the natural environment than some individual visitors, but the reverse may be at least equally common.

In any event, however, this issue is largely irrelevant. Park management agencies have to spend money on visitor management as well as conservation management, and in many parks the former consumes far more of their funds than the latter. Even if visitor fees are tied to visitor infrastructure, other funds are then freed for conservation management.

Administrative efficiency

As a source of income, it is in the land manager's interests to set and collect fees as efficiently as possible. Given that fee levels are subject to strong political constraints, which may prevent land managers from charging fees as high as markets would bear, the main focus is on minimizing the administrative costs of collection (Richer and Christensen, 1999; Rosenthal *et al.*, 1984). There are many components to such costs, including:

- the construction, repair and maintenance of fee collection booths and boxes and visitor-centre counters;
- the salary costs of people to staff toll booths or visitor centres, or collect fees from deposit boxes;
- the stationery costs for fee-collection envelopes, etc.;
- the salary costs for staff to answer complaints and queries about fees;
- the enforcement costs, including inspections, prosecutions, etc.;
- the costs of secure cash handling, storage and transfers;
- the salary costs for administrative, accounting and audit staff;

- the increased infrastructure costs occasioned by higher visitor expectations once fees are paid; and
- the increased liabilities occasioned by higher duties of care once fees are charged.

The administrative costs of collecting recreational fees have been estimated at around 20% of revenue for the US Recreation Fee Demonstration Project (USDI and USDA, 2001). This estimate does not incorporate all the components listed here. Where infrastructure and management systems to control visitor numbers, access and activities already exist, however, the marginal costs of collecting fees would be reduced accordingly.

Effectiveness as a direct visitor management tool

As a direct visitor management tool, visitor fees will generally only be effective if they change the behaviour of visitors in a way that helps the land management agency in meeting its overall objectives. For example, these may include: reducing overall visitor numbers; redirecting a particular recreational activity to a specific area; or encouraging visitors to reduce individual per capita impacts during particular activities.

Visitor fees are only one of a range of management tools available to achieve any of these goals. Fees will only be effective as a management tool if:

- they are large enough to influence visitor behaviour significantly;
- they change visitor behaviour in the way the management agency wants, rather than some different and possibly adverse way;
- they do not conflict with other management goals such as social equity; and
- their net cost is not greater, relative to their effectiveness, than that of alternative management tools.

These factors are not independent. For example, fees that are large enough to influence behaviour are also more likely to be inequitable. Hence, fees for tourism and recreation in public lands are more commonly used to raise revenue from visitors rather than to influence their behaviour directly. This revenue may then be used to offset visitor management costs.

As noted earlier, however, under some circumstances a small fee may have a large influence on behaviour, while under other circumstances a large fee may have only a small influence. In northern New South Wales, Australia, for example, camping fees commonly apply in public parks but not in public forests, and even though the fees are only a few dollars per person per night, local residents and habitual visitors tend to gravitate to the forests rather than to the parks (Ward, 2000a). This may not be due entirely to fees, however, since there are also fewer restrictions in forest areas. In south-western USA, recreational four-wheel-drive users apparently choose free-access beaches in preference to those that charge user fees (Schneider and Budruk, 1999). In Himachal Pradesh, India, in contrast, the state government charges a fee of US$350 per person per week for commercial heliski operations (Himachal Helicopter Skiing,

2001); but since the cost of a week's heliskiing is around US$7000 per person, the fee does not affect the number of visitors.

These elasticities in demand depend on a wide range of factors (Knapman and Stoeckl, 1995; Lindberg and Aylward, 1999; Lindberg, 2001a), including:

- the size of the fee and the visitors' personal convictions;
- their investment of time and money to reach a particular destination;
- the way in which the fee is packaged;
- the point at which the visitors became aware of the fee's existence;
- availability, distance and price of alternative sites for their preferred activities; and
- the time of year and degree of crowding.

Equity

Most public land management agencies in democratically governed nations, and parks agencies in particular, are required to ensure that any recreational opportunities they provide are available equitably. Even if this is not a legal requirement, it is likely to be a political one. From a practical park management perspective, equity is a minefield, since different social groups have widely differing conceptions of equity (Krannich *et al.*, 1999; Martin, 1999; Richer and Christensen, 1999; More and Stevens; 2000; Lindberg, 2001b). In addition, some argue for equity in principle, in a legal sense; whereas others argue for equity in practice, which may require active measures to counteract socio-economic differentials. For example, equity may include:

- Equity in principle between individual citizens: should what's available to one be equally available to all, at least nominally?
- Equity in practice between socioeconomic groups – should poorer people have an equal opportunity to enjoy public parks, even if they have lower ability to pay fees (More and Stevens, 2000)?
- Equity between citizens and foreigners – should the latter have to pay higher user fees? Should this still apply if the area is World Heritage and nominally available to all countries equally?
- Equity between nearby residents and those living further away – given that the former are likely to want to visit more often, should they pay lower fees per visit?
- Equity between people of different ethnic origin, urban/rural upbringing, religion, etc. – should people have equal opportunity to use public parks for their own preferred activities, even if these preferences differ between people with different social backgrounds?
- Equity between different user groups – should people have equal rights to use parks for different types of recreation, even if some types have far greater impact on conservation values and other users?
- Equity between individual visitors, non-profit recreational groups and commercial tourists – should they all have precisely the same rights and responsibilities and pay the same fees; or not?

- Equity between industry sectors – given that governments often subsidize other industry sectors through cheap access to land and primary resources and lax environmental standards, should the tourism industry get preferential access to public land of high scenic value, and if so should that include parks?

- Equity between tourism operators in different countries – given that other costs are higher in some countries than others, should tourism operators in high-cost countries get cheaper access to that country's public lands to offset the other international cost differentials?

Some of these questions may seem quite ridiculous, but all of them have been put forward quite seriously at one time or another. Land management agencies that impose user fees of any type are likely to be lobbied by a wide range of interests claiming inequitable treatment. It is perhaps a measure of their financial desperation that parks agencies charge visitor fees at all.

Individual or commercial usage?

A number of erroneous or misleading arguments have sometimes been advanced in attempts to gain increased privileges for commercial tourism in public protected areas. For example, the tourism industry has argued that it should have some special rights to parks, in the same way that graziers and ranchers have some special rights to public pastoral lands, loggers have some special rights to public forests, or miners have some special rights to mineral deposits.

This is incorrect for three reasons. The first is that these other industry sectors do not necessarily have any special rights in perpetuity, but simply because of historical land-use planning and current leases and contracts. As other uses such as tourism become more valuable in these areas, governments may well grant these new uses a higher priority than current land uses. A second and more fundamental reason is that the highest economic value of protected areas, and generally also their legal basis and highest management priority, is for conservation. Certainly, some jurisdictions have special recreational land tenures and, in those areas, recreation is the highest land-use priority, but those are few compared to protected area where conservation is the top priority. A third reason is a simple legal one: where public protected areas are required to provide for recreation, this establishes a duty for the management agency to allow individuals to enjoy these areas as private citizens for private recreational benefits, but not as commercial entities for commercial profit. Tour operators have rights to the same benefits as others if they enter parks as private citizens, but not if they enter as commercial businesses.

Similarly, it has been argued by some tourism interests that parks should operate in a more 'businesslike' manner. On examination, however, it becomes apparent that this is not at all what commercial tour operators want. If parks acted as businesses, they would charge for entry and activities according to what markets would bear, with no concerns for social equity. Just like airlines, they would charge higher fees for parks, seasons and activities in higher demand, and for bookings made at different times, to maximize income from those willing to pay, even if this disadvantaged those with fewer financial resources. Just like insurers, they would charge higher fees for visitors with a higher risk of costly environmental or social impacts or a higher likelihood of lodging compensation claims. They would install infrastructure only where increased fees could reap a profit from the investment. They would manipulate demand and supply by limiting area and times of access so that fees could generate maximum profit.

Private reserves can and do follow all of these strategies. They maximize profit for the landowner who, for private parks, is generally also the tour operator (Buckley, 2003a). In public national parks, however, the landowner and the tour operators are separate entities. Quite apart from the legal and social constraints on public park management, a strictly businesslike approach to commercial tourism would generate revenue for the park, not for the tour operator. From a private tour operator's business perspective, the highest profit can be generated if they can gain exclusive rights to particular areas or activities in public parks, at a price below that which their clients will pay. Where this has happened historically, the tour operators concerned have made large oligopoly profits. Commercial rafting in the Grand Canyon is perhaps the classic instance (McCulley, 1999; Grand Canyon Private Boaters Association, 2002). In reality, it appears that tour operators do not really want park managers to become more businesslike: they want park managers to grant them profitable privileges.

Ironically, tour operators and tourism industry associations in Australia, which have argued that parks should be more businesslike in their operations, have simultaneously complained that parks are competing with them by offering talks, guided walks and other visitor services in competition with private tour operators (Tourism Council Australia, 2000).

Public parks have public duties. Any public land management agency that gives away public rights to private interests without making reasonable efforts to ensure the best net return to the public, considering both cash income and economic, social and environmental costs, is in breach of its public duties. This may be of little concern if the rights concerned are small and short-term, such as a 1-year non-transferable tour operating licence. It is of much greater concern if the rights are large and long-term, such as a tradeable operating licence valid for many years or even in perpetuity, or approval for a commercial infrastructure development. Of course, these concerns apply to many public resource management agencies, not only parks. Logging and mining leases change hands at prices many times the value of capital investment; rights to collect crayfish or abalone, or indeed to operate taxis, trade at prices many times the annual income from the activity concerned.

It is often argued that the private sector is better at business than public land management agencies, so public national parks should contract out commercial operations rather than trying to run them themselves (Tourism Council Australia, 2000). This may sometimes be correct, but only so long as the park agency retains the right to control commercial operations so as not to interfere with its primary conservation goals, and only so long as the commercial partnership arrangements are negotiated and agreed freely and willingly by all parties, not as a result of political manoeuvring by commercial interests more powerful than parks staff. Partnerships work only by mutual consent, not coercion (Bramwell and Lane, 2000; Buckley, 2002a).

In addition, private businesses sometimes go bankrupt, sell off assets in firesales or get bought out and asset-stripped in hostile takeovers. If public parks enter into partnerships with private businesses, the public assets need to be protected. Finally, contracting out is itself a business process. There are certainly many instances where public agencies have improved efficiency by contracting out services to private providers, but there are also many instances where private contractors have made enormous profits at public expense, just as there are many instances where business partnerships have yielded a profit to one partner at the expense of the other.

Conclusions

Visitor fees for visitors in national parks and other public lands are not always efficient, effective or equitable, but they are widespread and likely to continue and increase as recreation in parks continues to grow far faster than government funding for park management. There are innumerable different mechanisms and models for visitor fees, and optimal fee structures, rates, collection mechanisms and allocation depend on the political, legal, economic and social context in which each park management agency operates. Currently, fees are generally used to raise revenue rather than as visitor management tools: where parks want to restrict visitor numbers or activities for environmental or social reasons, they generally use non-economic mechanisms rather than raising fees, for reasons of social equity. While many parks are coming to rely on visitor fees, these fees generally make up only a small proportion of their total budget and the costs of collecting the fees are relatively high. In some cases, there may well be a place for paying to play in parks, and hybrid funding models deserve further attention. As a means to fund the primary conservation function of protected areas, however, visitor fees alone do not seem to be the best option.

Acknowledgements

This reading is an edited version of Buckley (2003e), first published in the *Journal of Sustainable Tourism* 11, 56–73.

chapter 7

ENVIRONMENTAL MANAGEMENT

Diesel generator for stand-alone ecolodge. Note safety flooring, no oil spillage, lagged exhaust pipe, large muffler and heavily insulated walls.

REVIEW

Introduction

Environmental management is a term that first came into general use in the 1980s to describe the measures that an organization may take to minimize or otherwise manage its impacts on the natural environment. Even until the 1990s, tourism industry associations and government tourism promotion agencies were still arguing, quite incorrectly, that the tourism industry has negligible environmental impacts. Research organizations, however, pointed out that tourism can indeed have significant environmental impacts, and that a large proportion of tourism development and activities take place in areas with relatively undisturbed natural environments, often of high conservation value, so that these impacts are of particular conservation concern. They suggested that the same types of environmental management tool that had by that time been adopted in other industry sectors, such as mining and manufacturing, should also be applied in the tourism sector. It has taken well over a decade for this to happen in practice, and application of such tools is still very patchy and uneven, but they are in use. This chapter provides a brief introduction and review of the types of environmental management tools that are in common use within the nature, adventure and ecotourism sector. Some of these are also broadly relevant across the entire tourism industry, others only for particular activities or places.

The practical technicalities of environmental management seem to have received rather little attention in the academic literature on tourism. As outlined in the research section of this chapter, that literature has focused instead on the much more vague concept of sustainability. Practical examples of environmental management approaches are mentioned more often in industry publications, especially those relating to environmental awards and ecocertification (see Chapter 5). There seem to be rather few systematic analyses of environmental management practices, however, across entire industry sectors or regions.

Improvements in environmental management by individual tourism operators may be driven by: government laws and regulations; customer concerns and marketing manoeuvres; or the personal convictions of staff and owners. The relative significance of these factors determines the types of responses that operators and industry associations may adopt and how much they will invest. For example, they may: adopt low-impact designs, architecture, equipment and operating practices; hire environmental management staff; set up environmental education programmes for staff and clients; and devise a variety of self-regulation schemes or voluntary codes of practice.

All businesses, including tourism operations, are subject to constraints, which can be summarized as: money, markets, machines, land, labour and laws. Each of these constraints has an environmental component and, to be successful, any business must be aware of all of these.

Different issues for different subsectors

Environmental management issues may be divided broadly into those associated with use of the natural environment as a source of raw materials, the so-called green issues, and those associated with its use as a sink for waste products, the so-called brown issues.

Different environmental management issues, and different types of environment impacts, may be more or less significant for different components of the tourism industry and the ecotourism subsector in particular. There are different issues for accommodation, transport and other activities. Approaches adopted by a wilderness camping guide or balloon safari operator, for example, are necessarily quite different from those adopted by a large-scale resort, a hotel chain, or an international airline. In addition, some activities such as skiing or fishing are necessarily restricted to particular types of environments, with their own particular environmental issues.

Design issues for a small single-building ecolodge, or for a larger lodge or resort village with numerous independent cabins or villas around a central common area, are essentially similar to the issues for a private residential house. They include: issues relating to energy efficiency, such as shape and orientation, insulation and ventilation, heating and cooling, lighting and energy-efficient appliances; issues associated with water consumption, such as landscaping and bathroom and laundry facilities; and issues associated with wastewater and sewage treatment, including re-use or recycling of greywater, and the various technologies for toilets and sewage treatment. For larger, multi-storey tourist accommodation, the issues are essentially the same as for urban hotels or apartment buildings, except that in areas without access to municipal utilities, tourist accommodation will need its own power and water supply and waste treatment facilities.

For a large hotel or resort, low-impact technologies include both those for conserving energy, water and resources, and those for controlling pollution, particularly in relation to treatment of sewage. Energy-efficient design, insulation, demand management and energy audits are becoming commonplace in tourist accommodation worldwide. Most tourism accommodation needs power for heating and cooling, catering, cleaning and laundry, and for stationary plant such as irrigation pumps, sewage aerators and solid waste compactors. Low-impact practices start with the operation of pollution-control and resource-conservation technologies to achieve optimum design efficiency. This may also require redesign of staff work practices to complement relevant technologies, e.g. in order to separate recyclables. Impacts can also be reduced through redesign of facilities, e.g. landscaping for lower water, fertilizer and pesticide requirements. All these approaches can be incorporated into an environmental management system, which should include routine environmental audits of all aspects of facilities and operations.

Different types of transport also have enormously different environmental impacts. Even with the best technologies currently available, helicopters always use much more fuel and make much more noise than hiking, and the same applies for speedboats cf. seakayaks. The choice of transport is an important component in the design of a tour product, with significant environmental implications. Many types of tour products rely on mechanized transport to shuttle clients to an activity area, or as a logistic support mechanism, or as the basis for the activity itself. Similar considerations apply for the use of livestock, whether as pack or riding animals. The links between the design and markets for specialist tour products, land tenure and access considerations, and environmental management issues can be quite complex.

From an environmental management perspective, designing the transport component of a nature, adventure or ecotour involves at least three distinct components: the type of tour offered; the types of transport used; and measures to minimize local impacts of that transport. The type of tour restricts the potential types of transport, and the type of transport restricts the potential minimal-impact measures. Local minimal-impact measures, for different types of transport, may involve the details of equipment and accessories, the techniques with which they are used, and the management structures to support those techniques. Low-impact technologies and operating techniques are generally specific to the particular type of transport involved, but good environmental management practices always require an active involvement at all levels of the company structure: owners, retail sales, local operators and equipment suppliers, and trip guides (Buckley, 2006).

Good environmental design and low-impact technologies form the basis for an overall environmental management strategy, in tourism as in other sectors, but the way in which people use those technologies is equally important. Operational environmental management systems are particularly important in the tourism sector, where environmental management is less dependent on technology, and more on individual behaviour, than in many other sectors. Recycling bins don't work if no one uses them, and waste management systems or low-irrigation landscaping will generally only perform effectively with continual and competent maintenance. Similarly, minimal-impact bushwalking and backcountry camping techniques depend as much on individual behaviour as on technology. How an individual walks and where they camp and cook can be as important as their choice of footwear, shelter and cooking stoves.

At the other end of the impact scale, some helicopters are quieter than others; some can be fitted with so-called hush kits to reduce noise; and each machine produces blade slap under slightly different combinations of load, speed and other flying conditions. In addition, different animal species are differentially susceptible to helicopter noise and live preferentially in different parts of the landscape, so different flight paths will produce different impacts in different places. A strategy to minimize the impacts of helicopter noise on wildlife needs to consider all of these components.

Scale and site

Different types of tourism development and activity are appropriate for different areas. There are relatively few conservation reserves where conservation requirements make it necessary to prohibit all forms of tourism and recreational access. Equally, large-scale hotel accommodation or infrastructure would generally conflict with conservation goals in most reserve areas. Between these extremes lies a range of possible options.

Scale and site are critical in environmental management. An individual tourist resort, for example, may produce substantial environmental impacts locally during its operating life. Regionally, however, these impacts may be negligible, but if several similar resorts operate simultaneously in the same region, the cumulative impacts may again be substantial (Buckley, 1999a). If other regions in the country concerned have little tourism development, then overall impacts at national scale may be small (Buckley 1999a, 2003c); but if the country as a whole depends heavily on tourism, the national impacts may be significant on a global scale. Finally, the impacts of tourism must also be considered in the context of relative impacts from other industry sectors such as agriculture, fisheries, forestry, mining or manufacturing.

Site or location is as important as scale. The impacts of a new hotel in a metropolitan area are very different from those of a similar hotel in an otherwise pristine natural environment. The immediate inputs and outputs to and from the hotel may be the same, but their marginal impacts on the surrounding environments will be very different indeed. The total volume of sewage produced, and even the sewage treatment system used, may be the same irrespective of site, but the ecological effects of a given discharge of nutrients and bacteria into an oligotrophic receiving water body are likely to be quite different from the effects of a similar discharge into a water body whose nutrient and bacterial status are already affected by other discharges. A new development and associated infrastructure in a previously undisturbed area will require clearance of vegetation and fauna habitats, whereas a similar development in an urban area will not. Similarly, the ecological effects of an additional source of noise in an otherwise undisturbed natural environment are very different from those of a similar source in an already noisy urban area.

Current legal frameworks for development planning treat development proposals independently, whether these applications are assessed by local government agencies, or by state agencies with formal environmental impact assessment. With the growth of tourism development in recent years, therefore, planning frameworks are gradually being modified to take into account the cumulative impacts of multiple medium-scale developments. Such approaches include regional and local environmental plans, zoning restrictions of various forms, and increasingly, a requirement to consider cumulative impacts in formal EIAs.

Scale in time, as well as space, is as important as location. It is not simply that a larger development will generally have greater impacts than a smaller one if the two are otherwise similar. The aggregate impacts of several small developments or activities may be either greater or less than the impacts of a single larger one with the same total volume of clients. An airstrip that is used only intermittently will have lower impacts than one that is used continuously, but a single airstrip used heavily may have lower total impacts than two airstrips each used half as often. Most animals can survive a single loud noise, but many would be driven away by continuous or repeated noise such as road traffic or helicopter overflights. A single visitor casually throwing food to wildlife may have negligible impact, but a steady stream of tourists feeding parrots, wallabies or dolphins at regular times and sites generally does. At very low levels of use, the impacts of backcountry hikers in most environments may generally be minimized if each person takes a different path to disperse impacts, but at higher levels of use, total impacts may be minimized by concentrating the disturbance into a single restricted track or area.

Such issues arise frequently in relation to ecotourism. A single visitor picking up a shell or piece of coral from a reef flat, for example, may have negligible impacts. If visitors are numerous and each collects one item, however, the reef flats may soon become completely denuded. To avoid this aggregate impact, the only effective measure is a total ban on the removal of any items, as commonly enforced in most conservation reserves. Similarly, a single small-scale commercial ecotour operation in a national park may produce negligible impact relative to that of individual independent visitors. If the numbers and size of commercial operations increase, however, the aggregate impacts may soon become of major management significance.

Design and technology

As in any industry sector, the simplest and cheapest way of solving any environmental problem is not to create it. Enormous effort and expense has already gone, and will continue to go, into addressing environmental damage that could have been avoided by improved design. In the tourism sector there are two principal aspects to this: the engineering design of individual technologies, and the architectural and landscape design of entire tourism developments. Placing a building to catch afternoon sea breezes in a tropical climate, for example, or designing it for minimum energy absorption in a hot climate and maximum energy retention in a cold climate, is an architectural approach. Improving the efficiency of electricity generating plants to minimize waste emissions per unit power generated, on the other hand, is an engineering approach.

Architectural design approaches include: the location and layout of individual components of a tourist development within an overall site; the size, shape and structure of buildings and other construction; the choice of materials and design to suit those materials, etc. Many ecolodges contain examples of low-tech environmental design, incorporating materials such as wood, canvas and mosquito netting. Environmental design is equally important for large tourism resorts, however: for example, designing landscaping so that irrigation runoff is retained on-site; or designing kitchen areas so that catering residues can go straight to a composting system; or designing a boat mooring or reef platform so that anchor chains do not damage coral. The examples are endless.

There are many specific technologies, notably those involved in waste management and in the conservation of water, energy and other resources, which have applications in the tourism industry. Many, if not most, of these technologies also have applications in other industry sectors, and may have been developed for primary applications in those sectors. For applications in tourism, what is commonly needed is re-design or re-engineering, rather than re-invention of the technologies concerned. Examples include: the design of quiet and energy-efficient engines for different applications, and of low-drag vehicle bodies, aircraft fuselages and boat hulls; the design of water supply, intake and purification systems, and disposal of water treatment wastes;

the design of flush, low-flush, waterless, composting or pump-out toilet systems and associated sewage treatment plants; and so on. These are essentially engineering issues, which, in all but the simplest cases, require specialist expertise, and details are beyond the scope of this volume.

From the perspective of the tour operator or tourism developer, the critical issue is generally to select the most appropriate low-impact technology or design from amongst those available, rather than attempting to develop them from scratch. This applies both for accommodation, transport and equipment that are fully owned by the tour operator concerned, and also for accommodation, transport and equipment that are leased or supplied by franchisees or subcontractors, or otherwise incorporated into a tour package, e.g. by sales on commission.

The degree of flexibility differs greatly between different tourism operations. If a tour takes clients to a national park, for example, then the tour operator is likely to have little say over the design of toilets in the park's visitor centre. If a tour operator is building its own lodge on a private reserve, however, then it will generally have full flexibility to select toilet and sewage treatment systems to minimize impacts, subject to health and building regulations and client expectations.

Even when the design of a lodge, or facility, is completely under the control of a tourism developer or operator, the range of design parameters realistically available depends very greatly on the terrain and environment, notably on climatic conditions. A lodge in the Canadian Rockies, such as Aurum Lodge (Buckley, 2003a, pp. 166–168) needs very different design parameters from a lodge in subtropical Australian rainforest such as Binna Burra or O'Reilly's (Buckley, 2003a, pp. 102–103), or one in the sub-Saharan African savannas, such as those built by Conservation Corporation Africa (Buckley, 2003a, pp. 9–19; 2006, pp. 353–358).

Similarly, different four-wheel-drive vehicles produce different impacts, depending on their configuration as well as the way they are driven (Buckley, 1999–2001, 2004f). The impacts of motorized watercraft may depend on a range of factors including overall size, hull design, draught, engine type and capacity, propeller or impellor design and safety caging, and boat speed and handling (Byrnes and Warnken, 2004; Mosisch and Arthington, 2004).

ENERGY SUPPLY AND CONSERVATION

Most tourism operations and activities require energy in some form. For some minimal-impact backcountry travellers the only direct consumption may be food. Most tourism accommodation, however, uses electrical power for cooking, cleaning, heating water and, in larger hotels, for operating lifts, pumps, etc. Some tourist activities, such as downhill ski lifts, also consume large amounts of electrical power. For tourism operations in remote areas, energy supply and conservation is a major logistic issue with social and environmental connotations. This applies, for example, to trekking lodges in the Annapurna region (Nepal, 2007) or to wildlife lodges in remote areas in north-western Namibia (Buckley, personal observation, 2008).

Small-scale tourist accommodation in remote areas may rely on diesel generators to produce electric power, but large hotels and resorts generally draw their supply from the electricity grid. This creates local impacts associated with power lines, and remote impacts associated with power generation. Power-line impacts include vegetation clearance, disturbance to animal habitat, soil modification, electromagnetic radiation, and impacts associated with secondary access. The impacts of electricity generation itself depend on the fuel used. Most electricity generating stations are fuelled by coal, oil or gas. There are environmental impacts associated both with mining coal or producing oil or gas, and with transporting the fuel to the power station. All of these involve vegetation clearance, disturbance to fauna, noise and dust, etc. Coal mining may produce acid mine drainage; oil production involves the risks of spills and leaks. All thermal power stations produce carbon dioxide, which contributes to climate change. They also produce other gaseous emissions such as oxides of sulphur and nitrogen. Their cooling systems produce impacts on aquatic ecosystems. Coal-fired power stations also produce large volumes of fly ash. Anyone using electricity from the grid supply contributes pro rata to these impacts.

Transport also consumes energy. Most international tourism, in particular, involves longhaul air transport with high per capita fuel costs (Simmons and Becken, 2004; Folke *et al.*, 2006; Becken and Hay, 2007). In addition, the hub-and-spoke route design followed by most of the world's major air carriers means that actual total flight distances may be much greater than the direct path from origin to destination. Of course, increasing the proportion of direct flights would not necessarily increase the per capita energy efficiency, if there is a higher proportion of unfilled seats on direct flights. If an indirect connection using sectors between major hubs decreases the proportion of empty seats, it may increase the per capita fuel efficiency even though passengers travel further to reach their destinations. The broad financial goals of the airlines, which are generally aimed at filling seats, will also tend to lead to high fuel efficiencies for each passenger flown. The same general argument applies to substitution between few large and many small aircraft, whether within a single airline, or as a component of competition between airlines. It is in the economic interests of each airline to minimize fuel costs and maximize the proportion of seats filled.

There are some types of air transport, however, where major increases in fuel efficiency are possible. The most obvious of these is in the so-called flightseeing industry, where tourists pay for short aerial joyrides. There are many instances where the same area is served both by fixed-wing aircraft and by helicopters. For these short-haul flights, the economic and environmental goals are not necessarily coordinated: helicopter flights may be more profitable, but they use more fuel and create more noise.

Similarly, there are major differences in the fuel efficiencies of different watercraft and land-based vehicles. If both are fully laden, a large displacement-hull vessel will have a higher per capita fuel efficiency than a small planing hull, high-speed catamaran or hydrofoil, and a bus will have greater per capita fuel efficiency than a car. At this broad level, however, the choice of vehicle or vessel is likely to be made on the basis of speed and comfort rather than fuel efficiency. Even if a high-speed boat shuttle to an island resort, for example, has lower fuel efficiency than a slower ferry, it would still have much higher fuel efficiency than a light aircraft shuttle.

Within any one general class of vehicle or vessel, fuel efficiency can be improved through refinements in engine design, and streamlining of the hull or body. This can achieve substantial fuel and hence cost savings. As simple a measure as installing cab-top air deflectors on trucks, for example, increased fuel efficiency by 10–15%. Fuel efficiency also depends on operational practices: a planing boat hull driven in displacement mode just below the planing threshold, or a bus driven at just below top-gear freeway speed, consumes significantly more fuel per kilometre than if they were planing or cruising, respectively.

Many of these issues, of course, are by no means peculiar to the tourism industry. Boats, trains and trucks are used to transport goods in all industry sectors worldwide. To the extent that tourism corporations and individual tourists make use of energy from either stationary or moving sources, they contribute to the environmental impact associated with energy generation. The cumulative impacts of energy consumption by the tourism sector are large, and the cumulative savings that can be achieved by improved energy efficiency and energy conservation measures are both environmentally and economically significant on a global as well as a local scale.

One good example of energy conservation measures in practice in the tourism industry is the widespread adoption of demand management systems in large-scale tourism accommodation such as major resorts and international hotel chains. Insulation, energy-efficient light globes, and room-light master-switches operated by a door-key tag, for example, are now commonplace (Buckley and Araujo, 1997b). While smaller-scale tourism accommodation in general has taken less account of energy efficiency (Buckley and Araujo, 1997b), there is an increasing number of specialist ecolodges that have achieved high energy efficiencies through the use of, for example, passive solar design features and computerized energy management systems.

Water supply and conservation

Water conservation is a major issue for tourism accommodation, though less for other sub-sectors. Demand management, low-impact water treatment, and wastewater reclamation and re-use are important for hotels, resorts, golf courses, ski fields and other recreational facilities, whether urban or greenfields. Integrated water and waste management programmes can incorporate irrigation and runoff from managed turf, and disposal of sullage, cleaning and laundry wastes, sewage and garbage. Existing technologies in wastewater ozonation or ultraviolet irradiation, and in subsurface irrigation are being used in new greenfields tourism developments without municipal services.

There are some locations where water supplies are particularly scarce, or liquid effluents are of particular environmental concern. Water supplies may be scarce, for example, for tourist accommodation on small oceanic islands; or remote sites in arid, semi-arid or seasonally dry environments; or for locations within conservation reserves where the construction of surface dams would not be permitted.

Hotels and resorts use water for showers and toilets, laundry, washing and washing up, cleaning, and irrigation of lawns and landscaping. Lawns and landscaping can consume large volumes of water for irrigation, and ski resorts use large volumes for snowmaking. In some instances, this water is provided from local shallow aquifers, using bores or spear pumps, or by collecting surface runoff in special-purpose dams and reservoirs. More commonly, water is drawn from a reticulated supply. This may be a public system, managed by a local government or a national or provincial government water authority, or it may be owned and operated by a private water supply utility company. In either case, the supply may be from surface dams, natural rivers and lakes, underground aquifers or some combination of the above.

Whether the water supply is small-scale, local and dedicated, or by reticulation from a larger-scale regional or municipal supply system, there are pro rata environmental impacts associated with water consumption. These may include aquifer draw-down, salinization, depletion of natural rivers and lakes, modifications to flow regimes, interruption to surface flow by dams, flooding and associated disturbances to native vegetation and fauna by dams, impacts associated with disposal of sludges from water treatment plants, impacts associated with irrigation, and impacts associated with disposal of used water. Each of these may be addressed independently to reduce the environmental impacts per unit volume of water consumed, or they may be addressed jointly by reducing per capita water consumption.

Resorts, for example, can improve water conservation if they: replace water-hungry lawn grasses with drought-tolerant ground-cover plants; capture and use local rainfall runoff on site; re-use greywater for irrigation; use drip-feed or subsurface rather than overhead sprinklers for irrigation; and run irrigation systems at night rather than by day. Urban hotels can fit dual-flush toilets and low-flow shower heads, and adopt laundry management systems that allow guests to reduce the average laundry frequency for guest linen and towels.

Materials and recycling

The consumption or destruction of natural resources is one major category of impact for any type of human development activity. The supply of tourism products generally involves consumption of fuel and water at significantly higher per capita rates than for people staying at home. Mineral resources are consumed in manufacturing, from heavy earthmoving equipment to cameras and golf clubs. Timber and textiles, both from crops and synthetic sources, are consumed in the construction and manufacture of buildings, furniture and service items. Destruction of natural resources, notably native vegetation and fauna, occurs through clearance for new developments and facilities, through manufacturing of tourist souvenirs and curios; through hunting, fishing and capture of wildlife for tourist displays; and through disturbances such as increased noise, introduction of weeds, pathogens and feral species, and disruption of interspecies interactions. Even the supply of food and drink to people on holiday typically consumes more resources than if they stayed home. Most manufactured items, from the smallest to the largest and the simplest to the most complex, involve an enormous array of material and energy inputs in the chain from primary natural resources to final use and disposal by the consumer. The environmental impact associated with using a particular item includes not only those which may be created during the actual period of use, but also those involved in production, distribution and subsequent disposal of the item concerned. To quantify each of these steps and the associated environmental impacts precisely is an extremely complicated and difficult task, known as life cycle analysis. It is of particular significance for the tourism industry, which is the final consumer of a wide range of manufactured products.

There is relatively little scope for the tourism industry to reduce initial materials consumption, but two main approaches to reducing its impacts. The first is to improve environmental management during manufacturing, by introducing supply-chain certification and purchasing procedures that select suppliers with good environmental performance. The second is to improve recycling. The choice of reusable, recyclable or disposable service items by hotel, resort, airline, tour and boat operators, as well as individual tourists, has considerable environmental significance in aggregate. This applies both to individual items such as napkins, cutlery and toiletries, and to cleaning materials, office equipment, etc. Equally significant are actual procedures adopted, e.g. cleaning techniques, transport to recycling depots and landfill operations. Packaging, both in bulk and for individual items, is an allied issue.

Issues such as water and energy conservation, recycling, use of disposable items such as plastic cups and paper napkins, and selection of environmentally friendly materials such as biodegradable detergents are familiar in a domestic context to most people in developed countries, whether through the mass media or through their children's school education. In the tourism sector, the application of such domestic concerns to the workplace is straightforward. In addition to market pressures from clients for improved environmental management performance, therefore, many tourism businesses also experience internal pressure from their own staff. Indeed, many of the environmental programmes now espoused by major hotel corporations saw their origins in voluntary programmes by individual hotel staff.

Many remote-area game lodges and ecolodges have their own local recycling programmes, and some of the larger urban and resort hotel chains either have their own programmes, or take part in local municipal recycling schemes. Some South African game lodges, for example, provide paper scraps and candle ends to local villages, which remanufacture craft paper and candles that are then used in the same lodges. Large hotel chains such as Canadian Pacific Hotels established employee-run internal recycling programmes in the early 1990s (Canadian Pacific Hotels, 1993), and these later became a model for the International Hotel Environment Initiative (IHEI, 1995), which in turn became part of the International Tourism Partnership (2008). Recycling programmes are widely adopted because they allow tourist accommodation facilities to claim green credentials while at the same time cutting costs, as for energy-saving and water-saving programmes (Buckley and Araujo, 1997b). This also applies for bulk purchases of consumables such as cleaning products, which save on packaging and cost less, as long as they can also be used in bulk and do not have to be repackaged into smaller containers. In most developed nations, health regulations and customer expectations require that any guest toiletries provided must be new and individually wrapped, so there is little opportunity to save on packaging. Paradoxically, however, partially used toiletries may still be recycled for use by staff or charity programmes, as in the CPH case. In developing countries, in contrast, some upmarket lodges make a feature of refillable glass containers in each guestroom.

Opportunities for recycling in the tourism industry, as in other industry sectors, cover a wide range of timescales. Items such as catering residues and other organic garbage require attention on a daily basis, for example. Items of packaging can generally be collected and recycled on a weekly, monthly or longer basis depending on the volume and facilities available. Items such as building and construction materials, and aircraft fuselages, boat hulls and vehicle engines, may be available for recycling on a timescale of decades or longer.

At the longer timescales, recycling opportunities are generally beyond the scope of operating tourism corporations. Even at this scale, however, operating tourism corporations have the opportunity to enhance recyclability by purchasing items designed for disassembly or manufactured with recycling in mind. Similarly, for larger tourism operators at least, there is scope to seek out recycling opportunities when items are de-commissioned. This may be as straightforward as selling building materials on-site when an old hotel or apartment complex is dismantled, or having old plant and machinery collected by scrap metal merchants rather than hauled to a dump.

At slightly shorter timescales, operators can choose to purchase vehicles, whitegoods, electrical appliances, etc. whose manufacturers have adopted a cradle-to-grave environmental management approach, with individual components designed to be taken apart and re-used or recycled. Design for disassembly is becoming increasingly commonplace even for small items. Disposable cameras provide an example. Tourism operators can also aim to avoid purchasing items known to produce environmental impacts on disposal.

Most of the recycling opportunities in the tourism sector, however, occur at short timescales for items used in large volumes or quantities, such as catering residues, paper and cardboard, cans and bottles, partially used toiletries, waste oil, etc.

Catering residues and other organic garbage can be recycled in a variety of ways. In rural areas, food scraps can be used directly as stock-feed for pigs, chickens, etc., but this is rarely feasible in developed urban areas. Similarly, remote rural resorts and ecolodges can install integrated digestion systems for sewage, sullage and organic garbage. Even in relatively urbanized areas, composting of some organic garbage may be feasible, at least for those operations that include garden areas. Worm farms are also in use in some tourist resorts. In some local government areas, organic garbage may be removed from hotels by a waste contractor, municipal or private, but may still be composted at a waste disposal site, rather than mixed with other rubbish and dumped in landfill. Similarly, organic garbage such as lawn clippings, shrub prunings, etc. may be chipped and used as mulch on-site. In the Gold Coast tourism area in Queensland,

Australia, composting was more commonplace in lower-end tourist accommodation such as caravan parks, than in up-market hotels when this was examined a decade ago (Buckley and Araujo, 1997b).

Recycling aluminium, glass, PET plastics, and paper and cardboard is generally accomplished by adding the materials for recycling to the raw feedstock in a smelter, glass furnace or paper mill. From the perspective of the tourism industry, recycling of containers and packaging materials such as these is therefore a question of delivering them to an appropriate manufacturing plant. This generally involves separating recyclable materials as soon as possible after they have been used, keeping them free from contamination as far as possible, stockpiling them temporarily, and having them collected by or delivered to a private or public recycling agency. In some areas this may involve delivery to a municipal recycling depot, for example, and in others collection by a private waste management contractor.

From the tourism operator's perspective, the first requirement is to establish what collection systems are available and whether they pay for materials or charge for collection, and how often and in what volumes collections or deliveries must be made. An internal system for separating recyclables, cleaning them if necessary, and setting them aside for collection must then be established as part of routine operational practices. Guests and clients may be invited to assist, e.g. through provision of labelled recycling bins in private rooms and public areas. Such separation and collection systems need to be integrated with buying practices; there is little point in establishing a recycling system for one type of beverage container, for example, if beverages are then purchased in a different type of container.

Sewage and human wastes

The disposal of human wastes, whether mixed with water in the form of sewage or in their original raw form, is a significant environmental management issue for all segments of the tourism industry. Urban tourism accommodation and facilities, at least in the more developed nations, generally use flush toilets linked to reticulated municipal sewage collection and treatment systems. The precise type of sewage treatment thus becomes an issue for the tourism industry only in situations where tourists constitute a significant proportion of total population in the area concerned, or where the discharge of sewage, treated or otherwise, could significantly reduce the area's amenity value as a tourism destination. Coastal tourist towns, such as Australia's Gold Coast or Hawaii's Waikiki, provide well-known examples, but there are many more in coastal and island locations worldwide.

For self-contained tourist resorts not connected to municipal sewerage, stand-alone sewage treatment systems are required. There are still some places where untreated sewage is pumped directly into the ocean, or even into lakes and rivers, but this produces significant environmental and aesthetic impacts, which boomerang back on the polluter as well as affecting aquatic ecosystems and other users of the water bodies concerned. A wide range of primary, secondary and tertiary sewage treatment systems are available, produced commercially at a variety of scales.

The environmental impacts of discharging sewage are derived from two main constituents of human waste: microorganisms and nutrients. Some of the microorganisms in human gut contents are pathogenic, either to humans or to other species. A discharge of unsterilized waste, even if treated to some degree, can hence contaminate receiving water bodies with pathogens.

Sewage also contains nutrients, notably nitrogen and phosphorus in large concentrations, and in most sewage treatment systems, these nutrients, especially phosphorus, are discharged in treated effluent and are liable to cause eutrophification in receiving water bodies. This may include cyanobacterial blooms in fresh water, and smothering algal blankets and floating diatom blooms in the sea.

Clearly, such impacts depend on the volume and concentration of microorganisms and nutrients in the waste stream, and characteristics of the receiving water body including flow rate or tidal currents, temperature and pH, oxygenation and nutrient status, and prior microbiological status.

The discharge of liquid effluents is of particular concern in conservation reserves, especially where effluents drain rapidly into natural watercourses. The discharge of liquid effluents may also be prohibited or discouraged in situations where leachates might quickly contaminate underground aquifers supplying drinking water, or where runoff might contaminate surface water bodies used as water supplies.

One technology that is becoming increasingly commonplace in such circumstances is the substitution of composting toilet systems, or in some circumstances sealed chemical toilet systems, for flush toilets. Sealed fibreglass toilets, for example, are widespread in mountain national parks in the USA and Canada. Composting toilets of various designs are widely used in national parks and also in a number of Pacific Island nations.

For aircraft and coach operators, human wastes are generally held on board in chemical toilets until a particular journey finishes, when the toilets are pumped out for treatment in a fixed-site plant. Chemicals to reduce odour and inhibit fermentation are added to the sewage during transit. Such additives may be discharged or volatilized either in original or modified form at the treatment plant. From an environmental management perspective, the critical issue is the type and quantity of additives. Generally, these can be reduced by increasing the frequency with which the toilets are pumped out, and by improving toilet design to minimize the escape of air.

Portable toilets of various types are also used by some four-wheel-drive operators, boat operators and river-runners. In some areas, notably a number of rivers in the USA, the use of portable toilets is mandatory for all commercial tour operators. In the past, such toilets tended to be somewhat basic in construction, typically an army-surplus ammunition box lined with a plastic bag. Either lime or bleach was added to the faecal material to inhibit bacterial activity. Whenever a camp was moved, the plastic bag was sealed and a new one opened at the next camp. At the end of the journey, the entire contents were taken to an appropriate disposal facility or simply dumped in landfill.

More recently, however, these rocket-box toilets, or 'groovers' as they were known in the river-runners' vernacular, have largely been replaced with purpose-built stainless steel portable toilets with screw-on lids for transit, welded seams to withstand gas pressure during fermentation, safety valves to prevent dangerous pressure build-up, and screw-capped inlet and outlet nozzles where a high-pressure water hose can be attached to wash out the interior at the end of the journey, somewhat improving the much-despised task of cleaning out the rocket-boxes.

These toilets have been developed in response to three factors. The first is that many municipal waste disposal facilities have banned dumping of human waste, even in plastic bags, so that portable toilets can only be emptied in places such as caravan parks with facilities for cleaning out toilets in individual caravans; as noted above, these have restrictions on the chemicals that can be used to retard bacterial fermentation. The second is that as the adventure travel and ecotourism sectors have grown, operators have offered higher and higher standards of service in the competition for clients, particularly more wealthy clients. Since toilet facilities have often been perceived by clients as the low point in the facilities provided, there is a considerable incentive to invest in more comfortable systems. Finally, the third factor is that as the number of operators and their demand for improved portable toilets has risen, this has created a sufficient market to justify investment in the design, manufacture and distribution of more sophisticated purpose-built units.

Several different designs are currently available. For river rafters in the large rivers of the USA, for example, the most common model is designed to fit inside the army surplus rocket-box while on the river, first to protect it and second since the design of raft frames, and the guides' packing systems, allow for a container of these dimensions. A toilet seat is carried separately, and attached to the unit when it is set up at camp.

Such large rectangular units, however, being heavy and sharp-cornered, are impossible to carry in smaller craft such as seakayaks, and operators have shown considerable ingenuity in designing custom-built portable toilet systems for such circumstances. Some seakayak operators, for example, currently use a design based on a length of plastic drainpipe sealed at the base and capped with a screw-on lid during transit. At camp, it is set up vertically, and a bowl and seat screwed on to the upper end.

For individuals and small groups of backcountry hikers, backpackers, climbers and kayakers, even these smaller-scale portable toilets are not feasible. Minimal-impact disposal techniques in such circumstances differ with group size, visitor frequency and ecosystem type, and are a matter of some debate. In the past, the recommended technique was to concentrate all human waste in group pit latrines, as deep as possible. It has now been shown that in most environments, faecal material in pit latrines is very slow to break down.

The technique most commonly recommended in national-parks interpretive materials is the use of dispersed cat-holes, shallow burial at a few centimetres depth where plant roots and soil microflora are plentiful and breakdown relatively rapid. In some ecosystems, however, shallow burial may lead to excavation by native animals, so burial under heavy rocks is preferable. In coastal environments where the biological productivity of the terrestrial ecosystem is low, e.g. in very cold or arid areas, but tidal currents are strong and marine productivity is high, disposal in the sea may be the best option.

In high montane environments above snow line, microbial breakdown is extremely slow. Faecal material buried in snow is exposed during thaw, and material deposited in boulder scree or glacier crevasses is leached out in snow-melt. In areas of high visitor pressure, therefore, such as Mount Rainier in the Pacific northwest of the USA, park management agencies have instituted a so-called blue bag system. Climbers are issued with thick-walled blue plastic bags on registration for climbing or mountaineering permits, and are required to deposit faecal material in the bags, seal them and carry them to collection bins placed at intervals along heavily used routes. These are then removed periodically by helicopter or in some cases by snowmobile.

In desert environments, a few operators have adopted the use of surface smears rather than burial, on the grounds that this promotes rapid drying and sterilization by heat, desiccation and ultra-violet radiation. It also promotes rapid dispersal of pathogens in wind-blown dust, however, and rapid transport of nutrients into water courses by overland flow during rain events. The net impact of surface smears, relative to deep or shallow burial, remains untested.

Irrespective of the technique used to dispose of faecal material, the use of toilet paper or tissue provides another potential environmental impact of tourism in areas where toilets are not available. At one stage, park management agencies recommended that used toilet paper should be burnt *in situ* before the cat-hole was filled in. Following a number of fires traced to this practice, however, it is no longer recommended. The most dedicated minimal-impact operators currently avoid toilet paper completely, replacing it with small rocks, leaves, moss, snow, or whatever other natural materials are available on-site. This approach is not widespread, however, and used toilet paper is a significant contributor to litter in many heavily used recreational areas.

Washing and cleaning

All kinds of tourism operations involve cleaning, whether of people or things. Most routine cleaning processes use water and a variety of cleaning agents, and most discharge dirty water and spent cleaning agents in the form of sullage or wastewater. The choice of cleaning products, and the disposal of spent materials, is environmentally significant at all scales from integrated resorts to individual backpacker. In addition, some integrated sewage and garbage treatment systems also produce a wastewater effluent stream. The disposal or reuse of wastewater, sometimes in large volumes, is a significant environmental management issue for the tourism sector. As with other effluent streams, there are several approaches to reduce the overall impacts of cleaning and wastewater. The first is to reduce the total volume of water used. The second is to use less toxic or less concentrated cleaning agents to reduce the potential impacts per unit volume of wastewater discharged. The third is to recycle or treat wastewater before discharge. The fourth is to prevent or control release of contaminated water, e.g. by bunding washdown areas.

Cleaning agents vary enormously, from pentachlorophenol and similar agents used in mechanical and electronic cleaning applications, to individual cakes of hypo-allergenic soap in guest-room sinks or handbasins. For special-purpose cleaning agents used in limited volumes, the best strategy is generally to keep the particular cleaning operation concerned quite separate from other cleaning activities, and to collect spent cleaning agents locally so that they are not added to the main wastewater stream. Examples of such agents include organic solvents such as pentachlorophenol or toluene, volatile agents such as ethanol and methanol, paint thinners, petrol and kerosene, etc. This approach may also be feasible for concentrated cleaning products that are only used occasionally, such as those containing chemical scouring agents, fungicides and bactericides, etc.

In tourist accommodation, the principal sources of wastewater are from showers, laundry and room cleaning. The choice of soap and shampoos, laundry detergents and additives, and cleaning agents is hence critical to the net impacts of wastewater discharge. When biodegradable detergents first became available, for example, they were initially sold only in household sizes, not in industrial quantities. Most developed nations have established environmental standards for detergents and other cleaning agents, in relation to phosphate content and tests for biodegradability. Commonly, however, these standards are applied to labelling rather than to sale of the product itself.

For ecotours and independent travellers in wilderness areas, the release of detergents, soaps and other cleaning agents into otherwise unpolluted fresh water is potentially one of the more serious ecosystem impacts associated with wilderness recreation. Some ecotour operators and reserve management agencies have therefore prohibited the use of detergents completely. More commonly, they promulgate guidelines for minimal-impact use. For example, all cleaning should be carried out, and all cleaning and washing water should be discarded, well away (at least 50 or 100 m) from the nearest stream, lake or swamp area. First-stage cleaning at least should be carried out with water alone, or in the case of cooking utensils, natural scouring materials such as sand. Only biodegradable cleaning agents should be used, in minimum volume, for final stage cleaning only. Finally, all water from washing up, cooking and cleaning utensils should be strained before discarding, and foodscraps strained out should be added to food garbage.

Runoff from tourism facilities can also cause water pollution. Runoff from golf courses and other managed turf is commonly contaminated with fertilizers and pesticides. Runoff from roads, parking lots, garages and maintenance facilities, airstrips and hangars, and plant hardstand areas is commonly contaminated with petroleum residues. Engine oil from boats causes similar impacts.

Aircraft and vehicles produce wastewater in the form of washdown at airport hangars and coach depots, respectively. Typically, washdown water contains oil, solvents and detergents. If washdown water simply is allowed to run off to the nearest drain, these contaminants will flow to the receiving water body, whether freshwater or ocean. In addition, washdown water from vehicles, especially off-road vehicles, may contain weed seeds, fungal spores and other pathogens.

Washdown areas should therefore be bunded and, at the very least, wash water should be held temporarily in settling ponds so that sludge can settle out and oil can be skimmed from the surface before wastewater is discharged. Alternatively, it may be directed to an integrated treatment system, whether municipal or on-site, and/or reused for local irrigation.

Atmospheric emissions

The tourism sector is a significant contributor to global atmospheric emissions through the exhaust from aircraft, marine and vehicle engines, and pro rata contributions to atmospheric emissions from energy generation and manufacture of equipment, service items and consumables. Except for diesel-powered stationary plant, there are relatively few atmospheric emissions generated directly on-site by tourism accommodation and activities.

Tourism is a major contributor to total global motorized transport of people and freight. A high proportion of the total transport load in the tourism sector, measured in kg km, is people rather than goods; since people require a high volume per unit weight and want to travel fast, the net atmospheric emissions from transporting a given weight of people is higher than the average rate for a similar weight of freight. That is, the net emissions of greenhouse gases such as carbon dioxide, ozone-depleting substances such as chlorofluorocarbons, acid gases such as sulfur dioxide, and toxins such as carbon monoxide are higher on average for passenger miles in aircraft, high-speed ferries, recreational water craft, coaches and private cars than for transport of an equivalent weight of cargo.

For clients travelling internationally to take a local tour, the energy consumption and atmospheric emissions associated with local transport, even heavily mechanized, may be small compared to those of international air travel (Simmons and Becken, 2004; Hall and Higham, 2005; Folke et al., 2006; Becken and Hay, 2007).

Noise and disturbance

Impacts on noise levels are particularly significant for the transport and construction subsectors. Noise is also significant for all tourism operations in or near conservation reserves. Engine noise, overhead cablecars, overflying aircraft and even human voices can all cause major disturbance to wildlife as well as other human users. Some animal species can become habituated to human noise, but others may be driven away permanently just by voices and footfalls. Such disturbance, and its relation to visitor numbers and behaviour, is a major management issue for many conservation reserves worldwide.

Noise impacts are particularly significant for tourism developments located in or adjacent to areas of high conservation value. While the noise of aircraft landing and taking off at urban airports is a significant nuisance and social impact for local residents, the noise of tourist joyflights in light aircraft and helicopters, in and around scenic areas of conservation reserves, may have impacts on the local fauna that are much more significant ecologically.

While most conservation reserves have restrictions on overflights, they are not always well enforced or well observed and, even if they are, may still allow very significant noise impacts. The most common restriction, for example, is simply that aircraft may not fly below 300 m altitude except during take-off and landing at a recognized airstrip. This is a regulation enforced by national air safety legislation in most countries, and is not specifically associated with national parks. In areas with cliffs or canyons greater than 300 m in vertical relief, therefore, light aircraft may fly, and helicopters hover, below the lip of the cliff or canyon without infringing this regulation. Managers of conservation reserves often experience considerable difficulties in imposing ecologically effective restrictions on overflights, since they generally have no jurisdiction over air space, and national air traffic agencies have shown a marked reluctance to assist.

The noise of boat engines, though quieter than aircraft, carries a long way through the ocean, and whalewatching tours and other sightseeing boats that approach too closely or too rapidly can disturb marine mammals at the surface. Many countries now have codes of practice for whalewatching tour operators in an attempt to reduce such disturbance.

There are also many areas worldwide where conflicts over noise and disturbance have arisen between mechanized and non-mechanized uses of particular areas, including national parks and similar conservation reserves. The use of snowmobiles in Yellowstone National Park, USA, is a particularly well-known example, albeit principally for private recreation rather than commercial tours. As another example, there are many tour products where the activity on the tour itself is human-powered and low-impact, but where access to the area concerned is mechanized and potentially much higher-impact. Examples include four-wheel-drive-access mountain-biking tours, speedboat-access seakayaking tours, or helicopter-access river-rafting or mountain-hiking tours (Buckley, 2006).

Vehicle noise and human voices can also be significant sources of disturbance in many areas. Noise-sensitive animal species avoid road corridors and walking tracks, especially during periods of heavy use such as weekends and public holidays. Similarly, noise from tourist accommodation and facilities in or near areas of animal habitat can exclude many animal species from an area many times larger than the built-up area.

Accommodation and facilities produce a major noise impact during construction and a continuing noise during operations. Major sources of operational noise include vehicles arriving and departing, generators, electrical appliances, doors opening and closing, televisions and audio systems, and human voices. Even in wilderness campsites, human voices and the clash of cooking utensils can create a significant noise disturbance, especially in an otherwise quiet environment.

Besides noise, human activity can disturb animals through smell, provision of unusual food sources, interruption to daily movement patterns, or by modifying quantity, quality or access to water sources. All these types of disturbance can occur at all scales, from large resorts to individual backcountry hikers.

Smell disturbances, for example, can include: volatile components from diesel, petrol, or camp-stove fuels; perfumes and cosmetics; insect repellent and sunscreen; food and drink; and the smells of the human body itself. In Northern Hemisphere bear territory, for example, back-country travellers are careful not to carry perfumed soaps, and all food and even toothpaste must be used and stored at least 100 m from sleeping sites. In this case, of course, the concern is for the safety of the humans as well as the bears, but the importance of these precautions is a good indicator of how easily animals can be disturbed by unusual scents, and how sensitive their sense of smell can be relative to ours.

Disturbance to wildlife

Many animal species used for wildlife watching in commercial tourism are easily disturbed by humans even if the latter are quiet (Buckley, 2004b,g). The opportunity to interact directly with individual animals at close range, however, is one of the major attractions in many nature-based tours. Destinations that provide opportunities for visitors to approach animals closely are increasingly popular for tourists from urban areas who have previously seen such animals only in photographs or video, if at all.

The impacts of tourism on native wildlife, however, can be reduced greatly if tourists do not feed or touch individual animals, but remain at a sufficient distance and behave in a sufficiently non-threatening way that the animals will continue their normal patterns of behaviour without disturbance or stress. Such safe approach distances and behaviour may vary from one individual of a species to another, as well as between species. In particular, individuals of some species may become habituated to human proximity and activities, allowing a much closer approach distance than for individuals that are not so habituated.

If the individual animals concerned have never been subject to attack, injury or other threatening behaviour by humans, they may not recognize humans as threatening and may pay little attention to them. One well-known instance of this is in the Galapagos Islands, where all visitors are restricted to defined tracks. Many of the birds and reptiles for which the Galapagos are famous will rest or nest immediately adjacent to the tracks, apparently oblivious to camera-wielding visitors less than a metre away.

Even if an animal does not run away at the sight of a human, however, it may stop feeding and experience elevated pulse rates and adrenalin levels, which increase its energy consumption. Disturbances such as these may be critical for animals whose energy budgets are finely balanced, such as those overwintering in cold climates. The increased energy consumption associated with repeated stress from human visitors, for example, has been shown to affect the survival of overwintering animals in Yellowstone National Park in the USA.

In areas where hunting is commonplace, species that are commonly hunted are likely to be extremely wary, exhibiting stress at any sight, sound or smell of human presence, and exercising considerable ingenuity to avoid any human contact, even at a high energetic cost.

Codes of practice

Environmental management practices for a variety of tourism subsectors and activities have been assembled and distributed as guidelines and codes of practice by a range of organizations. Some of these are not specific to tourism, e.g. for green office practices or green purchasing policies. Many consist only of rather vague principles, not practical instructions.

Some, however, are detailed summaries of actual minimal-impact practices by leading tour operators, specific to particular activities and sometimes also to particular sites or ecosystems, and sufficiently comprehensive that an operator that follows all of the relevant recommendations can reasonably claim to have adopted best-practice environmental management for the subsector concerned. Well known examples include the Leave-No-Trace® series for various outdoor recreation activities, and the *Green Guide* series for various types of commercial outdoor tourism. There is also a series of longer but more general handbooks produced under the auspices of the UNWTO, in association with a programme called the Tour Operators Initiative for Sustainable Tourism (UNWTO, 2007).

There are also a number of instances where groups of competing operators have all agreed to adopt specified environmental management practices simultaneously. In general this has not happened until all the operators concerned were experiencing client complaints or loss of revenue through environmental deterioration, or could foresee a high probability of revenue loss in the immediate future. The best-known example occurred when the absence of adequate sanitary practices led to the wide-scale pollution of campsites in the Grand Canyon. All the operators concerned suffered the consequences, and it was in the interests of all to agree to improve methods for human waste disposal. Similarly, if a number of operators offer tours where their clients can feed, touch or handle native wildlife, birds, marine mammals, etc., and the high intensity of human interactions produces illnesses in the animal populations concerned, reducing their health or numbers, then it is equally in the interests of all operators to adopt lower-impact practices.

Of course, this rationale will only apply where tourism products concerned are critically dependent on a limited natural resource, such as river campsites, human-habituated populations of wild animals, or individual animals of a threatened or endangered species. Where the animals concerned are confined in so-called petting zoos or marine parks and can be replaced by capturing further individuals from wild populations, there is no economic incentive for the owners or operators of such facilities to ensure the survival of individual animals, and indeed there are many instances on record where animals have died in captivity and have simply been replaced.

Conclusions

Clearly, some of these environmental management approaches are principally a public-sector responsibility, some are private-sector, and some are individual. Very broadly, the largest-scale issues tend to be addressed by the public sector, with private-sector corporate approaches at a medium scale and individual responses at small scale. This is only a very broad pattern, however. For example, public-sector environmental management actions may include interpretive signs and educational materials intended to modify the behaviour of individuals, as well as actions by local, state and national governments and multilateral government agencies. Similarly, private corporations range in scale from single-person businesses to multinational corporations with resources larger than many small national governments.

Finally, though a single individual can clearly only act at an individual scale, some individuals have the ability to modify the behaviours of many others, and where large numbers of people independently make the same individual choices, either through similar personal convictions or through similar economic responses to market conditions, the aggregate effect may be as great as that of large public or private-sector organizations. Indeed, where groups of people make similar choices, government and corporations often change their policies, practices, products and prices in consequence, greatly magnifying the effect of the individual choices concerned.

RESEARCH

Sustainability

The sustainability, or otherwise, of the tourism sector as a whole has been the subject of numerous books over the past decade and a half. These include, for example, Eber (1992), McIntyre (1993), Nelson *et al.* (1993), Cocossis and Nijkamp (1995), Harris and Leiper (1995), McIntosh *et al.* (1995), Priestley *et al.* (1996), France (1997), Stabler (1997), Wahab and Pigram (1997), Hall and Lew (1998), Middleton and Hawkins (1998), Honey (1999), Singh and Singh (1999), Swarbrooke (1999), Bramwell and Lane (2000), Harrison (2001), McCool and Moisey (2001), Harris *et al.* (2002) and Mowforth and Munt (2003).

Several of these are edited compilations. The main themes, messages and conclusions from three in particular (Hall and Lew, 1998; Harrison, 2001; McCool and Moisey, 2001) are summarized in the readings for this chapter.

There are over two dozen journal articles during the past decade that address general issues of sustainability in tourism, from a variety of theoretical or political perspectives. These include contributions by, for example, Buckley (1996, 1999a), Drost (1996), Moscardo *et al.* (1996), Berry and Ladkin (1997), Brown and Essex (1997), Clarke (1997), Forsyth (1997), Hunter (1997), Wall (1997), Welford and Ytterhus (1998), Bramwell (1999), Hjalager (1999), Manning (1999), Robinson (1999), Briassoulis (2002), Casagrandi and Rinaldi (2002), Gössling *et al.* (2002), Hardy *et al.* (2002), Lovelock (2002), Ryan (2002), Twynam and Johnston (2002), Wight (2002) and Saarinen (2006).

The sustainability of specific tourism enterprises and destinations has been considered quite extensively, with case studies from, for example, Kenya (Sindiga, 1999; Curry and Morvaridi, 1992); South Africa (Spenceley, 2005); Scotland, both terrestrial (MacLellan, 1999) and marine (Woods-Ballard *et al.*, 2003); Nepal (Curry and Morvaridi, 1992; Devkota, 2005); the Indian Himalayas (Singh, 1991); Jamaica (Curry and Morvaridi, 1992); northern Thailand (Dearden, 1991); and Tenerife (Rodriguez *et al.*, 2008). Many of the books on sustainable tourism listed earlier also include comparable case studies from, for example, Belize, Canada, Crete, the Czech Republic, Dominica, Fiji, Goa, Indonesia, Madagascar, Malaysia, Nepal, New Zealand, Scotland, Spain, the UK, the USA and Zimbabwe.

Most recently Schianetz *et al.* (2007) reviewed tools to improve sustainability at tourism destinations; Bramwell and Lane (2007) noted the significance of audience and language in discussion of sustainability; Bohringer and Jochem (2007) concluded that currently available indices of sustainability are 'rather useless'; Hunter and Shaw (2007) argued that ecological footprints could provide a better option; and Kelly *et al.* (2007) found that tourists were prepared to pay for 'eco-efficiency'.

Codes and guidelines

Codes of conduct and behavioural guidelines for various types of tourist activity have been put forward by a number of authors and organizations over the past decade and a half. Early general discussions include Grotta (1992) and d'Amore (1993). Ethical codes and approaches have been considered by Fennell and Malloy (1995, 1999), Ewert and Shultis (1997), the World Tourism Organization (1999) and Holzapfel (2000).

Specific codes have been put forward by, for example, Stonehouse (1990) and Smith (1993) for the Antarctic; Giese (1998) for tourists watching Adelie penguins; Harris (2005) for aircraft flying near bird colonies in the Antarctic; the Australian Alps National Parks, for various mountain tourism activities; Leave-No-Trace® Inc., for various regions and activities in North America; the UK Countryside Commission for tourism in UK national parks; and the *Green Guide* series (Buckley *et al.*, 1999–2001) for various forms of outdoor tourism and recreation.

Collections and/or comparisons of codes extant at the time have been made by: Blangy and Nielsen (1993); UNEP (1995); Mason (1997) for the Arctic; Halpenny (2001) for marine tours; Buckley (2002c) for mountain tours; and Garrod and Fennell (2004) for whalewatching codes. Some of these comparisons (e.g. Buckley, 2002c) have found considerable similarities between different codes for the same activity; others (e.g. Garrod and Fennell, 2004) have found major differences. The distinction is perhaps that the codes compared by Buckley (2002c) all set out to be comprehensive, whereas those compared by Garrod and Fennell (2004) were compiled by dissimilar organizations with varying interests.

The degree to which tour operators actually comply or conform with such codes has been examined by Sirakaya (1997a,b), Sirakaya and Uysal (1997) and Sirakaya and McLellan (1998). Russell *et al.* (2008) found that the behaviour of commercial tour operators in protected areas, including compliance with rules, depends on their perceptions of the regulatory agency. Twynam and Johnston (1998), Parson and Woods-Ballard (2003) and Waayers *et al.* (2006)

tested what effects such codes have on tourists. Waayers *et al.* (2006), for example, found that tourists routinely breach the code of conduct for watching whales at Ningaloo in Western Australia. Holmes *et al.* (2005) tested how well such codes actually protect the environment. Specifically, Holmes *et al.* (2005) found that Royal Penguins experience raised heart rates when pedestrians approach within 5 m, the currently recommended minimum distance, and indeed, that an approaching pedestrian causes a greater reaction than a predatory skua flying overhead. That is, the current code of conduct, even if observed, is ineffective. In the marine environment, Michael *et al.* (2007) and Rouphael and Hanafy (2007) examined a variety of mechanisms to manage the impacts of divers, e.g. by monitoring broken coral.

REVISION

Site and scale

- Impacts depend on site and scale
- Aggregate impacts of development clusters
- Particular impacts in protected areas

Design and technologies

- Low-impact design and architecture
- Best-practice technologies
- For example for sewage treatment, greywater, garbage
- Low-noise, energy-saving, water-saving systems, etc.
- Quieter engines, emission controls

Management structures

- Environmental management needs all levels
- Owners or shareholders: message to retail clients
- On-ground: operational management, equipment
- Guides, frontline staff: instructions to clients
- Other staff: clean back-of-house operations
- Routine environmental audits

Long-distance travel

- Global atmospheric pollution
- Acid rain
- Ozone depletion
- Global warming
- Improve fuel efficiencies
- Reduce airport congestion

Local transport components

- Design tour products with low-impact components
- For example minimize high-impact transport
- Such as helicopters or speedboats (fuel, noise)
- Or vehicles or livestock in national parks

Engines

- Engine type and capacity affect impacts
- Anti-spill measures during refuelling
- Type, tuning, emission control to reduce exhaust impacts
- For example four-stroke cf. two-stroke for snowmobiles, watercraft
- Hush kits for helicopters

Accommodation components

- Design lodges for minimal impact
- For example insulation, natural lighting, efficient layout
- Staff and utilities as well as guest areas

Energy conservation

- Energy-efficient technologies
- For example energy-saving refrigerators and light globes
- Educational programmes
- Demand management devices
- For example room-light master keys

Water conservation

- Water-saving technologies
- For example low-irrigation landscaping
- Water-saving shower heads and washing machines
- Educational programmes
- For example laundry of hotel towels and linen

Resource conservation

- Reduce packaging
- Refillable food, beverage, toiletry containers
- Only if permissible under health laws
- Separate recyclables
- Glass, aluminium, paper and cardboard
- Compost organic garbage

Reduce water pollution

- Use best available treatment technologies
- For sewage, sullage and garbage
- Minimize fertilizers and pesticides
- For example lawns, landscaping, gardens
- Through selection of species and mixes
- Monitor runoff and leachates
- Use biodegradable soaps, detergents, cleaners

Use recycled products

- For example office paper
- Printer cartridges
- Furnishing materials

Codes and guidelines

- Leave-No-Trace® Inc.
- *Green Guides*
- UNWTO Tour Operators Initiative for Sustainable Tourism
- UNWTO handbooks
- TIES collections

Individual behaviour

- Choose low-impact transport
- Choose operators with good environmental management
- Minimize individually packaged and disposable items
- Choose tour providers that contribute to conservation
- Choose low-impact recreational activities
- Follow minimal-impact codes
- Especially in parks, backcountry, wilderness

REFLECTIONS

1. Choose any specific multi-day backcountry ecotour, real or imaginary, and briefly describe its major characteristics such as location, season, activity, group size, equipment used and so on. List the principal environmental management issues associated with your chosen tour, and the principal measures you could take to minimize environmental impacts. For the area, ecosystem and activity you have identified, what would be the single most significant ecological impact? Describe in detail the steps you could take to minimize, manage and mitigate that impact.

2. Many ecotour and outdoor tourism operators worldwide have a multi-tiered structure, with a central retail arm, local on-site operators and individual guides on seasonal contracts. How does such a structure affect day-to-day details of practical environmental management? What management structures would the owners of the retail company need to put in place to ensure best-practice environmental management during individual tours?

3. Suggestions are sometimes made that the aggregate environmental impacts of overnight visitors to a protected area or other pristine environmental might be reduced if they were accommodated in a permanent lodge rather than being distributed across a number of backcountry camping areas. What arguments could be made for and against this proposal? How would you assess which was preferable on balance? How would your considerations depend on: the type of environment, total visitor numbers, seasonality and similar factors?

4. Choose any individual ecotourism product, real or imaginary, and briefly describe its characteristics such as location, season, activity, group size, equipment used and so on. What codes of conduct and codes of practice can you find which would be relevant to environmental management for your chosen ecotour? What are the main points of similarity and difference between the various codes you have found? Are these codes realistic for practical commercial ecotour operators and, if not, why not?

READING 7.1. SUSTAINABLE TOURISM: A GEOGRAPHICAL PERSPECTIVE

This reading summarizes selected chapters from an edited volume by Hall and Lew (1998). Sixteen edited chapters provided commentaries and case studies in sustainable tourism from Anglophone members of the International Geographic Union and the Association of American Geographers. The first seven chapters are reviews that emphasize various historical, social and cultural aspects of sustainability, demonstrating that geography is a diverse discipline. The next eight chapters are case studies, ranging in scale from a single urban park in Canada to the entire Asia-Pacific region.

The technical chapters open with a historical summary by Michael Hall, who examined the role of tourism in the dedication of national parks. He summarized, 'The ideas behind sustainable tourism . . . translate to not shitting in one's own nest . . . Yet we all have to shit'. The next chapter, by Dick Butler, also presented a historical perspective and emphasized that sustainability is a global concept. For tourism, an evaluation of sustainability must include the impacts of bringing people and material resources to and from a particular site, over a period of time, as well as the local short-term impacts at that site. In addition, the interactions between tourism and other social and economic activities at the sites concerned must be included. Butler cited a report that concluded 'No example of the successful application of sustainable development of tourism had been found'. Taking this to its logical conclusion, Butler argued that: 'In some areas the best strategy for the environment, the local population and future generations may be no tourism development at all . . . Praising small-scale additions to the tourism scene while ignoring more significant ongoing problems does little to persuade the critical observer that many players are really serious about the application of sustainable tourism principles at a level that will make a great deal of difference.'

Heather Zeppel reviewed the involvement of indigenous peoples in the tourism industry. One common theme is the continued tension between community traditions and expectations, and the economic viability of tourism endeavours.

Pam Wight reviewed a range of standard environmental management tools with practical application in sustainable tourism. Some of these were developed in other industry sectors and subsequently applied to tourism. Others are approaches developed by national parks agencies for managing recreational visitors. Noting that 'tourism as a discipline seems to be lagging behind recreation', Wright argued that 'carrying capacity as a guiding concept has limited success outside the field of wildlife management, and cannot deal with the complexity and diversity of issues associated with tourism and recreation'.

Susan Place questioned whether so-called ecotourism in Costa Rica, which promotes itself internationally as a premier ecotourism destination, is in fact sustainable. Some Costa Ricans, she said, view the growth of tourism as the 'kidnapping of a nation'. She argued that: 'Although the Costa Rican government has paid lip service to nature-oriented tourism, it has offered little material help. On the contrary, among the casualties of structural adjustment were the park service, forest service and other resource conservation budgets.'

Bill Forbes described a programme to develop sustainable nature-based tourism in Curry County in southern coastal Oregon, USA. It seems that logging and commercial fishing provided high wages at the expense of the natural environment, and the social hierarchy was based on an ideal of the tough outdoorsman. Jobs in tourism were perceived as lower paid and lower status: 'babysitting for tree huggers'. Promoters of tourism development faced community opposition as serious as in the oft-reported cases of community opposition to tourism in less developed nations. Despite these difficulties, the development of nature-based tourism in Curry County was successful. Only one of the eight new tourism products, however, a US$19 million canopy walkway, was specifically designed to take tourists to old-growth forests.

A survey of 106 group trekkers and 385 independent trekkers in the Annapurna Conservation Area (ACAP) in Nepal in 1994 to 1995 found that group trekkers contributed more per capita to the Nepal economy as a whole, but independent trekkers contributed more to local village economies, and group trekkers consumed more fuel wood per capita than independent trekkers did. Trekkers were generally aware of environmental problems, including pollution and deforestation. Only four households in Tatopani, 2 days' walk from ACAP headquarters at Ghandruk, knew that ACAP existed. ACAP has a minimal-impact code, which suggests that tourists stay in lodges with appropriate waste control and fuel management. Apparently, however, as of that date none of the lodges fulfilled those criteria. This has changed subsequently, owing largely to the work of ACAP itself (Buckley, personal observation, 2007; Hum Bahadur Gurung, personal communication, 2008).

The book's final chapter, written by the editors, suggested that there were five lessons to be learned from 'geographic inquiry into sustainable tourism': (i) managing impacts must override market economics; (ii) implementation depends on scale and context; (iii) issues differ between developed and developing countries; (iv) locals must control resources; and (v) 'sustainable tourism development requires patience, diligence and long-term commitment'. Of these, lessons (ii), (iii) and (v) are probably unarguable. Lessons (i) and (iv) might well be contested by tourism developers. The editors concluded that: 'The goal of sustainable tourism development and its continuing inaccessibility provide a world of opportunity for stimulating research, discussion and action.'

Acknowledgement

This reading is condensed and revised from a review by Buckley (2000c), published in the *Journal of Travel Research* 39, 238–241.

READING 7.2. TOURISM AND THE LESS DEVELOPED WORLD

This reading is a review and summary of an edited volume by Harrison (2001). Harrison argued that: '[t]he notion of "sustainable tourism" is at best ambiguous and more often than not virtually useless . . . the tourism industry can be sustained for long periods, albeit at the cost of specific destination areas, environments, and communities.' He identified three key issues that shape tourism in developing countries: migration, commoditization and the roles of government.

Linda Richter suggested that '4-S tourism' needs four more 'Ss': security, sanitation, safe transport and sensible protection of built and natural heritage. David Weaver used his Caribbean experience to illustrate his classification into sustainable and unsustainable mass tourism, and both its 'deliberate' and 'circumstantial' alternatives.

Derek Hall examined tourism in post-communist societies, bemoaning 'economic geographers'. Brian King examined resorts in less-developed countries, comparing enclave tourism with developments integrated into local communities, anarchic development with rigid planning, large with small-scale development, and boosters with detractors. He concluded that '[t]he growing popularity of vast mega-resorts managed by transnational corporations is of ongoing concern'.

Frank Brennan and Garth Allen re-examined case studies of community tourism in Kwa-Zulu Natal in South Africa, and a dispute at Greater St Lucia Wetland Park. The conflict involved a mining company, a conservation agency and subsistence farmers at Dukuduku. They also described how at nearby Phinda, Conservation Corporation Africa successfully converted 17,000 ha of farmland to a private game reserve, while at Kosi Bay, a community ecotourism venture for 130 families from three tribes, set up by an NGO, failed apparently because of poor management and personal rivalries.

Indonesia is one of the world's most biodiverse regions, but as noted by Sheryl Ross and Geoff Wall, it also has the world's highest proportion of endangered species because of continuing clear-cutting of its forests. They suggested that in North Sulawesi, ecotourism is merely a small-scale add-on to pre-established parks, rather than a driving force for their establishment. The same applies in most developed nations. In nearby Fiji, Kelly Bricker described her experience in establishing a whitewater rafting and kayaking business. This involved complex negotiations with local landowner groups, establishment of a conservation reserve along the rivers, and arrangements for revenue-sharing.

Harrison concluded that 'tourism development is intimately linked to relationships of power', and that while there may be individual resorts, tour and transport operators, and even governments that try to promote sustainability, 'examples of good practice are comparatively rare'.

Acknowledgement

This reading is condensed and revised from a review by Buckley (2002d), published in *Annals of Tourism Research* 29, 1192–1193.

READING 7.3. TOURISM, RECREATION AND SUSTAINABILITY

This reading is a summary of an edited volume by McCool and Moisey (2001). The volume presented 16 case studies from around the world with the basic premise that 'tourism, particularly that which is based upon a region's natural and cultural heritage, contains both the promises of a better quality of life and protection of the region's heritage, as well as numerous pitfalls' (p. xi).

A 15-page introduction examined meanings, context, indicators, planning and knowledge for sustainable tourism, arguing that sustainable tourism is a 'guiding fiction', and that 'tourism is no longer the benign economic development tool that the boosterism of the past purported it to be'. The editors noted that 'tourism agencies are generally involved solely in promotion activities', and that this often becomes 'unbridled boosterism, with few acknowledgements of tourism's negative social and environmental consequences'. As it is, 'one agency may promote protected areas as a tourism destination, while another is responsible for managing the tourists and their impacts when they arrive'. These observations apply worldwide, and form a major barrier to the potential for tourism as a tool in sustainable development. McCool and Moisey also argued that sustainable tourism is a rather meaningless term unless quantitative indicators can be defined to assess progress. They noted that planning and development commonly involve so-called 'messy situations, where goals conflict or compete'. They also drew attention to the weakness of 'carrying capacity' approaches. Few of the case study chapters, however, addressed these issues specifically.

The central significance of environmental impacts and management in any consideration of sustainability was established in a review chapter on recreation ecology by Yu-Fai Leung, Jeff Marion and David Fennell. Chad Dawson examined the place of ecotourism in a tourism opportunity spectrum. Dimitri Ioannides looked at tourism life cycles in the Mediterranean, noting the routine hypocrisy of government ministers who talk green while approving, and indeed promoting, large-scale coastal tourism developments. Simon Evans noted the extreme crowding of national parks in the UK and argued that, to alleviate this pressure, public forests should be used for public recreation, and new community forests should be created around urban fringes. This would allow the national parks to fulfil their primary role of environmental protection.

Judith Meyer reviewed contentious issues past and present in Yellowstone National Park, such as the management of bears, bison, fires, snowmobiles and hotsprings. Once a wild place where tourists could watch wildlife and wade in warm water, Yellowstone has become a seething mass of self-drive tourists. Until a few decades ago, it was still peaceful in winter, but as Meyer notes, 'now those who come to the park expecting solitude and silence find crowds of people and the roar of snowmobiles'. Attempts by the National Parks Service to control these impacts have constantly been thwarted by tourism interests that want to expand winter tourism to extend their income throughout the year.

In conclusion, McCool and Moisey again asked whether sustainable tourism is a guiding fiction or a realistic endstate, and re-emphasized the need for indicators and the importance of public participation.

Acknowledgement

This reading is condensed and revised from a review by Buckley (2003d), published in *Annals of Tourism Research* 30, 271–273.

chapter 8

IMPACTS

Shower area of a private wildlife ecolodge in a desert area in Namibia. Note open slats for ventilation, low-volume hand-basin to reduce water usage, bucket to catch initial shower water during temperature adjustment, small taps as a subtle reminder that water is in short supply, and slatted floor with water collection tray beneath. Daytime lighting is through a slatted ceiling, covered by transparent plastic. Night-time lighting is from solar-powered electric ceiling light, with a battery bank under the room, or by candles on the window ledge.

REVIEW

Introduction

Minimizing impacts on the natural environment is a key criterion in all definitions of ecotourism. It is equally critical in managing land and water access for all forms of outdoor tourism, especially in protected areas. Effective management of environmental impacts requires both the ability to measure those impacts and an understanding of the mechanisms that produce them. These approaches constitute the field of recreation ecology, reviewed comprehensively by Liddle (1997).

The environmental impacts of ecotourism have been reviewed in detail more recently (Buckley, 2004a). This chapter summarizes the principal conclusions from that volume, focusing on aspects relevant to the operation and management of outdoor tourism businesses. That is, this chapter does not attempt to review the field of recreation ecology from a scientific perspective. For those wishing to pursue that perspective, the reviews in Buckley (2004a) and the compendium by Liddle (1997) provide a good starting point. The detailed measurement, analysis and comparison of ecological impacts, however, require expertise specifically in relevant environmental sciences. Information provided in this chapter is at a more general level, relevant for parks, recreation and outdoor tourism management.

The preceding chapter on environmental management focused principally on the practical steps that ecotourism operators can take to reduce their environmental impacts. This chapter delves deeper into the types of impacts and the mechanisms by which they are produced. It also considers impacts more from the perspective of a parks or land manager, rather than the tour operator. There are necessarily some areas of overlap between the two chapters, but in general, this chapter contains more detail on ecological issues, while the preceding chapter emphasizes engineering and management aspects.

Type, sites and scales

Different types of tourism activity, and different components of tourism products, create very different impacts, and opportunities to reduce those impacts differ correspondingly. In addition, different components and activities may take place in very different sites, with correspondingly wide variation in the ecological significance of the impacts they cause.

For an international client travelling to another country to take part in a nature, adventure or ecotour in a remote area, the greatest gross impacts at a global scale may well originate from international air travel and from hotel accommodation in gateway cities. Both of these, however, are largely beyond the control of either the client or the tour packager, except insofar as they can select airlines or hotel companies that take steps to reduce their impacts, or unless, of course, they elect not to take such a tour at all. Once on the ground or in the water at the final destination site, the volume of atmospheric emissions from transport, and solid and liquid wastes from accommodation, are likely to be much smaller. The impacts from disposing of such wastes, however, may be of considerable ecological significance at a local scale. In addition, there may be local impacts on plants and animals, sometimes including endangered species, both through direct disturbance and through indirect mechanisms such as fire and feral or invasive species. In any assessment of tourism impacts, therefore, both the type and the scale of impacts must be considered.

Accommodation, transport, activities

In establishing the types of impacts that any given tourism product may produce, it is useful to consider accommodation, transport and activity components separately (Tables 8.1 and 8.2). Accommodation may range from a backcountry bivouac to a luxury lodge, but in any case will generally require a supply of heat for cooking and water for drinking and washing, and the disposal of human waste, used washing water, food scraps and packaging (Table 8.1). Each of these involves significant design and operational choices, which influence environmental impacts. For a backcountry hiking tour, the choice between carrying in liquid stove fuel or using local firewood affects both the type and scale of impact. For a large lodge or remote-area resort, the choice is generally between: a power transmission line from the nearest town; on-site gas or diesel generators; or a combination of smaller-scale energy sources and energy-saving measures, which might include solar cells for electric lighting, gas or fuelwood for cooking, and direct solar heating for hot washing water.

In the case of transport, some activities and locations may be accessible via a range of different alternative transport mechanisms, from hiking to helicopters, seakayaks to speedboats. In other cases, mechanized transport is needed to reach a remote site, even though the activity on arrival is non-mechanized. In other cases again, the activity itself is mechanized, such as off-road safaris; or cannot function without mechanized transport, as in the case of heliskiing. Occasionally, accommodation, transport and activity are combined, as in the case of expedition cruises. Even in that case, however, the different components and their impacts (Table 8.2) can still be distinguished and considered separately.

Activities and ecosystems

The types, severity and consequences of impacts on soil, plants, birds and other wildlife that are produced by various types of outdoor activity, have been detailed by Liddle (1997) and Buckley (2004a). The latter concluded that despite considerable research, data on the environmental impacts of ecotourism are still sparse, clumped and crude (Buckley, 2004a).

There are now over a thousand individual published studies on the ecological impacts of human recreational activities, including commercial ecotourism (Buckley, 2004a), but there are hundreds of thousands of plant and animal species affected, and for each of these there are dozens of different effects that disturbance could produce. The multitudinous social science disciplines have not yet described the behaviour of our own species, and why should other vertebrates, at least, be any less complex? In addition, the ecological impacts of ecotourism

Table 8.1. Environmental impacts of accommodation and shelter.

Type of accommodation or shelter	Vegetation clearance or damage	Soil erosion and/or compaction	Wildlife disturbance or habitat destruction	Firewood collection and campfires	Solid wastes	Water pollution	Noise	Visual
Resorts, hotels: construction	Site clearance	Short term, during construction	Habitat cleared, noise		Construction rubbish, builders' rubble	Sediments	Construction plant	Construction site and plant
Resorts, hotels: operations	Tracks, etc.	Unsealed tracks, etc.	Shyer species leave area	Collected elsewhere, if used	Garbage, treated sewage	Sullage, increased nutrients	Machinery and motors	Conspicuous buildings and infrastructure, large vehicles
Fixed car or caravan camps	Site clearance initially and continuing, tracks, etc.	If ungrassed, and increasing with use	Habitat clearance, shyer species leave area	Large area often denuded	Garbage, litter, toilets	Sullage, increased nutrients, bacteria	Generators, car engines, chainsaws, radios, voices	Vehicles, caravans, large tents, equipment, campfires
Overnight car/ four-wheel-drive camps	Increasing with use	Increasing with use	Depends on frequency of use	Large campfires common	Litter, human wastes	Bacteria, soap	Car engines, chainsaws, radios, voices	Cars, large tents, campfires

Continued

Table 8.1. *Continued.*

Type of accommodation or shelter	Vegetation clearance or damage	Soil erosion and/or compaction	Wildlife disturbance or habitat destruction	Firewood collection and campfires	Solid wastes	Water pollution	Noise	Visual
Horse/hiker huts	Local site clearance, trampling	Localized, depends on soil type, etc.	Minor, localized	Large area often affected, regular large campfires	Litter, horse dung, human wastes	Bacteria	Saws, voices	Huts, cleared paddocks, campfires
Boat-access shore sites	Increasing with use	Bank erosion	Minor, localized	Large area often affected, regular large campfires	Litter, fish guts, human wastes	Petroleum residues	Outboard motors, voices	Boats, large tents, fires, clearance
Often-used bush camps	Localized, new tent sites	Localized, depends on soil type, etc.	Minor, localized	Depends on vegetation type: large area may be affected	Some paper, human wastes	Bacteria, soap	Voices	Small tents, fires
Single-use camps and bivouacs	Minimal or none	Generally none	Temporary or none	Minimal or none	Generally none	Generally none	Minimal or none	Minimal and temporary

Source: Buckley (1991a).

Table 8.2. Environmental impacts of transport and travel.

Means of transport or travel	Vegetation clearance or damage	Soil erosion or compaction	Wildlife disturbance, shooting or habitat destruction	Solid wastes	Water pollution	Air pollution	Noise	Increased fire risk	Weeds and pathogens
Light planes, helicopters	Airstrips only	Airstrips only	Depends on speed, altitude, frequency of flights	Empty fuel drums at remote strips	Refuelling spills	Engine emissions	Loud, but intermittent	Little or none	Airstrips only
Bus or car on road	Roads and verges cleared	Compaction and erosion on unsealed roads	Noise depends on traffic density; roads can act as barriers; road kills	Litter	Petroleum residues in runoff from roads	Exhaust fumes	Line source, volume depends on traffic density	Sparks, cigarette butts	Along road verges
Car or four-wheel-drive on tracks	Tracks cleared; tend to be widened and new tracks cut	Dust, gully erosion and compaction widespread	Road kill, noise, shooting	Litter	Turbid runoff	Exhaust fumes	As above	Sparks, cigarette butts	Along track verges
Off-road vehicles (ORVs) off track	Severe and extensive vegetation damage	Erosion widespread, depends on terrain and soil type	Widespread noise disturbance; ORVs used for shooting	Litter, human wastes	Campsites, etc.: bacteria, soap	Exhaust fumes	Major impact, since ORVs can enter otherwise quiet areas	Sparks, cigarette butts, campfires	Spread on tyres

Continued

Table 8.2. *Continued.*

Means of transport or travel	Vegetation clearance or damage	Soil erosion or compaction	Wildlife disturbance, shooting or habitat destruction	Solid wastes	Water pollution	Air pollution	Noise	Increased fire risk	Weeds and pathogens
Mountain bikes	Less severe than ORVs	Localized in heavily used areas	Disturbance in heavily used areas	Litter, human wastes	Campsites, etc.: bacteria, soap	None	Voices only	Cigarette butts, campfires	Spread on tyres
Horses	Trampling on horse trails	Localized, trails and holding paddocks	Minimal, unless riders rowdy or shooters	Horse manure	Nutrients, bacteria, downstream of holding paddocks	None unless very crowded	Voices only	Cigarette butts, campfires	Spread in fodder if carried
Hiking	Trampling on heavily used trails	Localized on heavily used areas	Generally minimal	Human wastes	Campsites, etc.: bacteria, soap	None	Voices only	Cigarette butts, campfires	Minimal, on boots and socks
Power boats	Campsites, shoreline and aquatic vegetation	Not applicable	Noise, fishing and shooting	Garbage at campsites, jetsam	Fuel residues, nutrients, bacteria, antifouling paints	Exhaust fumes	Engine noise	Campsites only	Campsites only
Unpowered watercraft	Generally none	Not applicable	Fishing only	Garbage and jetsam	Bacteria, soap	None	Voices only	Campsites only	Campsites only

Source: Buckley (1991a).

include effects on the physical as well as the biological environment, and effects on ecosystems and species assemblages and interactions as well as direct disturbance to individual species. So even though a thousand studies might sound a lot in tourism research, from an ecological perspective the entire body of impact research to date is but a bare beginning in the discipline of recreation ecology.

For effective management of visitor impacts in areas of high conservation value, as has often been said (Buckley and Pannell, 1990; Buckley, 2001a, 2004h) we need quantitative information on the impacts of different numbers of visitors in groups of various sizes, engaged in a range of activities with corresponding equipment, over different periods at various seasons in a range of ecosystems, and subject to a variety of management regimes, on a number of ecosystem parameters and components including individual species. To date we do have individual research studies that have addressed aspects such as visitor numbers and group size, activity and equipment, season and duration, ecosystem and management, but only in a small number of instances and for a small number of species and parameters.

Our need for knowledge may be likened to a vast multidimensional matrix linking all the various factors that may influence impacts on all the various ecosystem components (Buckley, 2004a). In each cell of the matrix, we need replicated studies, quantitative data, measures of uncertainty and predictive models. Our total current knowledge, in contrast, lies entirely within a tiny proportion of these matrix cells, and not a single cell is entirely filled.

Intercontinental differences

Current data on the impacts of ecotourism are heavily biased to a few geographic areas, notably North America and, in consequence, to particular ecosystems, species and ecotourism activities (Buckley, 2004a). For some combinations of impact categories, such as the impacts of pedestrian trampling on temperate grassland and similar vegetation, there is an established body of English-language ecological research by internationally recognized experts. For other types of impacts, and other parts of the world, there are valuable case studies but as yet no coherent and cross-referenced body of research.

There may be corresponding bodies of impact research in other languages from other continents, but if so there is very little cross-citation into the English-language literature. Chizhova (2004) and Magro and de Barros (2004), for example, do cite previous work published in Russian and Portuguese respectively, but not in such quantity as other authors cite work published in English. It would indeed be valuable for bilingual ecologists to compile English-language reviews of recreation-impact research published, for example, in Chinese, Japanese, Spanish or French.

Intercontinental differences in the apparent depth and breadth of recreation ecology research, however, cannot be ascribed solely to incompatibilities in language. For example, the literature cited in the various chapters of Buckley (2004a) show that there has been far less impact research in Australia than in North America, even though Australian scientists are well represented in the ecological literature as a whole. This pattern was also noted previously by Newsome *et al.* (2002a). Certainly, there are fewer people and hence fewer ecologists in Australia and, certainly, many ecologists in both continents perceive other ecological issues as more fundamental or urgent than measuring the impacts of ecotourism and outdoor recreation. At least equally critical, however, is access to research funding for applied recreation ecology. Much of the work in the USA and Canada has been carried out by a relatively small number of individuals supported by specialist institutions. In Australia, the federal government has provided very substantial funding since the mid-1990s for research in 'sustainable tourism', but only an extremely minuscule proportion of this has been allocated to research on ecological impacts.

Because of the strong representation by North American researchers, some particular ecosystems and activities have been studied much more intensively than others. Perhaps the greatest concentration of quantitative experimental research has been on pedestrian trampling of ground-layer vegetation, especially in open landscapes such as alpine meadows. This research is indeed applicable in similar ecosystems on other continents (Whinam *et al.*, 2003; Magro and de Barros, 2004). In other ecosystems, however, pedestrian trampling may be far less significant ecologically than other impacts of hikers, such as noise disturbance to birds and wildlife, or introduction of weeds and pathogens (Buckley, 1999a, 2001a, 2002e).

There is thus a strong need to expand research effort on the ecological impacts of ecotourism and outdoor recreation across a broader range of ecosystems and species. In particular, as many developing countries are currently promoting ecotourism as a means to fund protected area systems, it is important to extend recreation ecology research into relevant tropical and subtropical ecosystems to assist these countries in managing visitor access and activities.

In the developed nations, there is an additional trend, namely the expansion of outdoor sports and adventure recreation in public lands. Recreation ecology research therefore needs to devote additional attention to a broader range of activities by a broader range of people. For example, the increasing popularity of mountain biking and rock climbing has generated a pressing need for better data on their ecological impacts.

Trampling and weeds

Even for the most heavily studied impacts, such as pedestrian trampling on ground-layer vegetation, available data are still insufficient to yield quantitative predictive models except at the broadest scale. The only consistently available parameter that Cole (1995a, b) could identify to compare the results of vegetation trampling studies was the number of passes needed to reduce plant cover to 50% of its original value. Even with such a broad parameter, available data are not sufficient to predict the value of that parameter for a plant community not previously studied. Similarly, even though the effects of trampling on plant cover have now been studied experimentally for a range of ecosystems (Cole, 2004), there are very few where the effects of, for example, the distribution of hiker passes over time have been quantified. Again, even though there are some instances where soil as well as plant parameters have been measured for trampled areas, and even though there are cases where the influence of, for example, slope and moisture content on soil erosion have been considered, these are still not sufficient data to predict how many hikers can cross a specific hill before tracks start to erode out.

There are guidelines for choosing low-impact hiking routes and guidelines for building erosion-resistant hiking trails, but these are based on experience, not on predictions from impact research. Suppose that hikers routinely cross a particular hillslope, and a land manager wants to know whether to divert them around it to avoid an erosion scar and expensive rehabilitation or track-hardening works. To make that decision the land manager needs to know how many pedestrian passes will reduce plant cover to zero and initiate soil erosion, for a specific slope, soil type, plant cover and climate. Rarely, however, can we provide such an estimate with any degree of confidence. So the land manager must choose between caution and associated controversy from users, or waiting till damage has occurred and trying to repair it. For trampling of trails, perhaps waiting for damage is an acceptable management strategy: impacts can be detected easily and immediately, are generally only of local significance, and can be rehabilitated if required. For many other impacts, however, detection is difficult and delayed and ecological effects are diffuse and irreversible. If research data are so limited even for trampling, how much more serious is the deficiency for other types of ecological impact? Even for the relatively better-studied impacts, therefore, many more data are required before the mechanisms can be considered well understood.

Typically, trampling damage is also associated with other impacts from some activities, such as soil erosion or compaction, and the introduction or dispersal of weed seeds and fungal spores. Tourists, by definition, travel from one place to another, and in doing so they may transport weed seeds and soil and plant pathogens on their car tyres, footwear, clothing and camping equipment. Some people also travel with dogs and cats, and these pets sometimes escape and become feral predators.

An astonishing variety of plant seeds may be carried on socks, and in mud on car tyres. Fungal pathogens such as the dieback fungus *Phytophthora cinnamomi* may also be spread in soil, adhering to bulldozers, vehicles, boots or even tent pegs (Buckley *et al.*, 2004). The current distribution of *P. cinnamomi* in Tasmania, for example, suggests that it was introduced initially into state forests, and thence by hikers into national parks. Pathogens may also be carried internally. The best-known example is the protozoan *Giardia*, which has apparently been transported into previously uncontaminated water catchments by people moving from one catchment to another (Buckley and Warnken, 2002).

Tours that include horses may potentially introduce weeds and pathogens through seeds and spores in feed and dung. These can be avoided by allowing horses to eat only cleaned and processed feed, not only while they are in areas of high conservation value, but also for several days previously. This represents an additional expense, and it also requires staff and supervision to control what the horses eat before the trip actually starts.

Quality of impact science

From an ecological perspective, most past studies of ecotourism impacts are rather crude. Relatively few researchers have: used physiological indicators; calculated consequences at population scale; or examined impacts that are indirect, second-order, diffuse, evanescent, invisible to the naked eye, or delayed in onset. Such effects, however may be very significant ecologically.

Day visitors to heavily used sites in national parks, for example, could inadvertently increase the food available to common predatory bird species, and these more aggressive birds might also attack the eggs and nestlings of smaller bird species, some of them rare (Oost, 2007). The significance of such effects for populations and survival of these smaller species remains largely untested (Buckley, 2004g). Tracks created by backcountry hikers would perhaps increase the success of predators, native or introduced, in stalking small native mammals and ground-foraging birds, even where the tracks are faint and little travelled. Oversnow vehicles can crush the undersnow burrows of small mountain mammals (Sanecki et al., 2006), and helicopter overflights can drown out territorial, courtship and alarm calls by native birds.

In the Australian Alps, it has been suggested that habitat modification on ski slopes and hiking trails within Mt Kosciusko National Park has hastened the spread of particular introduced plant species, whose more showy flowers attract native insect pollinators away from endemic native species in the same plant family (Kelly et al., 2003). Since the continued survival of the native species depends on their ability to produce more seed than are attacked by seed-parasite insects, even a small reduction in pollination success could tip the balance towards extinction of the species concerned. To assess the ecological significance of this mechanism would require detailed long-term analyses by a plant reproductive ecologist, and this has not yet been done.

Indirect impacts such as these are difficult to identify without extensive field observations and almost impossible to quantify without carefully designed ecological studies. Such studies require ecological expertise, funding, equipment and time-scales (Buckley, 2002c, d). All of these are rare in tourism research. Of course, even with considerable additional research effort, the ecological impact of ecotourism, as with any other human activity, will never be precisely predictable. Individual animals, for example, behave differently from others of the same species. Indeed, they may react differently to two successive and similar disturbances, even if their usual behaviour is broadly predictable. Both wildlife ecologists and wildlife tour guides learn to identify individual animals and distinguish their likely reactions under different circumstances.

Overall, however, the clear conclusion from Buckley (2004a) was that a great deal more recreation ecology research is required in all continents, for a wide range of ecosystems species and ecotourism activities. Subsequent research is summarized later in this chapter.

Threshold processes

One particularly important issue in examining the impacts of human activity on natural ecosystems is the operation of threshold processes. Many ecosystems are resistant to external disturbances, e.g. through internal feedback mechanisms that act to counter small changes, but only as long as that disturbance is below a certain threshold. Once this threshold is exceeded, there is a qualitative change in the processes concerned, with major change to the ecosystem in consequence. As an example, a grassland can withstand a certain number of people walking across it with little or no detectable change, but if it is used as a regular thoroughfare, the grass will die and the soil will erode into a deep trench. Once this threshold is crossed, the grassland area is unlikely to recover even if people stop walking across it. The eroded section may even serve as the focus for further erosion, e.g. by runoff after rain. There is thus a threshold level of external disturbance, human trampling in this case, beyond which a major change in system behaviour occurs.

Typically, different ecosystems may have widely different thresholds for similar types of disturbance. The threshold level of trampling for plant and soil damage on an alpine scree slope, for example, is a great deal less than that of level temperate grassland. In some cases, such differences between thresholds can provide a useful measure to compare the responses of different natural environments to particular human disturbances such as those associated with tourism.

What this means in practice is that different types of human impact are more or less critical in different types of ecosystem. In desert environments, unsurprisingly, availability of water is likely to be the most critical factor for the survival of plant and animal species. In the wet tropics, water is rarely a limiting factor, but soil nutrients often are. In very harsh environments such as extreme arctic and alpine areas, soil and vegetation seem to be highly susceptible to trampling damage, but relatively resistant to the introduction of weeds, since most weeds do not have the necessary specialized adaptations to survive in such harsh environments. Subtropical rainforest, in contrast, is highly resistant to trampling damage, as its soils are spongy and its vegetation fast growing; however, it is highly susceptible to the introduction of weeds, which can easily survive and spread in such a favourable environment.

Whether planning major engineering earthworks or a small hiking tour, therefore, the relative importance that should be attached to quarantine measures, such as washing mud off heavy earthmoving equipment or hiking boots, differs greatly between these two ecosystem types. Similarly, a given level of noise, whether from human voices or construction machinery, is likely to have much greater impacts in a subtropical rainforest, where the ambient noise level is low and there are many noise-sensitive birds and mammals, than on a snowbound mountain top with no animals except the occasional eagle and other mountain climbers.

Conclusions

Recreation ecology is now a substantial and active research discipline worldwide, as indicated by the 2004 reviews listed in Table 8.3 and the subsequent publications listed in Tables 8.4 and 8.5. As the outdoor recreation and commercial ecotourism sectors continue to grow, their impacts in areas of high conservation value become increasingly significant. Ways to measure and manage these impacts, and understand and predict the mechanisms by which they occur,

Table 8.3. Reviews of the environmental impacts of ecotourism.

Type of impact	Chapter authors
Positive cf. negative	Buckley
Impacts of	
Long-distance travel	Simmons, Becken
Amenity migration	Johnson
Hiking on soils and vegetation	Cole
Horse-riding	Newsome *et al.*
ORVs	Buckley
Tour boats, marine	Warnken, Byrnes
Powerboats, freshwater	Mosisch, Arthington
Impacts on	
Polar ecosystems	Forbes *et al.*
Whales and dolphins	Higham, Lusseau
Birds	Buckley
Terrestrial wildlife	Buckley
Managing impacts	
Hiking trails	Marion and Leung
Campsites	Leung and Marion
Visitor perceptions	Manning *et al.*
Quota systems	Manning
Effectiveness of indicator systems	Buckley
Effectiveness of interpretation	Littlefair
Case studies	
Campsites, Prince William Sound, Alaska	Monz, Twardock
Dieback disease, Australia	Buckley *et al.*
In-stream bacteria, Australia	Warnken, Buckley
Four-wheel-drive vehicles, coastal dunes, Australia	Priskin
Macroalgae, Vancouver I, Canada	Alessa *et al.*
Various users, Itataia National Park, Brazil	Magro, de Barros
Hiking, Kavkazsky, Russia	Chizhova

Source: Buckley (2004a).

Table 8.4. Recent research on tourist disturbance to wildlife.

Species or group	Country	Disturbance and/ or behaviour	Reference
Polar bear	Canada	Tundra buggies, vigilance	Dyck and Baydack (2004)
Brown bear	Alaska, USA	Salmon intake	Rode *et al.* (2006)
Brown bear	British Columbia, Canada	Wildlife watching	Nevin and Gilbert (2005)
Brown bear	Sweden	Resorts	Nellemann *et al.* (2007)
Brown bear	Sweden	Monitoring	Bellemain *et al.* (2005)
Grizzly bear	USA	Farm food attraction	Wilson *et al.* (2005)
Brown bear	Slovenia	Denning	Petram *et al.* (2004)
Lions	Zimbabwe	Sport hunting	Loveridge *et al.* (2007)
Snow leopards	South-west Mongolia	Monitoring	McCarthy *et al.* (2005)
Carnivores and herbivores	Tanzania, Ngorongoro	Population decreases	Estes *et al.* (2006)
Mountain caribou	Canada	Fragments populations	Apps and McLellan (2006)
Gazelle, ibex	Saudi Arabia	Disturb at waterhole	Wakefield and Attum (2006)
Elk	USA	ATVs	Preisler *et al.* (2006)
Forest elephant	Asia, Africa	Monitoring	Blake and Hedges (2004)
Chimpanzee	Uganda	Human gut bacteria	Goldberg *et al.* (2007)
Marmots	USA	Sight and sound	Griffin *et al.* (2007)
Kangaroos	Australia	Roadkill	Klocker *et al.* (2006)
Rock wallaby	North-east Australia	Artificial feeding	Hodgson *et al.* (2004)
Subsnow mammals	Australia	Ski grooming	Sanecki *et al.* (2006)
Bottlenose dolphin	South-east Australia	Tour boats	Lemon *et al.* (2006)

Continued

Table 8.4. *Continued.*

Species or group	Country	Disturbance and/ or behaviour	Reference
Killer whale	British Columbia, Canada	Boats, energetics	Williams *et al.* (2006)
Manatees	Florida, USA	Boats, injuries	Nowacek *et al.* (2004)
Manatees	Florida, USA	Boats	Solomon *et al.* (2004)
Frogs, four species	Central Thailand	Noise, call rate	Sun and Narins (2005)
Podarcis lizards	Spain	Disturbance affects health	Amo *et al.* (2006)
Reptiles	Ontario, Canada	Deliberate roadkill	Ashley *et al.* (2007)
Yellow-eyed penguin	New Zealand	Visual	McClung *et al.* (2004)
Humboldt penguin	Chile	Heart rate increase from 150m sighting	Ellenberg (2006)
Puffins	Scotland	Weeds affect nesting	Fischer and van der Wal (2007)
Kittiwake, guillemot	Scotland	Visitor disturbance	Beale and Monaghan (2004)
Shorebirds	Global	Visual, noise	Yasue (2006)
Shorebirds	South Carolina, USA	Disturbance to roosting	Peters and Otis (2007)
Shorebirds	British Columbia, Canada	Visual, energetics	Yasue (2006)
Golden plover	Pennines, UK	Visual	Finney *et al.* (2005)
Whooper swan	Scotland	Visual	Ress *et al.* (2005)
Golden eagle	Scotland	Harassment	Whitfield *et al.* (2004a,b)
Ptarmigan	Scotland	Ski resort, crows	Watson and Moss (2004)
Woodlark	England	Hikers	Mallord *et al.* (2007)
Alpine grassland birds	Italy	Ski runs	Rolando *et al.* (2007)
Forest birds	South-east Australia	Monitoring	Cunningham *et al.* (2004)
Birds, mammal	New South Wales, Australia	Roadkill	Ramp *et al.* (2006)

Continued

Table 8.4. *Continued.*

Species or group	Country	Disturbance and/ or behaviour	Reference
Bees	Ontario, Canada	Pathogens spread from apiaries	Colla *et al.* (2006)
Ghost crab	Brazil	Vehicles	Neves and Bemvenuti (2006)
Intertidal species	Central Chile	Parasitism	Loot *et al.* (2005)
Fish, various	Austria	Boats	Wysocki *et al.* (2006)

Note: For research prior to 2004, see Buckley (2004a,b,g).

become more important for land managers. For ecotourism operators, minimizing impacts is a key concern, but so also is offsetting them, through active contributions to conservation. These are considered in the next chapter.

RESEARCH

Research on the ecological impacts of ecotourism was reviewed in detail 4 years ago (Buckley, 2004a). The review chapters in that volume and their authors are listed in Table 8.3. Major themes for future research, emerging from that review (Buckley *et al.*, 2006), are summarized below, and expanded further in the reading for this chapter.

One major theme is to compare impacts from the same recreational activities in similar ecosystems, between different continents. For example, do arctic/alpine plants respond to trampling in the same way on Mt Kenya as Mt Wilhelm, Aconcagua as Annapurna, Brooks Range Alaska as Western Arthurs Tasmania? If not, how and why do these responses differ? Do rainforest birds react to human noise in South-east Asia as in northeast Australia, in Guinea as in Guatemala? How do the energetic consequences of disturbance by boaters or anglers differ between migrating shorebirds in North America, Europe, Siberia, Western Australia? Are differences related to climate, food supplies, species' life histories or recreational patterns?

A second major theme is to compare the relative significance of different types of impact in different ecosystems. As noted above, trampling impacts may be critical for alpine scree vegetation and negligible for tropical rainforest, while the reverse may apply for disturbance to birds by human voices, but such comparisons have not yet been made in any systematic way.

A third major theme is to identify and test subtle and indirect mechanisms of recreational impacts on particular plant and animal species and communities in different ecosystems, by applying other specialist ecological disciplines to recreational activities. Examples might include pollination ecology, fire ecology, ecotoxicology, population ecology, predation ecology, reproductive ecology, foraging ecology and energetics, and many more.

Considerable recent research in recreation ecology has been published since the review volume (Table 8.3) edited by Buckley (2004a). This research has continued both along traditional lines, and in new directions such as those suggested in priorities outlined above. Research that has focused finely on impacts that are difficult to detect but may yet be highly significant ecologically includes work on the microbiological impacts of hikers swimming in rainforest creeks, and on the effects of differently coloured spotlights on nocturnal marsupials. Complex ecological impacts currently under study include: the effects of trackside weeds on the pollination success of native plant species; the effects of food supplementation by tourists on the community ecology of bird populations, including nest predation effects; and the effects of small trails made by backcountry hikers on predation of small mammals by quolls and feral dogs.

One particular issue that has vexed recreation ecologists and protected area managers for some years is the degree to which an education and interpretation programme can reduce visitor impacts, actual rather than self-reported. Controlled experimental tests are not easy to design (Marion and Reid, 2007), but have been carried out successfully for guided walks in a rainforest World Heritage area (Littlefair, 2004; Buckley and Littlefair, 2007; Littlefair and Buckley, 2008). The links between recreation ecology research and protected area monitoring have been reviewed more generally by Hadwen et al. (2007, 2008).

Research on the impacts of human disturbance on various animal species has continued as summarized in Table 8.4. In addition, several more theoretical publications have appeared. Beale and Monaghan (2004) provided a conceptual framework to apply the considerable body of ecological research on predator–prey relationships, by suggesting that tourist disturbance could be seen as 'predator-free predation'. Interactions between humans and actual predators and prey were examined by Graham et al. (2005). Most recently, Preisler et al. (2006) reviewed statistical methods that can be applied in analysing the responses of animals to human disturbance.

Three types of impact have received particular attention in recent research. Several authors have examined roadkill and associated effects. Aresco (2005) found that the females of three species of turtle in Florida, USA were more likely than males to be killed on roads, with consequent population effects. Boarman and Sazaki (2006) found that desert tortoise populations were lower within 400 m of a road than at greater distances, probably because of roadkill. Ashley et al. (2007) found that some motorists run over reptiles deliberately. Roadkill of kangaroos, wallabies and other Australian marsupials has been studied at three sites, two in New South Wales (Taylor and Goldingay, 2004; Ramp et al., 2006) and one in the outback (Klocker et al., 2006), and the effect of snow grooming on small mammals in the Australian Alps was examined by Sanecki et al. (2006), who found substantial indirect impacts from crushing of subniveal burrows.

The role of tourism in spreading weeds into sub-Antarctic islands has been examined experimentally by Whinam *et al.* (2005), who found that velcro on outer clothing carries weed seeds from previous sites and travels. Weed seeds can also be spread by recreational riding or packhorses (Newsome *et al.*, 2008), and are often associated with roads and other tourist infrastructure (Pickering *et al.*, 2007). Once present, weeds can affect rare native plant species (Pickering and Hill, 2007), e.g. by reducing pollination (Bjerknes *et al.*, 2007). Tourists have also been implicated in spreading parasites in: birds in the Galapagos Islands (Wikelski *et al.*, 2004); lizards in Spain (Amo *et al.*, 2006); and intertidal food webs in Chile (Loot *et al.*, 2005). Pathogens have also been detected spreading from introduced to native bumblebees (Colla *et al.*, 2006).

Finally, the ecological and population effects of habitat fragmentation, often an unintended consequence of tourism and associated infrastructure and development, have received increased attention during the past few years. There are general reviews of relevant research by Henle *et al.* (2004a), Melbourne *et al.* (2004), and Driscoll and Weir (2005), and a review of effects on population dynamics by Wiegand *et al.* (2005). Recent research on particular species or groups, post-2004, is summarized in Table 8.5. In summary, habitat fragmentation can have widely different effects on different species. Some species will cross a narrow, little used or dirt road but not a wider, heavily used or tarred road. Some suffer significantly depressed populations up to a kilometre or more from a road. Some can survive in quite small fragments but may not breed successfully. Some survive only in large undisturbed wilderness areas. Some are dependent on other species that need large patches. Some cannot or will not cross even a narrow barrier, even to follow other species they depend on. The overall effect is that any form of fragmentation, e.g. by roads, power lines, fences, firebreaks, or even walking tracks, is likely to affect some species, but is unlikely to affect all species equally.

REVISION

Minimizing impacts is a key factor in ecotourism

- Minimal-impact management is a defining criterion
- Needs an understanding of impact mechanisms
- Management tools and technologies to reduce impacts
- Indicators to assess effectiveness of these approaches

Different impacts from different tour components

- Accommodation: tents, cabins, lodges, hotels
- Transport, ground: foot, bike, horse, ORV
- Transport, water: kayak, raft, yacht, motor vessels, cruise ships

Table 8.5. Recent research on impacts of habitat fragmentation and edge effects.

Species, taxa	Country or region	Reference
Wolves	Canada	Shepherd and Whittington (2006)
Mountain caribou	British Columbia, Canada	Apps and McLellan (2006)
Rainforest marsupials	Australia	Turton (2005)
Greater glider	SE Australia	Cunningham *et al.* (2004)
Greater glider	SE Australia	Lindenmayer *et al.* (2004)
Squirrel glider	Victoria, Australia	van der Ree (2006)
Lemuroid ringtail possums	Australia	Wilson *et al.* (2007)
Antechinus agilis	Australia	Banks *et al.* (2005)
Two rodent species	Amazon, Brazil	Jorge (2008)
Scarlet tanager	Pennsylvania, USA	Fraser and Stutchbury (2004)
White-starred robin	African tropics	Githiru and Lens (2005)
Yellow-faced honeyeater	Australia	Boulton and Clarke (2003)
Pigeons	Northern Territory, Australia	Price (2006)
Birds in secondary forest	Atlantic forest, Brazil	Harris and Pimm (2004)
Forest birds	SE Madagascar	Watson *et al.* (2004)
Waterbirds, buffer zones	UK	Jackson *et al.* (2004)
Birds	Brazil, Amazon	Lees and Peres (2006)
Birds	UK	Bennett *et al.* (2006)
Spotted salamander	USA	Rittenhouse and Semlitsch (2006)
Desert tortoise	California, USA	Boarman and Sazaki (2006)
Lizards	Australia	Fischer *et al.* (2005)
Cane toads	Australia, tropical	Brown *et al.* (2006)
Ants and plants	Amazonia, Brazil	Bruna *et al.* (2005)
Palm fruiting	Mexico, tropical	Aguirre and Dirzo (2008)
Beetles, 34 species	New South Wales, Australia	Driscoll and Weir (2005)
Various	India	Barve *et al.* (2005)
Review, various species	Various	Henle *et al.* (2004a,b)
Review, modelling	Various	Melbourne *et al.* (2004)

SE, South-east

- Transport, air: balloon, light plane, helicopter, airliner
- Activities, e.g. climbing, diving, birdwatching

Crossovers between components

- For example backcountry hiking tour includes foot travel, camping
- Some raft and kayak trips use helicopter access
- Expedition cruises have on-board accommodation but off-ship landings

Accommodation

- Water supply
- Heat, light, power
- Sewage treatment and disposal
- Washing, cleaning, greywater
- Wastes: from packaging, food, etc.

Water supply

- Supply: creeks, boreholes, dams, municipal
- Quality, treatment: filters, treatment systems, sludges
- Volume, scarcity: desert waterholes, mountain streams, urban supplies
- Particular uses, e.g. snowmaking

Heat, light, power

- Camping: fuel stoves, campfires, candles, flashlights, headlamps
- Campfires: minimal-impact practices
- Lodges: gas, generators, firewood, microhydro
- Generators: noise, exhaust
- Urban hotels: municipal supplies
- Greenfields resorts: power line impacts

Sewage treatment and disposal

- Individual catholes for off-trail backcountry hiking below treeline
- And for little-used rivers, coastlines, etc.
- Carry-out systems (bags, tubes) for heavily used climbing routes
- Self-contained boxes for heavily used rafting routes
- Composting toilets on trails and campgrounds in temperate and subtropical areas
- Pump-out toilets on trails and campgrounds in arctic and alpine areas
- Some lodges also use composting systems
- Most fixed accommodation uses flush toilets
- Variety of septic tanks and small-scale treatment plants

- Urban hotels and resorts connected to municipal sewers
- Pump-out systems for smaller boats from ports, marinas
- Marine sewage treatment systems for ocean-going ships

Washing, cleaning, greywater

- Camping: biodegradable soaps and detergents only
- All washing well away from water sources
- Lodges: greywater tanks, soakaways, evaporation systems
- Some areas require greywater plumbed into septic tank
- This reduces effectiveness of tank and requires much larger soaks
- Self-contained greywater and sewage systems for islands
- Urban: municipal systems

Wastes

- Camping: pack in, pack out
- Lodges: bulk purchases to minimize packaging
- Separation and recycling: paper, glass, plastic, metal, organics
- Wide variety of local recycling programmes
- Composting systems, mulches, worm farms, etc. for food wastes
- Lodges near towns can use urban recycling programmes
- Ships must follow MARPOL and should bring solid wastes home

Transport

- Toilets, wastes, washing: as for accommodation
- Fuel consumption and efficiency
- Engine exhausts, air pollution
- Engine noise
- Transport of weeds and pathogens
- Trampling damage from feet, hooves, tyres
- Anchor damage from boats
- Secondary impacts from roads, tracks, trails

Weeds and pathogens, terrestrial

- Weed seeds, fungal spores, etc. carried in mud
- On vehicle tyres, hiking boots, horses' hooves
- Also in horse and livestock feed
- And even mud on tent pegs
- Various cleaning procedures and quarantine measures
- Sludge in carwashes contains many weed seeds

- Fungal spores on vehicles and boots
- Weeds carried by horses in feed
- Different species with different transport mechanisms

Invasive species, marine and aquatic

- Marine and aquatic species transported on boats
- On hulls and in ballast water
- Control by anti-fouling, onshore ballast treatment
- Insects can also be carried on boats, e.g. attracted by lights
- Of particular concern in conservation areas used only by recreational boats

Trampling damage

- Wheels, hooves, boots, all crush plants
- Extensive research on trampling damage and recovery
- Different types of effect at different trampling intensities
- Different plant species more or less susceptible
- Generally grasses are less susceptible than woody plants or other herbaceous plants
- Different ecosystems more or less resilient
- Soil invertebrates also affected

Soil damage by vehicles

- Depends on ecosystem, tyre load, driving style
- And on number of passes, soil type and moisture
- Removes plant cover, then erodes soil
- Multiple trails extend damage
- Creek and dune crossings especially susceptible

Crushing damage to wildlife

- Vehicles on beach crush crabs and burrows
- Also beach-nesting birds, including rare species
- Oversnow vehicles crush subsnow space, tunnels
- Restrict foraging by overwintering wildlife
- And force them to snow surface where vulnerable to predation

Secondary impacts of roads and trails

- More people access area once trail exists
- In forests, predators use trails to hunt native wildlife
- In dry areas, fires often started by vehicles
- In woodland areas, roads act as wildlife barriers
- Weeds move into undisturbed areas along road verges

- Slope erosion often starts from roads and tracks
- Noise from roads and tracks disturbs wildlife
- Overall effect is loss and fragmentation of conservation areas

Anchor damage from boats

- Recreational boats anchor away from port
- Anchor chains scrape seafloor in circle
- Damage to reefs and corals especially
- Use permanent moorings to restrict area damaged
- Conceal moorings using underwater buoys, or may attract fishing boats

Noise and visual disturbance

- Construction, generators, clatter
- Overflights, vehicles, boats, off-road
- Human voices, bright colours, movement
- Different animal species respond differently
- Individual animals also respond differently
- Can become habituated to particular noises
- But may still be disturbed by different sounds

REFLECTIONS

1. Choose any particular type of ecotourism activity and any particular ecosystem in which it is carried out, and list the major types of environmental impact in decreasing order of ecological significance, giving reasons for your ranking.

2. Choose any single type of ecological impact commonly caused by ecotourism activities, and describe how you would design an experiment or monitoring system to measure it quantitatively. How would you ensure that your experimental design: (i) could distinguish between human impacts and natural variations in the environmental parameters measured; and (ii) could distinguish between impacts from tourism and impacts from other sources?

3. Many ecotourism operations include a birdwatching, whalewatching or other wildlife-watching component, and often the individual animals concerned can become habituated to particular types of tourism and tourist behaviour. Would you say that this in itself represents an environmental impact, either positive or negative, or would you say that it is environmentally neutral, effectively no impact? Would your answer depend on the ecology and life history of the particular species concerned? Give reasons and examples to support your answers.

4. To what degree can research results on the impacts of ecotourism for a particular activity in one ecosystem be applied to the same activity in a different ecosystem? Choose one particular ecotourism activity and illustrate your answer with examples from several ecosystems.

READING 8.1. RECENT RECREATION ECOLOGY RESEARCH IN AUSTRALIA

Why do we need recreation ecology research in different countries? Recreational impacts differ considerably between activities and between eco-systems, and Liddle (1997), Sun and Walsh (1998) and Buckley (2004a) used these criteria to structure their reviews of research literature; but do findings from one country apply to comparable ecosystems elsewhere?

Different continents and geographical regions have different flora and fauna, even if they have structurally similar vegetation types. Considerable effort has been devoted to identifying the differences as well as the similarities, e.g. for coral reefs (Dubinsky, 1990), coastal heaths (van der Maarel, 1997) or tropical rainforests (Primack and Corlett, 2004).

Except at the crudest level such as wholescale vegetation clearance, recreational impacts are different in different continents. The broad types are similar, but the specific mechanisms, the quantitative relationships and the shape of stress–response curves may depend on the terrain, climate, evolutionary history of plant and animal species and communities.

In addition, people in different countries tend to take part in different recreational activities, using different equipment and in different ways (Weaver, 2001; Buckley, 2004i; Chizhova, 2004; Magro and de Barros, 2004). Land management authorities also use different resource and visitor management tools and techniques. These human differences, however, can be adjusted for much more easily than the ecological differences outlined above.

It is hard to make reliable intercontinental comparisons, because recreation ecology research effort has been heavily skewed to northern developed nations with strong science research funding programmes (Buckley, 2005b). Land management agencies in southern and developing nations have wrongly assumed that research from the UK and the USA applies globally. In Australia, the tourism industry has captured research funding programmes and suppressed research on impacts.

Australia is one of the world's 17 megadiverse regions (Barlow, 1994; Williams *et al.*, 2001). Its flora and fauna have many endemic species, and are generally well adapted to fire, drought and low soil phosphorus, but not to large placental grazing mammals with hard hooves, or to pests and pathogens from elsewhere. We could thus use comparisons between semi-arid ecosystems in Australia, southern Africa and north America, or between subtropical forests in Australia and South-east Asia, to examine how similar recreational activities may produce different impacts in structurally similar but functionally different ecosystems.

Most recreation ecology research in Australia has been on high-impact activities within protected areas, carried out at management level and thus relevant for international comparisons. This includes activities such as: off-road driving (Priskin, 2003, 2004); horse riding (Whinam *et al.*, 1994; Whinam and Comfort, 1996; Newsome *et al.*, 2002b, 2008; Phillips and Newsome, 2002); mountain biking (Goeft and Alder, 2001); heavily used backcountry hiking trails

(Whinam and Chilcott, 1999, 2003; Whinam *et al.*, 2003; McDougall and Wright, 2004); camping (Turton *et al.*, 2000; Smith and Newsome, 2002; Talbot *et al.*, 2003); swimming in freshwater dune lakes (Hadwen *et al.*, 2003, 2005); scuba diving on coral reefs (Rouphael and Inglis, 1997; Plathong *et al.*, 2000; Rouphael and Inglis, 2002); power-boating in freshwater lakes (Mosisch and Arthington, 2004) and coastal seas (Byrnes and Warnken, 2004); and whalewatching in New Zealand (Higham and Lusseau, 2004).

There is also recent work on the impacts of infrastructure, such as: roads and power lines in rainforest (Goosem, 2000; Turton, 2005); roads and formed tracks in alpine and subalpine areas (Jones, 2000; Johnston and Pickering, 2001; McDougall, 2001; Johnston and Johnston, 2004; Hill and Pickering, 2006); and tourism infrastructure on coral reefs and islands (Walker, 1991). Most protected area management agencies in Australia also carry out monitoring, but this is generally unpublished and not intended as research.

Several recent Australian studies have advanced recreation ecology research at a global level. Two studies have tested the asymptotic stress–response curve proposed as a general model for the impacts of recreational trampling in North American eco-systems (Cole, 2004). Rouphael and Inglis (2002) found that impacts of divers on coral reefs are both spatial and temporally heterogeneous, and do not necessarily increase with increasing use. Some individual divers cause so much more damage than others that their impacts mask any cumulative effects from larger numbers alone.

Growcock (2005), studying trampling and camping in burnt and unburnt alpine and sub-alpine vegetation, found that the stress–response curve is commonly sigmoidal, with very little vegetation damage below a lower threshold of use, rapidly increasing damage at intermediate levels, and little increase in damage at the highest levels. The thresholds represent transitions between different types of impact. Below the lower threshold, there may be physiological effects on plants, but not loss in cover. Between the lower and upper thresholds, there is a loss in overall cover caused by death of individual plants, some species before others. Above the upper threshold, the living plant cover is largely gone, and the principal impact is loss of leaf litter and soil.

These impacts have been identified and quantified previously (Cole, 1995, 2004; Monz *et al.*, 1996; Liddle, 1997). The strength of this previous work was to identify one parameter – number of passes yielding 50% cover loss – to compare results from different times and places. The key contribution of Growcock's (2005) approach is that it allows the disaggregation of a rather generalized parameter – loss of plant cover – into a series of successive ecological effects each with its own identifiable mechanism.

There have also been several methodological innovations. Giese *et al.* (1999) used artificial eggs with monitoring devices and remote telemetry to examine physiological stress suffered by nesting penguins approached by tourists. Bridle and Kirkpatrick (2003, 2005) examined the breakdown of human waste of various types, in various ecosystems, and under various weather conditions, using novel forms of synthetic human waste.

Some recreational impacts are hard to detect but still significant ecologically. Various nocturnal marsupial species, for example, respond differently to spotlights of different colours as well as intensities. Warnken and Buckley (2004) distinguished microbiological impacts of hikers swimming in rainforest creeks, from the numerically much larger changes due to natural rainfall fluctuations. Buckley *et al.* (1998) identified previously unrecorded waterborne pathogens, introduced by tourists, in pristine Australian rainforest creeks.

Recreational impacts can occur through complex ecological mechanisms. There is recent Australian research on: effects of trackside weeds on pollination success of native plant species; effects of food supplementation by tourists on community ecology of bird populations (Oost, 2007); effects of backcountry hiking trails on predation by quolls and feral dogs; and effects of snow compaction on small marsupials that travel through subniveal space (Sanecki *et al.*, 2006). One particular issue that has vexed recreation ecologists and protected area managers for some years is the degree to which an education and interpretation programme can reduce visitor impacts, actual rather than self-reported. Controlled experimental tests are not easy to design, but have been carried out successfully for guided walks in a rainforest World Heritage area (Littlefair, 2004).

Transport of weeds is a major recreational impact in Australia (Lonsdale and Lane, 1994). Whinam *et al.* (2005) found ~1000 weed propagules on clothing and equipment from 64 expeditioners to sub-Antarctic islands. Hill and Pickering (2006) examined weeds alongside formed walking tracks in the Australian Alps. Raised steel-mesh walking tracks have far less impact than gravel, paved or informal tracks. In Australia, tourism use of protected areas is a major factor in the spread of the root rot fungus *Phytophthora cinnamomi*, which threatens a wide range of plant species, many of them already at risk of extinction from other causes (Kelly *et al.*, 2003; Schahinger *et al.*, 2003; Buckley *et al.*, 2004; DPIWE, 2005; Turton, 2005).

Introduced foxes are a threat to many native marsupials in Australia. In the Australian Alps, foxes occur at higher densities immediately around ski resorts, leading to increased predation on native marsupials (Green and Osbourne, 1994). Snow grooming in winter increases predation even further, since compaction of subniveal space forces native marsupials onto the snow surface where they are more vulnerable to foxes (Sanecki *et al.*, 2006). Even minor additions of nutrients by tourists can result in significant impacts in some Australian ecosystems. In freshwater dune lakes on Fraser Island, a World Heritage site, increased use by tourists causes algal growth, both by direct nutrient input and through resuspension of sediment (Hadwen *et al.*, 2003, 2005; Hadwen and Bunn, 2004). Similar mechanisms were reported for rainforest streams by Warnken and Buckley (2004).

Despite such research, we do not know whether Australian species and ecosystems behave like international counterparts. Are trampling impacts in the Australian Alps different from North America because of the species or the experimental design? Do birds on Australian lakes or shorelines take flight at similar distances from approaching tourists as those in North America or Europe? Do vehicle passes along a sandy beach crush the same number of tern eggs or burrowing crabs? Do marsupials subject to spotlighting behave similarly to placentals?

Key opportunities for international comparisons include the following. We could compare types and intensities of impacts from the same recreational activities in similar ecosystems on different continents, and the relative ecological significance of different types of impacts in different ecosystems. We could set out to identify and test subtle and indirect mechanisms of recreational impacts on particular plant and animal species and communities, by applying other specialist ecological disciplines such as pollination ecology, fire ecology, ecotoxicology, population ecology, predation ecology, reproductive ecology and foraging ecology. We could also examine the indirect impacts of tourism and recreation in altering ecosystem functions, e.g. in dune lakes, snow country, rainforests and coral reefs.

Acknowledgements

This reading is modified from Buckley *et al.* (2006), a presentation to the MMV3 conference.

chapter 9

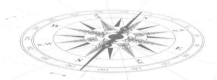

CONSERVATION

Oryx are one of the most beautiful antelope, and a particular tourist draw in parts of Africa and Arabia. There are a number of different species. This southern African species, the gemsbok, has long, near-straight horns. There is also a scimitar-horned species in Arabia.

REVIEW

Introduction

This chapter examines specifically how commercial tourism in general, and ecotourism in particular, can and sometimes does contribute to conservation of the natural environment. It does not set out to cover the topic of conservation as a whole; this is a very large and complex topic, about which many books have been written. There is extensive research, for example, about: why conservation is important, for humans as well as the other species being conserved; the economic value of conservation, through various mechanisms; priorities for conservation, both at landscape and ecosystem scale and the scale of individual species; the ecological aspects of conservation, in terms of species biology and community ecology; and the political, social, economic and legal practicalities of conservation, from funding for parks to legislating for endangered species to enlisting local community support. It is in these last-mentioned fields that ecotourism may have a significant role.

There is also an extensive research literature on the management of existing protected areas (e.g. Hendee and Dawson, 2002; Lockwood *et al.*, 2006). This includes the management of visitors, including commercial tourists as well as private individuals. Management tools include ways to raise funding through tourism and otherwise enlist tourists in conservation management, as well as ways to minimize visitor impacts. The former are considered briefly in this chapter, and in more detail in Chapter 6, Economics. The latter are considered in Chapter 8, Impacts. Further information on these and other aspects of protected area management is available in books such as those by Lockwood *et al.* (2006).

As outlined in Chapter 1, different stakeholders have different views as to whether a contribution to conservation of the natural environment is an essential defining criterion for ecotourism. For related sectors such as adventure, cultural and nature tourism, more broadly, it is not. Ultimately, however, it is the contribution to conservation that is the critical distinction between ecotourism and nature tourism more generally. There are many tours that rely on natural attractions and that include interpretation and environmental management measures, but that still produce significant environmental impacts. There are a number of instances, for example, where breeding colonies of seabirds or local populations of marine mammals have suffered impacts from tourism based specifically on viewing those species.

Leading examples of ecotourism operations worldwide, in contrast (Buckley, 2003a) have indeed established commercial operations that do make a net positive contribution to conserving those natural environments upon which they depend. Irrespective of marketing terminology, from an environmental viewpoint, these companies are significantly different from the tourism industry in general, and it is this difference that constitutes the concept of ecotourism, at least from an analytical perspective. Contributions to conservation can occur by many different mechanisms, and measures to generate a net positive contribution may include reductions in negative impacts as well as improvements in conservation benefits. In addition, both costs and benefits may be considered at various scales: a local benefit may be offset by a global cost, or vice versa. There is thus an enormous range of variation between, on the one hand, hotels or tour operations that simply comply with applicable environmental legislation; and on the other, companies that deliberately use tourism to fund private conservation reserves or otherwise make a significant contribution to conservation. To determine if any particular tourism enterprise makes a net positive contribution to conservation is far from straightforward: it requires a detailed comparative accounting of costs and benefits through all relevant mechanisms (Buckley, 2003b). Such accounting approaches are explored further in Chapter 14, Accounting. In this chapter, the various mechanisms by which tourism can contribute to conservation are considered.

Suggested indirect influences

It is often suggested, by tourism industry associations and government tourism promotion agencies, that the outdoor tourism industry could contribute to conservation merely by exposing its clients to the wonders of the natural world. The suggestion made is that simply seeing some beautiful scenery or a rare plant or animal species should lead commercial tour clients to lobby to protect them. In fact, however, this seems to be wishful thinking at best, and more probably, a profit-motivated political argument to gain commercial access to protected areas. There seems to be no actual test or evidence to show that a nature or ecotourism experience converts commercial clients to conservation lobbyists (Beaumont, 1998; Lee and Moscardo, 2005). Certainly, many ecotour clients are indeed concerned about conservation, and some devote time, money and effort to conservation causes and organizations. It is more likely, however, that conservation-minded people simply choose conservation-oriented holidays, than that the holidays make them conservation-minded. For some individual tourists, a particular ecotourism experience might indeed be a life-changing event. For this indirect mechanism to generate a net conservation benefit, however, the marginal change in behaviour by these few would have to outweigh the impacts of the many, and there is certainly no evidence that this is the case.

Funding private reserves

Perhaps the clearest way in which tourism can contribute to conservation is through funding the establishment and/or operation of private conservation reserves. There are a number of well-known examples in southern Africa (Buckley, 2003a), and smaller numbers in other countries. If a reserve is funded entirely through tourism, then the tourism operation has to generate a sufficient surplus from the service and hospitality components, to cover the operating costs of conservation management. In practice, this is rarely possible unless the property has an icon attraction for which there is a strong demand. In most instances, this is scenery and/or wildlife, whether it be the Big Five and similar species in southern Africa, seals or seabirds on temperate coastlines, or red cliffs and rock wallabies in arid Australia. In addition, since the need to cover conservation costs means that prices must be relatively high, clients will then expect a high level of service quality, and this in turn will increase prices still further. The most successful model for private conservation reserves funded by tourism hence seems to be through up-market luxury game lodges with skilled staff who can provide a particularly memorable wildlife watching experience, often with animals that are at least partially habituated, and that may be managed to maintain particular population densities. This is the model employed, for example, by large multi-country operators such as Conservation Corporation Africa and Wilderness Safaris, and more localized lodges such as Sabi Sabi and Chitwa Chitwa (Buckley, 2003a, 2006).

Payments to national parks

Many national parks and other public protected areas charge various entry, camping and activity fees, for individual visitors, for commercial tour clients, or most commonly for both. These fees may be kept for local use by the individual park concerned, redistributed within the parks system or paid into the general government treasury of the country or state concerned. This choice is often controversial but, in any event, it is outside the control of an individual tour operator. Likewise, these fees are generally mandatory, not at the discretion of the individual tour operator. To the extent that they are retained within the protected area management agency, they do indeed contribute to conservation. Since per capita fees charged are generally well below the per capita cost of running visitor infrastructure, however, there is generally no net contribution towards the conservation function of the protected area, i.e. each additional visitor imposes a net cost against the government-funded budget of the protected area management agency. From an overall policy perspective, this is perfectly reasonable, since protected areas are funded through the tax system as a public good, for recreation as well as conservation; but it does mean, at least in most developed countries, that a commercial tour operator paying mandatory fees to take clients to a public protected area cannot legitimately claim that those fees make a net contribution to conservation.

Some tour operators do indeed make net contributions to public conservation agencies, especially in developing countries where central government budgets for protected areas may be extremely low, and where domestic visitors pay very low or zero fees while international visitors pay significantly higher fees. In this case, especially if commercial tour clients make up a significant proportion of total international visitors, then these tour operators may indeed make a net contribution to conservation – but only if the fees collected are in fact used by the country concerned for conservation management in its parks system. If, as in many developing nations, these fees are simply collected by the central government treasury and used for general purposes, then the link to conservation is broken. In such cases, commercial tour clients may be contributing to the economic and community well-being of the country concerned, but not necessarily to conservation. Again, however, both the collection of these fees and their subsequent use are generally beyond the control of individual visitors, tour clients or tour operators.

In-kind contribution to parks agencies

In addition to any mandatory fees and charges, some tour operators with strong links to particular public protected areas have elected to make direct in-kind on-ground contributions to local conservation management in those areas specifically. A number of examples are summarized in Buckley (2003a).

Such contributions may be considered in three main categories: staffing, equipment and services. There are instances, e.g. in Africa, where private commercial tourism operators pay staff salaries for park rangers and anti-poaching patrols in public protected areas. There are also examples where tour companies have purchased and provided four-wheel-drive and other vehicles for park rangers to use on patrol, as well as a range of other equipment. In the third category, provision of services, the most common example is probably monitoring, where commercial tour operators that routinely visit more remote parts of a public protected area may serve as informal patrols. Since they usually visit to a fixed schedule and have no enforcement capability, however, they are an extension to park ranger patrols rather than a replacement. There are also examples where particular individual tour operators with appropriately qualified staff may carry out ecological monitoring exercises, typically in their own immediate operating areas (Buckley, 2003a, p. 116). Less common categories of services include, for example, programmes where a tour operator may pay a bounty for animal snares turned in by local residents, as one measure to combat poaching. A programme of this type is reported, for example, by Robin Hurt Safaris in Kenya (Buckley, 2003a, pp. 212–215).

Support for conservation organizations

Instead of trying to convert tour clients to conservation lobbyists, some ecotour operators simply support NGOs that lobby for conservation. There are four main mechanisms for such support. In some cases, tour operators have provided free transport and accommodation for conservation researchers, and for conservation groups bringing politicians to inspect current or potential conservation areas, as in the case of Khutzeymateen Sanctuary in far north-western British Columbia, Canada. Another example is provided by Walindi Plantation Resort in Papua New Guinea, which provides land free of charge to a local environmental NGO, Mahonia na Dari (Buckley, 2006, pp. 172–174).

The second mechanism is that some tour operators run trips specifically for non-profit organizations, with a significant proportion of the trip price going to the organization concerned. Some of the organizations involved, though by no means all, are devoted to conservation. The proportion of the total price going to the non-profit organization can be quite significant, e.g. up to 20%. Since this organization assembles the group, however, the tour operator saves on marketing costs. This approach, known in the tourism industry as the not-for-profit (NFP) market, operates principally out of the USA.

In a distinct but related approach, some of the larger conservation organizations offer their major donors special trips to areas where their funds have been used for conservation. Particular ecotour operators are commonly selected to run these so-called high-donor trips. To the extent that these tour operators may discount trip costs and prices, this could be considered a contribution to conservation. In some countries, there are also regular annual events where tour operators donate places on particular tours, and these are auctioned off. If the proceeds are then given to an environmental organization, such auctions may represent contributions to conservation. Sometimes, however, the proceeds are simply used to fund tourism or ecotourism events or promotions.

A number of ecotourism and cultural tourism operators also make direct cash donations to particular conservation or community causes, funds, organizations or trusts. In some cases, these organizations or trusts were set up by the tour operator itself, specifically to contribute to a particular local conservation or community need. In other cases, they are large-scale conservation organizations or community charities. In a few cases these donations are substantial, but more commonly they are relatively small, often because the company making the donation is itself small. For a small community in a country with a relatively weak currency, however, even a small donation in hard currency can sometimes generate significant benefits.

Instead of contributing to conservation or community causes themselves, many ecotourism and cultural tourism operators encourage donations from their clients instead. Various mechanisms are in use, differing considerably in subtlety. One of the less subtle, but none the less commonplace, techniques is for a company to add a small environmental charge to every guest's or client's bill, and remove the charge only if the client objects. A more subtle approach is to offer clients the opportunity to inspect conservation or community projects already under progress, make a passing reference to how much satisfaction other donors have experienced, and leave it to the client to initiate further discussion. Between these extremes, a variety of intermediate approaches are in use, typically involving a mix of written and verbal information and requests. In addition, tour operators with programmes such as these will generally mention them in marketing materials, and use them to apply for various tourism awards, so donors receive a degree of reflected glory.

Motivations, outcomes and scale

There are many different reasons why a tourism operator might establish a private conservation or community support programme. In some cases, certainly, such programmes may be driven by the personal convictions of the company's founders, who see tourism as a means to support conservation or local communities. In many other cases, however, these programmes represent a low-cost or cost-free marketing manoeuvre, or an essentially political ploy to obtain preferential treatment from government agencies, to maintain good relations with neighbouring landholders or residents, or even as a staff motivational technique. Often all these elements may be combined, and different participants may have different motivations, especially in a large tourism corporation.

From a conservation perspective, what matters is not the motivations so much as the outcome. A tourism operator that makes a successful and significant contribution to conserving a critical population of an endangered species, as occurs for some of the private game lodges and reserves, does indeed deserve recognition as a significant contributor to global conservation. A company that collects funds from its employees and government grants to carry out environmental programmes, which it might well be required by law to undertake anyway, probably does not. If in addition, the company's contribution represents only a few points of a per cent of its annual revenue, and it spends more on advertising its environmental awards than on the programme itself, then even the least cynical observer must surely suspect ulterior motives at a corporate level, no matter how sincere the person who put together the programme.

Similar distinctions apply where tourism operators contribute to non-profit organizations and associations. Where contributions are made to reputable conservation and community NGOs, it is reasonable to infer a genuine interest by the tour operator concerned. Not all NGOs, however, necessarily do what their names might imply. Many are so-called astroturf, fake grassroots groups put together for political purposes, to promote particular commercial interests. A local community fund established and operated entirely by a single tour operator may indeed be a mechanism to channel clients' concerns into practical projects, but it might also be a mechanism to maintain exclusive access rights, e.g. by funding school scholarships for the children of local leaders. Such scholarships might still be well deserved; the issue is simply that contributions to local community funds may not necessarily be entirely altruistic.

Political support for conservation

One possible mechanism for ecotourism to make a net positive contribution to conservation of the natural environment is direct political support for conservation by the tour operators concerned, especially in competition with other more environmentally damaging industry sectors (Edington and Edington, 1986).

The potential role of the commercial ecotourism sector as a political supporter for protected areas, especially as an alternative to other commercial activities with greater environmental impacts, has been mentioned on many occasions. Cohen and Richardson (1995) suggested 'megamarketing' ecotourism as a competitor to other industries, and McKercher (1998) suggested that conservation groups should maintain a working relationship with tourism interests even when their ideologies diverge. Vrslovic (1996) suggested that ecotourism had the potential to displace logging in Tierra del Fuego, and Massinga (1996) made more confident but perhaps unwarranted pronouncements for Mozambique. There seem to be rather few instances, however, where tour operators, tourism developers or government tourism agencies have actually lent political support to conservation campaigns (Buckley, 2002a, 2004c).

Attempts to promote ecotourism as an alternative to logging in Australia (Buckley, 2003e), Indonesia (Buckley, 2002f) or Papua New Guinea; to hydroelectric dams in China; or to whaling in Iceland (Parsons and Rawles, 2003) have been largely unsuccessful. Tourism ventures have indeed commenced in many such areas, but they have not halted developments in other industry sectors, so there has been little or no contribution to conservation.

One of the main conclusions reached from the case study review by Buckley (2003a) was that in practice, ecotourism can contribute to conservation only where the legal and political framework for conservation is already in place before tourism development begins. In that case, ecotourism can provide a financial engine for conservation efforts. Without that framework, early and well-intentioned ecotourism operations may indeed commence and make initial contributions, but later and less-principled tourism developers are likely to swamp any such efforts through large-scale, high-impact development. Similar issues have also been noted by Isaacs (2000) and Kruger (2005).

Partnerships

One of the mechanisms that tourism industry advocates often mention in the context of conservation is the so-called partnership approach (Buckley, 2002a, 2004c, j). Typically, the partnerships proposed are between individual tourism enterprises, and protected area management agencies. Partnerships sound good, but they may not always be as good as they sound. At worst the term may be employed simply as a rhetorical device to achieve political ends solely for profit. Typically, in such cases, a tourism developer or entrepreneur may use the term as a means to gain exclusive or preferential access to a public protected area in a manner that would not be permissible for commercial enterprises more generally. For example, a property developer may want the right to build private tourist accommodation inside a national park, or a tour operator may want vehicle access along a management trail, or exclusive rights to operate a particular tourist activity.

Even if tourism entrepreneur and conservation management agency are indeed both willing to enter a partnership on an equal footing, it is unlikely that they will have the same goals, or the same concept for the partnership. For example, a parks agency may have in mind that commercial tourism operators should contribute to infrastructure funding, since their clients benefit from this infrastructure. Tour operators, however, may want a say in the management of the park, solely on the grounds that they are its main commercial users.

Commercial tourism operations have been granted access to public protected areas and other public lands under a wide variety of different arrangements, some standardized and others negotiated individually. Some of these arrangements have been referred to as partnerships by the tour operator, the management agency or both. Few, if any, however, have actually yielded a demonstrable net benefit for conservation.

A useful distinction can be drawn on the basis of scale. At one extreme, there are relatively small-scale and low-impact commercial operations carrying out the same activities, in the same places, and at similar scales as small guided groups of private individuals visiting the same protected areas. At the other extreme, there are large-scale tourism development corporations, which want protected area management agencies to provide them with special access, permits, operating conditions or other rights at a sufficiently large scale that they affect conservation practices, or the rights of other recreational visitors, or the finances or operating conditions of the particular protected area concerned.

Closely related to scale is the issue of reversibility. A large parks agency dealing with a number of small operators running mobile tours can, if necessary for conservation reasons, reduce the impacts of commercial tourism operations. For example, it may decide not to renew permits, it may limit the total number of vehicles or vessels, it may limit the number of sites available for commercial access or the number of days when they are open, or it may impose particular equipment or operating requirements. There may be barriers to each of these. Where permits have been issued in perpetuity, for example, they cannot simply be cancelled without compensation. Where permits have been issued in the past but not previously used to the full, levels of use and impact may grow even without the issue of any further permits, a problem known as latency. These barriers, however, are not insurmountable.

Where a large corporation has been granted a long-term land lease to develop and operate a substantial tourism hotel or resort, however, as occurred in the early days of the North American parks services, it is not realistically feasible to demand that the resort be dismantled and removed. The same applies, perhaps with even greater force, to tourism developments on other public lands, such as ski resorts on Forests Service land in the USA. In addition, once a large private-sector tourism corporation has started operations in a national park or other public land, there will be political pressure for it to remain commercially viable, even if this requires continual expansions in the scale of operations. A tourism developer in the state of Victoria, Australia, for example, took legal action against the State Government to demand the right to expand, claiming that its operating permit gave it the right to run at a profit, and that expanding was the only way in which it could do so. The government ended up paying substantial compensation at taxpayers' expense (Buckley, 2004j).

It is these larger-scale, one-off or ad hoc tourism development proposals to which the terminology of partnership is more commonly applied. The argument most often advanced by those promoting tourism development proposals or agendas within public protected areas, is that the private sector has greater experience in commercial business operations than parks agencies. This may or may not be true, but it is largely irrelevant. Parks agencies are perfectly capable of running commercial businesses if they want to, as demonstrated by examples such as the Ontario Parks Service. Usually they don't, because their goal is to provide equitable access to recreational opportunities, not to make a profit. If and when they do decide to use a particular tourism opportunity to generate funds that can support conservation and public recreation, there is no reason why they should give away that opportunity to a private commercial enterprise for less than its full commercial value. As noted in a US legal review of the issue some years ago, there is no obligation for parks agencies to operate only the unprofitable parts of their portfolios.

Mutually beneficial partnerships between tourism operations and protected area management agencies are indeed possible, but under rather more stringent agreements than are generally proposed by tourism developers. Most critically: (i) any commercial tourism operations in a national park or similar area should comply with that park's overall management goals and strategies, not conflict with them; and (ii) the commercial terms should provide benefits to the parks agency as well as the private operator, and those benefits should be commensurate with the assets that the park is contributing. These assets include not only the scenery and the setting for recreational activities, and specific attractions in the form of wildlife and vegetation, but also publicly funded infrastructure, and a wide range of information materials that effectively provide free advertising. The fact that these assets are provided as public goods to non-commercial visitors does not make them any less valuable, nor does it provide any automatic right for private businesses to use those assets for commercial profit. Just as commercial tour operators are not under any obligation to offer tours in a particular park, but do so only if they expect to gain a net benefit, parks agencies are under no obligation to provide opportunities for commercial tourism operations, and can decide to do so only if they expect to receive a net benefit.

Conclusions

Contributing to conservation is a key issue in ecotourism, especially if a triple-bottom-line approach is taken. A rather small number of leading operators make clear and unambiguous positive contributions to conservation, principally through private reserves. A much larger number make much smaller or more ambiguous approaches through a variety of mechanisms. Some also encourage their clients to make such contributions. This is one of the roles of ecotourism guides, examined in the next chapter.

RESEARCH

The possibility that ecotourism could contribute to conservation by providing funds and resources on the ground, whether to private reserves or public protected areas, has been proposed repeatedly (Henning, 1993; Buckley, 1994a, b, 2003d; Buglass, 1995; Gössling, 1999; Lindsey et al., 2005). There do indeed seem to be some successful examples, albeit relatively few. The global review of ecotourism case studies by Buckley (2003a), for example, identified barely 50 operations making demonstrable contributions to conservation. Significantly more of these were in sub-Saharan Africa than any other region. Additional examples include contributions to the conservation of: wild dogs in South Africa (Lindsey et al., 2005); parrots in the Caribbean (Christian et al., 1996); harpy eagles in the Peruvian Amazon (De Roy, 1998); various species in Bahia, Brazil (de Oliveira, 2005); endangered hawks, falcons and eagles in Greece (Svoronou and Holder, 2005); and sea turtles, tree kangaroos and mahogany gliders in Australia (Tisdell and Wilson, 2002, 2004; Tisdell et al., 2005).

NGOs have historically been enthusiastic in promoting ecotourism as one of the benefits of conservation (e.g. Ziffer, 1989; Zethoven, 1995). Indeed, arguably the World Wide Fund for Nature (WWF) owes its entire existence to this approach. The form of tourism originally envisaged by WWF was hunting by wealthy Westerners, but arguably this is little different from modern African parks and game reserves used for lodges, photo safaris and, in some cases, also for hunting safaris (Buckley, 2003d). Rather few specific case studies of NGO involvement, however, seem to be documented in the tourism research literature. Sisman (1994) described the operation of an NGO named Green Flag International, but this no longer seems to exist. The role of a local NGO at Oaxaca has been described by several authors, including Barkin and Pailles (1999) and Barkin and Bouchez (2002). Transboundary conservation in the Zambezi region, according to Sithole (2005), owes some of its success to a local NGO, the

Zambezi Society. A number of the ecotourism case studies summarized by Buckley (2002a,b, 2003a) also include involvement by NGOs (Table 9.1).

Table 9.1. Case studies of NGO involvement in ecotourism.

Continent and country	Site or case	NGO	Other stakeholders
Africa			
South Africa	Ngala	WWF	Conservation Corporation Africa
Zambia	Kasanka NP	Kasanka Trust	Zambia Wildlife Authority
Seychelles	Cousin I	Birdlife Seychelles	Global Environment Facility
Namibia	Spitzkoppe	WWF	Other NGOs, local community
Namibia	Nyae-Nyae	WWF	Namibia government
Asia			
China	Great Rivers	The Nature Conservancy	Government of China
Indonesia	Togian Islands	Conservation International	Local NGO, Togian Consortium
Indonesia	Gunung Halimun	Wildlife Preservation Trust (USA)	NGOs, private sector
Nepal	Himalayas	Kathmandu Environmental Education Foundation	Various
Philippines	Noslek Arbor	Conservation International	Philippines government, locals
Australia			
Australia	Warrawong	Earth Sanctuaries	
Australia	Mornington	Australian Wildlife Conservancies	Donors
Australia	Mareeba	Mareeba Wetland Foundation	Private landholder

Continued

Table 9.1. *Continued.*

Continent and country	Site or case	NGO	Other stakeholders
Americas			
Brazil	Fazenda Rio Negro	Conservation International	
Panama	Wekso Ecolodge	Conservation International	Naso community
Belize	'Baboon' Sanctuary	Belize Audubon Society	Eight local villages
Belize	Toledo guesthouses	WWF, TNC	USAID, Belize government
Belize	Cockscomb Basin	Belize Audubon Society	
Mexico	Cuatro Cienegas	TNC, Pronatura Noreste	Local NGO
Europe			
Greece	Dadia-Lefkimi-Soufli	WWF Greece	Government of Greece
Greece	Prespa	WWF Greece	Other NGOs, governments

Source: Buckley (2003a).

Recent research on the conservation implications of ecotourism has generally confirmed and extended earlier findings. Fisher and Christopher (2007), for example, noted that most of the world's areas of highest biological diversity, the biodiversity hotspots, are also areas with high levels of poverty. The fact that many of these areas are also international nature tourism destinations, as noted some years ago by Conservation International, thus gains additional importance since tourism may provide the funds required to alleviate poverty. This still remains more potential than practice, however, as many of these hotspots are under continuing pressure from logging, mining and oil explorations, and tourism is rarely powerful enough to prevent these impacts. Indeed, these industries may instead provide significant barriers to ecotourism, as reported in Gabon by Laurance *et al.* (2006). The importance of tourism revenue finding its way to local residents, if it is to be effective in conservation, has been shown again by Marshall *et al.* (2006), who found that more orang-utans are currently killed by blowdarts than through habitat loss.

The perennial difficulties in managing large carnivores in protected areas adjacent to livestock farming were re-examined for the Serengeti by Holmern *et al.* (2007). Differences among resident attitudes to conservation in the Annapurna Sanctuary in Nepal were reported by Allendorf (2007) who found, not surprisingly, that those who received economic benefits through tourism held more favourable attitudes to conservation. While some birdwatching tourists also take part in conservation activities (McFarlane and Boxall, 2006), a recent study of birdwatching tour operators in the UK found 'a lack of willingness to adopt ecotourism principles if they interfere with business operations', and 'a reluctance to translate good intentions into practice' (Jackson, 2007).

In recent research, Törn *et al.* (2008) found that almost 60% of residents in an area of north-eastern Finland were sympathetic to nature conservation and neutral in their attitudes towards tourism; about half this number were critical of conservation and neutral to tourism; and the remainder were neutral to conservation and critical of tourism. Household income from tourism was not one of the factors determining these attitudes. In The Netherlands, Beunen *et al.* (2008) suggested that so-called gateway communities could, under certain circumstances, prove an effective tool for managing visitors to protected areas.

REVISION

Key component of ecotourism

- If ecotourism does not contribute to conservation
- Then it is just an economic activity like any other
- Therefore conservation aspects are key to ecotourism

Potential indirect political mechanisms

- Ecotours might change clients into conservation activists
- Argument used by tourism industry to provide access to parks
- Compared with parks agencies using recreation to create political constituencies
- No reliable evidence that it actually happens
- Even if it did, no net conservation benefit unless three criteria all met: (i) activism due to ecotourism experience; (ii) activism effective in improving actual conservation outcomes; (iii) conservation outcomes outweigh impacts of all clients in aggregate
- Therefore this indirect mechanism unlikely

Private conservation reserves

- Purchase, rehabilitate, re-stock, fund through tourism
- Intensive conservation and wildlife management
- Tourism income has to cover conservation costs too
- So generally up-market lodges
- Especially for wildlife watching

- Successful examples in Africa, Americas, Asia
- Best prospects for ecotourism to help conservation

Contributions to public protected areas

- For example paying for rangers, vehicles, equipment
- Distinguish from mandatory fees required by permit
- More common in developing countries
- Examples in *Case Studies in Ecotourism* (Buckley, 2003a)

Contributions to conservation groups

- For example NFP tour operations
- Principally in USA
- Run commercial tours for NFP organizations
- Proportion of package price goes to that NFP organization
- Also levy and donation systems from clients

Scale of contributions: conservation cf. marketing

- Many tour operators make relatively trivial contributions
- And use these for marketing, ecocertification, award applications, etc.
- Few help conserve endangered species or habitats
- Those that do are often conservation organizations funded by tourism
- That is, not tourism operations interested in conservation

Partnerships: what industry wants

- Tourism and entrepreneurs propose partnerships, with parks agencies in particular
- Want preferential or exclusive rights
- For example to build commercial accommodation, facilities, infrastructure
- Or to operate particular activities in particular places
- Or even to control access and collect fees

Arguments proposed by industry

- Private sector may be more experienced at tourism operations
- Can free up parks staff for core conservation work
- Can provide capital for facilities otherwise funded from parks budget

Problems with industry proposals

- Private sector aim is profit from paying customers
- No particular concern for equity or impact

- Parks agency aim is conservation
- With equitable opportunities for public recreation
- As long as minimal impacts on conservation
- Why should parks agencies give away opportunities for revenue?

Criteria for conservation benefit from private-tourism involvement

- Facilities that parks agency wants anyway
- Provision for alternative facilities for visitors who can't pay for private service
- Sufficient financial return to parks agency for net contribution to conservation
- Outweighing impacts and opportunity costs

REFLECTIONS

1. List three different ways in which ecotourism can potentially contribute to conservation of the natural environment, and provide two examples of each. Relative to the size and scale of the ecotourism operations in each of your six examples, how significant are the contributions to conservation in each case? How would you rank these contributions from most to least significant, and for what reasons?

2. On the basis of published case studies, private game reserves funded through tourism seem to be proportionately more common in sub-Saharan Africa than in other continents or subcontinents. Do you think that this pattern in published case studies accurately reflects real patterns or not, and on what evidence? If it does, what reasons can you suggest why this pattern should have arisen? Based on these reasons, should it be feasible to copy the African model in other continents? Or do different continents need different models, or perhaps have them already?

3. In your country, would you say that protected area management agencies generally encourage people to visit parks, or discourage them, or encourage them in some areas and for some activities but discourage others? Give examples and evidence. Is any distinction made between private individual visitors, and commercial ecotour clients, and if so what? At a global scale, would you say that commercial tourism in public parks and protected areas makes a positive contribution to conservation, or not? What evidence is there to support your view?

4. Do you think that people visiting parks should have to pay fees? Does this depend on: whether they are visiting as private individuals or commercial tour clients; whether they are local residents or long-distance tourists; whether they come from the country the park is in; the type of activity in which they want to take part in the park; whether they want to stay overnight; or any other factors? Explain your answers. If fees are charged, do you think the money collected should be: used only for a particular purpose such as visitor infrastructure or search-and-rescue operations; kept at the particular park concerned, but with no restrictions on the type of expenditure; kept within the parks service, but not necessarily at the park where it was raised; or paid into the central government revenue? Would your answer depend on the particular type of fee, the degree of development of the country concerned, or any other such factors? Explain your reasoning in each case.

5. Some ecotourism companies now sponsor a variety of community and conservation projects by selling products such as souvenirs, wristbands etc. Do you think this is a useful approach? What other mechanisms can you suggest for ecotourism clients to contribute to conservation, through either financial or non-financial mechanisms?

READING 9.1. TOOLS AND INDICATORS FOR MANAGING TOURISM IN PARKS

Recreational pressure on conservation reserves is continuing to grow worldwide. Increasing numbers of private individuals and commercial tours are visiting national parks, World Heritage, and other conservation reserves, public lands, wilderness areas and fragile environments. This increases both actual and potential environmental consequences, and also the management effort and investment required to control impacts and maintain the primary conservation function of the areas concerned (Lindberg and McKercher, 1997).

Land managers in different jurisdictions have traditionally used different approaches to organizing tourism and recreation. Broadly, the main options are either to harden the natural environment against visitor impacts, or to influence visitor numbers and behaviour so that impacts in different areas are kept within limits (Cole *et al.*, 1987; Buckley and Pannell, 1990; Buckley, 1994a; Harroun and Boo, 1996). Hardening typically involves construction of tracks and boardwalks, campsites and fireplaces, toilet facilities, etc. Visitor management may involve regulations, educational programmes, and fees and charges.

Regulations can include constraints on numbers of visitors permitted or forbidden in different areas at different times of year; the activities they may undertake; and the equipment they may use. The most widely used regulatory technique is zoning, where different areas are set aside for different activities or sets of activities. Seasonal closures, such as those associated with hunting and fishing licences and use of open fires, are also common. Limits on visitor numbers (for example, by setting a fixed total quota for overnight camping, with an associated permit allocation system) are widespread in heavily used national parks and other wilderness areas in many countries. Other common types of regulation include bans or restrictions on motorized vehicles and watercraft, pack animals and pets, fires and firearms. Prescriptions of maximum party size provide another example. Education programmes may include interpretive centres, trackside signs, guided activities and the like. Education and regulation may be linked, for example if leaflets or videos are followed by a test, which must be passed to obtain a permit for access or a particular activity.

Fees and charges, such as those for entrance, overnight camping, and commercial permit, are now levied by many parks and other protected areas, both public and private. Most of these appear to be designed to raise revenue rather than influence visitor behaviour. Most charges levied directly on individual visitors are relatively low. Some indirect charges, however, levied through licence and franchise fees paid by commercial tour operators, are substantial (Driml and Common, 1995; Eagles, 1995).

Historically, different approaches to managing tourism in conservation reserves have been emphasized at different times, in different conceptual frameworks. Examples include carrying capacity, recreational opportunity spectra, limits of acceptable change, and visitor impact management planning (Lindberg and McKercher, 1997; Lindberg *et al.*, 1997).

There is little to be gained from arguing the merits of one approach or another. It seems more useful to recognize that they can all be considered as different aspects of a single all-encompassing monitoring and management strategy – or the M&M Toolkit – with four essential aspects.

1. No tool is innately superior to any other. Different tools are better for different purposes. For some tasks, any one of a number of tools could suffice. Other tasks require several to be used together. Sometimes it is obvious which one will be best; sometimes it takes skill and experience to select the right tools in the right sequence. The size and type of the tool must match the magnitude of the task. A sledgehammer is not required to crack a nut, but a wild pig cannot be killed with a popgun.

2. The toolkit does not define the tasks. The methods available, and their effectiveness and costs, may limit what goals are achievable, but they do not determine how to choose between the achievable goals.

3. One must be able to tell when a task needs to be done, as well as how urgent and how serious it is. This is not always straightforward. If major environmental impacts have already occurred at a particular site, it will generally be obvious that remedial works and rehabilitation will be required, and measures taken to prevent the impact recurring. Both of these steps are likely to be expensive, and it may still prove impossible to rehabilitate the area fully. If the impact could have been predicted or detected at an earlier stage, and certainly before it reached any threshold of irreversible change, then it could have been overcome or avoided much more cheaply and easily. As with any toolkit, preventive maintenance generally needs less effort and smaller tools than major repairs. While some impacts are detectable by the naked eye of the park ranger well before they are likely to affect critical ecosystem functions, others are not, and in fact can only be detected with relatively sophisticated scientific methods and statistical analysis. The monitoring component in the M&M Toolkit is thus critically important.

4. In order to use any particular tool one must know what it is for and how well it works, in different potential applications. Before it can become part of the routine toolkit, any tool must first have been tested in different situations. Sometimes this leads to the invention of new tools, or improvements to old ones. Again, in the context of managing tourists in wilderness areas, this is not always straightforward. Ideally it requires quantitative measurements of the impacts of different numbers of tourists, engaged in various activities, on a range of environmental parameters in a range of ecosystems, under alternative visitor management regimes (Buckley, 1994a).

Once the toolkit analogy is made, all of the above is self-evident, especially with the benefit of hindsight over several decades of park and wilderness management. It is still a useful conceptual approach, however, for several reasons. It emphasizes that different approaches may each have a place in appropriate circumstances; that the sustainable use of wilderness areas for tourism and recreation requires the management of people within the natural environment; and that management relies on monitoring of the state of the environment, changes caused by tourists, and changes as a result of management.

Conceptually, many parks and wilderness managers have long since embraced all these philosophies. Monitoring, however, is generally at the eyeball level so most management actions are not taken until impacts are clearly apparent to the naked eye. At this point, there are typically few options available, especially because it is politically much more difficult to reduce visitor numbers or activities than it is to limit them before numbers increase or activities commence. The most common response of park managers is to harden the environment against ever-increasing numbers of tourists. This in turn consumes an ever-increasing portion of management budgets. This approach in turn forces managers to levy increasing visitor fees to cover the cost of infrastructure. To break this vicious cycle, managers need to devote more of their budgets to monitoring the state of the environment, and testing the effectiveness of management tools, before impacts become irreversible. The establishment of monitoring programmes, and selection and application of management tools, are choices that can only be made by land managers. Research groups can assist, however, by compiling and analysing data from past impact measurements; improving the design of monitoring protocols; establishing the relative effectiveness of different environmental parameters as general indicators of ecosystem health or impact; and testing the effectiveness of management tools.

Acknowledgement

This reading is a much condensed version of Buckley (1999b), first published in *Annals of Tourism Research* 26, 207–210.

chapter 10

GUIDING, EDUCATION AND INTERPRETATION

Two male lions walk along a road between two safari vehicles in a private game reserve. Note that both the lions and the tourists are very relaxed.

REVIEW

Introduction

Environmental education is a key component in almost all definitions of ecotourism. In commercial ecotours, this is provided principally by guides. The importance attached to this component by tour companies and clients is indicated in commercial marketing materials, which commonly feature individual guides and quote client endorsements.

In addition, parks agencies commonly use a variety of interpretive approaches both to educate visitors about the area and to encourage them to minimize their impacts. Most of these materials are in the form of printed signs and leaflets, but some parks also offer guided walks and ranger talks. In addition, some public land management agencies promote minimal-impact guidelines produced by independent organizations, notably the Leave-No-Trace® series in the USA. One of the arguments often put forward by tourism industry associations to lobby for commercial access to public conservation reserves, is that the educational aspects of such tours can change the subsequent lifestyle behaviours of their clients. In fact, this claim seems to be quite unfounded, but it is made so often that it is also explored here.

Finally, there is a small but distinct educational tourism sector in its own right, which is also described in this chapter.

Guiding skills

Role of guides

Tourism includes individual tourists and private groups as well as commercial tours, and travel agents sell packages that include unaccompanied transport, activities and accommodation. One of the principal defining characteristics of most commercial tours, however, is that they have a leader or guide who is familiar with the itinerary, local conditions and languages, and can shepherd the clients through the various logistic arrangements more safely and less stressfully than if they were on their own. That is, good guides are a key component of commercial tour products.

More expensive tours may have several guides and leaders at different levels. For a large group booking, for example, the client group may have a nominal leader who serves as a contact point for the group but little else. The tour company may provide a trip leader who handles all the logistics and is the clients' first point of contact for any problems or requests, and who is responsible, on the tour company's behalf, for ensuring that the clients are satisfied with their trip and experience. Where the retail tour packager uses local on-site operators for particular components, those operators in turn may provide their own local guides who join the tour for one particular sector only, taking responsibility for that company's component. Finally, there may be instructors or other staff with particular duties such as rowing rafts, handling horses, tracking game or pointing out plants, birds and other wildlife.

Given such a wide and varied range of responsibilities, it is not surprising that working as a tour guide is a highly skilled profession. In particular, it requires a combination of so-called hard and soft skills. Hard skills refers to the ability to carry out a particular activity oneself, and soft or people skills means the ability to teach others about it, keep them happy while doing so, and maintain consensus and avoid conflict in a group. It is for this reason that several countries now have guide certification schemes. Best known of these is the highly professional programme by the Field Guides Association of South Africa, FGASA. In other countries, including Australia, there are several different and overlapping schemes.

For a typical adventure or ecotour, a wide range of different people are involved in designing and constructing the tour and assembling the clients, but once the tour actually starts, almost all the responsibility lies with the tour guides. These are the company representatives with whom the clients have by far the greatest personal contact, and whom they praise or blame for everything that goes right or wrong. When clients write letters or comments back to the tour company after a trip, it is the guides whose names they mention, and if the trip went well, they may specifically request the same guide for a repeat visit, or recommend them to friends. Not surprisingly, therefore, tour companies go to considerable effort to retain well-known and popular guides, and feature them in their tour advertising.

Logistics

As noted in the previous section, some tours have multiple guides with different roles. For many tours, however, there is only a single guide, with many roles. The most basic role, generally speaking, is to manage the group's logistics. This includes knowing the itinerary, holding group vouchers, managing group check-ins at airports and hotels, collecting and redistributing passports, allocating rooms and room keys and checking that keys are returned, making sure that habitual laggards get onto coaches and airport transfer buses in time, and dealing with innumerable difficulties and requests, some major and same minor. In an adventure tour, guides may have the additional responsibility of teaching clients how to carry out a particular outdoor activity, from putting up a tent to paddling a seakayak, riding a whitewater raft or a mountain bike, navigating on land or sea, or a wide range of other skills.

Health and safety

From a tour operator's perspective, briefing clients on safety issues is essential, if only for insurance. This may include basic reminders about sunstroke or hypothermia; information on snakes, sharks, crocodiles, bears, ticks, spiders, stinging trees, contaminated water, malarial mosquitoes, etc.; training on how to handle boats, skis, climbing gear, etc.; and briefings on fires, cyclones or avalanches. Depending on the type of tour and clientele, some operators focus on training their clients and then leaving them to fend for themselves, whereas others shepherd their clients closely at all times and rely on direct instructions to keep them out of harm.

Most tour companies have some form of medical screening process, which is supposed to ensure that clients are physically and mentally fit and healthy enough to take part in the tour concerned, and also insist that clients carry appropriate health insurance, sign a disclaimer, consult their own doctors for vaccinations and prescription pharmaceuticals, and bring their own medical supplies. Despite all these precautions, clients sometimes do get sick or injured, or put themselves and the group at risk. In such circumstances, it will be up to the guide to take care of the sick or injured patient initially, and to minimize risk and disruption for the rest of the group.

In the past, guides would often travel with an extensive medical kit. Currently, however, in some developed nations only licensed medical practitioners are permitted to give a prescription drug to another person. Thus a guide, or even another client, who does something seemingly so innocuous as to give a sick companion prescription antibiotics from their own supply, could be liable to criminal prosecution as well as civil litigation if the patient's condition were to become worse. Clients are expected to seek pre-trip medical advice from their own practitioners and bring their own prescription medications.

In practice, therefore, guides need to take three steps in regard to safety. First and most important is to watch and manage what the clients do, so they do not put themselves at unnecessary risk in unfamiliar terrain or with unfamiliar activities. This includes everything from, for example, watching for signs of altitude sickness, dehydration or hypothermia, to helping less athletic clients in or out of a boat or vehicle, to checking that they have appropriate clothing and footwear. It is now increasingly commonplace that even remote-area adventure and eco-tours may include clients who are urban residents with little outdoor experience or skills and a relatively low level of fitness, and guides have to be ready to assist them.

The second step is to maintain a first aid kit, including a large supply of band-aids or similar small dressings to give out to clients who did not bring their own, for the innumerable small scratches and blisters that they will inevitably incur. The third step is that every tour needs an emergency medical evacuation plan to get a seriously ill or injured client or indeed guide to hospital quickly and safely. In some countries, there are organized systems, such as the Royal Flying Doctor Service in Australia, or the Medical Air Rescue Service in southern Africa. In others, every arrangement may be a one-off.

Culture and society

Both for safety and for client comfort and satisfaction, one of the other duties of a tour guide is to introduce clients to new and unfamiliar cultures. The opportunity to experience different cultures and societies is a major driving force for many tourists, and a major selling point for many tourism products. Knowledge about those cultures may be important both to reduce risks, whether from poisonous plants and animals or angry locals, and to increase enjoyment, through greater appreciation of people and places.

Typically, information that guides provide for clients may have both formal and informal components. Formal components may include, for example, the ceremonial gifts and greetings that are traditionally expected when entering lands belonging to various indigenous peoples. They may include particular cultural or religious requirements, such as taking off one's shoes, laying ceremonial scarves in the temples of various Asian nations, sharing a bowl of kava in Fiji, or not walking through a village between 5.00 p.m. and 6.00 p.m. in Samoa. Informal information may include, for example: where it is safe to walk and where it is not; what to eat and drink and what to avoid; what constitutes a fair price for various artefacts and souvenirs; how to greet or leave someone politely; what to wear in different circumstances; and a range of small and subtle differences in body language between different cultures, which could potentially cause offence if clients were not aware of them.

From this kind of information, it is a very small step to cultural interpretation, where the guide explains to the clients something about the history and social structure of the people they are visiting, their lifestyles and their views of life, their art and material culture, and their social rules and traditions. This applies as much for tourists travelling from one developed nation to another, or one developing nation to another, as for those travelling between developed and developing nations. These aspects are considered further in Chapter 11.

Client satisfaction

Many tourists want to learn about the countries they visit. Not all: even for tours advertised specifically as ecotours, some clients only want to consume the same food and drink as they do at home, lie in the sun, buy souvenirs and enjoy the company of other members of the same tour group. Many, however, want to learn something. It may be a skill, such as scuba diving or sailing, or it may be knowledge, typically about the country or culture they are visiting. Even if a particular tourist did not set out to learn about local culture, but simply to meet some local people, they are likely to be pleased if learning comes as a painless incidental bonus. One of the distinguishing characteristics of ecotourists, according to most definitions, is a keen interest in understanding and learning about local ecosystems and communities in the areas they visit, whether through their own enquiries or through a high-quality educational component in commercial ecotours.

Client satisfaction will only increase in this way, however, if the tourist feels they have been given something they want, not forced into something they do not. This requires market research to match educational offerings to tourist preferences. It may be as simple and informal as a guide asking a small tour group what they would like to know, or it may involve extensive surveys to assist in the design of international packages, which incorporate formal education as well as other components.

In most of the mainstream tourism market, any educational component is informal and incidental to the main selling point. A national study of coach tours in Australia a decade ago (Weeks, 1996) found that the quality of environmental education in mainstream Australian coach tours was relatively poor. One of the differentiating features of ecotourism is a focus on high quality environmental education as an integral part of the product. The educational quality of commentary and conversation by guides, in both content and delivery, hence becomes an important component of client satisfaction. Some ecotour operators do indeed offer very high-quality training programmes.

There are many different measures of quality in education. These may include: the accuracy, relevance, completeness and level of information; the degree of retention of this information by those taking part in the educational programme; and the efficiency of delivery, i.e. information retention per unit time and resources in delivery. Customer satisfaction, however, does not necessarily depend on any of these. An interesting style of delivery, for example, generally aids in the retention of accurate and relevant information, whereas if the delivery is boring, participants may pay no attention to the information, no matter how accurate and relevant. Equally, however, tourists may be perfectly satisfied and indeed pleased by an intriguing presentation or patter, even if the content is irrelevant, erroneous and quickly forgotten. One of the distinguishing skills of leading ecotour guides is the ability to convey accurate and relevant information, to clients with a wide range of different backgrounds and prior knowledge, in an interesting and informal style.

Guide training

Most ecotour guides learn their skills from many different sources, some formal and some informal. As with most professions, training is an essential prerequisite, but no substitute for experience. Basic training in ecology and environmental sciences, and also in the structure of the tourism industry, is available through a wide range of university courses. Rather few, however, combine these two fields. University courses are also available in areas such as outdoor education, and parks and recreation management. Once again, however, few courses combine these fields with either ecology or tourism.

A range of private training organizations, and one or two public agencies such as national parks services, provide short courses in basic safety and minimal-impact skills for particular environments. There are many 1- and 2-day courses in first aid, and in the USA at least there are organizations offering 6-week specialist courses in wilderness medicine. Organizations such as the National Outdoor Leadership School offer field courses from a few weeks to a few months, with a strong focus on minimal-impact wilderness travel techniques. Similarly, a range of private commercial and NFP organizations provide training in wilderness travel, outdoor activities and adventure sports skills. Many adventure travel operators train their own staff, essentially by assigning them as apprentices with more experienced staff. Some of the larger ecotourism operators, such as Conservation Corporation Africa, run formal multi-level training for their guides, which covers a wide range of environmental knowledge and practical field skills. Guides trained by companies such as these are in considerable demand by other operators.

Guide motivations

Different people may have many different reasons to take up tour guiding as a profession, but in ecotourism in particular there is commonly a significant vocational component. For some, certainly, guiding is simply a way to see the world and stay outdoors. For others, it is a personal contribution to protecting the natural environment. It is important to recognize, however, that as in other professions, ecotour guides are often likely to experience conflicts between motives and interests. For example, one may lead groups of clients into the back-country to teach them minimal-impact travel techniques, only to discover that these very groups may well be the principal source of impacts in the area concerned. One may become an ecotour guide to educate city dwellers about the importance of protecting the natural environment, but find it hard to tell whether the net environmental benefits of such education outweigh the environmental costs of the travel involved in the tours. Individual guides with a strong personal environmental ethic and commitment to minimal-impact practices and lifestyles, may find themselves working for nature-based tour companies that pay only lip service to environmental protection, and may face an uphill battle to improve this situation. For those who establish their own ecotourism business, there is often a conflict between the desire to be out in the field acting as a guide, and the need to be back in the office managing the business. None of these issues should prevent people taking up tour guiding as a profession, but forewarned is forearmed.

Interpretation on tour

Understanding local ecology

In any kind of nature or ecotour, interpretation by the guide includes locating, identifying, and pointing out different plant and animal species, and explaining their behaviour, life histories and interactions, to build up a coherent picture of the landscape and environment. This may include geography and geology, history and modern land use as well as biology and natural history.

Most tour groups contain clients with very different levels of knowledge and interests, and it is a challenge for any tour guide to provide environmental information that enhances the client's experience without either being patronizing or pretending to know more than they actually do. A tour guide may well find that while one of the group wants to debate global environmental politics, a second wants to know which plants are edible, and a third expects the guide to identify every corner-of-the-eye glimpse of brown flying feathers. To satisfy the experts without losing the interest of the less experienced is often a demanding task, but for many tour guides it is also a rewarding one. There are enormous differences between clients in the level of sophistication required. For some, it may be enough to distinguish a kangaroo from a koala, a warthog from a wildebeest, or a salmon from a stickleback. Others want to distinguish a Grant's gazelle from a Thomson's, a red-necked wallaby from a pretty-faced, a jack pine from a loblolly. Others again want to know Latin names and identifying features for three different kinds of *Spinifex* grass or sagebrush, or ten different thornbills, hummingbirds or woodpeckers, or 600 different species of eucalyptus. Some have their hearts set on seeing a particular species, be it whales, gorilla or quetzal; others are equally interested in everything.

For many ecotourists and ecotour guides, identifying species is only a first step, equivalent to naming the components of a system. The next, and for most people more interesting step, is to learn how the ecosystem functions. This may include information on physical environmental parameters, such as seasonal weather patterns and the effects of floods, storms and droughts, and information on plants and animals, including what they eat, where they live, what they do and how they interact with each other. Again, this may range from an anecdotal snippet of information provided by a guide in conjunction with a plant or animal species identification, to descriptions of recent scientific research results on, for example, the chemistry of pheromones involved in interactions between groups of plant and insect species, or the dynamics of interactions between individuals in a large group of social animals such as a troop of baboons or a mob of kangaroos.

Descriptions of ecosystem processes are usually more interesting if illustrated by case studies. To say that tourist litter can affect animals, for example, is true but relatively unexciting. The message is much more memorable if one describes, for example, how predatory fish swallow the glittering ringpulls from beer cans if they are thrown overboard, killing the fish, or how male satin bower birds collected the blue caps from two-litre plastic milk containers to decorate their bowers, and many were strangled by the retaining rings until the milk retailers changed the colour of the caps. For a suitable audience, the story of the Western Australian jewel beetles who attempted unsuccessfully and indeed fatally to copulate with the dimpled brown rings on old-style beer bottles is guaranteed a high level of interest and retention.

In educating tourists about environmental components or processes, the question of scales in space and time is important. Most people tend to be more familiar with components and processes at approximately human scales, particularly those that can be observed by the unaided human senses. They are less familiar with components that are very large or very small, or processes that occur over very large or small scales in time or space. Ecotours can provide opportunities to illustrate the range of scales, from stargazing at night to filtering microscopic pathogens out of drinking water.

Minimizing impacts

For many ecosystems and environmental parameters, the effects of an individual trained in minimal-impact techniques and concerned to employ them, is orders of magnitude less than the effects of individuals who neither know nor care how to control their impacts. Training in the skills needed to reduce individual impacts in the immediate environs is therefore a common and important component of many ecotour operations, particularly those that take smaller groups into backcountry and wilderness areas. This includes how to behave in person, and how to use equipment. Commonly it requires a combination of common sense and specialist knowledge, e.g. in relation to animal behaviour.

Education of tourists to allow them to reduce their environmental impacts may be considered at four different levels of detail. The least technical is simply a general attitude towards protecting the environment, to encourage individuals to make extremely basic common-sense decisions where impacts are obvious. The second level, applicable to all outdoor users, comprises broad rules of thumb that apply across a range of ecosystems, e.g. in relation to litter, fire, noise, vehicles, pets, firearms, and so on. These can be conveyed through simple signs or other written materials. The third level includes specific techniques, which require knowledge or skills not routinely possessed by the general population, often related to a particular activity or ecosystem, e.g. minimal-impact hiking or horsepacking, and camping, cooking and cleaning. These are documented in various minimal-impact guidelines, but are perhaps most effectively taught through practical demonstration by a guide. At the highest level, the individual learns how to study an unfamiliar environment and evaluate their own practices with sufficient skill to minimize impacts even without rules of thumb or prior experience in that environment (Buckley, 1996b).

As well as learning how an ecosystem works and how to minimize their own impacts on it, many ecotourists are equally interested in other human impacts in the area concerned. This may include, for example, issues such as: the conservation status of particular plant and animal species, both locally and throughout their global range; the effects of air and water pollution; the impacts of logging, farming, fishing or mining; and indeed, the impacts of large-scale tourism development including resorts, marinas, golf courses, downhill ski-lifts, etc. Environmental education programmes offered by some ecotour operators go one step further, and use minimal-impact training during the tour as a model for clients to reduce the impacts of their lifestyle overall, when they have left the tour and returned home.

Knowledge retention

No matter how valuable the information or entertaining the presentation, training is of little use unless the trainees can remember and apply the knowledge and skills involved. To be effective, therefore, an education programme needs to incorporate mechanisms to enhance retention. These will depend on the type of information and the interests of the trainees or clients. One useful technique is a test of some sort. These can be practical, e.g. demonstration of a bush craft skill, ability to identify plants and animals, etc., or theoretical, e.g. by presenting a group with a hypothetical scenario and asking what they would do and why.

Where the critical issue is attitude or behaviour rather than knowledge or skills per se, one of the most effective training tools is the development of a group ethic. A commercial ecotour guide or group leader cannot force clients to adopt minimal-impact practices or police them at all times to ensure that they do. Most groups will include some members who are already concerned to minimize impacts, and who will quickly learn and apply techniques and practices suggested by the guide or leader, and other members with little experience or interest. The latter commonly learn to minimize impacts not through supervision from the guide, but through indirect supervision and assistance by other members of the group. It is part of the guide's task to foster development of a cooperative group ethic, which helps all its members learn and apply minimal-impact techniques or other skills and knowledge, rather than disintegrating into competing subgroups where some members cause impacts and the others try to remedy them.

Education in parks

Interpretive tools

Education is also one of the primary tools in the park or land manager's tourism tool kit. If tourists can be persuaded to behave so as to minimize per capita impacts, then other more intrusive management tools, such as hardening the physical environment or restricting numbers or activities, may be unnecessary. As in most educational processes, there are many different potential ways to deliver the same information, and different ways are more efficient and effective for different people in different circumstances. Parks agencies rely principally on signs and leaflets, and less commonly on ranger or video presentations.

Signs and notices are generally the simplest delivery mode. At their most basic, they are also very inexpensive, e.g. printed, photocopied or mimeographed paper notices tacked to wooden notice boards at trailheads. The effectiveness of different formats depends on how actively the reader is seeking the information in the sign concerned. If wilderness users are accustomed to signing in at trailheads, for example, and to the display of up-to-date advisory notices in conjunction with sign-in forms, they are likely to find notice boards and read the notices even if they are relatively small and inconspicuous. If they are not accustomed to such a procedure, however, or do not appreciate its safety benefits in case search and rescue may be required, then people are unlikely to read inconspicuous signs on notice boards, and larger, more colourful and more distinctive notices will be required in order to be effective. Signs advising bans on open fires, pets, vehicles or specific activities such as abseiling commonly fall in this category. Between these extremes are signs providing information on species identification, biodiversity and biogeography, characteristic ecosystem processes, and similar information on the natural environment. Such signs need to be brief, informative, eye-catching and accessible.

Apart from being printed in multiple copies for individuals to keep, rather than a single copy for individuals to peruse briefly, information leaflets and brochures tend to be similar to interpretive signs in type of content, level of detail, and layout and format. As with signs and notices, they range from relatively crude black print on a single background colour, to high-resolution glossy materials with full colour separation. In many national parks and other government-run backcountry and wilderness areas, printed materials are used to accompany interpretive signs.

A few national parks use site-specific video information about particular areas or environments, sometimes coupled with minimal-impact guidelines, in large-scale interpretative centres in national parks and similar areas. Much less common, but potentially very useful, are interactive training videos intended to ensure that backcountry travellers have at least a basic understanding of safety and environmental issues before they are granted a permit by the land management agency. Denali National Park in Alaska used a touch-screen video training programme for many years to teach backcountry hikers and campers about safe behaviour in grizzly bear country, and this approach could easily be adapted to train and test whether visitors know how and where to walk, camp, cook and clean to minimize impacts in wilderness areas. This does not guarantee that people will use that knowledge, but it would at least check that they possessed it.

Behavioural change

Education will only be a useful tool in managing tourism in natural environments if it is actually effective in reducing human impacts. To reduce per capita impacts, education must change individual behaviour, by giving those individuals new skills that they are already keen to apply, or by changing their attitudes so they are keen to apply skills they already possess, or both.

It is relatively easy to test whether people claim their attitudes have changed, by straightforward survey or questionnaire techniques. It is more difficult to test whether their attitudes have in fact changed, and arguably it does not matter, except in so far as it affects their behaviour. Determining if and how people's behaviour has changed, however, as distinct from whether they say their behaviour has changed, requires direct observation under circumstances where the people concerned either do not know they are being observed, or are unlikely to change their behaviour in response to observation. This is more difficult again.

Arguably, it does not really matter if and how people change their behaviour, except in so far as it alters their impacts. Ideally, therefore, to assess the effectiveness of education programmes in ecotourism we need to quantify how these education programmes affect their net per capita impacts. This, however, is most difficult of all, principally because of the obstacles to obtaining a properly matched and representative control group or groups. As a result, surveys of claimed changes in attitude or behaviour following education programmes are relatively common, but measurements of actual changes in behaviour are rare, and controlled measurements of actual changes in impacts even more so (Medio *et al.*, 1997; Littlefair, 2004; Buckley and Littlefair, 2007; Marion and Reid, 2007; Littlefair and Buckley, 2008).

Post-trip learning

Portability

Different types of knowledge and skill can be transported and applied with varying degrees of success in different environments and circumstances. Basic techniques for using map and compass, for example, are universal, but despite this, a person used to navigating in the mountain ranges of North America can easily become confused in tropical rainforests or in flat open subtropical savannah woodland. Techniques for building an iglu, quinzhee or snow cave differ according to weather and snow characteristics, which vary with latitude, altitude and relative humidity as well as precipitation patterns. Similarly, local dead branches may be the least-impact cooking fuel in a fire-prone temperate or subtropical forest or woodland, while in arctic or mountain areas wood may be scarce and re-growth slow, so the least-impact source of heat for cooking is portable stoves using alcohol or petroleum-based fuels carried in from outside. The types of vegetation that suffer least impact from camping differ from one environment to another, and so do the least-impact techniques for disposing of human wastes. Overall, therefore, what is learnt in one environment may not necessarily be applicable elsewhere.

Competency

Many outdoor education courses incorporate aptitude or competency tests as part of a graduation or certification procedure. Some also offer different levels of instructor certification. Formal testing of minimal-impact skills is rare, but techniques such as campsite inspections provide continual informal practical tests. Without formal tests, there are no statistics on the success rate of minimal-impact training, but it seems clear that almost anyone can learn basic minimal-impact backcountry travel and camping skills for particular activities in particular environments, as long as they have sufficient interest. The same applies to general environmental information, or the ability to identify the larger, more common or more distinctive plant and animal species in any particular ecosystem. The ability to figure out minimal-impact techniques for an unfamiliar environment, or to make a broad and approximate identification of unfamiliar plant or animal species, requires a much broader knowledge base and is much harder to learn.

Lifelong learning

One of the claims sometimes made for ecotourism is that lessons about environmental management issues and personal environmental impacts, learnt during an ecotourism experience, may be translated to changes in the ecotourist's lifestyle once the holiday is over. For example, it might lead people to consume less water, energy and resources, recycle more, buy more environmentally friendly goods, contribute time or money to conservation efforts of various kinds, or give greater weight to environmental and conservation issues when voting in elections or taking part in other political processes. Whether this is of any global significance would depend on how many people are affected and how much they change. To date there seem to have been no published studies on the degree to which changes in individual attitudes and behaviour while on holiday carry over to changes in individual attitude or behaviour back at home and at work.

One of the defining characteristics of an ecotourist is an interest in learning from people and places visited, whether it be a greater appreciation of the wealth of different landscapes, vegetation types and biological species in different parts of the world; an understanding of different lifestyles and cultures; or an insight into the different environmental management issues faced by people living under very different conditions in different parts of the globe. Certainly, travel to different parts of the world can bring home just how much variation there is in wealth, poverty and material standards of living, and how the differences influence the type and quantity of natural resources and manufactured products that people consume, and the type and quantity of wastes they produce. To see first-hand how much of the day a villager in a developing country may spend collecting fuel and carting water, for example, provides a new perspective on reticulated electricity, gas and water supplies, just as communal toilets in the country areas of central Asia provide a new perspective on reticulated sewage. Similarly, the sight of archaeological artefacts such as an Anasazi granary or an Australian Aboriginal grindstone can provide a considerable contrast to the supermarkets and delicatessens of modern developed nations.

Resource and land use conflicts

Many clients on commercial ecotours are interested in the environmental implications of different energy sources, whether firewood or fuel stoves on the trail, or transmission cables, on-site generators or wind and solar power for ecolodges. At a broader scale, they may be interested in the various competing uses of wilderness areas. For example, this may include infrastructure such as roads, accommodation or ski-lifts; access or prohibition for motorized transport such as off-road vehicles, trail bikes, snowmobiles and powered watercraft; and ethical and safety conflicts between different user groups such as hikers, hunters and horsepackers.

In many parts of the world, tourism may have a part to play in conflicts between extractive industries and the conservation of endangered species. Well-known examples include: the impacts of logging on the spotted owl in the USA or long-footed potoroo in Australia; the impacts of industrial fisheries on marine mammals and turtles; the impacts of hydroelectric power generation on migratory freshwater fish, such as salmon in the north-western USA; the impacts of offshore oil exploration and production on marine mammals, e.g. in the Arctic and southern oceans; the impacts of livestock grazing on native predators such as wolves, puma, dingo, tiger, lion or leopard depending on continent; and the impacts of mineral leases in conservation reserves.

Some ecotours can also illustrate multiple land-use practices, either simultaneous or sequential. Some tours, for example, take place on current or former farms, in current or past production forests, or in areas used for commercial as well as recreational fishing. Such multiple uses are not without their own conflicts. Some farmers now operate farm tours where clients are invited to take part in routine farm activities. Unless this is the case, however, farmers would generally not take kindly to tourists getting mixed up in farm activities. Similarly, many publicly owned forest areas espouse multiple use in their management plans, and a number permit tourist activities in some areas. These areas are generally well separated from active logging operations, however, and public access to the latter is commonly restricted. The same applies for fisheries where sailors, seakayakers or commercial tourist cruises may use the same waters as prawn trawlers, salmon netters or longliners. When they are not working, the commercial fishermen may welcome tourists and be glad to talk to them, but where they are working, tourists are best to stay clear.

Publicizing environmental issues

Potentially at least, however, there are several possible mechanisms by which concerned travellers might help to bring about changes in environmental policies and practices once they return home. Even in developed Western nations with democratic systems of government, constitutional rights to freedom of speech, and active mass media corporations attempting to publicize social controversies, it can be very difficult for environmentally concerned citizens to bring instances of major environmental damage to the attention of the general public and the electorate at large. In countries with military governments and state-controlled print and electronic media, it can be well-nigh impossible for local residents to be heard. Tourists may have greater freedom.

Tourism is thus potentially a powerful tool to publicize hidden problems in nations where this is otherwise difficult, and this applies to the social as well as the physical and biological environment. International inbound tourists bring foreign exchange and contribute to the balance of payments, and nearly all national governments are keen to maintain or increase revenues from inbound tourism. Individual tourists who are concerned about environmental damage or social injustice can have significant effects on such revenues through a number of different mechanisms. They may simply decide not to return, cutting repeat business. They may discourage their friends from visiting. They may complain to tour operators, leading them to change itineraries. They may complain to travel agents, leading them to change their recommendations to other clients. They may publicize the issues concerned in their own countries, e.g. through letters to travel magazines, affecting the decisions of other potential tourists. Most powerfully, they may publicize these issues through blogs, leading to very rapid and far-reaching negative publicity. Equally, tourists can and do use any or all of these avenues to provide positive publicity for particular destinations and encourage others to visit them too, increasing tourism revenues for the country of destination in the process.

In addition to their role in publicizing social and environmental problems in destination nations, some tourists feel sufficiently strongly about such problems to spend money or change their voting patterns in their own countries in an attempt to resolve them. Of course, the ability of any group of individuals to influence a national government, and the ability of any national government to influence other countries, are both limited, the former by the structure of domestic political arrangements in democratic Western nations, and the latter by the constraints of independent national sovereignty, and of international agreements. If a major development project or policy in another nation is particularly large or environmentally damaging, however, information brought back by tourists from the country concerned may be sufficient to trigger wide-scale political action from other people who are already concerned about global environmental issues.

Educational tourism subsector

Educational teaching tourism

In addition to the role of environmental education and interpretation within ecotourism more generally, there is a specialist educational tourism subsector that overlaps to some degree with ecotourism. Some schools and universities offer existing courses, packaged with accommodation and transport, with formal assessment and credit towards a qualification. Some tour companies specialize in packaging tours for special-interest groups, including an educational component for tax purposes. Some specialized training organizations offer study tours, short or long, with a specific on-site educational programme led by recognized experts, often drawn from educational and research organizations. In this educational tourism subsector, the educational component is a core or integral part of the product.

Environmental research tourism

In addition to tours where clients pay to be taught about the natural or cultural environment, there is also a market for tours where clients pay to assist in environmental research, under the direction of a qualified scientist. This model has been popularized and used worldwide by the US-based corporation Earthwatch. Under this model, participants pay a substantial up-front package fee for the privilege of travelling to a research site and assisting physically in a scientific research project, under the immediate direction of a well-known scientist. This may involve some technical training at the outset, to ensure that all the Earthwatch team can carry out the research tasks required with adequate skill. The participants are called volunteers rather then tourists, and the fees paid are intended to cover expenses, but these expenses include staff salaries, travel and accommodation costs, and Earthwatch is a successful commercial venture, so even if it is not one in name, it is very similar to a specialist tour company in nature.

Outdoor education sector

There is a large and long-standing outdoor education industry worldwide, which has many similarities with modern commercial ecotourism but whose historical links are with the education sector rather than the tourism industry. This sector includes: outdoor education programmes in schools, colleges and universities, whether publicly or privately funded; NFP outdoor education associations and community organizations, whether for children or adults; and short-term courses offered by private companies, e.g. for corporate team-building and leadership development.

A common feature of most such programmes is that with few exceptions, the teaching curriculum is not centred on the workings of the natural environment in which it is based. Their main aim is not to teach people about the natural environment, but to use the natural environment to teach something else. They use the natural outdoor environment to teach bushcraft and survival skills, technical skills such as rock-climbing technique, organizational skills such as team-building and leadership, and personal skills such as self-confidence, motivation and self-reliance. They may treat the natural environment as a set of obstacles and opportunities, a set of challenges and resources, or a giant adventure playground, but rarely do they treat it as a complex and self-sustaining natural ecosystem.

Certainly, there are exceptions. Some outdoor education programmes do incorporate instruction on the natural environment for its own sake and interest, rather than a means or barrier to survival, and some incorporate minimal-impact skills in their training for backcountry travel and camping. The US National Outdoor Leadership School, for example, focuses heavily on minimal-impact skills, and all of its instructors are expected to be competent in that regard, but not all can teach course participants about plant and animal identification, life histories and interactions.

Conclusions

Ecotour guiding is a skill and a profession that requires abilities to organize logistics, to socialize with and entertain a variety of different clients, to maintain coherence among divergent groups, and to impart a wide variety of information in an interesting manner. These are not trivial skills. Environmental education features strongly in many definitions of ecotourism; perhaps because it is this component that provides jobs for specialist guides. Different ecotourism operators, tours and guides, however, have different interpretations of both content and delivery. Environmental education may encompass: broad-scale global or regional environmental issues; identification and life histories of plant and animal species encountered during the tour itself; techniques to minimize individual impacts on natural and social environment; and sometimes, information on environmental impacts or mismanagement at the sites visited, derived from other sources.

It is often claimed that education reduces impacts, but there are rather few demonstrated examples. It is also claimed that informal educational outcomes of commercial ecotourism experiences may lead clients to alter their lifestyles, but there is in fact no evidence for this. There is an educational tourism subsector and a separate outdoor education industry, both with strong but largely unacknowledged practical links to commercial ecotourism.

RESEARCH

Guiding and interpretation

The role of guides in ecotourism, and their contribution to the clients' experience, has been considered by, e.g. Weiler and Davis (1993), Thomas (1994), Aiello (1998), Markwell and Weiler (1998), Moscardo (1999) and Haig and McIntyre (2002). The fundamentals of good interpretive practice have been considered by Ballantyne (1995), Moscardo (1996, 1998, 1999), Knapp and Barrie (1998), Kimmel (1999), and Staiff *et al.* (2002).

The kinds of knowledge that tour guides consider important, and the degree to which they actually possess such knowledge, have been examined by Jacobson and Robles (1992), Ballantyne and Hughes (2001) and Hall and Piggin (2002). The particular advantages and issues associated with training local residents or community members as ecotour guides have been considered by Paaby *et al.* (1991) and Jukofsky (1998) in Costa Rica and Vieitas *et al.* (1999) in Brazil. Masberg (1996), on the other hand, considered what tour clients want their guides to tell them, and Klenosky *et al.* (1998), Stein *et al.* (2003) and Hill *et al.* (2007) investigated what motivates tourists to learn from their guides, how they use the information that guides provide and whether they are satisfied as a result. Lemelin and Smale (2006) found that tourists viewing polar bears in Canada simply count how many bears they see; interpretation, in that case, apparently did not influence satisfaction. Research on the experiences of commercial ecotour clients is summarized in Table 10.1.

Several studies have tested how effective interpretation can be in educating ecotourists about environment and heritage. Examples include Forestell (1993), with regard to whalewatching; Amante-Helweg (1996); Munn (1998) with particular reference to macaws; Schaenzel (1998); and Moscardo (1999). Orams and Hill (1998) examined whether interpretation may affect the behaviour of tourists feeding dolphins. Medio *et al.* (1997) tested whether interpretation can reduce the environmental impacts of divers on coral reefs. Littlefair (2004) carried out particularly rigorous tests of the effectiveness of best-practice interpretation in reducing the ecological impacts of guided ecotourists in a subtropical rainforest World Heritage Area. This topic was also reviewed by Marion and Reid (2007) with commentary by Buckley and Littlefair (2007). Most recently, Medeiros *et al.* (2007) found that interpretive signs can reduce visitor impacts on little terns, an endangered beach-nesting species, in Portugal.

Table 10.1. Surveys of ecotourist experiences.

Continent and country	Site or topic	Reference
Africa		
Kenya	Tsavo West National Park	Akama and Kieti (2003)
Uganda	Kibale National Park	Obua and Harding (1996)
Zambia	Mfuwe Lodge, South Luangwa NP	Husbands *et al.* (1994)
Americas		
USA	Carolinas, Georgia	Silverberg *et al.* (1996)
USA	Wyoming, overflights	Tarrant *et al.* (1995)
USA	South-east, two parks	Floyd *et al.* (1997)
USA	North Carolina	Meric and Hunt (1998)
Asia		
Borneo	Bako National Park	Chin *et al.* (2000)
Oceania and Antarctica		
Australia	Fogg Dam, Northern Territory	Chirgwin and Hughes (1997)
Australia	Grampians, Victoria	Chhetri *et al.* (2004)
New Zealand	Sub-Antarctic islands	Cessford and Dingwall (1994)
Antarctica	Regional	Maher *et al.* (2003)

REVISION

Tours have guides

- Guides or leaders are a defining characteristic of tours
- Clients may be passed from host to host or guide to guide
- But an unaccompanied group is a group, not a tour

Guides have many roles

- Logistics, planning, troubleshooting
- Safety, health, risk management

- Handling finance and formalities
- Information, explanation, interpretation
- Cultural introductions, client social comfort
- Need mix of hard (technical) and soft (people) skills

Guides are key to client satisfaction

- Tour marketing materials feature quotes about guides
- Good guides are in personal demand from repeat clients
- The more upmarket the tour, the higher the expectations from the guide
- If anything goes wrong, the guide is first to be blamed
- And is expected to fix the problem

Logistics

- Guides handle pre-booked tour components
- Keep the group on schedule
- Organize group check-ins
- Handle passports and permits, etc.

Safety

- Guides check client skills and equipment
- And group gear including first-aid
- Guides instruct clients what to do and what not to do
- Guides generally have formal qualifications in relevant outdoor skills
- For more adventurous activities, guides may also be qualified as instructors

Health

- There are legal rules about medicine in most countries
- Only qualified medical practitioners can administer prescription drugs
- Tour operators generally tell clients to get pre-trip medical check
- And bring their own medicines
- But guides often have first-aid qualifications
- For many operating areas, first-aid skills are mandatory
- Some backcountry guides also have paramedic training
- Irrespective of qualifications, guides need to monitor client health
- And manage rest, hydration, etc.
- If emergency evacuation is needed, guide is generally responsible

Cultural introductions

- Many tour clients unfamiliar and uncomfortable overseas
- Guide has to introduce new customs and cultures

- Can include greetings, language, food
- And religion, art and lifestyle (e.g. hunting, fishing)

Information and interpretation

- Clients have endless questions
- But they don't like to be lectured
- Different clients have different interests
- Guides must keep clients enthusiastic
- And ensure equal attention for all clients
- Critical skill for a good guide
- Can consume endless time and energy

Education and environment

- Ecotourism includes environmental education
- Different categories of environmental information
- Local facts, e.g. species identification, geology
- Broader debates, e.g. land use, climate change
- Technical instructions, e.g. minimal-impact practices
- Most people remember short stories and snippets best

What works best?

- Signs: attention, problem, action
- For example 'Warning! Collapsed track. Take detour'
- Spoken: instruction, reason, role-model
- For example 'Keep quiet, rare birds, easily disturbed' – and speak quietly
- Use a client question as an opportunity for information
- 'Teachable moments'

Parks interpretive materials

- Ecotours can also use materials provided by parks
- Interpretive signs and leaflets most common
- Sometimes ranger talks and walks
- Also videos and visitor centres
- Different expectations in different countries

Post-trip learning

- Skills cf. knowledge, localized cf. portable
- Lifelong learning: natural history, resource use
- Occasionally, lifestyle changes, political activism

Educational tourism subsector

- Specialist educational tours
- Environmental research tours
- Outdoor education sector

REFLECTIONS

1. Do all tours necessarily have guides, and if not, under what circumstances do commercial tours operate without guides? Provide examples.

2. List four major roles or functions that a tour guide will generally fulfil. Choose any individual ecotour product, either specific or generic (e.g. half-day hiking tour in subtropical rainforest; 10-day sea-kayaking tour in high arctic; lodge-based game safari in southern Africa). Describe how the guide or guides would fulfil each of the four roles you have identified, for that particular type of tour.

3. Many ecotour operators advertise environmental interpretation by their guides as a key component of the tour, sometimes listing the guide's academic qualifications (e.g. in biology) as well as their professional qualifications (e.g. in first aid or outdoor skills). What different types of environmental interpretation would an ecotour commonly incorporate, and what skills and knowledge would a guide need to deliver them?

READING 10.1. EDUCATION TO REDUCE IMPACTS

Minimizing visitor impacts is a critical component of protected-area management. Teaching visitors to reduce impacts is preferred to enforcing regulations, but does education actually reduce impacts? Littlefair (2004) used controlled experiments to carry out such a test.

The education programme tested involved verbal interpretation by skilled guides working with ecotourists in a subtropical World Heritage rainforest in Australia. Education for different groups taking the same guided walk was modified experimentally to include five levels: a control group with no environmental information; general environmental education but no minimal-impact information; verbal appeal for specific behaviours; role model demonstration by the guide, and both appeal and role model.

Actual impacts were measured using three parameters that could be zeroed between tours: noise, litter and shortcutting. Each programme was replicated for a number of tours. Actual behaviour was observed covertly during each tour, and impacts and self-reported behaviour measured immediately afterwards.

There were five main results: (i) minimal-impact education can indeed reduce actual visitor impacts; (ii) education only reduces some types of impacts; (iii) environmental education without minimal-impact messages does not reduce impacts; (iv) different interpretive approaches are differentially effective for different types of impact; and (v) self-reported behaviour did not match actual observed behaviour, so results from studies relying solely on self-reported behaviour must be treated with caution.

These results apply for verbal interpretation for guided ecotourists, not necessarily for signs or leaflets aimed at the general public. We need to test for different types of visitors, impact and educational materials, and, since wilfully uncaring visitors can produce much more impact than informed caring visitors, parks will still need laws and rangers.

Acknowledgements

This reading is a modified version of Buckley and Littlefair (2007), first published in the *Journal of Sustainable Tourism* 15, 324–325.

READING 10.2. AMERICAN OUTDOOR EDUCATION IN THE AUSTRALIAN TROPICS

The US National Outdoor Leadership School (NOLS, 2007) is a large NFP outdoor education organization based in the USA. It runs 2-week, 1-month and 3-month wilderness courses that teach core wilderness environment and survival skills, and a range of different backcountry travel skills including climbing, mountaineering, kayaking, cross-country skiing, etc. It operates in North, Central and South America, East Africa, Central Asia and Scandinavia, and is generally well respected worldwide.

In 1996, it ran its first semester course in Australia. A 1-month sector of this was a descent of the Drysdale River in the Kimberley region of north-west Western Australia, using open collapsible canoes. This was only the second descent of the Drysdale River; the first was by Operation Raleigh in 1988 using square-ended inflatable canoes (Buckley, 2006). There were three instructors and 14 students on the river section. Two of the instructors were Australian, but had worked for NOLS in the USA for many years previously. The third was a US instructor specializing in river travel. There were 14 students, all American, 18–23 years old, four of them women. I travelled with the group as a research scientist.

NOLS espouses and teaches a best-practice minimal-impact philosophy, to the extent that a single grain of rice or splash of dried coffee grounds discernible at an abandoned campsite is considered unsatisfactory. It uses a small-group teaching technique, where groups of three or four students share the same tent and cook together.

As with most such groups, the level of understanding and interest in minimizing impacts differed considerably between individuals. The tent-group approach, however, uses a group ethic in training at two different levels. First, the members of each tent group supervise each other's camping, cooking and cleaning techniques, help in teaching each other specific skills and techniques, and are jointly responsible for checking the cleanliness of the campsite before departure each morning. Second, once the tent group itself has checked its own site, a member of another tent group, or sometimes an instructor, is asked to recheck it. This procedure works well.

While the tent-group approach has been standard NOLS practice for decades and is well tested, the Australian wet–dry tropics were new terrain for instructors and students alike, and two significant issues arose that provoked group debate.

At the time of year when the course was run, the Drysdale River has a relatively low flow. At a number of points, it divides into multiple channels running through dense thickets of *Pandanus* screw-pine. Navigating in fragile collapsible boats, in fast-moving water, round tight corners in narrow channels obstructed by screw-pine branches entailed a significant risk of damage to the boats, which in turn would have placed the party as a whole at risk since the going was slower than anticipated and food supplies limited.

On some occasions, therefore, one of the instructors used a pocket saw to cut through the soft stems and branches of the screw-pines in order to make an easier passage. This raised considerable debate, both with the other instructors and between the students, as to the significance of the environmental impact caused, and the degree to which it could be balanced against safety considerations. The group did not have the knowledge to assess long-term impacts, because they did not know how much damage to branches was caused naturally during wet-season floods, nor how rapidly the *Pandanus* would re-grow following damage.

Some of the group believed that cutting a few branches was an insignificant impact. This group also moved rocks on the streambed to prevent damage to the boats in the smaller rapids. Others argued that if tourists started using the river routinely for canoe trips, and each group cut a few branches, the *Pandanus* thickets might suffer considerable cumulative damage. This could be of particular concern since the thickets provide one of the few habitat areas for the endangered purple-crowned wren. This group argued that it was inconsistent that on the one hand, the instructors insisted that students scrub away tiny spills of dried milk powder from exposed rocks, for example, and used fuel stoves rather than dead wood for cooking, while on the other hand they were prepared to cut live branches impeding their progress downstream. No consensus was reached by the students, because instructors' concerns over safety forced them to act on their own judgement without a conclusive group mandate.

The second debate was potentially much more significant. As well as the river section, the course was intended to incorporate a rock-climbing section, and a (separate and subsequent) period spent with the Bardi Aboriginal people, under instruction from Aboriginal guides. Most of the students expressed a very strong interest in Aboriginal culture, and the group had brought a number of books on this topic. They were also keen to see examples of Aboriginal rock art, with which the Drysdale River escarpments are richly endowed. There are several different styles of painting, some of them many thousand years old.

As well as the three river instructors, the course had two climbing instructors who had travelled separately by four-wheel-drive to a pre-arranged point downstream, where there was a large escarpment that could potentially provide a site for rock climbing instruction. Not surprisingly, however, the same rocks that the instructors had picked out as most suitable for teaching rock-climbing techniques also proved to contain the most outstanding examples of rock art. This provoked considerable and heated debate as to whether a rock art site should be used for climbing instruction.

From a technical perspective, there were two distinct issues: physical damage to the paintings and cultural impacts associated with the site's value to Aboriginal people. Those who were in favour of climbing argued that they would, of course, not be climbing on the actual paintings themselves, and they would not be leaving bolts or other climbers' protection devices permanently in the rock. Although walking back and forth between tents and climbing routes might leave visible tracks in the dead grass, this would be a temporary impact, which would be negligible compared to the effects of fire, given that the Kimberley is a highly fire-prone environment and the tall grass is burnt naturally every year or two. In fact, the area was later firebombed by the land management agency as part of a fuel reduction programme, while the group was still camped there, destroying some of the group's equipment. Hence the only possible physical impact on the paintings themselves would be a slight increase in the concentration of airborne dust, of which a minuscule amount might potentially adhere to the paintings. Those opposed to climbing, however, argued that the paintings had survived for thousands of years precisely because they had suffered no disturbance whatsoever, being situated in caves and protected from casual visitors by Aboriginal customs. Hence even a small increase in dust deposition would be a greater impact than they had experienced in the past.

In relation to cultural impacts, there were three distinct subsidiary issues. The first was whether the nearest Aboriginal people now living in the area should be considered as the modern representatives of the Aboriginal people who had made the paintings in the past. The second was whether Aboriginal people, either there or elsewhere, would in fact object to Europeans practising technical rock-climbing techniques so close to their paintings and within the boundaries of the site as a whole. The third was whether any European group, particularly one from another country, had any rights at all to be debating what Australian Aboriginal people might or might not think, or rather, whether they should simply recognize that rock art sites were generally areas of considerable cultural importance to Aborigines, so the European group should therefore leave the vicinity immediately.

Individuals concerned about such cultural issues raised a number of analogous scenarios in attempts to convey their concern. For example, they asked whether Europeans would consider climbing the interior walls of a European art museum, even if they were not climbing over the paintings themselves or otherwise harming them physically. They asked whether other recreational activities involving specialist equipment would be appropriate in areas of high conservation value, e.g. the construction of ski resorts and golf courses in national parks. Finally, they asked whether the pro-climbers would still be so keen to climb if Aboriginal elders were watching them do so, and how they would feel about reporting their actions to the Aboriginal people with whom they were about to spend several weeks of their life.

During the debate, several cross-cutting divisions of opinion became apparent. One of the most important was a cultural division between instructors. Some of the instructors were familiar with the Anasazi cultures and artefacts in arid south-western regions of North America. These individuals argued that while cultural artefacts of this type were certainly worthy of respect, they were also relatively commonplace and therefore not of outstanding universal value. It seemed to be difficult for the Australian instructors to get across that the Kimberley rock paintings were at least 10 and probably 30 or more times older than the Anasazi remains, and indeed, that they were among the eldest surviving human artefacts in the world, being contemporaneous or older, for example, than Neolithic cave paintings in southern Europe. This division of opinion among the instructors was somewhat disconcerting for the students. Though used to the instructors setting them practical problems to solve, they expected to be able to turn to the instructors for a definitive solution. The division of opinion among the instructors made it difficult for a group ethic to operate among the students.

Interestingly, however, the group ethic was re-established when someone suggested that those who wanted to climb should do so, and those who didn't should not. This instantly raised the response that those who climbed would then be inflicting an immediate cultural impact on those who believed personally, for whatever reasons, that the group should not climb in the rock art site. They also argued that NOLS generally propounded the precautionary principle in relation to impacts on the physical environment, i.e. if you don't know what impacts an actions will have, don't do it. Given that the group clearly did not have enough information to assess the potential cultural or long-term physical impacts of climbing at the site concerned, the philosophy or approach that the instructors had been teaching in regard to other types of action should also be applied in this context. Once these points were raised, the group ethic did begin to operate again, with the general consensus that in view of the many uncertainties, it would be preferable not to climb at the rock art site, even though this would mean the complete loss of the rock climbing section from the course as a whole.

Arguably, this outcome was a vindication of the group-discussion educational techniques used by NOLS, as well as its general minimal-impact philosophy. Of course, if the opposite outcome had occurred and impacts had in fact been inflicted, a radically different conclusion might be reached and, in fact, a similar NOLS course the following year also camped at the same site, despite knowing that the rock art was present.

chapter 11

COMMUNITY

Locals assembling for the Naadam cultural festival at Renchinlkhumbe, Mongolia. Photo courtesy of Claudia Ollenburg.

REVIEW

Introduction

This chapter focuses on the social costs and benefits that ecotourism may generate for local communities. It considers the various ways in which communities may be involved in ecotourism, and the various types and mechanisms of impacts, both positive and negative. It does not aim to review the broader topic of community-based tourism or community ecotourism as a specialist subsector.

Community involvement in ecotourism

Local communities may be involved in ecotourism and related subsectors in a number of different ways. First, local communities, including indigenous and traditional communities, may own the land or water where tourism operations take place, or may own rights of use through either modern or traditional legal systems. It may thus be up to the local community to decide whether to issue a lease or an operating permit to a tour operator, and if so under what conditions. Second, local community members may have direct commercial involvement in ecotourism enterprises, as owners, as employees or as contractors. Third, local community members may be involved in commercial dealings with ecotourism operations, as suppliers of goods or services. Fourth, locals may be perceived by tourists as part of the tourist attraction, something worth looking at. Fifth, irrespective of which of these mechanisms may be involved, nearly all communities that are visited by tourists experience some form of social impact – positive, negative or both.

The relationships between tourists, tour operators and host communities depend greatly on the cultural and socio-economic differences between visitors and residents. Where the two are very similar, as in most domestic tourism, the social impacts of tourism are related principally to crowding, cross-subsidization and competition for resources. Where they are very different, as in most ecotourism from developed to developing nations, the interactions are commonly more complex.

Some authors currently argue that economic benefits to local communities should be one of the defining criteria for ecotourism, but this view is not universally accepted. More commonly, community ecotourism is recognized as one particular type of ecotourism, with a primary focus on involving local communities and providing them with social and economic benefits. It is also widely recognized that local communities can have a strong influence, positive or negative, on the conservation outcomes of ecotourism projects or enterprises, and that this in itself provides a strong reason to design ecotourism projects to include such community benefits.

There is an extensive literature on the political aspects of socioeconomically asymmetric interactions between tourists and host communities (e.g. Mowforth and Munt, 2003). Theoretical analyses of this nature, however, are beyond the scope of the current volume, which takes a more practical tone. In particular, given that ecotourism can be expressed in triple-bottom-line terms (Buckley, 2003b), this chapter examines the factors contributing to the social bottom line, whether positively or negatively.

Community division and crime

Human communities are heterogeneous. There are significant differences both between and within individual communities. In almost any community involved or influenced by tourism, different people will be affected differently. Such differences within individual communities can easily outweigh differences between communities in the same region, though perhaps not between rich and poor nations. One of the principal community effects of any kind of tourism development, therefore, including ecotourism, is an increasing degree of division within that community between those individuals who gain from tourism and therefore support it, and those who lose from tourism and therefore oppose it. Generally speaking, the more important tourism becomes as the source of income within the community, the greater the intensity of such polarization. Indeed, there are some traditional communities that have chosen not to accept tourists at all, in order to avoid the consequent community impacts. The Province of Arunachal Pradesh in the eastern Himalayan part of India, for example, adopted this approach in the 1990s (Shackley, 1995b), though during 2007 it reopened for limited international tourism.

Because of the influx of cash and strangers, growth in tourism is often associated with growth in crime, particularly in areas where tourists are significantly wealthier than local residents. Locals stealing from tourists, however, is not the only manifestation of this effect. As some locals become wealthy from tourism and others grow increasingly envious, this can lead to an increase in property crimes between members of the same resident community. Where different tour operators are competing for control of lucrative opportunities, this can generate an increase in violence, and where tourism brings a large influx of foreign nationals into a particular destination, this may attract organized crime from their countries of origin. Organized criminals from a number of Asian nations, for example, apparently now operate in the major Australian tourist destinations, and organized crime from Russia in various parts of Europe.

Cultural change

Particularly in communities where tourism has brought cash incomes and Western community goods to the younger generation, growth in tourism may lead to the erosion of traditional social and community structures, with effective power shifting from elders with knowledge and respect, to younger people with cash. At the same time, where aspects of traditional culture form an important component of the tourism attraction, these may be preserved in a commoditized form specifically for tourists, even if they are no longer adhered to by local residents. Examples may include dress and dances, art and architecture, cooking and cultural activities.

Tourists create social and cultural impacts on host communities as well as impacts on the natural and physical environment. Cases where the cultures of local communities have been modified by tourism are now commonplace. Sometimes the host community welcomes these changes; sometimes it resists; and sometimes it simply increases turnover, with those opposed to the change moving elsewhere.

Tourism can contribute to the trivialization of cultures, with rich tourists treating indigenous cultures as entertainment, and formerly isolated and self-sufficient communities adopting a cargo-cult mentality towards rich visitors. Tourism is not the only such influence. In most parts of the world, television is now a far more pervasive source of information on consumer goods and lifestyles in the richer developed Western nations, and traders have brought new goods and information to isolated communities since time immemorial.

Distinctions have often been drawn between individuals whose aim is to assimilate into the host community and themselves be changed by this process, even if only temporarily, and those who bring their own social and material culture with them as far as possible, viewing the culture of the host community purely as entertainment. Clearly there is a continuum between these extremes.

Even those who try to adapt themselves to the host culture as far as possible, will still contribute inadvertently to cultural impacts. The first outside visitor to a closed community, for example, though unlikely to change its social fabric, will still bring different objects, clothing and language, and a new awareness of different cultures elsewhere. At the other extreme, where a host community receives millions of visitors a year, it will be modified by the sheer task of providing infrastructure, and by the associated economic and employment opportunities.

In areas where local communities are already familiar with television portrayals of Western society, ecotravellers who try, with the best intentions, to minimize their cultural impacts by wearing local clothes, eating local foods and adopting local customs so as to blend in to local society, may find themselves in the perverse situation that they are looked down upon by those very locals as being mean, poor or low class relative to the locals' perception of Western society as a whole.

Between these extremes is a wide range in which the aggregate cultural impacts of tourism depend strongly on the behaviours of the individual tourist: preferences and prices paid for transport, accommodation and food; appreciation of local languages, art and music; willingness to comply with local customs and take part in local events; and behaviour towards individual people, whether rude or respectful, uninterested or intrusive. Not surprisingly, cultural impacts can be reduced considerably by education about the host community, including its history, social structure, attitudes and customs.

There are many potential sources for such information, ranging from published books to the local people themselves, and including information compiled, printed and distributed locally by host communities, and lectures and commentaries by tour guides. Some of these focus on factual information about the culture concerned, others are intended to influence the attitudes of individuals towards cultures other than their own.

Role of ecotour operators

One of the criteria used, at least by some analysts, to distinguish ecotourism from mainstream forms of tourism development is the degree to which it attempts to overcome or minimize these various negative effects. Most of them, however, are internal within the community, may not be immediately apparent to tourists or even a tour operator, and cannot easily be resolved without an unwarranted level of interference in internal community affairs. There are various ecotourism projects, for example, where payments for leases or operating permits are put into a central fund to be spent at the discretion of community elders. There are other cases where such funds are held by the tour operator until the community chooses what particular project, such as a school or health centre, it wants the funds used for. Broadly speaking, the greater the degree of involvement by an expatriate tour operator, the greater the risk of potential paternalism, but the greater the discretion given to individual community members, the greater the risk of potential misuse of funds. Some examples are summarized in Buckley (2003a).

Employment, labour and entrepreneurship

In addition to attempts to minimize negative social impacts, ecotourism can generate a range of positive social impacts. The most straightforward of these is that it brings money to the community, in the form of leases, employment, purchases and entrepreneurial opportunities. In some areas where land is held in traditional ownership so that the local community can effectively decide whether to make it available to commercial tour operators, the community may demand jobs as the price of admission. In other areas, such local employment may be the price of political support, which the tour operator needs to maintain its position. The type of employment available, however, depends on the type of tourist product and the skills of local residents. Front-of-house staff in upmarket ecolodges, for example, need to have training and experience in hospitality service skills. Some companies have therefore set up staff training programmes, to the point where luxury lodges are managed by local residents who have worked their way through the company over a period of years. This approach is only feasible, however, in cultures that accept promotion based on capability rather than nepotism.

As the proportion of a local community employed in tourism continues to increase, the availability of labour for other occupations may begin to decrease accordingly. In some subsistence communities, this may even reduce the availability of food. Examples are reported where certain community tasks, historically carried out as a form of community service, have lapsed because people now expect payment. There are also examples where residents in communities receiving income from tourism have themselves begun to employ residents from neighbouring communities to carry out domestic or agricultural tasks such as looking after livestock.

Commercial opportunities associated with tourism extend well beyond direct employment. There are usually also opportunities to supply goods and services on contract. Upmarket lodges in developing nations, for example, may purchase fresh food from local gardens. Local boat owners may be hired to shuttle tourists from island lodges to nearby beaches or surf breaks. Locals may manufacture artefacts for sale to tourists as souvenirs, and they may put on performances that they charge tourists to watch. Some examples are summarized in Buckley (2003a).

Commodification

Where artefacts are manufactured, or performances staged solely for tourists, this is referred to as commodification. If the tourist versions are different from the originals, e.g. by being simpler or shorter or just by losing cultural meaning, this is referred to as loss of authenticity. For example, a dance traditionally performed for a particular purpose on a particular date, may be repeated on other dates solely to earn money. Such approaches are not restricted to traditional cultures – Western cultures are equally susceptible. For example, some private game parks in South Africa have apparently started offering clients the opportunity to watch when wildlife are being darted with tranquillizer guns in order to move them for management purposes. This apparently proved so popular that some of these operations began darting animals unnecessarily, simply so they could charge tourists to watch.

Conclusions

Local residents and their communities may gain or lose from commercial ecotourism in a variety of ways. The most commonly cited costs are breakdowns of traditional practices and community structures, and increased inequities, social division and crime. The balance between these factors influences whether local communities are generally in favour or against providing access for commercial ecotourism. Access issues are examined further in the next chapter.

RESEARCH

General discussions of community involvement in ecotourism are provided by Sproule (1996) and Harper (1997). Specific mechanisms for communities to become involved have been put forward by, for example, Healy (1994), Ashley and Row (1998), Beeton (1998) and Hulme and Murphree (2001). The risks that community traditions may become commodified were outlined over a decade ago by King and Stewart (1996) and have also been considered by Mowforth and Munt (2003). Some specific published examples of community involvement in ecotourism are listed in Table 11.1. Some of these have been reiterated many times. An additional nine case studies are presented in a book by Chambers (1997).

The social and cultural impacts of ecotourism and related tourism subsectors on local communities have been studied quite extensively, notably in a book by Wearing and Neil (1999). General reviews of social impacts include, for example, Din (1988), Dogan (1989),

Table 11.1. Ecotourism and local communities.

Continent and country	Area, case	Reference
Africa		
Egypt	St Katherine Protectorate, Sinai	Grainger (2003)
Cameroon	Korup National Park	Gilbert et al. (1994)
Ghana	Two towns	Teye et al. (2002)
Kenya	Maasai Mara	Berger et al. (1996)
Kenya	National Parks	Akama (1996); Sindiga (1995)
Tanzania	Selous Game Reserve	Gillingham and Lee (1999)
Tanzania	Serengeti, Ngorongoro	Johnsen (1998)
Uganda	Budongo Forest Reserve	Langoya and Long (1997)
Mozambique	Tchuma Tchato	Wilson (1997)
South Africa	KwaZulu Natal	Foggin and Munster (2000)
South Africa	KwaZulu Natal, Western Cape	Binns and Nel (2002)
South Africa	Natal	Ward (1997)
South Africa	Richtersveld National Park	Boonzaier (1996); Khan (1996)
South Africa	St Lucia	Baskin (1996)
South Africa	Umzimvubu, Transkei	Powell (1996)
South Africa	Various	Koch et al. (1997)
Zimbabwe	CAMPFIRE Project	Child (1996)
Zimbabwe	Hwange National Park	Potts et al. (1996)
Zimbabwe	National, 30 years	Heath (1992)
Americas		
Canada	Pond Inlet	Grekin and Milne (1996)
Canada	Rocky Mts, British Columbia	Williams and Hunter (2002)
Canada	West Arctic	Notzke (1999)
USA	Hawaii	Liu and Var (1986)
USA	Mt Rogers, Virginia	Jurowski et al. (1997)
Belize	Baboon Sanctuary	Alexander (2000)
Belize	Baboon Sanctuary	Horwich (1998)

Continued

Table 11.1. *Continued.*

Continent and country	Area, case	Reference
Belize	Cockscomb Basin	Horwich *et al.* (1993)
Belize	Crooked Tree Sanctuary	Steinberg (1993)
Belize	Gales Point	Belsky (1999)
Belize	National	Lindberg and Enriquez (1994)
Belize	Possum Point	Kangas *et al.* (1995)
Brazil	Amazonas	Wallace and Pierce (1996)
Caribbean	Dominica	Slinger (2000)
Caribbean	Various	Briereton (1991)
Costa Rica	Monteverde	Wearing and Larsen (1996)
Costa Rica	Monteverde Cloud Forest	Lober (1992)
Costa Rica	Ostional	Campbell (1999)
Costa Rica	Tortuguero	Lee and Snepenger (1992)
Costa Rica	Tortuguero	Hummel (1994)
Costa Rica	Tortuguero National Park	Hummel (1994)
Ecuador	Capirona	Colvin and Dembner (1996)
Guatemala	Maya Forest	Norris *et al.* (1999)
Guyana	Rupununi	Shackley (1998b)
Honduras	Rio Platano	McCain (1997)
Peru	Taquile Island	Mitchell and Reid (2001)
Europe and Russia		
Austria	Alps	Kariel (1989)
Finland	North-east	Törn *et al.* (2008)
Greece	Dadia-Lefkimi-Soufli	Svoronou and Holden (2005)
Greece, Spain	Various	Kousis (2000)
Russia	Various	Poirier and Ostergren (2002)
Sweden	Jukkasjarvi	Hanneberg (1994b)
Turkey and UK	Comparative	Liu *et al.* (1987)
East Asia		
Borneo	Sarawak	Zeppel (1998)

Continued

Table 11.1. *Continued.*

Continent and country	Area, case	Reference
China	Xishuangbanna	Tisdell and Xiang (1998)
Indonesia	Tangkoko DuaSudara	Kinnaird and O'Brien (1996)
Indonesia	Bali area	Mardini (1995)
Japan	Osaka	Yamamoto *et al.* (1998)
Laos	Various	Laird (1993)
Mongolia	Cultural landscape	Buckley *et al.* (2008)
Nepal	Annapurna	Gurung and de Coursey (1994)
Nepal	Annapurna	Gurung (1998)
Nepal	Annapurna Conservation Area	Gurung and de Coursey (1994); Nepal (1997, 2000)
Nepal	Chitwan	Bookbinder *et al.* (1998)
Nepal	Kosi-Tappu Wildlife Reserve	Heinen (1993)
Nepal	Makalu-Barun Conservation Area	Mehta and Kellert (1998)
Philippines	Balicasag and Pamilacon Marine Parks	Christie *et al.* (2002)
Sri Lanka	Various	Gunatilleke (1992)
Taiwan	Tawushan	Lai and Nepal (2006)
Oceania		
Australia	Aboriginal people	Altman (1989)
Australia	Central Australia	Ryan and Huyton (2002)
Australia	Cocos Islands	Carlsen (1999)
Australia	Djabugay people	Dyer *et al.* (2003)
Australia	Halls Gap	Guevara (1996)
Australia	North Queensland	Sofield (2002)
Australia	North-west Queensland	Stoeckl *et al.* (2005)
Fiji	Nadi	King *et al.* (1993)
Maldives	National	Brown *et al.* (1997)
New Zealand	Rotorua and Kaikoura	Horn and Simmons (2002)
New Zealand	Rural areas	Mason and Cheyne (2000)

Brown *et al.* (1997) and Doan (2000). Residents' perceptions and attitudes have been recorded by, for example, Liu and Var (1986), Liu *et al.* (1987), Allen *et al.* (1988, 1993), Ap (1992), King *et al.* (1993), Ap and Crompton (1998), Mason and Cheyne (2000) and Teye *et al.* (2002). Impacts on community health were considered by Bauer (1999a), and impacts on indigenous hosts by Hinch (1998). Attempts to involve local communities in tourism enterprises, specifically in order to give them greater control over social impacts, are described by Darrow (1995) and Campbell (1999).

The effectiveness of community-based protected areas has been examined by: Nepal (1997) and Gurung (2008) in Nepal; Christie *et al.* (2002) in the Philippines; and Grainger (2003) in Egypt.

REVISION

Models and issues

- Impacts of tours on local communities
- Community involvement in tour operations
- Community ownership of tour operations
- Traditional practices as tourist attractions

Differential impacts

- Generally some people gain from tourism, others lose
- Gain may be from employment, business, social or political capital
- Those who profit typically support tourism
- Tourism typically increases prices, e.g. of food, land, etc.
- People outside the industry suffer from higher costs
- Those who lose typically oppose tourism
- Polarization increases as scale of tourism grows

Social costs

- Range of potential social costs
- Increasing crime
- Envy of wealthy tourists
- Inequitable costs and benefits (as above)
- Breakdown of traditional social structures
- Commoditization of culture

Employment in tourism operations

- Direct employment in tours and lodges
- Training, qualifications, customer service attitudes

- Opportunities in management positions
- Some tourism companies have in-house up-skilling systems
- Tourists often can't distinguish locals from other nationals
- Risks of nepotism, bribery, kickbacks to get jobs
- From operator perspective, risk of unhelpful staff

Entrepreneurial opportunities

- Subsidiary tourism business, e.g. local tours from lodges
- Contract services, e.g. transport, cleaning, gardening
- Wholesale opportunities, e.g. food supplies
- Retail opportunities, e.g. artefacts

Authenticity and commodification

- Staged authenticity: pretending to be traditional
- Cultural performances: song, dance, ceremony
- Difficult for tourists to tell how locals view this
- Cultural tours may be used as tool to attract donations
- And to sell artefacts manufactured purely for tourists
- Or mass-produced and bought in for resale

Community-owned tourism

- Wide range of different arrangements
- Lease tourism operating rights on community-owned land
- Revenue-sharing or profit-sharing agreements
- Direct community shareholding in corporation or partnership
- Tourism operations owned in common by entire community
- Tourism operations owned by particular community members
- Local politics and profit, no guarantee of equity

REFLECTIONS

1. What are the various social impacts, both positive and negative, which ecotourism and related types of tourism development can produce within resident host communities? How might these differ depending whether the community is large or small, rich or poor, indigenous or Westernized? Give reasons and examples to illustrate your answers.

2. Local community members may be involved in ecotourism operations as owners, as guides, as active hosts involved in the tourism product (e.g. through accommodation or artefact sales), as neutral hosts (providing the setting, but not directly involved), or as a tourist attraction. Provide an example of each of these categories. In each case, how will different community members experience the social impacts of tourism, depending on their degree of involvement? Which categories are likely to cause the greatest degree of community polarization or conflict, and why?

3. Identify any particular individual community that you have lived in, visited or are familiar with, and that is a destination for tourism at least to some degree, and describe your own experiences in interacting with tourists.

chapter 12

ACCESS

Multi-day camp set up by a commercial cross-country ski tour group, a little below the treeline in the Snowy Mountains, Australia. Guide at far left, making tea. Skis and poles stuck upright to prevent caking with frozen snow. Tents are elliptical domes designed to withstand severe storms.

REVIEW

Introduction

Every outdoor tourism product needs a place to operate and a way to get there, whether it is a fixed-site lodge or a mobile tour activity. Generally this involves two distinct but related issues: first, legal permission to use a particular area for a particular purpose; and second, the physical means to get equipment, staff and clients to the area concerned, and the costs and risks in doing so. In some cases, notably the use of national parks and other protected areas by larger-scale or higher-impact types of commercial tourism activity, the legal issues of access can prove quite controversial. In other cases, notably the more remote areas and extreme environments, the more critical issues are the costs, time and difficulties in bringing clients and equipment safely to the operating area. In a few cases, e.g. commercial climbs on Mt Everest, both aspects of access can provide very significant obstacles for commercial tour operators.

The legal technicalities of access rights and responsibilities in different jurisdictions and tenures are beyond the scope of this chapter. The same applies for the engineering technicalities of access infrastructure such as roads and bridges, airstrips and helipads, jetties and boat ramps. Rather, this chapter presents the issues involved in obtaining access to the tour operating area, from the perspective of a commercial outdoor tour operator. It focuses on mobile tour operations, and does not cover the procedures required to obtain development approval for fixed-site tourist accommodation and infrastructure.

Public cf. private land

Historically, in many countries, tour and safari operators and outfitters could gain permits to access public lands through a straightforward application procedure and nominal fees. Currently, however, in most countries and places, the process is much more complex. In developed nations, it may require an entire suite of subsidiary permits before applying for the principal one. In developing nations, it may require protracted negotiations with local officials at various levels, sometimes with side payments under various guises.

Access to privately owned or community-titled land will generally require site-specific negotiations with the owners, who are likely to be particularly concerned about indemnification from any potential liabilities. They are also likely to require some form of commercial lease, and may want preferential employment opportunities for family or community members.

Public land tenures

In most countries, the overall distinction between public and private lands is generally clear, but the details can be rather complex. Many countries have multiple levels of government, multiple agencies within each level, and multiple types of land and water tenure controlled by each agency. For example, there may be parks and protected areas at national or federal, state or provincial, and local government levels, each with its own management agency and management plans, including those for commercial tourism operations. Two otherwise identical pieces of public beach or forest, for example, may permit entirely different sets of outdoor recreation activities, at entirely different charges, if one happens to be controlled by a local government and the other by a state government.

In addition, governments at all levels own and manage lands that are allocated principally for primary production activities such as forestry, but that are also available for recreation and commercial tourism. Perhaps the best known example worldwide is the Wilderness Areas in lands managed by the US Forests Service, which are used very extensively for recreation. Finally, governments at all levels also manage lands set aside specifically or principally for recreation, ranging from small-scale public parks set aside by local government authorities, to large-scale recreation reserves managed by state and national agencies. Even though such areas may be allocated principally for recreation, however, does not necessarily make them available for commercial tourism operations. Commonly, only particular activities are permitted, and then only under licence.

In addition to the various government bodies, laws and regulations within any one country, some areas of land and water also have special international designations, such as World Heritage, Biosphere Reserves, Ramsar Wetlands and so on. Even though these areas are still managed locally by the country concerned, such designations may add an additional level of complexity to the permitting process for commercial tourism operations, since they may bring the area into the ambit of national heritage legislation as well as regional or local control.

Private land tenures

Similarly, lands that are perceived and operated as privately owned, in the sense that the owner has exclusive rights of use and occupation, may actually be held under a variety of different legal arrangements depending on the country and land use. There may be a broad distinction, for example, between private freehold and private leasehold, even if the leases are for 99 years or longer and can be bought and sold between private individuals. The particular rights conferred by a freehold title may differ between countries, and between subsidiary jurisdictions in a single country, depending on the details of the legal system used. The boundaries of a freehold property may be defined in a variety of ways, either cadastrally or with reference to natural features such as riverbanks or high-tide marks. Different parcels of either freehold or leasehold land may come with different permitted, prohibited or restricted land uses and activities, either through the type of title as in a pastoral lease, or through planning schemes and other legal or quasi-legal instruments. All of these may affect whether a private landholder can operate a private tourism business on their land, or permit an independent tour operator to do so, and under what circumstances.

Lead time and ecocertification

These complexities can indeed be daunting for a new ecotourism start-up unfamiliar with the formalities involved. Business plans for any such enterprise certainly need to factor in the time required to put all these permits in place. In addition, many such permits have a limited life and must be renewed at intervals. Since most commercial tourism marketing has a relatively long lead time, measured in years at least, it becomes critical for operators to know some years in advance, whether they will have access and operating permits for particular areas in the future.

As a result, tourism industry associations and government tourism agencies have expended considerable effort in political lobbying to promote access to protected areas by commercial tour operators. This has taken three main forms. The first is general political lobbying to argue that commercial operators should have access. This is considered further later in this chapter. The second involves attempts by some government tourism portfolios to take over the permitting procedure from protected area management agencies under the guise of 'simplification' or 'a one-stop shop'. These attempts have generally not been successful, because it is the parks agencies that have the relevant legal responsibilities.

The third, and perhaps the most widely adopted in practice, has been to establish ecocertification programmes for outdoor tour operators and then lobby for preferential access or permit conditions by certified operators. This has been the approach adopted over more than a decade, for example, by the industry association Ecotourism Australia, and it has indeed achieved a degree of success in negotiating extended lease terms for its ecocertified members. The Great Barrier Reef Marine Park Authority, for example, currently runs a scheme known as the High Standard Tourism Programme, which offers 15-year leases to commercial tour operators certified by Ecotourism Australia, compared with 6-year leases for those that are not.

There is, in fact, some doubt as to whether this is legally valid under Australian law, since it requires that the tour operator establish a commercial relationship with a specific third party, i.e. the certification agency, as a condition of a commercial relationship with the second party, i.e. the protected area management agency. To date, however, it does not seem to have been challenged, and it seems likely that this approach will continue to be extended to other areas.

Permit conditions

The precise conditions of operating permits can be quite complex. Typically, they may have up to three main aspects or components. The broadest are conditions that apply to the tour operator irrespective of the activity or site: for example, that it be a properly registered company, that it have adequate insurance, that it indemnify the landholder against any lawsuit by its clients, that its guides have adequate safety skills and first aid training, and so on. The second type of conditions applies to the activity undertaken. For example, they might specify safety equipment, maximum group size, client-to-guide ratios or professional training requirements for the guides. They may also specify where the activity can be carried out, at what times of year and what times of day, and any other restrictions such as booking procedures, quotas, anti-crowding measures, and so on. The third category of conditions are typically applied to specific individual sites, with restrictions at a more detailed level: for example, mooring points for dive tours on coral reefs, belay points for abseiling tours on cliff faces, or regulations for use of launching points in lakes and rivers, etc.

Appropriate activities

In determining whether to issue an access and operating permit to a particular tour operator, and if so under what conditions, land owners and land managers have three sets of factors to consider. The first is whether such an operation can fit in successfully with other uses of the land or water concerned. For protected areas, this is conservation; for other public or private lands used for outdoor tourism, it will generally be some form of broad-scale primary production such as agriculture, forestry or fisheries. In some cases the main concern is for safety of tourists, e.g. on narrow tracks used by large logging trucks. In other cases, it may be the loss of the tourist attraction, e.g. through clearfelling or commercial fisheries. In others, it may be the potential impact of tourism on primary production, e.g. through leaving gates open and allowing stock to wander. For national parks and other protected areas, the principal concern is the potential impact of tourism on plants, animals, soil and water conservation.

User conflicts

The second major consideration, for agencies issuing tourism operating permits, is interactions with other users from the tourism and recreation sector itself. This may include both other commercial tour operators, and in the case of publicly accessible areas, private individual visitors. Conflicts between different user groups are commonplace, and may potentially involve the landowner or land management agency. Such conflicts fall into two broad categories: those within the same activity, and those between different activities. The first category is typically related to crowding, where many people want to undertake the same activity at the same time and place. Many land management agencies, for example, have had to introduce complex advance booking systems to control crowding on hiking trails, raftable rivers, designated camping areas, and cliffs routinely used by rock climbers. The second category, conflicts between different activities, commonly arises from asymmetry of impacts, where one set of users disturbs another. Hunters, for example, typically disturb wildlife watchers, birdwatchers and photo-safari clients. River rafters, not to mention jet-boaters, may disturb recreational riverbank anglers. In general, users with motorized equipment such as vehicles, powerboats or aircraft tend to disturb those without; users with livestock or wheeled equipment, such as horse riders and mountain bikers, may disturb those without, notably hikers; and users who disturb wildlife, such as trail runners or joggers, may disturb those who want to watch wildlife. There is now an extensive literature analysing such conflicts, and land managers have various ways to separate different user groups in either time or space.

Legal and commercial issues

The third type of consideration for the landowner or land manager is the commercial aspects of any permits issued. These may include, for example, the legal mandate of a land management agency, or the planning and land-use controls affecting a private landowner; potential legal liabilities of various types; any contractual obligations to other users or to other stakeholders such as land trusts; and finally, the actual fees charged, the costs and mechanisms for collecting them, and the additional costs incurred by the landowner or land manager in permitting commercial tourism operations.

These aspects are by no means straightforward. From a commercial perspective, fees and charges to run commercial tourism operations on land owned by someone else are akin to a lease or rental payment. Unlike rents and leases for commercial or residential property, however, or even private-sector agricultural agistment arrangements, access and activity fees for outdoor tourism are not set in a freely clearing competitive market. To take one simple example, in some jurisdictions the potential legal liability of landowners or land management agencies for any injuries incurred during specified types of outdoor recreation on that land, is limited by statute. In others, it is not, so the landowner must obtain an enforceable indemnity from the tour operator against any potential claims from its clients, or must obtain its own insurance against any such claims and pass the premium costs on to the tour operator, or both. As another example, if a private landowner is negotiating access and activity arrangements with a commercial tour operator, and that same tour operator could also obtain a permit to use a nearby area under public land tenure where such fees are subsidized by public funds, that is likely to limit what the private landowner can charge.

In public lands such as forestry areas that are also used for primary production, tourism and recreation may be seen principally as public relations exercises, and fees cross-subsidized by timber sales. This is not necessarily the case, however, and some forestry agencies now generate many times more revenue from commercial tourism than from commercial logging.

In publicly owned protected areas, there is a somewhat different set of complexities, relating principally to distinctions between independent recreational visitors, and commercial tourism operations. Most protected areas allow a range of low-impact recreational activities and provide considerable publicly funded infrastructure to help visitors enjoy the parks' natural environments. They may charge entry and camping fees, but such fees cover only a small proportion of the total costs of visitor infrastructure, let alone the total costs of managing the park. If commercial tour operators can gain access to protected areas and their visitor infrastructure under the same conditions and at the same cost as private visitors, then they can gain a considerable financial advantage, since they do not have to pay the full commercial cost of land and infrastructure. It is therefore not surprising that outdoor tour operators, and their industry associations and government representatives, continually lobby for commercial tourism operations to have access to public protected areas and other public lands. Effectively, such access represents a public subsidy to commercial enterprises.

Invalid political arguments

There are at least four conceptually distinct arguments, none of them valid, which are put forward by tourism industry proponents who want guaranteed rights of access to public protected areas for commercial tourism operations. The first is that other industry sectors such as farming and forestry have historically been allocated extensive areas of land, and the tourism industry is now economically larger than either of these. While this may provide an argument for reallocating land from forestry or farming to tourism, however, it does not provide any justification for commercial tourism access in protected areas. The second argument is that the private sector has greater skills and experience than the public sector in running profitable businesses. This, however, does not provide any reason why parks agencies should hand over profit-making opportunities to the private sector, particularly since parks provide visitor facilities as a public service, not as a commercial enterprise. The third argument is that visiting a protected area may convert people into political lobbyists in favour of parks. There seems to be no evidence, however, that this actually happens; even if it does, it provides a justification to encourage private visitors, not necessarily commercial tourism operations. The fourth argument is that commercial tour clients are essentially no different from independent visitors, except that they have paid for a guide to accompany them. In reality, however, there may be several significant differences. The legal relationship between a parks agency and a tour operator, and between a parks agency and a tour client, is different than between a parks agency and an independent visitor. The political relationship between protected area management agencies and a large industry sector is different than between the same agency and independent individuals. Finally, people in large groups generally do not behave in the same way as smaller groups or individuals.

Successful approaches

In most parts of the world, commercial tourism operations are part of the portfolio of visitors to public protected areas, and this is certainly likely to continue. There may indeed be circumstances under which commercial tourism operations can help management agencies to provide recreational opportunities, and sometimes also to achieve conservation aims. There are good arguments that public land management agencies need to understand the commercial aspects of running a tourism operation in order to design and manage their permitting and zoning systems effectively. These arguments, however, do not create any particular right of access to protected areas or other public lands, by commercial tour operators or the tourism industry more generally. To gain such access, therefore, a tour operator will generally need to demonstrate to the land management agency that its proposed operations: will comply with the agency's own management plans and goals, will create minimum marginal impacts, and if possible, will assist the agency in its conservation goals, its recreation goals or both.

Fee structures

For commercial tourism operations on private land, or large-scale tourism developments on public land, commercial arrangements are typically negotiated individually and are rarely published. For smaller scale tours on public lands, especially public protected areas, there is generally a standard schedule of charges, which is publicly available. Both the structures and the amounts of such fees, however, differ considerably between countries, between different agencies in each country, and sometimes between different individual parks or regions. Generally, such fees include two components: a fixed annual application or renewal fee, and recurrent fees charged per person, per person per day, per vehicle per day, etc. for entry, overnight camping and/or particular activities. Where similar recurrent fees are charged for individual visitors, these usually provide a benchmark for the recurrent fees charged for commercial tour clients. In some cases, however, the latter may be charged either a higher or lower fee, depending on the type of tour and the policies of the agency concerned.

Permit fees charged to commercial tour operators by parks agencies in Australia, for example, include: application fees ranging from US$50 to US$300; annual fees up to US$2000 but commonly <US$300; and entrance fees per client equal or similar to those charged for private recreational visitors (Buckley *et al.*, 2003b). These fees are minuscule relative to the commercial benefits received. Similar reviews have been carried out under the aegis of the Recreation Fee Demonstration Program in the USA (Watson, 1999). An international comparison was carried out by Lindberg (2001a) on behalf of The International Ecotourism Society some years ago.

Special stipulations

In addition to all the considerations above, permits and licensing arrangements for commercial tourism operations in protected areas and other public lands, often contain a set of stipulations requiring: operators to carry specified equipment; guides to possess specified skills and qualifications; and both staff and clients to observe particular environmental management practices. Such stipulations may cover, for example, use or prohibition of fires or firearms; procedures for disposing of human waste; and quarantine rules for vehicles, livestock and humans. In some areas, there are also mandatory requirements to carry particular safety equipment, such as capsicum spray in areas with a history of aggressive confrontations between bears and backcountry hikers. In most cases, the conditions applied for commercial tourism operations will be similar to those applied for individual visitors, except that in the case of a group, only the guide may be required to carry safety equipment. There are also instances where commercial tour operators have permits to carry out activities such as climbing or abseiling, which may be banned for the general public.

Physical access

Physical access to an operating area is as critical as legal access. For many commercial ecotours, this presents no difficulty since the operating areas are accessible on paved or formed public roads and have paved public parking areas. For many of the more remote or adventurous tours, however, the logistics of access are a major part of the tour's design and cost structure, and may be one major reason why clients purchase commercial tours rather than attempting the same trip independently. There are game and wildlife-watching lodges reached only by light plane, river rafting put-ins accessible only by helicopter, islands accessible only by boat, remote desert regions reached in a convoy of four-wheel-drive vehicles, lakes reached by floatplane, and many mountainous and other areas reached only on foot or sometimes on horseback.

Often there may be different options at different costs. Most backcountry hikers, mountaineers and rock climbers, for example, get to their favourite areas on foot; but more recently, some have started using helicopters instead. Cash-rich, time-poor skiers, snowboarders, scuba divers, game fishers and perhaps even surfers, may send a luxury charter vessel to their preferred playground and then have themselves flown in by floatplane or helicopter. Such approaches, however, are very much the exception rather than the rule, and fall within the realm of adventure rather than ecotourism.

Client logistics

For the vast majority of ecotours, the principal issue for managing access is to synchronize the collection or arrival of clients, in either their own transport or a tour operator minibus, with that of guides and equipment. For local tours, this may be as simple as specifying a meeting time and place, and making sure that the lead guide has contact phone numbers for all the clients in case one does not show up. For tours that include several intermediate transport steps between an international gateway and the actual operational site, a tour operator has to decide whether to: package the domestic and local transport into the product price; leave individual clients to make all their own travel arrangements; or arrange all the clients' travel but charge separately from the tour itself. In some cases, lodges and local tour operators may have special arrangements or even cross-ownership with local airlines or air charter businesses, so that there are commercial as well as logistic advantages in making clients' travel arrangements. For tours that are run only once or twice a year and use specialist equipment, there may be an additional incentive to make sure that everyone travels on the same plane, because group equipment can then be divided between the clients and carried as checked baggage so as to avoid freight charges.

Conclusions

Gaining access to a suitable operating area may be extremely straightforward or remarkably complex, depending on the activity and land tenure. Physical access may simply involve driving up and walking in, or it may require expedition vessels and helicopters. Legal access may be open to anyone, or may require a complex set of permits, and it may be free, or costly. These issues influence where commercial ecotourism enterprises choose to operate, and what they charge their clients.

RESEARCH

Tools for managing tourist access and activities in protected areas have been described, analysed and categorized in a number of well-known books on park and wilderness management. Examples include Hammit and Cole (1997), Pigram and Sundell (1997), Butler and

Boyd (2000), Eagles and McCool (2002), Hendee and Dawson (2002), Buckley *et al.* (2003a), Lockwood *et al.* (2006) and Pigram and Jenkins (2006).

The issues have also been reviewed and discussed by, e.g. Brown (1989), Jim (1989), Cole and Hendee (1990), Heberlein *et al.* (1996), Manning *et al.* (1996), McCool and Stankey (2001) and Manning (2004). Zoning approaches have been considered by Leung and Marion (1999), McIntyre *et al.* (2001) and Lusseau and Higham (2004). Techniques that rely on limiting numbers, e.g. through carrying-capacity approaches, have been critiqued by Lindberg *et al.* (1996), Buckley (1999d), McCool and Lime (2001) and McCool and Stankey (2001), and illustrated by Symmonds *et al.* (2000). McCool and Lime (2001) for example, describe the carrying-capacity approach as 'a seductive fiction, a social trap, or a policy myth'. Approaches that rely on education have been described by Mallick and Driessen (2003), and tested by Medio *et al.* (1997) and Littlefair (2004). The role of marketing and demarketing is considered by Beeton and Benfield (2002) in Australia and Kastenholz (2004) in Portugal. The actual behaviour of small tourism operators in UK national parks has been examined by Dewhurst and Thomas (2003). Responses to various charges and regulations by recreational anglers in Yellowstone National Park, USA have been compared by Kerkvliet and Nowell (2000). Relations between tour operators and regulatory agencies were examined recently by Russell *et al.* (2008).

Monitoring is an essential component of any strategy to manage commercial tourism operations in protected areas, whether it relies on rangers (Gray and Kalpers, 2005), researchers or community involvement (Freeman, 2004). The role and use of monitoring data have been reviewed recently by Moore *et al.* (2003), Buckley and King (2003), Pullin *et al.* (2004), Danielsen *et al.* (2005 a, b) and Hadwen *et al.* (2007, 2008). Pullin *et al.* (2004), for example, found that in the UK 'the majority of conservation actions remain experience-based', with little use of scientific evidence. Individual case studies are summarized in Table 12.1.

REVISION

Component of ecotourism products

- Every tour needs an operating area
- Commonly the area is a key component of the attraction
- Operators need permission for entrance and activities
- As commercial tour, not as private individuals

Types of tenure in use

- International protected areas: World Heritage, Biosphere Reserves
- National protected areas: national parks and marine parks
- Other public lands, e.g. USFS Wilderness Areas
- Multiple-use land, e.g. public forests, rangeland, rivers

Table 12.1. Case studies, monitoring tourism in parks.

Continent and country	Region, ecosystem or feature	Reference
Africa		
Kenya	All parks	Olindo *et al.* (1991)
Americas		
Canada	Bow Valley, Banff	Ritchie (1998)
USA	Wilderness	McCool and Stankey (2001)
USA	Campsites	Cole (1981, 2004)
USA	New Jersey West	Burger *et al.* (1995)
Cayman Islands	Stingray tourism	Shackley (1998b)
Europe	Protected areas	Simpson (1996)
Asia		
China	Tianmushan National Park	Li (2004)
Oceania		
Australia	Western Australia parks	Dowling and Sharp (1997)
Australia	Western Australia whalesharks	Davis *et al.* (1997)
Australia	Michaelmas Cay, Queensland	Muir (1993)
Australia	North New South Wales rafting	Buultjens and Davis (2001)
Australia	Tasmania WHAs	Bennett *et al.* (2003)
Australia	Australian Alps	Pickering *et al.* (2007); Hadwen *et al.* (2007, 2008)
New Zealand	National	McIntyre *et al.* (2001)
New Zealand	Dolphins	Lusseau and Higham (2004)
Sub Antarctic	Islands	Hall and Wouters (1994)
Global	WHAs	UNEP/UNESCO (1993)
	WHAs	Shackley (1998c)
	Caves	Cigna (1993)
	Coasts	Carlson and Godfrey (1989)

WHAs, World Heritage Areas

- Local-government areas, e.g. beaches, lakes
- Private conservation reserves, including riverine rights
- Private farmland and other private landholdings
- Areas controlled by international treaty: Antarctic, High Seas

Access issues

- Who, what, when, where
- Fees and permits
- Particular requirements and prohibitions
- Commercial cf. non-commercial use
- Comparison across jurisdictions
- Differences between tenures
- Conflicts between different types of use
- Competition among similar users
- Quotas and preference systems

Who, what, when, where

- Generally, who has permission to enter which areas
- Under what circumstances
- To carry out what activities
- At what times of year or day
- In which particular sites
- All of these aspects may be controlled in detail
- Standardized cf. negotiated systems

Motorized use, livestock, paddlers, hikers

- Some protected areas off limits for all recreation
- Some allow hikers only
- Some allow canoeists and kayakers, some don't
- Some allow mountain bikes, some only on trails, some not at all
- Similarly for horses, llamas, etc.
- Motorized access especially controversial
- Generally allowed in large flat parks, e.g. in arid areas
- Not in smaller mountain areas
- However, many US national parks have road access
- And some allow snowmobiles in winter

Fees and permits

- Can be very simple or very complex
- Commonly, entry fees and permits are separate from activity fees and permits
- Commercial operations distinguished from individual recreational visitors
- May have more or fewer rights
- May pay higher or lower fees

Fee and permit systems worldwide

- Different systems in different countries
- Some charge high fees, some zero
- Many developing countries charge differential fees for foreigners
- International review of fee systems
- Recreation Fee Demonstration Program in the USA
- Detailed review of Australian parks systems

Fees and permit systems, Australian parks

- Australian parks: different in each state
- Different combinations of fees per vehicle, per person
- Various single-entry, short-stay, season-pass fees
- Passes for single, several, or all-state parks
- Camping fees combine per site, per vehicle, per person
- Separate fees, e.g. for commercial photography

Particular requirements

- For example, skills qualifications to lead outdoor activities
- Insurance requirements for tour operators
- First-aid requirements for trip leaders
- Self-contained toilets or bags on some trips
- Fire bans at river rafting campsites
- Safety equipment, e.g. compass or GPS
- Nosebags for feeding livestock

Particular prohibitions

- For example, no fires at particular places, times
- No fixed bolts at many climbing routes
- No powered watercraft in many river stretches, especially in some seasons
- No firearms in many protected areas

Commercial cf. non-commercial use

- Legal distinction irrespective of group size, activity
- Access for private recreation does not imply right of access for commercial tour
- Permit systems are generally different
- For some sites and uses, tour operators have preferential access
- For some, tour operators have pre-allocated quota
- For example, river rafting on Colorado Grand Canyon

- Competitive events and training programmes may also be commercial uses
- Conflicts if local recreational users can't access favourite sites

Comparison across jurisdictions

- Different countries, states have different access control
- For example horses allowed in many parks in the USA but few in Australia
- Commonly reflects historical uses
- In Australia, different access conditions for national parks in different states
- Developed countries may be either more or less expensive than developing countries

Differences between tenures

- Protected areas commonly have relatively detailed and stringent access controls
- Other public lands may have either more or less access
- For example some public forests open to four-wheel-drives, horses, fires; others closed
- Cf. USFS Wilderness Areas, managed similarly to parks
- Areas managed by local governments have highly variable access rules and rights
- Access controls may be changed at short notice
- For private land, most access is at landholder discretion
- Except for public rights of way in some countries
- Landholders may be concerned about carelessness, liability, privacy
- Therefore may allow access only to organized clubs with insurance and controlled activities

Conflict between uses

- Well-researched topic
- Most common conflicts between motorized and non-motorized use
- For example jetskis cf. surfers, motorized cf. oar rafts
- Snowmobiles cf. cross-country skiers
- Also between hikers and horse riders, mountain bikers
- Issues of safety, peacefulness, aesthetics
- Asymmetry in conflicts: hikers suffer but don't inflict impacts
- Conflicts also between consumptive and non-consumptive uses
- For example hunters cf. hikers, anglers cf. kayakers
- Each restricts opportunities for others
- Conflicts between motorized users, e.g. heliski cf. snowmobile
- Due to competitive consumption of resource – fresh powder

Managing conflicts between user groups

- Most common approach is to separate them
- For example different zones, trails, camps, seasons

- Separation may be by regulation or differential attraction
- And/or by marketing/demarketing
- Educational approaches to reduce social impacts also common
- But generally less successful
- High-impact tour operators may seek private land
- Lobby groups well developed, especially in the USA
- For example Blue Ribbon Coalition

Competition among users

- Whenever recreational resources are scarce
- Resources include quiet, solitude, wilderness
- Crowding selects for different users
- Recreational succession, 'Disneyfication'
- Frontcountry crowding produces indirect backcountry impacts
- Land managers' tools to control crowding and competition
- Quotas, group size limits, advance booking, demarketing
- Also physical access and infrastructure limits
- Competition includes private cf. commercial
- Many examples: rafting campsites, kayak playholes, surf breaks, climbing routes, hiking trails

Managing crowding and competition at individual sites

- Carrying-capacity concepts: social, economic, environmental
- Shortcomings of carrying-capacity approaches
- Quota systems: establishment, allocation, operation
- Advance bookings via permit systems
- On-arrival allocation, e.g. to backcountry hiking areas
- Group size limits as adjunct to quotas: widely used

Quota allocation systems

- Fixed cf. variable
- Grandfathering: fixed quota based on past use
- Competitive tendering: highest bid gets quota
- First-in: electronic or telephone bookings
- On arrival: can't book till you get there
- Lottery: pre-register, random allocations
- Stratified lottery: random within groups, years, etc.

Defining quotas

- How broadly or narrowly defined is the site?
- For example a whole mountain, a single pegged campsite

- How broadly or narrowly defined is the time?
- For example a year, a season, a single day, a short time bracket
- How broadly or narrowly defined is the activity?
- Access for any activity, cf. highly detailed specifications

Examples of tightly defined systems

- Boat cruises in the Galapagos Islands
- Summer raft trips on many US rivers
- Hiking and backcountry camping in many national parks
- Including heavily used parks in Australia, Canada, New Zealand, the USA

Setting and taking up quotas

- Converting a general concept to a legal management number
- Estimates rely on understanding of likely impacts
- Also on intended visitor experience
- Preferable not to allocate all estimated quota initially
- In case estimates proved too generous

Latency

- Particular problem if not all allocated quota taken up at first
- So when impacts are detected, too late to recall quota
- This problem is known as latency
- Can be addressed by use-it-or-lose it policy
- Or by increasing fees and charging for unused quota

Enforcing quota

- Needs on-ground or on-water patrols
- Or aerial surveillance in some cases
- Can be deputized to volunteers, tour operators, other users
- But they need regulatory backup

REFLECTIONS

1. What, if any, are the critical differences between access to a national park or similar protected area for private recreation by a group of friends visiting as individuals, a group of children on an organized school outing, or a commercial ecotour? What are the differences from the perspective of the park management agency compared with the perspective of an individual participant? Explain why these distinctions might be important, and why.

2. Imagine that you are the owner of a large farm, ranch, station, estancia, etc. used principally for livestock grazing, but that also includes areas of native vegetation, opportunities for various ecotourism or adventure tourism activities, and a small site containing prehistoric artefacts protected by law. Individual friends and neighbours, non-profit clubs and commercial tour operators have all asked your permission for access to your land. What issues would you need to consider in deciding whether to grant access, to whom, and under what circumstances? What approach would you use to check that your requirements were being followed?

3. Using their websites, check access rules for horses, mountain bikes and off-road vehicles in national parks and other public lands in at least three different countries (e.g. Canada, the USA, Australia). How do these rules differ between individual parks, between parks and other public lands, and between countries? How might such differences have arisen? Are they logical, in view of the environmental impacts and management considerations for the activities concerned? If not, why not?

4. Some areas allow access for various types of outdoor tourist activity, but prohibit particular practices or equipment. For example, they may allow rockclimbing but prohibit fixed bolts or boltguns; they may allow bowhunting but not firearms; or they may allow fishing, but only catch-and-release using barbless hooks. Identify an example of such a restriction on access for a particular activity and explain: (i) why it was imposed; (ii) how it is enforced; and (iii) how successful it may be.

5. Many areas allow access for particular activities only at specific sites or in particular zones. Name four possible reasons for such restrictions, and give two examples of each.

READING 12.1. PRINCIPLES FOR TOURISM IN PROTECTED AREAS

Ecotourism businesses need accessible natural environments, and many of them are in national parks or other protected areas, but the parks were set up for conservation and public recreation, not tourism. So how should they deal with commercial tour operators? Market to them, keep them out, ignore them, licence them, charge them, compete with them, restrict them, form partnerships with them? Or perhaps all of the above, in different times and places and circumstances? In practice, the politics are complex, and different in every country, but the same issues arise repeatedly, and there are some basic principles that can be applied broadly. These are listed below and then examined in more detail.

Preamble

- No economy without environment.
- Sustainability is a social process.
- Parks are critical for conservation.

- Parks are underfunded.
- Tourism is a large industry.
- Tourism in parks is growing.
- Parks are valuable for tourism.
- Tourism is fundamentally different from recreation.
- Tourism can provide recreational experiences.
- Tour operators can provide valuable visitor interpretation.
- Parks-use conflicts are increasingly commonplace.
- Commercial tourism in public parks is a politically charged issue.
- Parks and tourism have different goals.
- Commercial agreements aren't automatically win–win.
- These principles are for IUCN Category II protected areas.

Principles

- Parks are for conservation first.
- Parks are for recreation second.
- Only low-impact recreation should be in parks.
- Tourism has no special right to parks.
- Planning for parks and tourism needs a regional ecosystem approach.
- Partnerships need consent not coercion.
- Any user fees should reflect management costs including conservation impacts.
- Tourism facilities in parks should provide a net benefit for conservation.
- Commercial tour operators should meet all the costs they impose on parks.
- Commercial tour operators should pay a resource rent.
- Marketing should match park plans.
- Parks agencies need a range of staff skills.

Supporting information – preamble

No economy without environment. Technological inventiveness gives the human species enormous adaptability to changing environmental conditions at a local scale. At a global scale, however, the human species is entirely dependent on the natural environment for air, water, food, warmth, shelter and ultimately survival. Conservation, in the sense of maintaining a functioning planetary ecosystem, is hence the single most critical priority facing human societies. Ultimately, the entire human economy and the whole of human society is underpinned by the natural environment.

Sustainability is a social process. The practicalities of conserving natural environments, however, depend upon human social structures and individual behaviour, i.e. on the human environment including economic and other social factors. Sustainable development is therefore conceptualized as a triple bottom line: environmental, economic, social.

Parks are critical for conservation. National Parks and other protected areas, though not sufficient on their own, are the single most critical core components in global conservation of biodiversity.

Parks are underfunded. Public funding for many parks agencies has failed to keep pace with increasing visitor numbers and management costs, and the agencies are being compelled to recoup part of these costs from visitors and tour operators.

Tourism is a large industry. While precise figures depend on definitions and differ between countries, overall the tourism and travel sector makes up around 10% of the global economy. It is a huge and varied sector, a major earner of foreign exchange in many countries, and a major source of employment in rural and regional economies as well as cities and gateways.

Tourism in parks is growing. The scale and scope of commercial tourism activities in public protected areas continues to increase. This reflects three broad social trends: increasing total visitor numbers in parks; increasing range of recreational activities in parks; and increasing proportion of outdoor recreation carried out through commercial tour operators.

Parks are valuable for tourism. The natural environment provides major tourism attractions in the form of scenery, wildlife and wild flowers, and opportunities for outdoor activities. While these attractions may occur on land under various private or public tenures, in most countries the best known and most accessible are in public national parks. Parks provide commercial opportunities for tourism entrepreneurs in the form of high-quality attractions with publicly funded access, infrastructure and marketing. They also provide major international market differentiation between tourism destinations.

Tourism is fundamentally different from recreation. Using parks for commercial profit differentiates commercial tourism operations from individual recreation, even if the activities are identical. There are three particularly important differences: (i) legal obligations and liabilities are very different, especially in the event of personal injury or environmental impacts. This is one reason why commercial tourism operations need permits in almost all protected area systems. (ii) Duties of protected area management agencies towards the general public, such as equity of access, do not necessarily apply to commercial entities such as tour operators. Even where a particular park allows a particular recreational activity by individuals, this implies no obligation to allow similar activities by tour operators. (iii) Tourism is an industry, which provides employment and income and maintains political lobbying organizations. If activities by individual visitors cause impacts in a particular area, parks agencies can close the area or restrict the activities. Where impacts are caused by commercial tourism, however, it is often extremely difficult for parks agencies to restrict their access or activities, not only because of contractual obligations, but because of political lobbying.

Tourism can provide recreational experiences. Because of large-scale social changes, an increasing number of people prefer to purchase guided and packaged nature and adventure tours, rather than undertaking the same activities as an individual. This commodification of recreation provides commercial opportunities for tour operators. Such tours can provide experiences of natural and cultural environments to people who might otherwise not enjoy them. However, they need not necessarily be in public protected areas; they may well be on private land or other public lands.

Tour operators can provide valuable visitor interpretation. Commercial tour operators have a valuable role to play in presenting and interpreting natural areas to visitors, as long as their activities are consistent with management objectives for particular protected areas.

Park-use conflicts are increasingly commonplace. Interactions, competition and sometimes conflicts between conservation, public recreation and commercial tourism in national parks are becoming increasingly frequent in most countries. The same applies for conflicts between different recreational user groups, particularly between types of use with different levels of impact, such as those with motorized vehicles or livestock, and those without. Criteria are therefore needed to establish priorities for different uses in cases of conflict.

Commercial tourism in public parks is a politically charged issue. Many people in democratically governed nations hold strong opinions in regard to the use of publicly funded parks for private profit.

Parks and tourism have different goals. The primary goal of private entrepreneurs is profit, in tourism as in any other industry sector. It is unrealistic to expect that a private profit-making entity would share the same goals as a public authority charged with broad and long-term responsibilities on behalf of an entire state, nation or the whole world.

Commercial agreements aren't automatically win–win. Commercial agreements between parks agencies and tour operators can be beneficial to both under appropriate conditions, but these conditions will not occur automatically. Without appropriate principles, the current political context in some countries risks a 'political firesale' of public protected areas to private commercial interests, or at best, continual conflicts and ad hoc decisions.

These principles are for IUCN Category II protected areas. The principles for tourism in protected areas proposed below are relevant to national parks in the sense most commonly used worldwide, i.e. at a level of protection equivalent to the World Conservation Union (IUCN) Category II, 'Ecosystem conservation and recreation'. Purpose, priorities and principles are different for other IUCN categories, and for private land, land reserved for indigenous peoples and First Nations, and for public land under other forms of tenure, such as forestry, farming or unallocated Crown land.

Supporting information – principles

Parks are for conservation first. The highest value of protected areas to human societies and economies is in maintaining supplies of breathable air, drinkable water and living biological diversity. Environmental conservation and ecological integrity are recognized as the highest management priorities in the establishing legislation for protected area systems in most countries and jurisdictions. Even where conservation is not the top priority in law, however, it is none the less the most valuable function of protected areas.

Parks are for recreation second. Recreation has major value for physical, mental and emotional health and well-being of individuals. Public recreation is the second highest value use of protected areas for human societies and economies.

Only low-impact recreation should be in parks. There is now a very large global outdoor recreation industry, which overlaps the clothing, specialist equipment manufacturing, entertainment and real estate sectors. Many forms of outdoor recreation, however, involve large-scale fixed infrastructure, motorized equipment, or horses and other riding animals or packstock, all of which can produce relatively high impacts on the natural environment and other park users. The same applies for some forms of non-motorized recreational equipment in some ecosystems, depending on the level of use and behaviour of the visitors. Recreation is a valuable use of parks, but where recreation conflicts with primary conservation values, its type, timing, location and intensity must be managed to limit impacts. Management may include educational approaches.

Tourism has no special right to parks. Tourism interests have no preferential right of access or operation in protected areas, except as granted by the land management agency. Tourism operations in parks are a privilege, not a right. Tourism can be one valuable use of protected areas, but this is not the primary function of protected areas, and the social value of tourism is less than the value of conservation and public recreation.

Planning for parks and tourism needs a regional ecosystem approach. (i) Protected areas are the single most critical component in biodiversity conservation, but conservation measures are also needed outside parks, e.g. for additional habitat area, for animal corridors and to reduce impacts on parks. (ii) Parks are often icon attractions for nature tourism, but tourism accommodation and transport infrastructure are generally outside the park; many tourism activities and opportunities can be provided on other public and private lands nearby, and marketable tourism products generally require a suite of potential experiences of which activities in the park will be only one. (iii) High-impact industrial or residential development near parks commonly affects both conservation and tourism. (iv) The economic significance of nature and adventure tours is commonly small compared with that of associated resort–residential development, and this in turn is small compared with the economic scale of amenity migration in some regions. Where amenity migration is a significant factor, long-term economic effects of parks on neighbouring land values far outweigh short-term effects through tourism revenues.

Partnerships need consent not coercion. Partnerships between protected area management agencies and private commercial tourism interests can provide benefits for both, in some circumstances, but only where all parties can decide freely whether to enter into any such partnership, and can negotiate freely on the terms of any agreement. Such agreements need to recognize that the aims and interests of tour operators and protected area management agencies may be very different, and provide for each to assist the other in reaching those different goals, without threatening the core priorities of either: i.e. ecosystem conservation and public recreation opportunities by protected area agencies, and commercial viability for tourism operations.

Any user fees should reflect management costs including conservation impacts. In different parks and jurisdictions, there are commonly social, economic and legal arguments both for and against the imposition of user fees of various possible types, rates and applicability. The costs of managing a protected area for visitors include the costs of conservation management as well as the direct costs of visitor management and infrastructure. In some cases – e.g. the effects of accommodation on water quality – it is possible to distinguish impacts and management costs associated with commercial tourism, public recreation, and other anthropogenic influences both current and historical. In other cases – e.g. weed control – it may be very difficult to make such a distinction. Most protected area management agencies are public authorities that receive public funding to provide public benefits. Public benefits include conservation and public recreational opportunities. Commercial tourism is a private benefit, but where the activities are similar to public recreation, the management costs may be hard to differentiate. Similar considerations apply, for example, to use of the public road network by vehicles used by individual or commercial transport respectively. Arguably, commercial users of protected areas should meet the full incremental or marginal management costs associated with that commercial use. In practice, however: (i) these costs are hard to define precisely; and (ii) some small-scale commercial tours, though clearly distinct from private recreation in a legal sense, may be almost indistinguishable in a social sense. In practice, therefore, a system of commercial permits for smaller operators, and negotiated partnership agreements for larger operators, is generally the most workable approach. Any such system, however, must respect the overriding authority of the protected area management agency to determine whether commercial tourism is permitted and, if so, under what conditions. It must also maintain the overriding management priority of ecosystem conservation.

Tourism facilities in parks should provide a net benefit for conservation. For example, facilities may decrease the impacts of existing uses or projected future uses, or provide educational opportunities that lead users to reduce their lifestyle environmental impacts.

Commercial tour operators should meet all the costs they impose on parks. This includes the costs of: (i) providing for their operations; (ii) monitoring compliance with permit conditions and possible impacts; and (iii) remediation of any impacts detected.

Commercial tour operators should pay a resource rent. That is, they should provide a return to the public, via protected area management agencies, for the privilege of conducting a private business using a public resource.

Marketing should match park plans. Permit conditions for commercial tourism in protected areas should include restrictions on marketing materials. This is needed to ensure that both the protected area and the tourism operation are presented accurately, and to allow strategic use of marketing as one component in visitor management.

Parks agencies need a range of staff skills. Protected area agencies need staff with specialist skills in visitor management and perhaps also tourism, economics and marketing, as well as ecology and natural resource management.

Acknowledgements

A first version of these principles was presented to the Australian Academy of Science Fenner Conference on Nature Tourism and the Environment, Canberra, Australia, in September 2001. Several revised versions have been published subsequently, e.g. by Buckley (2002e), in the *Journal of Ecotourism* 1, 75–80.

chapter 13

POLICY AND PLANNING

Ecotourism student group in Chitwan National Park, southern Nepal. Photo courtesy of Khalifa al Khalifa.

REVIEW

Introduction

Ecotourism planning has gradually grown in importance as the ecotourism sector has grown in scale. Local areas and entire countries, as well as individual national parks and similar areas, now have their own ecotourism plans and strategies. The focus of such strategies varies in line with their functions. Those produced by tourism promotion agencies typically concentrate on marketing, whereas those produced by land management agencies typically feature the spatial distribution of different activities. Plans produced by mixed stakeholder groups often focus on infrastructure, since this is a shared interest.

This chapter considers the policy contexts for ecotourism planning by relevant government agencies, at various spatial scales. Industry associations commonly provide input to such plans, but ultimately, policy and planning are principally government functions.

It is worth noting a rather different use of planning phraseology in the concept of ecotourism programme planning (Fennell, 2002), which refers to the design of ecotourism experiences as part of a single ecotourism product, whether commercial or non-profit. In this usage, the emphasis is on the various practical and psychological stages associated with an ecotourism experience, including periods before, during and after the actual tour itself, and on how the tour operator can plan a programme to maximize what the participants get out of the experience. These aspects are not examined in this chapter.

Basic features of ecotourism plans

A variety of similar ecotourism, nature-based tourism and adventure tourism plans have been produced by government agencies in different parts of the world (Buckley *et al.*, 2001b). Many of these plans fail because they are put together by agencies that do not have the legal mandate or the funding to implement them. Others are overshadowed by master plans and marketing programmes for the tourism industry more generally, which rarely consider ecotourism principles and may not even incorporate ecotourism strategies produced by the same agency (Buckley, 2004k). In addition, the intentions of ecotourism plans may be frustrated by large-scale developments, either in tourism or in other industry sectors, approved without reference to the ecotourism plan.

Key features of ecotourism plans that are effective and successful at national scale may be summarized as follows (Buckley, 2004k). Perhaps the overarching issue is that land-use planning needs to consider all land uses simultaneously, to ensure that adequate areas are set aside for conservation and tourism and protected from damage by other industry sectors. For example, land-use plans need to protect water and sea, especially rivers and coastal waters, against industrial and agricultural pollution. Plans need to provide for full conservation of existing protected areas including national parks and reserves, with adequate management funding, and they generally need to establish new areas for tourism and conservation, with basic management funds. They need to provide protection for wildlife, including measures against poaching, and measures for rescue and conservation of the endangered species that form a primary tourist attraction. This may include joint lobbying, information gathering, education and local community development projects by tourism and conservation interests, to overcome wildlife poaching and illegal trade in endangered species and body parts.

Typically, ecotourism plans will also provide for international marketing of natural and cultural heritage as a basis for a globally competitive tourism sector, and local marketing of natural and cultural attractions, to establish tourist expectations that can be satisfied. Plans need to provide for adequate environmental management within the tourism industry, to minimize its impacts on the natural and cultural environment on which it depends. In most countries, this includes independent environmental impact assessment, managed by the environment portfolio, for major tourism developments in any geographical area or land tenure. At a national scale, an effective ecotourism plan is likely to need routine processes and criteria, including environmental criteria, for screening investments in tourism development and infrastructure, and routine systems for public environmental reporting and performance monitoring of tourism operators.

Plans may include components for environmental audit and certification of tourism developers, operators and tour guides, and guidelines or regulations for best practice environmental design, technology and management. They may include incentives, awards and perhaps tax concessions for tourism companies with high levels of environmental performance, and penalties for poor environmental performance, such as fines, cancellation of operating permits or exclusion from national marketing programmes. Particularly in protected areas, plans may involve user charges to fund public costs of managing tourism including environmental monitoring. Finally, plans may include environmental education both by and within the tourism sector, to generate respect for nature and culture within domestic as well as international tourists.

The policy contexts for these various components are considered below, commencing at a broad national level across all land tenures, and finally focusing on national parks and protected areas where planning for commercial ecotourism is particularly critical.

Broad policy instruments

Environmental policy instruments relevant to tourism may be considered in three main categories: prescriptive or regulatory, economic or market-based, and advisory or suasive. Prescriptive instruments include laws and regulation at all levels of government, notably in relation to land-use planning, development approval, environmental impact assessment, waste management and pollution control. In addition to statutes that refer specifically to environmental issues as above, broader laws relating to directors' duties, lender liability and insurance are also relevant, together with corporate and individual liabilities under laws of contract, tort and nuisance.

Economic and market-based measures include, for example: direct grants and government budget allocations to particular programmes, made at the discretion of elected officials or their government representatives; competitive grant programmes within particular portfolios, with a more formal structure and longer duration; and a wide range of environmental taxes, charges, levies and rebates, which provide economic incentives for tourism corporations to improve relevant aspects of environmental management, but without placing them under a statutory obligation to do so.

Advisory or suasive instruments rely largely on non-binding plans and strategies, guidelines, publicly funded marketing campaigns, and educational programmes and material at all scales. These include: material distributed internationally, nationally, regionally and locally through television, radio, print media, mail-outs, travel agents, the internet, etc.; government-funded educational materials in schools and universities; and interpretive signs and materials produced by public land management agencies.

In practice, governments rely largely on: direct funding of management and mitigation works by nature conservation agencies; educational and interpretative material in conservation reserves; environmental impact assessment for large-scale development projects; planning and development approval procedures for smaller tourism development projects; and competitive grant funding through government tourism portfolios, to encourage directed research, regional ecotourism planning and infrastructure development.

Multiple land use: conflicts and synergies

In some areas, tourism continues to co-exist with other land uses, rather than replacing them or being replaced – multiple rather than sequential land use. To a large degree this distinction is a question of scale: a series of sequential land-use changes, occurring at different times in small adjacent areas, means that at any given point in time the combined area will be subject to multiple land uses. Equally, a large area may be permanently zoned or subdivided into smaller areas with different land uses, so that even without sequential land use changes, the area contains a mosaic of multiple uses.

Multiple land use is a term subject to multiple misuses. At its most basic, it is simply a recognition that a parcel of land under a single land tenure does not all have to be used for the same purpose at the same time. An area of public or private land can be used partly for tourism and partly for commercial or conservation, for example. At its best, it describes a process of land capability assessment and land use planning for a combined set of sustainable economic and conservation activities. At its worst, however, it is a term used as a political sop to enable continued environmentally damaging exploitation of natural environments by a single industry sector, with lip-service alone to other potential activities.

Multiple-use management of publicly owned state and national forests provides an excellent example. Lands managed by the United States Forest Service, for example, include designated wilderness areas of high conservation value, not available for logging, and actively managed for conservation and recreation. Typically they have visitor information centres, detailed back-country maps, wilderness rangers, trailhead route registration systems and zoning to separate potentially conflicting uses such as hiking and horsepacking.

At the other end of the spectrum, however, there are public forests in other parts of the world and indeed other parts of the USA, where multiple-use principles are nominally espoused in the policies of the managing agency, but where management in practice caters entirely to logging and wood-chipping, and access for recreational or other activities is permitted only where it has no effect on logging operations. Indeed, there are public forests in Australia where access has been completely denied to the public, with police enforcement.

Intermediate between these extremes are dominant-use approaches where logging is clearly given priority, but logging operations are modified to some degree to permit other activities such as tourism to occur concurrently. The Tasmania Forestry Service, for example, issues permits for river-rafting and road-based tour operators, but with the proviso that they are in so-called working forests and tourists must expect to see logging tracks, recently cut coupes, or indeed active logging operations in train. Heliski operators in the Canadian Rockies operate principally in public forests, with some cooperation in management to provide 'glading' of heavily treed ski runs.

Similar issues occur in relation to other industry sectors. Prince William Sound, in Alaska, USA, for example, supports both commercial tourism and commercial fisheries. The commercial salmon fisheries are operated by a relatively large number of small trawlers, which fish principally in estuaries and inlets. The salmon fisheries are regulated by opening and closing particular inlets to fishing for short periods at different times of year, and when any particular area is open, it becomes extremely crowded as the fishing boats take it in turns to trawl, according to a system they have devised within the industry. At such times, the small power boats, yachts and sea kayaks, which operate most of the coastal tourism industry, are well advised to stay clear, and in that sense the fishing industry is the dominant use. Over a full year, however, any given area is open for tourism for a much longer total period than it is open for fisheries and, in practice, there appears to be little conflict. Such conflict as does occur appears to be more within the fishing industry, between local boats and boats that have come north for the season, and within the tourism industry, between large single or multi-day cruise boats and the rapidly growing seakayak sector.

Dams and river-based tourism operations provide another example. The construction of a dam, whether for water supply, flood regulation or hydroelectric power generation, modifies the recreational potential of the river concerned very considerably. Upstream, the dam forms an artificial lake, which may or may not be open to public access, and where different recreational uses such as angling, canoeing, waterskiing and even large commercial marinas may or may not be permitted. Depending on rainfall patterns and draw-down regime, the lake may have a relatively constant volume, or its height may fluctuate dramatically. River flows that were formerly controlled by rainfall and runoff patterns may now be determined principally by the dam-controlled release pattern. This in turn may depend either on demand for power, as in the case of the Glen Canyon dam on the Colorado River in Arizona, USA, or on the demand for irrigation water, as for many dams in New South Wales, Australia.

Tourism operations based on the natural scenic beauty of the river channel and surrounding areas are likely to be severely curtailed by a dam, both upstream and downstream. Those that rely on river flow, such as white water rafting and kayaking, will be affected by the change in flow regime. At one extreme, if dam releases are zero or small most days, and high-volume releases are rare and unpredictable, commercial raft companies may no longer be able to operate at all. At the other, there are examples where dam operators have been required to guarantee a minimum release volume for a specified number or set of days every year, specifically to allow continued recreational use to the river.

Overall, therefore, it is clear that concurrent use of land or water for tourism and other activities is perfectly feasible. It is also clear that a multiple-use management regime is unlikely to be equitable unless tourism receives recognition as a sector whose significance and rights are similar to any other.

Planning tools for tourism in parks

Use of National Parks, World Heritage areas and other conservation reserves for tourism and recreation continues to grow worldwide, and most national parks services and reserve management agencies now have to manage for tourism as well as conservation. Indeed, as noted in earlier chapters, in some countries the political pressures for increased tourism are making it increasingly difficult for reserve managers to maintain the primary conservation function of lands and waters under their control and responsibility. To cope with this growth, parks agencies have a range of policy, planning and management tools to address the impacts of visitors, whether individual recreation or commercial tourism (Buckley, 1998c, 1999c). In addition to physically hardening the natural environment against impacts in various ways, parks agencies may apply spatial planning approaches such as controlling tourist numbers, equipment or activities in particular areas or at particular times, or they may adopt a policy of educating visitors so that they use equipment and behave in such a way as to minimize their individual impacts.

Broadly speaking, parks agencies tend to use educational approaches at low visitor densities, spatial planning and regulation at intermediate densities, and physical engineering at highest visitor densities. Once visitor numbers have reached high levels, it is politically difficult for land managers to restrict them to lower levels. Similarly, once a particular activity or a particular type of equipment has become commonplace, it is difficult to restrict its use. Instead, park managers spend increasing proportions of their operational budgets on engineering construction and maintenance. This may include, for example, access roads, carparks, barriers, etc.; formed, gravelled, paved or duckboarded tracks and tent sites; toilets, taps, drains, etc.; tables, benches, garbage bins, fireplaces, barbecues, etc.; boat launching ramps, jetties and other special facilities.

In a few countries, notably Australia, there seems to be a perception by the tourism industry that national parks and conservation reserves are public lands allocated for tourism and recreation, whereas in fact, these lands are allocated primarily for conservation, with recreation as a secondary function. Overall, it is clear that if nature-based tourism is to continue growing as it is at present, recreational use of national parks and other reserves of highest conservation value will necessarily have to be restricted to minimal-impact activities, such as hiking, bushwalking and camping, and non-motorized means of travel such as rafts and kayaks, cross-country skis and snowshoes, etc. Higher-impact recreational activities, including those that require motorized travel, livestock or higher-impact infrastructure, will need to focus their growth in other public lands. To achieve this will require a shift in attitude in the industries concerned, and the relevant government land management agencies.

Managing tourism and recreation in other public lands

Most countries have large areas of publicly owned and managed lands in various categories, not only national parks. In many countries, there are large areas of leasehold agricultural land, e.g. in south-west USA and south-central Australia. Lessees may treat this as private property, but government management agencies often retain rights to permit public recreational use as well as private use for livestock grazing. There are state and national forests in most countries, of which only a proportion is leased to logging and wood-chipping companies at any given time. There are various categories of vacant or unallocated public or Crown land, ranging from small parcels set aside historically as part of urban and local planning procedures, through the blocks of federal lands throughout much of the western USA, to large expanses in desert and arctic areas, used by indigenous peoples but not allocated to private tenure under modern land zoning procedures. There are public lands nominally set aside for purposes such as road and rail reserves, jetties and harbours, airports, military and defence activities, etc., but not necessarily in current use for the nominated purpose. There are coastal and marine reserves, which may or may not be treated as national parks, and, at a local scale, there may be areas set aside from subdivision or construction as part of local planning procedures, e.g. wetland areas prone to flooding. All of these areas are potentially available for tourism. Of course, they will not all be attractive to tourists and tourism entrepreneurs. Some of them are already used by the tourism industry in an informal way: coastal reserves provide a good example in many countries. Others give formal recognition to tourism as one potential land use, even if it is a relatively minor one at present: rangelands and forests provide good examples.

The planning issues associated with using public land for tourism are the same as those applying to any form of multiple and sequential land use, as outlined earlier. For example, is any of the land to be allocated to tourism as a dominant long-term land use, and if so, what security will tourism operators have in order to encourage them to invest in infrastructure, new tours or facilities, or even advertising materials that feature the areas concerned? If leases to tourism operators cover the same geographical areas as leases for other commercial purposes, then what mechanisms are there to ensure the rights of each are maintained, and will they use the same access roads and other infrastructure?

If tourism is to be encouraged in a small section of a large parcel of land under government tenure, as for example in some of the USFS Wilderness Areas, or the widely spaced waterholes in the central Australian cattle country, what access will tourists have, and what measures are in place to prevent them from interfering with the principal land use? Whether justified or not, it is a common cause of complaint by pastoralists that tourists leave gates open and bring in weeds on their vehicles. Similarly, logging trucks expect an unimpeded passage down logging roads in public forests, and oil exploration vehicles expect exclusive use of seismic tracks in desert dunefields. If tourists use the same roads, complaints or accidents are likely unless there is a deliberate multi-use strategy in place.

While some public lands, such as the USFS Wilderness Areas in the USA, are effectively of similar wilderness quality and conservation value as national parks, many other public lands have been subject to impacts from land uses such as forestry or agriculture, with consequent impacts such as access roads and tracks, partial vegetation clearance, etc. Such areas may hence be well suited to higher-impact tourism and recreational activities involving, for example, vehicles, power boats, snowmobiles, mountain bikes, campfires, fishing, hunting, pack animals, pets, etc. Indeed, there are strong arguments for excluding these higher-impact activities entirely from national parks and other high-quality conservation reserves, and restricting them to other public and private lands.

In practice, the greatest difficulty in using public lands for tourism seems to be one of perception. The forestry industry perceives that it has the prerogative to log and woodchip in public forests, whereas in reality it has such rights only if the relevant government agencies grant it a lease, licence or permit. Government forestry agencies have duties to manage public forests on the public's behalf, and in many areas, recreation and tourism are preferable to logging on economic as well as social and environmental grounds (Ward, 2003).

Similarly, farmers and graziers generally perceive public leasehold farm and range land as dedicated indefinitely to farming and grazing, irrespective of potential environmental damage and low economic returns. Government land agencies responsible for such lands have taken a similar approach. It is interesting to note that where farmers have turned to tourism as a more profitable enterprise, this has almost universally been a private initiative on the part of individual farmers, typically on freehold farmland, rather than a public initiative on the part of leasehold land management agencies. Interestingly, as of late 2007 there was a controversy in New Zealand, where sheep farmers were lobbying to convert leasehold to freehold not for farming reasons, but to gain rights to recreational use and residential subdivision.

Planning for tourism growth and change

One of the more contentious planning concerns for ecotourism and related sectors is that of growth and change through positive feedback. This is known as recreational succession within the parks management literature, or tourism lifecycles within the destination development and tourism marketing literature. Essentially, it recognizes that the characteristics of individual tourist destinations change over time.

Areas that are initially unknown save to explorers, scientists or local residents gradually become known as goals for more adventurous independent travellers. Depending on the costs and difficulty of access, they may then become part of the international backpacker circuit or the target for specialist safaris or expeditions. As the number of visitors increases, local residents modify their behaviours and lifestyle either to seclude themselves, or much more commonly to profit from a fledgling tourism industry.

As soon as tourists can visit the area with a reasonable degree of safety, commercial adventure travel operators will start to offer bare-bones trips there. This leads to increased development of tourism infrastructure, and increased demand for commercial transport and accommodation from tourists who expect, and are prepared to pay for, a higher standard of comfort. That provides commercial opportunities for the development of permanent tourism accommodation on site, at gradually increasing density. To keep their businesses profitable, the owners advertise the destination to potential customers. Local entrepreneurs begin to offer tours to local attractions, and some local residents start to make their living entirely from tourism.

As tourism becomes an increasingly important component of the local economy, and tourism-related construction and urbanization increases, the local property industry, tradespeople and professionals come to depend increasingly on tourism for their continued livelihood. By this stage, the original character of the area is greatly modified, and the natural or cultural attractions that originally brought visitors to the region are replaced increasingly by urban attractions associated with the growing tourism industry itself: bars, shows, nightclubs, casinos, shopping, etc. If urban density and visitor numbers increase sufficiently, ultimately it becomes profitable to develop wholly artificial tourist attractions such as theme parks and, if these become large enough, they may ultimately take over as the primary tourist attractions for the area as a whole. The best known example of this, of course, is Disneyland in Los Angeles, now replicated elsewhere. Similarly, Australia's Gold Coast offers Sea World, Dream World, Koala World, Frozen World, Movie World, and so on.

The broad progression outlined above has been observed historically at a large number of locations. The trends occurring at a single location over time, from the smallest-scale adventure travel to the largest-scale mass tourism, parallel the patterns of segmentation within the tourist industry at any given time. Just as each individual tourism product is slightly different, however, the precise pattern of development at different sites also differs. In addition, the pattern of development at any one site is affected by the pattern of development in the world as a whole, so the development history of a remote area recently discovered by travellers is likely to be quite different from that of a remote area discovered by travellers decades or centuries ago, because of differences in transport and communications as well as changes in global politics.

Tourism destination life cycle

In its broadest form, the latter stages of the progression outlined above have been described as a tourism destination life cycle (Butler 1972, 2006). Butler's model, which has been cited extensively in the tourism research literature, suggests that if growth is unchecked, tourism destination areas eventually collapse under the weight of their own urbanization. The amount of tourist accommodation on offer continues to increase, but the attractiveness of the area to tourists begins to decrease. Accommodation providers are forced to engage in competitive price-cutting, decreasing profitability and reinvestment. Accommodation and facilities become increasingly dilapidated and less attractive, in a continuing vicious cycle, and eventually the area ceases to attract tourists at all.

In addition, during this downward spiral phase, there is likely to be a marked increase in petty and organized crime, a downward trend in property values relative to other destinations, and a general decrease in welfare for local residents as well as tourists. It has been argued that this has already happened in Miami, Florida and Waikiki, Hawaii in the USA, and the Gold Coast in Australia. Butler argues that the terminal, declining phase of the cycle can be reversed, and the tourism destination rejuvenated, if a major new attraction is provided. Again, the most commonly cited example is Disneyland in Los Angeles. Since neither Miami nor Los Angeles has ever been primarily a tourism destination, however, it is not clear that the economic success or otherwise of Disneyland has any general significance for areas such as Waikiki and the Australian Gold Coast.

The destination lifestyle model recognizes that there have been broad similarities in the development trajectories of many different tourism destination areas. These similarities occur only at the broadest level, however, and the model is therefore much too general to be useful in practical tourism planning. Even from an analytical perspective, it permits only the broadest of testable hypotheses about the future development pattern in any particular location. In addition, such hypotheses are testable only for the earlier stages of development, since in the later stages the model allows for alternative trajectories, with no testable criteria to determine which will be followed in any particular case. Even for the earlier stages, since the model acknowledges that different areas develop at different speeds but does not specify what factors influence that time scale, it can only be tested in very broad and general terms.

While the tourism development cycle provides a broadly useful core framework for modelling the development of tourism destination areas, therefore, it needs to be refined to a significantly improved level of detail before it can be applied or tested at individual locations. This detail can be achieved in several possible ways. The simplest is to construct partial models that apply only to particular types of tourism development or destination area, but describe the development trajectory in more detail for that specific category. An example is the resort development model of (Smith, 1994), which was developed for beachside tourist towns in South-east Asia. To construct a detailed tourism development model that applies for a wide range of destination and development types is a much more complex task. A variety of regional planning models is available, and some of these are applicable, though not specific, to tourism development. They tend to focus on spatial modelling, emphasizing the geographic rather than historical differences between sites.

To account for the details of development trajectories at different destinations, both historical and geographic factors must also be incorporated. Geographical factors include climate, topography and the precise locations of natural features such as mountains, cliffs, rivers, lakes and beaches and human infrastructure such as harbours, roads and airports, all of which are predictable. Historical factors include changes in airline fuel prices, the promulgation of new legislation, or the arrival and actions of an individual entrepreneur, and these factors are generally not predictable. Tourism development trajectories at individual destinations are influenced by both.

Recreational succession and carrying capacity

The earlier phases of the progression outlined above are commonly described as recreational succession. This term could reasonably be applied to the entire progression, but as noted above, the later stages have more commonly been described under the rubric of the tourism development cycle. Recreational succession has been described for a large number of natural areas subject to tourism, including many national parks. One of the most typical characteristics is that, if left unchecked, numbers and crowding continue to increase, and so do the degree of mechanization and consequent environmental impacts.

The people who visit during the earlier successional stages typically place a strong value on lack of crowding, and are prepared to take a high degree of personal responsibility and if necessary risk in order to achieve quiet and solitude. The value of their recreational experience is greatly reduced if they are compelled to share the area with other visitors, particularly if the latter have more intrusive behaviour patterns and create greater impacts. Despite this conflict between different groups of visitors, however, when the visitors actually present on site at any given time are asked if they are satisfied with their experience, the majority say yes. The explanation for this apparent paradox is that visitors typical of the early successional stages, who would be highly dissatisfied with the levels of noise, crowding, mechanization and infrastructure development found in the later stages, no longer visit the site concerned, so they are simply not there to be questioned about visitor satisfaction levels.

As the number of people visiting national parks and other fragile environments continued to increase over recent decades, some management agencies took the step of limiting visitor numbers to a pre-determined maximum threshold, through a variety of mechanisms. For example, if the management agency bans motorized vehicles, restricts overnight camping to designated campsites, and limits the total number of campsites available, that effectively restricts the total number of visitors more than a half day's walk from each roadhead. Broader systems simply limited the total number of people in the park, through a road entrance turnstile system. More sophisticated measures may divide the park into zones, with only one group permitted in each zone at any one time, and priority determined by a booking system.

Any such approach requires a mechanism to determine what the threshold visitor number should be. This led to the concept of carrying capacity, a term that sparked considerable controversy. Much of the debate was carried out at cross-purposes, however, with arguments being largely semantic rather than technical. For any given area, it is possible to define a range of different carrying capacities based on different criteria. Ecological carrying capacity may be conceptualized as the number of visitors that produces no detectable, or at least no irreversible, ecological change to the ecosystems in the area concerned. Social capacity may be defined as the density of visitors at which the number of meetings, sightings or other unplanned interactions between individuals or groups begins to reduce their enjoyment of the experience. Where visitors have to pay to be in the area concerned, and the amount they are prepared to pay per capita decreases with crowding, then economic carrying capacity may be defined as the number of visitors that maximizes net revenue, real or notional, i.e. number of visitors times per capita payment less infrastructure and support costs.

It is clear from the above that carrying capacity is a very ill-defined concept and of little practical use in a management context. Because of recreational succession, the social carrying capacity of an area increases over time, as the characteristics of the visitors will generally change over time. For visitors who crave solitude and wilderness, social carrying capacity might be as low as one person per $100\,km^2$ in areas traversed by foot, or one or two orders of magnitude lower in areas traversed by vehicle, such as deserts. For visitors who have come for night-life and associated social interactions in the final stage of Disneyfication, a density of hundreds of thousands of people per km^2 may be perfectly acceptable. Hence social carrying capacity is meaningful only under a predetermined management regime that prevents recreational succession and filters the types of visitors in a particular area.

Similar considerations apply to economic carrying capacity. If allowable activities in an area are predetermined, and visitors are charged an entrance fee as for a zoo or private wildlife park, then the economic carrying capacity is the number of visitors at which this total revenue is maximized. Conceivably, this could be determined by the maximum amount individuals were willing to pay per capita when visitor numbers were so high that no more people could be physically squeezed into the space concerned. More generally, however, it is presumed that people would pay less as crowding increased, so that economic carrying capacity would be determined by two functions: the willingness of different people to pay for entrance if they were the only visitor; and the reduction in willingness to pay as crowding increases. Clearly, if this approach is used to set visitor numbers in a national park, high crowding and ecological damage are likely to result. Note also that this approach depends critically on the assumption that permissible activities are predetermined, so that recreational succession is stalled. If a public reserve or a private zoo or wildlife park can be sold for high-rise residential development, for example, its economic carrying capacity for nature-based recreation may soon become irrelevant.

At first glance, it might appear that ecological carrying capacity is a valid, useful and readily applicable concept, but in fact it, too, suffers major limitations as a management tool, unless much more precisely defined. The difficulty is that all visitors create some impacts, so if ecological carrying capacity is defined as the threshold of zero impact, then conceptually it will always be zero. Of course, zero impact is itself a somewhat empty concept, since for practical purposes an impact is only known to be non-zero if it is detectable, but to define ecological carrying capacity as a threshold of zero detectable impact is still not very helpful. The threshold at which an impact is detectable depends on the parameter measured, the detection technologies, the patterns of natural variation, the sampling design and the degree of sampling effort.

Instead of using a conceptual zero impact threshold, or a threshold of zero detectable impact, as a criterion for determining ecological carrying capacity, in practice it is only feasible and useful to specify an impact threshold by reference to some predetermined degree of anthropogenic impact occurring in addition to natural variations in the parameters concerned. Such limits may be specified as a function of that natural variation, or as an arbitrary threshold set simply for planning and management purposes. Thresholds set in this way have been termed limits of acceptable change (LAC).

From a practical management perspective, the concept of limits of acceptable change can be converted into an operational form much more easily than the concept of carrying capacity. It does, however, depend strongly on a reliable and well-designed environmental monitoring programme. This is needed both to establish the limits of acceptable change, and to determine when they are being approached or exceeded. Even if the LAC thresholds are specified in absolute terms rather than as a function of natural variation, baseline information on natural variation in space and time is still necessary to set the LAC, for several reasons.

First, LAC must be specified in terms of particular environmental parameters, and a detailed knowledge of ecosystem function in the area concerned is required to select appropriate parameters. Such knowledge is rarely available. Second, if the specified acceptable change is too small relative to natural fluctuations, it will be very difficult and expensive to detect, but if the specified acceptable change is too large relative to natural fluctuations, then major environmental damage could result before any remedial action is taken. Third, if the specified LAC threshold is within the range of natural variation, it will be largely meaningless and may trigger attempts at remedial action that are destined to failure.

Few protected areas, therefore, rely solely on carrying capacity or LAC approaches in planning and managing either private visitation or commercial tourism. In reality, they use a range of different monitoring and management approaches with a strong pragmatic component. Commercial ecotourism operators planning to make use of either protected areas or other public lands need to appreciate the difficulties facing the land management agencies, and the range of tools and approaches these agencies commonly make use of.

Conclusions

There are many different facets and specializations to ecotourism policy and planning, from the broadest environmental policy and land-use planning measures applicable to a wide range of industry sectors, through to the fine details of recreational carrying-capacity estimation and associated monitoring and management tools. Different measures are based on different views of human social behaviour, and different people respond in different ways to measures of different types. Effective plans and policies thus need a mix or basket of measures that take account of these variations and provide non-intrusive or 'light-touch' mechanisms for well-intentioned tourists and enterprises, backed up by a safety net of more heavy-handed tools for those who ignore the former. To evaluate how successful such measures may be requires an accounting system. This is considered in the next chapter.

RESEARCH

Broad regional planning approaches for ecotourism and sustainable tourism have been considered by, for example, Inskeep (1987), NcNeely and Thorsell (1989), Buckley (1991a), Lindberg *et al.* (1998) and Ahn *et al.* (2002).

Such approaches have been applied in, for example: the Caribbean islands (Albuquerque and McElroy, 1992); coastal Indonesia (Smith, 1994); Western Australia (Dowling, 1993; Mason and Moore, 1998; Lewis and Newsome, 2003); Vietnam (Smith, 1998); and Saskatchewan, Canada (Weaver, 1997). The use of geographic information systems was illustrated in northern Ontario by Boyd *et al.* (1994) and more generally by Bahaire and Elliott-White (1999). Planning for ecotourism development in parks specifically has been examined by, for example: Norris (1992); Boo and Lindberg (1993); Boyd and Butler (1996); Agardy (1993) for three marine parks; Hill *et al.* (1995) for Heron Island, Australia; Davis (1999) and Hemmings and Roura (2003) for the Antarctic; and Guclu and Karahan (2004) for Turkey.

Reference books on ecotourism policy and related issues include Hawkins *et al.* (1995), Bornemeier (1997), Weaver (1998), Briassoulis and van der Straaten (2000), Fennell and Dowling (2003), Lück and Kirstges (2003) and Diamantis (2004).

The volume edited by Fennell and Dowling (2003) includes case studies from: the Americas; Europe; China and Kyrgyzstan; and Australia, New Zealand and Antarctica. The compilation by Lück and Kirstges includes three cases from sub-Saharan Africa, three from Latin America, and two from the Asia-Pacific region. The book edited by Diamantis (2004) has a rather broader scope, not restricted solely to policy. It does, however, include a general chapter on ecotourism policy by Hall (2004b), and case studies from Dominica, the Korean demilitarized zone, Texas, the Canadian Arctic, Chile, Portugal, eastern Europe, Thailand, Vietnam, East and South Africa, and Australia.

General discussions of ecotourism policy have been provided by Pigram (1990), Buckley (1991a), Cater (1993), Cater and Lowman (1994), Bramwell and Sharman (1999) and Baker (2005). Examples from specific countries or regions are summarized in Table 13.1.

REVISION

Different spatial scales
- National strategies: broad marketing goals
- Regional plan: mix marketing, infrastructure, attractions
- Local plans: groups of individual sites and operations

Table 13.1. Case studies of ecotourism policies.

Continent and country	Region	Reference
Africa		
Egypt	Southern Sinai	Shackley (1999)
South Africa	National	Koch *et al.* (1997); Parker and Khare (2005)
Americas		
Haiti	National	Paryski (1996)
North and South	Entire region	Edwards *et al.* (1998)
Canada	National	Scace *et al.* (1992)
Canada	Northwest Territories	Hinch and Swinnerton (1993); Wolfe *et al.* (1993)
Mexico	National	Cothran and Cothran (1998)
Belize	Forest	Primack (1998)
Bonaire	National	Parker (1999)
Costa Rico	National	Lumsdon and Swift (1998)
Dominica	National	Burnett and Uysal (1991); Weaver (1991, 1993); Douglas (1992); Esprit (1994); Cater *et al.* (1996)
Guatemala	Forest	Primack (1998)
Ecuador	National	Wilson and Laarman (1988)
Ecuador	Galapagos	Buckley (2003a); Heslinga (2003)
Panama	National	Ayala (1998)
Peru	Amazonia	Yu *et al.* (1997)
Europe		
Europe	Regional	Simpson (1995)
Greece	Crete	Briassoulis (2003)
Portugal	National	Cavaco (1995)
Yugoslavia	Islands	Klaric (1991)
Asia		
Himalayas	Regional	Sharma (1998)
China	Selected areas	Lindberg *et al.* (1997)
Sikkim	National	Rai and Sundriyal (1997)
India	National	Singh and Singh (1996)

Continued

Table 13.1. *Continued.*

Continent and country	Region	Reference
India	Arunachal Pradesh	Shackley (1999)
Vietnam	National	van Lanh and MacNeil (1997); Jansen-Verbeke and Go (1995); Smith (1998b); Buckley (2004k)
Laos	National	Laird (1993)
Thailand	National	Tourism Authority of Thailand (1996)
Malaysia	Sarawak	Chan (1994); Yong (1994)
Oceania		
Indonesia	Siberut	Persoon *et al.* (1998)
Pacific Islands	Regional	Krausse (1995); Burns *et al.* (1997); Fagence (1997); Weaver (1998)
Niue	National	De Haas (2000)
Samoa	National	Lindgren *et al.* (1997); Simmons (1998)
Solomon Islands	Rennell Island	Overton and Purdie (1997); Hviding and Bayliss-Smith (2000)
Solomon Islands	Guadalcanal	Rudkin (1996)
Australia	National	Australia Department of Tourism (1994)

Planning context

- Overall aims of strategy or plan
- Who it includes
- Who it is aimed at
- Who has authority and responsibility for implementation
- Funding

Planning basis

- Legal or statutory basis if any
- Procedural and substantive requirements
- Practical market and political contents
- Who's writing the plan?

Consultation

- Identifying stakeholders
- Levels: information, consultation, participation

- Involvement, engagement, ownership
- Critical for effective multi-stakeholder implementation
- Informal, formal, legal/judicial

Types of plans

- Spatial plans
- Marketing strategies
- Programme planning

Policy instruments

- Regulatory or coercive
- Economic or market-based
- Suasive or educational

Multiple land use

- Forestry, rangelands, fisheries, hydropower
- Opportunities for multiple or sequential use for tourism
- Conflicts can occur if tourism has no rights
- Some successes, some failures

Tourism in parks

- Education and interpretation
- Quotas, zoning, regulations
- Fees and charges
- Hardening and infrastructure

Recreational succession and life cycles

- Type of tourist changes over time
- Positive feedback from impacts and infrastructure
- Parks use term recreational succession
- City destinations refer to tourism life cycles

Carrying capacities

- Economic, social, environmental capacities
- Shortcomings and difficulties
- Limits of acceptable change as alternative
- Relies on understanding ecology
- And on effective monitoring

REFLECTIONS

1. List three reasons why a country might wish to compile a national ecotourism strategy or policy. What kinds of organizations would need to be involved in, or affected by, such a strategy or policy? What approaches could be used to engage them both in the preparation and the implementation of the strategy? What kind of organization should take the lead in each of these processes, and why? What types of issues should such a document address? What other types of strategies, plans and policies would it need to link in to in order to be effective?

2. How might the management agency for an individual national park or similar public reserve go about preparing a management plan for commercial ecotourism operations within the park? Who, if anyone, would it need to consult from outside the parks agency? Should it also consider lands adjacent to the park tenure, and if so, why and how? What types of management tool or mechanism could the park plan use to manage commercial ecotourism operations, including their interactions with independent visitors?

3. Identify either: (i) a specific national or regional ecotourism strategy document, or (ii) a specific management plan for a particular park or similar area, which includes components related to commercial tourism. Briefly summarize the major features of the plan you have identified, and provide a critique of its good and bad points, including items it may have omitted or considered in insufficient detail. Consider, in particular: the data and information it is based on; the process used to prepare it, including any consultation; the particular measures it proposes to achieve its aims; and the likelihood that it would be implemented successfully, including funding, legal and organizational aspects.

4. Would it be feasible to construct an ecotourism plan or policy that covers several nations at once, e.g. for an entire continent or subcontinent? Give an example of a region where you think this would be appropriate. What would be the main components you would include in such a regional policy? If the UN World Tourism Organization were to commission you to produce a global ecotourism strategy, how would you extend and expand your approach from continental to global scale?

chapter 14

ACCOUNTING

Passive solar water heater, widely used for stand-alone ecolodges and camps in areas with sufficient sunlight. This heater provides ample water for one double guest room.

REVIEW

Introduction

If ecotourism is different from mainstream mass tourism in any meaningful way, those differences should be measurable. The process of making such measurements is a form of accounting. Since critical differences may be social or environmental as well as financial, environmental or triple-bottom-line accounting approaches are needed. Indeed, a triple-bottom-line approach is one way to conceptualize ecotourism (Buckley, 2003b).

Accounting approaches are also very valuable within the ecotourism sector itself. If ecotourism enterprises, industry associations or government agencies adopt measures intended to minimize the negative environmental and social impacts of tourism and to increase the positive social and environmental impacts, accounting approaches are needed to measure the success or effectiveness of such measures, to decide which work best, which to continue or discontinue, and which should receive highest priority.

Financial accounting is a well-established discipline for which there are many textbooks, university courses and business training manuals, and this chapter does not attempt to duplicate or summarize any of that material. Rather, it concentrates on other aspects of accounting that are relevant to the assessment of sustainability and the achievement of ecotourism's environmental and associated social goals. There is a developing research literature on environmental accounting and on sustainability accounting more generally, but much of this is at a rather theoretical level.

Practical protocols for individual ecotourism enterprises to carry out routine triple-bottom-line accounting, in the same way as they currently carry out routine financial accounting, are not yet available. This chapter examines the issues involved in producing such protocols, and suggests what factors ecotourism operators, tourism ecocertification programmes and other relevant stakeholders can consider meanwhile in attempting to generate triple-bottom-line accounts for ecotourism. For each issue, analogies are drawn with corresponding issues in financial accounting to illustrate the complexities. Triple-bottom-line approaches attempt to calculate net environmental, social and financial performance independently but concurrently. They do not attempt to establish exchange rates or equivalencies between these three components.

There is, in addition, an entire field of economics that does indeed attempt to calculate monetary values for a wide range of environmental goods and services. These approaches may be used, for example, to estimate economic values for environmental damage costs, either for comparison between alternative developments or activities, or in order to estimate net economic benefit of a particular development or activity after taking environmental damage into account. Such approaches can be very valuable, for example, in comparing alternative land uses such as tourism or logging in public forests, or in determining an optimum level of visitor use for an area that has both conservation and recreation value.

Environmental accounting parameters

Any kind of accounting needs measurements, preferably comparable and quantitative. One of the principal characteristics of money is that it is, in most circumstances, a measure of value. There are innumerable potential quantitative environmental parameters that might be measured and compared, but most of them describe a physical state rather than a value. Values may be applied to those physical states, but different people may apply different values to different parameters. For environmental accounting to become broadly meaningful, therefore, it must identify parameters that are not only measurable, but that are considered significant or important by a majority of the people who might use the results of the accounting exercise concerned. The choice of such parameters may therefore differ between places and change over time, depending on other circumstances. For example, in developed countries most people are concerned about the survival of endangered species. Populations of these species thus become potentially significant parameters in environmental accounting. Different parts of the world, however, have different endangered species, so the precise population parameters required will vary accordingly. In addition, new species become endangered at intervals, and some endangered species recover, so this also affects the choice of parameters for environmental accounting.

Air and water quality are also of broad concern to people in developing as well as developed nations. Once again, there are many different parameters that measure different aspects of air and water quality, and while the same physical parameter describes the same physical aspect of air or water no matter where it is measured, the relative significance of different parameters differs between people in different parts of the world. To take just one example, in some water supplies a brown colour indicates high turbidity from sediment, which may potentially contain microbiological contaminants that pose a risk to human health. In areas that obtain their water from peaty lakes, which are naturally stained brown by humic acids, however, brown coloured water does not present any kind of risk. In comparing water quality across the two sites, therefore, a simple and easily measured parameter such as colour is of little use. A turbidity parameter based on measurements of actual suspended sediment would be more relevant; a basic bacteriological parameter such as total coliforms would be better, and the concentration of key pathogens, such as individual bacterial or protozoan species, would be more meaningful still (Warnken and Buckley, 2004). As an indicator of fish habitat, however, turbidity would be a more useful measure than most microbiological indicators, since fish species such as carp can survive in highly turbid water, whereas those such as trout cannot.

There are also many different parameters for measuring money, in the form of different currencies. Some of these are freely tradable, others not; some are valuable in most of the world, others not; some have much the same value to different people in different places, whereas others are valuable only to some people in some places. For all but the most obscure currencies, however, there are markets or other conversion mechanisms so that measurements made in one currency can be expressed in others. This is very rarely the case for social or environmental parameters. The concept of social or environmental bottom lines suggests that even if social and environmental values cannot be expressed in financial terms, they can at least be aggregated into a single measure in each case. To date, however, there is not in fact any agreed method for aggregating different environmental parameters into a single summary measure. Instead, any company reporting its environmental performance has to select a basket of different measures, and there is as yet no commonly agreed basket. The closest approach, perhaps, is that taken by certain ecocertification schemes, which specify a predefined set of environmental performance parameters against which all certified applicants will be measured. As noted in Chapter 13, however, the measures used in such schemes may be chosen more for convenience than ecological significance.

Scales and protocols

Choice of particular parameters is not the only difficulty facing environmental and social accounting approaches. Equally critical are other aspects of accounting, which also apply for financial measures: for example, the scale of the accounting unit, and distinctions between stocks and flows. Environmental accounting approaches can be applied at a national scale, as in the calculation of so-called green gross national product (GNP), or at the scale of individual ecotourism enterprises, or anywhere in between. At the scale of an individual enterprise, for example, it is perfectly possible for one component of a large tourism corporation to achieve positive social and environmental outcomes, even if the remainder of the corporation creates considerable net social and environmental impacts. In any accounting exercise, therefore, it becomes important to specify the boundaries of the accounting unit quite precisely.

Even though financial accounting is far more straightforward than social or environmental accounting, there is still no single universally adopted financial accounting system. Rather, there are a number of different financial accounting protocols and conventions, and each of these can give a somewhat different picture of an accounting entity's financial position. As one example, Australia's various protected area management agencies gradually changed from cash-flow to accrual accounting systems around the year 2000, with unanticipated but significant practical implications for their actual management practices. As another example, different corporations or accountants may differ as to what they consider an extraordinary item and what they would include in routine annual accounts. They may also have different systems for reporting the current value of future risks and opportunities, and they use different discounting rates for reporting the current value of future income or expenditure.

When Australia's protected area management agencies used a cashflow accounting system, for example, they did not need to know what their many items of visitor infrastructure were worth in financial terms. They could, if necessary, calculate what it had cost them to construct those items and what proportion of that value might have been lost through nominal depreciation. There was no particular reason to make such a calculation, however, because the items concerned were not available for sale, and it was much more important to know which items they intended to repair or replace in any given year, and how much cash would be required to do so. Once they switched to accrual accounting, however, they had to assign a financial value to every physical asset.

Finance cf. economics

One common area of confusion in triple-bottom-line accounting is the distinction between financial and economic aspects. Both are measured in money, but while financial accounting refers to assets and cash flows for an individual enterprise or entity, economic accounting involves a broader scope, to include issues such as monetary inputs and multipliers in regional communities, relative returns to the public purse from alternative uses of a natural resource, or the value of time invested in a particular outdoor recreation activity. From a triple-bottom-line perspective, where the accounting entity is an individual commercial ecotourism enterprise, it is the financial accounts that measure the enterprise's commercial success. Various economic measures may also be relevant, but principally as an indicator of contributions to local communities or as ways to measure non-market values. Generally speaking, these represent contributions to the social rather than the financial bottom line for the enterprise concerned, since the effects are experienced by the broader community rather than the enterprise itself.

Typically, tourism development brings both economic benefits and economic costs to host communities. The benefits include new employment and entrepreneurial opportunities, and secondary effects through increased financial flows within the local economy, and marketing of the area as a whole as well as the individual tourism enterprises. Economic costs, which can be considerable, include the expense of constructing and maintaining infrastructure at a scale sufficient for tourists as well as local residents, and the costs associated with increased crime, congestion, conflict and health-care requirements. These economic costs and benefits are not necessarily experienced by the same individual members of the local communities concerned. Broadly speaking, in developed countries at least, the benefits accrue principally to private retail businesses, which gain an increased supply of clients. The costs are borne principally by the ratepayers who fund the local government authority and, to a lesser degree, by taxpayers throughout the state or country concerned. In traditional societies in developing nations, benefits are more likely to accrue to those people, often younger, who have adopted an entrepreneurial and cash-oriented lifestyle, whereas costs are more likely to be borne by those people, often older, who are responsible for maintaining community structure and harmony.

Social/economic anomalies

While some social costs and benefits can be expressed in economic terms, others cannot, or if they are, the economic values assigned are controversial and not generally accepted. One of the most commonly contested issues is whether the value assigned to advantages or disadvantages experienced by an individual person should be measured according to that person's income, converted to a single currency equivalent at applicable exchange rates, or whether it should be measured in human terms irrespective of income, and if so what those terms should be. There are many examples that illustrate this issue. When developed Western nations began to calculate GNP, for example, work carried out by housewives or other unpaid home carers was not included, because they did not receive a direct cash income for the labour and expertise involved.

As an even more controversial example, the allocation of funds for health care in different countries and communities provides a measure of the economic value ascribed to human life and health. Because different countries have very different total wealth, and may also have different budget priorities, the average expenditure on trying to keep individual people alive when they become sick, old or injured, can vary enormously from one area to another. Similarly, death benefits under superannuation schemes (pension funds) and payouts under life insurance programmes also differ enormously between countries. Does this mean that the value of your life depends on where you live and what you earn? Should the value of an individual human life be considered a more fundamental and universal measure? If the latter view is adopted, it would necessarily imply that currency exchanges at market rates are not in fact carried out at par, but involve enormous gains and losses in value as measured in human life equivalents.

These anomalies can be viewed from a variety of different perspectives. It could be argued that medical expenditures and insurance payouts do not measure the value of life, even indirectly, but merely measure specific functions of particular social institutions. Alternatively, one can argue that the life of a particular individual person has different values to different people, so that even if these values can be measured in economic terms, there is no consensus as to which is the appropriate value to choose or use.

Social accounting parameters

From a triple-bottom-line accounting perspective, the critical conclusion from the above is simply that social costs and benefits cannot be converted into monetary measures with any degree of consensus, so non-monetary social parameters are needed for any form of social accounting. As with environmental parameters, however, there is no single social measure that can be used to express all the different potential social costs and benefits of a particular tourism operation.

Even if no attempt is made to express the value of life in financial terms, for example, the question remains as to whether all human life should be accounted as of equal value. Consider, for example, a health threat that can be expressed as a proportional increase in the probability that a person will die in the following 12 months. Does a given increase in that probability for an 80-year-old person who is already ill represent the same social cost as a corresponding increase in probability for a healthy child, or not? Similarly, does the availability of new jobs in a community that people are leaving because of lack of employment, represent the same social benefit as new jobs in a community that is already wealthy and growing? Does a job that offers a cash income to a person previously relying on subsistence agriculture, represent the same social benefit as a job that offers the same cash income to a person who already had another job at a comparable pay rate? There are no generally agreed answers to these questions, and most attempts at social accounting do not even ask them. If social accounting is ever to reach the same level of precision as financial accounting, however, these are the kinds of issues that will first need to be addressed.

Crude and incomplete accounts

Similar considerations apply for environmental accounting. As a professional and academic discipline, environmental accounting has already become quite sophisticated, with a great deal of methodological research already available. The level of detail provided in corporate environmental accounts, in contrast, is typically very low indeed. One way to appreciate just how crude such corporate environmental accounts really are is to convert an environmental accounting statement to a financial analogue, and consider how it would compare with financial accounting as actually practised. For example, a company may report merely that it has taken a few tenths of a per cent of its operating revenues, or even less, and used those funds to purchase technology with lower environmental impacts than previously. Imagine if a forestry or fisheries corporation reported merely that it had taken a few tenths of a per cent of its total annual fish or timber harvest, and traded it for a slightly higher-yielding financial investment – but said nothing at all about what they did with the remainder of the harvest. Such a report would hardly satisfy shareholders, investors, auditors or the stockmarket, let alone comply with accepted professional accounting procedures. Or imagine that a company's financial reports showed that it had made profitable investments with a few tenths of a per cent of its total operations, but failed to mention that it had incurred substantial losses on the remaining 99% plus. Yet this is directly analogous to a corporate environmental report that describes the company's environmental expenditure without describing its overall environmental impacts using the same parameters. The issue is not to criticize the environmental investments that some corporations do indeed make and report, but simply to point out that these reports are so incomplete that they cannot be described in any meaningful way as accounting.

Selecting standardized indicators

At the research level, two alternative approaches are in use, in the same way as for social accounting: those that endeavour to express environmental values in financial terms, and those that attempt to establish physical parameters for environmental accounting, with no conversion to monetary values. As with social accounting, the difficulty with the latter approach is that different environmental parameters are rarely interconvertible. A suite of parameters is therefore needed to provide a reasonably complete picture, and that suite may differ between commercial activities and between regions or ecosystems. A considerable proportion of environmental science research sets out to measure changes in environmental parameters, including those produced by human activity such as tourism and recreation, but this research is not generally thought of as environmental accounting. In particular, there has been little attempt to standardize the parameters measured, specifically because research on impacts has not been designed as an accounting tool. Some of the current comparative studies in recreation ecology are indeed attempting to standardize parameters used, and the same applies for various tourism ecocertification programmes, but the particular parameters used are chosen more for convenience than ecological significance.

Productivity measures

There have been one or two attempts to develop broadly applicable environmental accounting measures based on energy, but these suffer from severe shortcomings and are not in general use. Biological productivity is one such measure, i.e. the annual increase in plant biomass on a unit area of ground. This is a useful measure in agriculture, where one of the major aims of the industry is to increase crop biomass produced per unit area. It is also one of the major distinguishing features between so-called biomes, i.e. large-scale regional ecosystem types: the biological productivity of a tropical rainforest, swamp or coral reef is much greater than that of an arctic or alpine ecosystem, and there is a broad general gradient of decreasing productivity from the tropics to the poles and from lowlands to mountain tops. As a measure of environmental performance by a corporate entity, however, biological productivity has extremely limited applicability. The same applies to the concept of 'embodied energy' put forward by Odum (1988) several decades ago. His idea was that it should be possible to calculate the total amount of energy that has gone into the production of any manufactured item, whether simple or complex, taking into account the energy used in growing biological raw materials and in providing tools and labour to carry out manufacturing processes. This may indeed be theoretically feasible, but it is not very useful for any practical purpose.

In effect, therefore, there are two functionally distinct approaches to environmental accounting: those that aim to estimate monetary values for environmental goods and services, and those that aim to identify ecologically critical environmental parameters, which can be measured and compared directly. From a triple-bottom-line perspective it is the unmonetarized environmental parameters that are most important, because the parameters used are chosen for ecological significance rather than convertibility. In any case, any parameters that can reliably be converted to monetary terms can simply be included in the financial bottom line. Most research in environmental accounting, however, has in fact focused on these attempts to estimate economic values.

Stated-preference valuation

Two different types of approach are used to assign monetary values to environmental or social goods and services that are not routinely bought and sold. Stated-preference approaches essentially rely on asking people what something is worth to them. There is a large and complex theoretical literature, with numerous case studies, testing how people's answers are affected by their circumstances and by the way the question is phrased. More sophisticated versions of stated-preference valuation approaches go by names such as choice modelling or conjoint modelling, and are described and illustrated extensively in the academic economics literature. All of these approaches, however, suffer from one fundamental difficulty, which no amount of design sophistication can overcome. There are many environmental goods and services for which individual people essentially have no rational mechanism to estimate values, because neither they nor anyone else knows enough about how the natural environment actually functions. For something such as recreational access to a protected area, even if this has historically been made available free of charge, individual people have something in their own experience against which to compare it and hence provide a meaningful estimate of value. For something they have never heard of and never expect to encounter, such as a rare species in another country, even this vague comparative approach is not feasible.

Even where people are indeed familiar with the environmental goods or services concerned, they may still provide highly inaccurate estimates of value. For example, in most developed nations, urban residents are accustomed to having water for drinking, washing and other uses such as lawn irrigation provided at a low or zero marginal unit cost, because they have already paid for water supply and treatment infrastructure through the tax or local-government rates system. If additional water supplies are provided by the same mechanism, the value that people will place on each additional unit will be low, because the cost they currently have to pay for each unit is low. If municipal water supplies cease to be drinkable, e.g. because of a pollution event, then the value they will place on each additional litre of water is the price they have to pay to buy bottled water in the nearest supermarket. This is typically several orders of magnitude greater than the rate per litre of water delivered by the municipal system. Likewise, if tap water can no longer be used for watering garden plants because of water restrictions imposed during drought, and plants can only be kept alive by buying water from other sources, then the value of that water depends on how much people value their garden plants. The point of these examples is to demonstrate that while increasingly sophisticated choice or conjoint models can extract stated values from people with greater precision and less risk of bias, this does not produce anything meaningful if those people do not have any such values to be extracted, because they do not have any information on which to base such a value. Despite these difficulties, there are many cases where stated-preference valuation approaches have indeed been used in contexts relevant to ecotourism and outdoor recreation. These are summarized later in this chapter.

Revealed-preference valuation

Revealed-preference valuation approaches, in contrast, attempt to estimate the financial value of goods and services that are not traded, by establishing functional relationships with those that are. If a commercially caught fish species breeds only in mangrove areas and moves into the open ocean only once adult, then the mangroves have a financial value related to the commercial sales of the fish species concerned. If people spend large amounts of money on boats and tackle for recreational angling, and also invest large amounts of their time, then those figures can be used to estimate the value of the fish they catch, even though those particular fish are not bought or sold. If the same fish species is also harvested commercially, then the recreational angling value can be compared with the commercial fishery sale price to determine which is a higher-value use for the fish stocks concerned. If people travel long distances to take their holidays in national parks, and buy equipment for use when they get there, then these expenditures indicate the value that people place on visiting that park, even if they are not charged any entrance or activity fees. If people will pay a price premium to buy a house or land with, for example, a particularly scenic view or easy access to outdoor recreation opportunities, then that premium indicates the value they place on the view or access, respectively. Each of these examples illustrates one commonly used revealed-preference valuation technique: productivity functions, travel costs, and hedonic pricing, respectively. Each of these approaches also has applications in ecotourism and related areas, for example in making policy decisions related to natural resource management, or in setting fees for commercial use of public protected areas or other public lands. Examples are summarized later in this chapter.

Techniques that rely on estimating financial values for environmental goods and services, using either revealed-preference or stated-preference approaches, can sometimes be useful in making policy decisions on the management of protected areas and natural resources. They are of rather limited value, however, in calculating an environmental bottom line for an ecotourism enterprise or similar entity. For that purpose, the most useful parameters are those that are ecologically significant.

Green and brown issues

In identifying and selecting specific environmental parameters that might be used in environmental accounting, it is useful to draw a broad distinction between so-called green and brown aspects of environmental management. The former are those relating to use of the natural environment as a source of materials or services as inputs to the human economy, the latter refer to the use of the natural environment as a sink for waste outputs from the human economy. In broad terms, the green issues refer to consumption of natural resources and threats to endangered species; the brown issues refer principally to air and water pollution. While there are indeed links between these, e.g. where water pollution threatens endangered aquatic species, in general these two types of parameters are not interchangeable or interconvertible, so any environmental accounting approach either needs to include both, or to identify which is more significant in a particular instance.

One of the difficulties with many tourism ecocertification programmes is that they focus only on relatively unimportant brown issues, which happen to be easily measurable, ignoring green issues or indeed other brown issues that may be much more significant ecologically but far more difficult to quantify. In accounting for the environmental performance of a chain of urban hotels, for example, energy and water consumption are meaningful measures. To certify a mechanical appliance as energy efficient is ecologically meaningful, because it involves a comparison between similar devices manufactured specifically to produce a particular output, such as heating or cooling food or living space, transporting loads, or cleaning clothes or dishes. In such circumstances, the outputs are quantifiable and comparable, and the energy and/or water consumed per unit output provides information that is useful in reducing the environmental footprint of the people purchasing and using the appliance concerned.

For a protected area management agency, in contrast, energy and water consumption by parks staff and visitor centres are far less significant ecologically than the success of the organization in maintaining air and water quality within the parks estate, and contributing to the conservation of threatened species and ecosystems, which is the primary function of protected areas.

To compare the energy and water consumption of a parks agency with that of an urban hotel or resort, therefore, is almost completely meaningless. It would be more significant ecologically to compare the contribution of the parks service in providing habitat for threatened species with the role of the urban hotels in reducing habitat for threatened species. This occurs through a range of indirect mechanisms, such as the impacts of: quarries and logging for building materials; woodchipping for paper production; climate change associated with energy generation and consumption; and flooding and modification to river flow regimes associated with water supply dams and water extraction schemes. Of course, people use all these resources when they are at home as well as when they are on holiday, but per capita consumption generally increases on holiday for a variety of reasons, and the marginal increase represents a net cost to the global environment.

If a single set of environmental accounting parameters were to be applied simultaneously to both urban tourist accommodation and remote national parks, as is indeed currently attempted by some tourism ecocertification programmes, then areas of endangered ecosystems and populations of threatened plant and animal species are more important environmental accounting parameters than water or energy consumption.

Accounting effort

To produce an ecologically meaningful environmental accounting scheme, therefore, the current highly simplistic approaches used by tourism ecocertification programmes have very restricted application, essentially in comparing very similar urban products where very basic brown measures can provide an adequate surrogate indicator of ecological footprint. For broader environmental accounting purposes, and particularly for ecotourism and other tourism products involving areas of high conservation value, a much more sophisticated approach is required. Such an approach would combine elements of community and population ecology, recreation ecology and impact assessment, and ecological footprint analysis to express the activities of a tourism enterprise in terms of changes to populations and conservation status of endangered species, ecosystems and other green indicators.

This would indeed be a large task. It would involve: research to quantify the various ecological linkages involved; practical testing to develop an accounting protocol based on such research; and an annual data collection effort by each of the enterprises compiling environmental accounts. There are two critical issues. The first is that enormous effort has been, and continues to be invested into financial accounting to carry out comparable tasks. If we want environmental accounts to be as meaningful and detailed as financial accounts, we must expect to invest comparable time and effort. Currently, however, the investment in environmental accounting is extremely minuscule relative to investment in financial accounting.

The second critical issue is that ultimately, environmental accounting is a more complex exercise than financial accounting. Even though, as noted earlier, financial accounting has its own complexities introduced by multiple currencies and accounting protocols, these complexities pale into insignificance compared with those of the natural environment. For environmental accounting to become comparable in scope and accuracy to financial accounting, therefore, would actually involve a higher level of investment than currently occurs for financial accounting. At present, however, this second consideration has not yet been brought into play, since as outlined in the first consideration, there is a long way to go before actual investment in environmental accounting even begins to approach that in financial accounting.

Evaluating triple-bottom-line approaches

Given the many shortcomings outlined above, is it indeed worth pursuing triple-bottom-line accounting at all? It is indeed, for two main reasons. The first is that the conceptual approach focuses attention, and to some degree also research effort, on issues explored earlier in this chapter, such as the relative ecological significance of different environmental indicator parameters in different subsectors of the tourism industry. It also helps to demonstrate just how crude our current tourism ecocertification programmes are, and how much more information would be needed to determine whether actual retail tourism products marketed as ecotourism do in fact comply with the principles of ecotourism articulated at a theoretical level.

The second reason why triple-bottom-line approaches are important is that some tourism enterprises, albeit a very tiny proportion, actually do seem to have achieved a bottom line that is positive on all three dimensions. Because of all the accounting difficulties outlined above, it may be difficult to express in quantitative terms exactly how positive the social and environmental bottom lines may be, but in one or two cases at least, the social and environmental contributions are sufficiently substantial that they do clearly outweigh corresponding social and environmental costs. Other than this relatively limited number of tourism enterprises, the only corporate entities worldwide that can claim a positive triple bottom line are certain environmental non-government organizations run along corporate lines. That is, those few ecotourism enterprises that do generate a positive triple bottom line would seem to demonstrate that unlike any other industry sector, it is in fact possible for tourism to be sustainable in an accounting sense. Examples of tourism enterprises that do appear to fulfil these criteria are considered in Buckley (2003a, 2006).

This conclusion, however, must be tempered by four additional considerations. The first is that these enterprises represent only an extremely tiny fraction of the tourism industry as a whole. By far the majority of tourism enterprises describing themselves as sustainable or indeed as ecotourism do not in fact generate a positive triple bottom line. The second is that those enterprises that do seem to yield a positive triple bottom line have a number of similarities with the conservation NGOs, which can also make such a claim. All of them ultimately seem to use tourism, plus donations in the case of the NGOs, to fund conservation on private land.

The third consideration is that this mechanism only works as long as there are people with money who are prepared to pay to visit private conservation reserves where they can gain exclusive or preferential viewing opportunities for spectacular scenery or wildlife, or outdoor recreation or adventure opportunities, with a high level of hospitality service. Generally speaking, this is only feasible as long as there are significant disparities in income between the staff and the clients of such enterprises. Insofar as equity is considered one of the defining criteria for sustainability, this model thus involves a certain degree of paradox. Where a tourism enterprise contributes to increased income and improved social welfare of local residents, however, this represents a positive contribution to the social bottom line.

The fourth issue is that most of the clients for ecotourism enterprises of this type travel long distances to visit them, generating significant atmospheric carbon dioxide emissions in the process. Thus, even if these enterprises achieve a positive environmental bottom line at the local scale, this may be offset by the environmental costs of long-distance air travel. These factors are not readily commensurate, adding an additional accounting difficulty. Overall, it appears that a triple-bottom-line accounting approach is indeed a valuable tool in the ecotourism sector, and one that deserves further development and refinement.

Conclusions

One of the major shortcomings in analyses of so-called sustainable tourism has been that there are no reliable measures of sustainability, so no way to judge whether the tourism industry as a whole, or an individual tourism enterprise, is becoming more or less sustainable. Triple-bottom-line accounting approaches, though far from perfect, do provide such an approach and are hence worth pursuing. In particular, it appears that there are a small number of leading ecotourism operators that may well be the world's only commercial business enterprises that can realistically demonstrate a positive triple bottom line. This provides a basis for evaluating the overall achievements of ecotourism as a philosophy and a business model. Such an evaluation is attempted in the next chapter.

REVISION

Triple-bottom-line basis

- Environmental, social, financial
- Costs and benefits, stocks and flows
- Needs quantifiable commensurate indicators or measures
- Requires equally detailed data on costs and benefits
- Need similar effort for social and environmental as for financial accounting

Scale and time period

- Product, company, region, country, world?
- Quarterly, annual, 5-year?

Financial cf. economic

- Questions of scale
- Financial accounts are typically for single corporate entity
- Economic bottom line includes external effects
- For example, multipliers and linkages
- But job creation may be categorized as social benefit

Financial accounting

- Many practical manuals and programmes for small-business accounting
- Financial accounting is a recognized profession with defined legal frameworks
- Corporate financial accounting has detailed prescriptions, procedures and protocols
- Even so, there are many different accounting methods and systems
- Financial bottom line in annual accounts is specified with high precision
- But it depends heavily on accounting conventions, so is rarely unambiguous
- Different countries and jurisdictions have different accounting laws and protocols
- A company's financial bottom line depends on country where accounts are compiled

Scale and entity

- Different accounting systems used for product, corporation, government, country
- Flexibility in attribution of corporate costs and benefits to particular products
- Requirements for tax accounting differ from accounting for market valuations
- Government budget processes differ from corporate accounting
- System of National Accounts to calculate GNP has own protocols
- Disagreement over financial bottom lines is not unusual

Economic accounting

- Distinction between financial and economic accounting depends on scale and entity
- For ecotourism, financial accounts are for business owners, inside company
- Economic accounts are for broader community, outside company
- Salaries, local contracts, purchases are financial cost to company but economic input to community
- Commonly expressed as number of new jobs, through employment or entrepreneurial opportunities
- Economic benefits include secondary effects such as multipliers and marketing
- Economic costs are those incurred by community because of private-sector tourism

- For example, road maintenance, traffic delays, higher prices, increased crime
- Overall, economic bottom line is part of social rather than financial bottom line

Social accounting

- Accounting difficulties as no single unit to measure all social costs and benefits
- Some social components can be converted to monetary terms
- But effective conversion rates may be highly contested
- For example, which is more basic: a person's livelihood, or a unit of currency?
- Does the social value of time wasted in traffic depend on the person's salary?
- Is the value of new health services measured in construction costs or extra years of life?
- Does the value of improved health depend on a person's age and social status?
- Many other social impacts are even more difficult to quantify
- Alternative approach is to ask people if they feel worse or better off because of tourism
- But this is very crude cf. financial accounting

Environmental accounting: monetary approaches

- Many attempts to express environmental costs and benefits in economic terms
- Entire academic disciplines of environmental and ecological economics
- Valuation approaches are very highly contested and uncertain
- Different individual people set enormously different values on various environmental components
- Scientific knowledge of quantitative relationships between ecosystem functions and human economy is very sparse
- Public and political knowledge of these links is even poorer
- Main approaches are revealed-preference, stated-preference

Revealed and stated preferences

- Revealed preference: deduce economic value placed on environment from observed human behaviour
- Examples: travel-cost, hedonic pricing, production-function approaches, etc.
- Stated preference: ask people what environment is worth
- Contingent valuation, choice modelling
- Large literature on shortcomings, improved models
- All valuations measure human perceptions of environment, not ecological parameters

Conversions between components

- Triple-bottom-line implies accounting for each component
- Requires quantitative measurement of social and environmental as well as economic costs and benefits

- Some social and environmental costs and benefits can be expressed in economic terms, but with many difficulties
- Information collected for environmental accounting very limited cf. financial accounting Need for audit

Environmental accounting: non-monetary approaches

- Various attempts to measure environmental values in non-monetary units
- E.g. 'embodied energy' – quantitative but ecologically irrelevant
- Conservation outcomes can be accounted using biodiversity measures
- For example, population changes for rare species, overall species richness, etc.
- Currently, no single measure to weigh, for example, wildlife conservation against water pollution
- Even comparing, for example, area of habitat gained cf. area lost is uncertain, since it depends on degree of protection, conservation value, etc., cf. degree of damage, potential rehabilitation, etc.

Some practical paradoxes

- Accounting schemes include what's quantifiable, not necessarily what's critical
- For example, ecocertification programmes may include carbon credits from paying for plantations
- But ignore biodiversity losses from clearing, noise, feral animals, weeds and pathogens, pollution, etc.

Accounting in future

- Triple-bottom-line accounting is a useful concept
- It provides a valuable framework to consider impacts and management
- It may catalyse research on social and environmental indicators and impacts
- But it can also distract attention from ecological issues and impacts
- And may use social and financial aspects to dilute attention to more critical ecological concerns

Is a positive triple-bottom-line possible?

- Yes, but very uncommon
- Best examples seem to be private conservation reserves funded by ecotourism
- With positive returns to local communities and conservation
- Case study: Conservation Corporation Africa
- And similar wildlife tourism operators worldwide
- Some environmental NGOs may also qualify
- Majority of ecotourism operators, however, do not

- Even those that do depend on funds from rich ecotourists
- That is, local net gains depend on global imbalances
- Also impacts from long-distance travel
- But valuable none the less

REFLECTIONS

1. Using examples, consider how tourism might change the patterns of crime within a local community. What possible parameters might you use to quantify such changes? How would you measure each of these parameters? What approach could you use to compare different parameters and to aggregate them into a single numerical measure?

2. If exposure to tourism persuades people to take paid jobs and buy consumer goods, rather than farming to grow food for their families, is that a social cost or a social benefit? How can you justify your argument? Identify some practical examples.

3. What is meant by a triple bottom line, and why is a single bottom line not enough? What are the advantages and disadvantages of a triple-bottom-line approach in describing the performance of a tour operator? How could triple-bottom-line accounting be improved, with specific application to the tourism sector?

4. Can you identify any individual ecotourism product or organization that in your view can justifiably claim to have a positive triple bottom line? Describe the product or organization, what it does, and why you think each of its bottom lines is positive.

5. What is the distinction between a financial bottom line and an economic bottom line, as applied in the ecotourism sector? Identify some practical examples.

6. Identify any particular outdoor tourism product, either fixed or mobile, and list the factors you would consider, both positive and negative, in assessing its environmental bottom line. What data would you need to quantify each of these factors, and how could these data be collected or measured? If the data were of different types or different factors, how would you weigh them against each other to calculate an overall environmental bottom line?

7. If tourism in and to a particular isolated local community grows gradually from zero to a major component of the local economy, how is the aggregate social bottom line for tourism in that community likely to change, and why? List the factors you would consider in making your assessment, the ways in which their values might change with the development of tourism over time, and methods you could use to quantify or assess each component.

READING 14.1. A TRIPLE-BOTTOM-LINE APPROACH TO ECOTOURISM

Introduction

Ecotourism is a complex concept. The *Quebec Declaration* (UNEP/WTO, 2002), the top-level output of the International Year of Ecotourism, uses over 80 words and at least five distinct criteria. These boil down to: nature-based product, minimal-impact management, environmental education, contribution to conservation and contribution to communities; but it is still difficult to define whether an individual product or project qualifies as ecotourism (Buckley, 2003a,b). Can we express the concept of ecotourism in a way that is both more precise and more succinct? Is the concept of ecotourism necessarily nebulous, a series of scales in five different dimensions? Does it matter? Perhaps it does. For ecotourism to exert any significant influence on large-scale practice and policy, for example, governments will want economic statistics, and to collect these, statistical agencies will need clear criteria.

Sources of uncertainty

The current lack of precision may be considered in four categories. The first source of uncertainty is about each criterion independently. For example, must the product be nature-based, or can it also be culture-based? If the former, where is the dividing line? If the latter, which cultures and cultural manifestations are included? If an indigenous tour guide describes plant and animal names, traditional uses and mythology, is that nature or culture-based? If visiting the cultures of indigenous peoples living traditional lifestyles is ecotourism, what about indigenous peoples on their own land but with oil royalties and Western speedboats or snowmobiles? If that would qualify, then why not, say, English country estates? If poverty is a precondition, why not ghetto gangs? Similarly, sustainability is vague, and minimal-impact means little without a comparative framework. For example, is it enough for a helicopter tour to use a low-noise machine, or should the client have to walk? What if a parks agency promotes helicopter over-flights in preference to hiking on fragile landforms?

The second source of uncertainty is in combining criteria. Must they all be satisfied, or only some, and if so in what combination? To what degree can good performance on one criterion compensate for poor performance on others? Can a green spiel from the guide compensate for a company's impacts on the environment, or is that merely hypocritical? Historically, it is this issue that has been debated most in defining ecotourism. In particular, commercial interests in some countries have focused strongly on nature-based products, with limited attention to management and education, and little or none to conservation or communities.

The third source of uncertainty is in quantifying performance against each criterion. If a company makes a contribution to conservation, for example, which represents only a few tenths of a per cent of revenue, is this large enough to count? If not, what should the threshold be? If a hotel simply puts placards in guest rooms, telling guests they can save water by not having their towels washed every day, is this a significant improvement in environmental management? If a lodge prints brochures advertising a walk in a nearby park, is that environmental interpretation?

The fourth source of uncertainty is in baselines or benchmarks for comparison. If company A barely complies with relatively stringent environmental standards in one country, whereas company B far surpasses much lower standards in another country but still does not match the actual performance level of company A, which should be judged closer to ecotourism principles? In addition, different types of tour operations typically have very different options available to improve environmental management. Instead of assessing what an enterprise has achieved relative to minimum legally mandated standards, should we assess performance relative to best practice by similar enterprises elsewhere?

Inputs and outputs

The questions listed above ultimately boil down to just two independent issues: the environmental input and the environmental output. The environmental input is the primary attraction: not the level of service or facilities provided as part of a product package, but the geographical factor that has led the tourist to a particular destination. The environmental output is the overall net global cost or benefit of the tour operation to the natural environment. This is an accounting question, which requires the identification, quantification and summation of all costs and benefits through all potential mechanisms, of which there are many.

Importantly, this approach completely bypasses the service components of a retail tourism product, effectively treating it instead as a black box. From a business perspective, these components are vital, but they do not differentiate ecotourism from any other form of tourism. In particular, if an interpretation programme keeps clients happy but does not reduce their impacts, then it is a component of service rather than a contribution to the environment.

This conceptual approach does not move the meaning of ecotourism outside its currently accepted boundaries, but can clarify them considerably. In particular, it highlights a number of critical issues, some on the input side and some on the output.

One such distinction is between nature and culture, natural and social environment. Historically, 'local communities' have been an oft-quoted touchphrase in the ecotourism literature, but with confusion between input and output aspects. On the input side, the critical question is whether an attraction that relies principally on some aspect of human culture, rather than nature alone, should be considered ecotourism. On the output side, the question is whether purely social costs and benefits are significant in themselves, or only insofar as they affect the impacts of those societies on the natural environment.

Fortunately, though significant both in principle and in politics, this distinction is rather unimportant in practice. Cultural tours do not seem to be marketed as ecotours in practice, except for traditional cultures with strong links to local natural environments. Equally, practical case studies indicate that for ecotourism to assist in conservation of the natural environment, it must provide some benefit, tangible or otherwise, for people in a position to protect that environment.

Under the conceptual approach suggested here, minimal-impact management is not a fundamental criterion in itself, but a way to reduce environmental costs, and the critical issue is to assess the total cost, not how much it may or may not have been reduced relative to various alternative possible benchmarks. Environmental interpretation is not a goal in itself, but simply one of many potential mechanisms to produce an environmental benefit. Again, it is the benefits that matter, more than the mechanism.

Under this approach, ecotourism is tourism that satisfies both the input and output criteria as outlined above. In practice, tourism products that yield a net benefit for the global environment are nearly all nature based, but this need not necessarily be so. The proprietor of an urban hotel, for example, could use profits to establish private conservation reserves. This is uncommon, but not unknown.

It would certainly be convenient if there were distinct terms to identify the input and output factors separately. Phrases such as 'tourism in a natural setting', however, are too vague, for the reasons outlined earlier. To date, most attempts to define the input aspect more precisely have done so by aggregating subsectors. The term NEAT (Buckley, 2000a), for example, aggregates more contemplative nature tourism with more excitement-based adventure tourism. The term ACE (Fennell, 1999) adds the cultural component to the mix, subject to all the issues discussed earlier. While useful analytically, however, such acronyms do not seem to have been adopted in marketing materials or policy documents.

One term that has been proposed but little used is geotourism (Stueve *et al.*, 2002). Currently, this term is used in two distinct senses. The original use of this term is as shorthand for geological tourism, travelling to see rocks (Dowling and Newsome, 2006). The alternative use is as shorthand for geographical tourism, i.e. tourist attractions, either natural or cultural, that are specific to one geographic place. In this sense, geotourism excludes business travel, VFR, MICE, 3S, generic resorts, casinos, theme parks and similar forms of mass tourism. If you travel to see particular scenery or wildlife or experience a particular local culture, climb a particular mountain or kayak a particular river, then in this sense you would be a geotourist. If you want to lie on the beach, visit nightclubs or casinos, play golf or go bungy jumping, however, and don't particularly care where, then you are not. Only if you insist on a specific casino, golf course or bungy jump, such as Las Vegas, St Andrews or Karamea Bridge, respectively, would you qualify as a geotourist under the geographical usage.

Triple-bottom-line accounting for output

On the output side, the most promising approach is triple-bottom-line accounting, where environmental, social and financial costs and benefits are assessed independently, and the company is not in credit unless all three bottom lines are positive. This is not the same as sustainability, in the fundamental sense of keeping the planet in a liveable state. It is, however, a useful step, which recognizes that such sustainability can only be achieved through major changes to human social structure and behaviour, and that social and environmental accounting may be one tool to promote such changes.

All definitions of ecotourism also include sustainability as a key criterion, but this has done little to clarify its meaning. The underlying issue of sustainability is clear enough: if the human species causes too much damage to the rest of the planet, then that species will not survive, and meanwhile the more damage to the planet caused by current human generations, the worse shape the planet will be in as a resource for future generations.

Establishing social structures and institutions that can change human behaviour sufficiently to reduce present-day damage to the global environment, however, is almost intractably difficult, because of the complexity of current human societies. Sustainability is fundamentally about human interactions with the natural environment, but any attempt to get there depends on human interactions with other humans. Hence the triple-bottom-line approach, including money and politics as well as the planet. Of course, the triple-bottom-line approach is subject to widespread political misuse: an excuse to divert attention away from environmental issues, disguise environmentally destructive practices and policy, dilute environmental research efforts and disarm environmental activists. Used constructively, however, the triple-bottom-line concept may perhaps lead voters and consumers to weigh the environmental and social aspects of products and policies as well as price and profit.

Businesses in all industry sectors have begun preparing triple-bottom-line sustainability assessments, similar to the various corporate environmental reporting initiatives over previous decades. In most of these, the social and environmental components are a great deal less detailed than the financial figures. For example, they may list the appointment of environmental advisors, the adoption of an environmental management system, or the sustainability report itself as environmental achievements, with no attempt to account for environmental costs and benefits across the company's entire operations. For comparison, a company's financial statements would not be well received by regulators and sharemarkets if they said only that the company thought money was important, had established a financial management system and had appointed some financial advisors!

At present, corporations and governments have much more detailed financial information than environmental or social, but this is largely because they spend far more effort on collecting financial information. For any organization to show that it has a positive social or environmental bottom line, in any meaningful accounting sense, it needs to identify and quantify all the direct and indirect environmental and social costs and benefits of its entire operations, and calculate the difference between the benefits and the costs. This is very different from arguing that money and jobs outweigh environmental costs. A positive triple bottom line means a net improvement in conservation of the natural environment and a net social benefit for local communities, as well as a net profit for shareholders and/or a net gain for national or regional economies.

Strictly speaking, a distinction can be made between a financial bottom line for shareholders, and an economic bottom line for a regional economy. The latter, however, may be viewed as part of the social bottom line, contributing to society beyond the shareholders themselves.

Very few organizations worldwide can demonstrate a positive triple bottom line. Most of these are environmental organizations, environmental technology and services companies, or ecotourism enterprises. Of these, the first two are established specifically to counteract or remediate the environmental impacts of other sectors. Currently, tourism seems to be the only major industry sector where there are individual commercial enterprises, which generate net gains for conservation, communities and shareholders simultaneously. These enterprises seem to be precisely what we think of as ecotourism, which can therefore be conceived of as geotourism with a positive triple bottom line.

Advantages of a bottom line focus

While fundamentally the same as more complex definitions of ecotourism such as that used by UNEP/WTO (2002), the conceptual approach proposed here does differ in emphasis, as noted earlier. Instead of listing environmental education and management as criteria or goals in their own right, the triple-bottom-line approach treats them simply as mechanisms, with the goal and criterion being the positive triple bottom line.

This focus on the bottom line has several advantages. One often-asked question is, why make such a fuss about ecotourism when there is no equivalent term in other industry sectors, or certainly not one of sufficient significance to have its own UN International Year? The reason, surely, is that while enterprises in other sectors can indeed take steps to reduce their operational environmental impacts, their environmental bottom line is still negative. It is only in tourism that there is a realistic opportunity to produce a positive environmental and indeed social bottom line at the same time as a positive economic bottom line. It is thus the positive contribution to conservation, either directly or through local communities, which makes ecotourism worth worrying about. These bottom line contributions, therefore, are the key defining feature.

The key advantage of the bottom-line focus is that to assess a bottom line requires a full and transparent accounting of all the costs as well as the benefits. Done thoroughly, this forces both the ecotourism enterprise and also its shareholders, clients, staff, regulators and local communities, to identify and weigh up those costs and benefits much more fully than is common at present. It is no longer enough simply to list a few benefits and ignore the costs. This in turn should eliminate many of the enterprises that might be described as fake ecotourism or ecotourism 'lite': where the cosmetic addition of an environmental interpretation programme or a minor improvement in environmental management is used to lay claim to the ecotourism title, even if overall the social and environmental impacts of the enterprise are quite severe. One of the major weaknesses of most tourism ecocertification schemes, for example, is that an enterprise can gain green ticks for hiring good interpretive guides, or indeed for buying plantations far away to offset its carbon dioxide emissions, even if its operations cause loss of biodiversity through disturbance in a national park or clearance of habitat for endangered species. Certification can be a valuable tool, but easily abused – just as Iraq wanted a UN blue tick for its weapons programme.

Practical examples

So, are there in fact any examples of geotourism with a positive triple bottom line? Yes, but not many (Buckley, 2003a, b; UNWTO, 2002). There are private companies that have bought areas of freehold land and established them as conservation reserves funded by ecotourism. Often this includes rehabilitation of vegetation and restocking with wildlife. If the net environmental benefits from the private reserve outweigh the environmental impacts of the tourism operations, then the environmental bottom line is positive. Some of these companies also include community development programmes, e.g. through funds established for community health and education facilities, so the social bottom line may also be positive. Some of these enterprises are very strong economically, while others have suffered a series of vicissitudes. Since they still survive, however, the financial bottom line must also be positive overall. These enterprises can thus lay a justifiable claim to a positive triple bottom line.

There are also a number of ecotourism enterprises, either privately or communally owned, which operate successfully on community lands. Where such enterprises allow these communities to retain their lands in a relatively undisturbed state rather than clearing them for agriculture, leasing them for logging or hunting native animals for bushmeat or wildlife trade, then a positive triple bottom line is also possible. Similar considerations may apply where large environmental NGOs buy land for conservation and operate ecotourism ventures there, or where public land management agencies turn their hand to tourism from other primary production sectors, or where aid programmes establish ecotourism ventures as a long-term source of community income.

As in all accounting exercises, defining the boundaries of the accounting unit is a critical step in assessing a triple bottom line for a tourism or ecotourism enterprise. Just as a large business may have profitable and unprofitable subsidiaries, a tourism company may own or operate particular lodges or tours that do have a positive triple bottom line, and others that do not. Thus, for example, the ecotourism certification programme in Australia offers ecocertification for individual tourism products, not entire tourism companies (Ecotourism Association of Australia, 2007). If a private reserve and ecolodge, for example, can demonstrate a positive triple bottom line in its operations, it makes no difference whether the initial investment capital was provided by shareholders, a bank loan or a private corporation that may also have interests in mining or manufacturing, farming or fisheries. For the investor, the net bottom line for the ecotourism enterprise is simply one component to be added into its overall accounts. From the viewpoint of the individual ecotourism operation, the source of capital is irrelevant.

Conclusions

The main defining characteristics of ecotourism fall into two categories, namely environmental inputs and environmental outputs. The inputs are the natural and associated cultural features in a particular geographic place, which serve as attractions for tourists. The outputs are the net costs or benefits for the natural and social environment. Ecotourism can hence be viewed with a geographically defined input, and a positive triple bottom line. There are several advantages to this approach: (i) it clarifies the meaning of ecotourism without redefining it; (ii) it bypasses the service components that are common to tourism in general, not distinctive to ecotourism;

(iii) it treats environmental management and interpretation as means, not ends; (iv) it requires an accurate accounting of environmental and social, as well as financial, costs as well as benefits; (v) it differentiates ecotourism from tourism products with a mere veneer of green; and (vi) the tourism products and organizations that are generally viewed as the world's best practice in ecotourism do comply with this definition.

Acknowledgements

This reading is a shortened and revised version of Buckley (2003b), first published in the *Journal of Ecotourism* 2, 76–82.

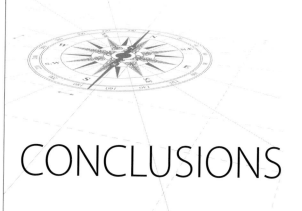

chapter 15

CONCLUSIONS

Perhaps the most famous of the arches which gave Arches National Park in Utah, USA its name. Note figure at centre left, indicating scale of rock formations. This park is heavily visited.

REVIEW

Introduction

This concluding chapter identifies and examines four major trends in ecotourism and related sectors, and uses these projections to predict ecotourism business opportunities, policy implications and research priorities for the next decade or so.

The four main trends may be summarized as follows. Continuing global urbanization drives continuing growth in outdoor tourism, but the principal focus is on the outdoors as part of tourism products. There is lots of rhetoric about environmental management, but little has changed in reality. Few tour operators currently contribute to conservation, but the number of private reserves is increasing. Links between the outdoor tourism industry and the property, equipment, clothing and entertainment sectors are increasing.

Over the past quarter century, the ideas and approaches associated with ecotourism have indeed proved quite influential, and this continues currently. Certainly, much of the mainstream tourism industry still has rather rudimentary environmental management practices, and most of the outdoor tourism sector sees nature purely as part of its products.

There has been a gradual trend for urban hotels in developed nations to adopt low-key environmental management measures, but at the same time, high-impact resorts and resort-residential developments in areas of high conservation value continue to be proposed, approved and constructed. A small but growing number of medium-scale commercial nature tourism enterprises, however, both fixed-site and mobile, have successfully adopted ecotourism principles, including significant contributions to conservation and local communities as well as environmental management and education. These companies are likely to play an increasingly important role in global conservation, particularly as climate change increases the importance of conservation management on private land.

The key goal of ecotourism is to reduce the net environmental impact of the tourism industry. Mechanisms may include minimal-impact management measures, education, community involvement, private conservation, contributions to public protected areas, expansion of ecotourism enterprises and mainstreaming of ecotourism principles. While there are successful examples of each of these, overall progress has been limited. Adoption of low-key environmental management measures is the most widespread approach. Establishment of private conservation reserves and expansion of global nature tourism retailers with environmental awards are currently the most significant.

Ecotourism goals and evaluation approaches

Ecotourism has been debated in theory and attempted in practice for close to two decades. A recent review by Weaver and Lawton (2007) examined patterns in published academic literature. That review did not, however, attempt 'to determine whether the goals of ecotourism are now being achieved'

(Weaver and Lawton, 2007). This chapter aims to complement that earlier review by assembling evidence specifically to test such a proposition. To avoid repetition of Weaver and Lawton (2007), only the rather limited literature that presents practical evidence is cited.

To assess whether they are being met, the goals of ecotourism must first be made explicit, and this depends on the precise definition adopted. There are many reviews, recapitulations and reconceptualizations of such definitions (Buckley, 1994a, 2003b; Fennell, 2001; Weaver and Lawton, 2007). Some of the criteria proposed, notably community involvement issues, remain contested (Weaver and Lawton, 2007; Buckley, 2008) and are hence not examined here. Excluding these, the four main defining criteria identified nearly 15 years ago (Buckley, 1994a) remain valid: nature-based product or setting, minimal-impact or 'sustainable' manage-ment, environmental education component, and a contribution to conservation.

While there has been very considerable debate over the precise criteria defining ecotourism, discussion of goals has been less explicit. Some of the criteria are simply questions of defi-nition, not goals as such: for example, reliance on the natural environment as the principal setting and attraction. Some are no different from those of the tourism sector more gener-ally: for example, any private business must make a profit if it is to remain financially viable, even if it receives start-up capital from development assistance funding (Weaver and Lawton, 2007). Some remain contested: for example, whether ecotourism must necessarily play a role in poverty alleviation for local communities in developing nations, or whether that is just one of many roles that ecotourism can play (Weaver and Lawton, 2007; Buckley, 2008).

Some, however, are real-life goals: that may or may not be achieved; where progress is at least potentially measurable; and that can clearly differentiate ecotourism from tourism more generally. It is these that are the focus in this assessment. In particular, the key goal of ecotour-ism, embodied in some form in all definitions and discussion, is that it aims to reduce the net impact of tourism on the natural environment.

There are three principal aspects to this, which may be seen either as mechanisms or as subsidi-ary goals. The first is to reduce gross per capita negative impacts, e.g. through minimal-impact environmental equipment, management and education, and possibly through post-tour life-style changes by clients. The second is to offset negative impacts by generating positive contri-butions to conservation, e.g. through the establishment or support of private reserves, through contributions to protected area management agencies, through support of local communities and conservation organizations, and possibly through post-tour political action by clients. The third is to extend these approaches as broadly as possible throughout the tourism sector, e.g. by enlarging individual ecotourism enterprises to mainstream scale, or by successfully promoting the adoption of ecotourism principles and practices throughout the entire tourism industry.

Evaluating progress by the ecotourism sector, even progress in mainstreaming ecotourism principles, is a very different exercise from evaluating environmental progress by the tour-ism industry as a whole, or progress towards so-called sustainable tourism (Weaver, 2007a, b). Commercial ecotourism takes place largely in relatively pristine natural environments, commonly with some formal conservation status or community ownership (Buckley, 2004d; Weaver, 2008). Its effects on these areas, whether negative or positive, direct or indirect, are identifiable and at least conceptually testable and quantifiable. Sustainability, in contrast, is not defined with sufficient clarity to be measured or evaluated across the tourism industry as a whole, and may never be (Wheeller, 2007). The evaluation of ecotourism attempted here can draw on an extensive quantitative natural-science and social-science literature related to protected area management and outdoor recreation, which as yet has no corresponding equivalent in, for example, the urban hospitality sector.

Of course, ecotourists also use international air travel (Simmons and Becken, 2004; Folke *et al.*, 2006) and stay in city hotels (Wheeller, 2007), and a full footprint analysis of the ecotourism sector would need to account for the associated social and environmental consequences of those components as well as the non-urban activities that form the principal attractions. These components, however, are no different from the rest of the tourism industry. Progress towards ecotourism goals can still be assessed, for those aspects and components that differentiate ecotourism from the sector as a whole. These are the components associated with the particular areas where ecotourism activities take place. This evaluation hence focuses on those areas rather than the urban and air travel components of commercial tour packages.

Sources of data on each of the themes and subthemes identified above differ greatly in detail. There are apparently only two large-scale published compilations of ecotourism case studies (UNWTO, 2002; Buckley, 2003a), and only some of these case studies include information on environmental management practices. The former was a country-by-country compilation of submissions from relevant national government tourism agencies. The latter used both a larger net and a finer mesh. It screened over 500 individual tour products that advertised themselves as ecotourism, and documented and analysed about 170 that did in fact meet at least some of the defining criteria for the sector. About 50 of these were audited on-site, and information on the remainder was derived from reputable independent published sources. These case studies hence provided a relatively reliable and comprehensive set of data from which to derive general patterns. There is also an analysis of the geography and certain characteristics of 188 published ecotourism case-study evaluations (Kruger, 2005) but this does not identify the specific case studies considered or list the sources of data, so it is of limited value in the present context.

There are several related but restricted sources of relevant data. There are numerous compilations and analyses of the various tools available to land managers, especially parks agencies, to monitor and manage the impacts of visitors including commercial ecotour operators (Lockwood *et al.*, 2006). There are several reviews of the types and degree of impacts produced, under the rubric of recreation ecology (Liddle, 1997; Buckley, 2004a). There is an extensive literature on environmental education and interpretation in outdoor tourism and recreation (Black and Crabtree, 2007) but very little on its effectiveness in reducing impacts (Littlefair, 2004; Marion and Reid, 2007; Littlefair and Buckley, 2008). Nor, apparently, have there been many published attempts to calculate the overall environmental footprints of particular ecotourists (Folke *et al.*, 2006).

Information on private reserves supported by ecotourism, and on ecotourism operators' contributions to conservation organizations and public protected area management agencies, is available from the case-study compendia as above and from information released by the parks, reserves and NGOs themselves. There is limited information on cash donations made by ecotour operators or clients to community or conservation funds. There are few if any rigorous published investigations into any post-tour political role that ecotour clients may play. Bauer (1999b) interviewed tour clients on an Antarctic expedition cruise, but found that they did not consider themselves as environmental advocates.

Data on the scale of individual ecotourism enterprises are obtainable, but not systematic. There have been very limited attempts at comprehensive national surveys. In most cases, one must rely on anecdotal evidence to identify candidate companies for detailed investigation, which can then be pursued through corporate reports, stock exchange disclosure statements and similar sources, albeit only for public corporations. This approach has been attempted for particular outdoor tourism subsectors such as the commercial surfing industry (Buckley, 2006), but not yet for the ecotourism sector as such.

The extent to which ecotourism principles may have diffused more widely into the mainstream tourism sector is even more difficult to gauge. There is a very extensive academic literature on this topic, most of it using terminology such as sustainable tourism, but very few hard data. Many of the publications concerned consider only a single measure by a single corporation, with no attempt to set it into any overall environmental accounting context. A parallel but also unreliable source of information is the literature on tourism ecocertification. This majority of relevant publications describe the existence, scale, intentions or occasionally the operational structure of such schemes, but very few attempt to assess their aggregate environmental outcomes.

Overall, therefore, the data available to assess how well ecotourism may have achieved its key goals are far from comprehensive. With this caveat, the various themes outlined above are now addressed in full.

Reducing negative impacts

Evaluation approaches

There are a number of steps that can be taken to reduce the negative environmental impacts of ecotourism. The first is to identify the types, mechanisms, intensity, scale and ecological severity of impacts from different activities in different ecosystems, and ways to measure them. This forms the discipline of recreation ecology. To assess progress on this front, we can: consider how accurately we can predict the ecological impacts of any specified ecotourism activity in ecosystems of high conservation value; establish criteria to distinguish effective indicator parameters; and examine how well these criteria are met by monitoring programmes currently in use.

The second step is for ecotourism enterprises and land managers to adopt minimal-impact equipment and technologies, in order to reduce such impacts. Progress can be assessed by considering what types of tools have been adopted, how broadly, and with what outcomes.

The third approach is to educate ecotourists to recognize and reduce their own impacts during the ecotourism experience itself, and test how effective such education actually is, both in changing behavioural patterns and in reducing aggregate environmental impacts in consequence.

Finally, to test whether ecotourism experiences may reduce individual impacts subsequently, once tourists have returned home, would require some form of statistically valid quantitative measurement and comparison of the ecological footprints of some sample of ecotourists both before and after they took their tours.

Impacts and indicators

Most ecotourism operations use areas that are significant for conservation as well as scenic. Tour operators and land managers need to know what types of impacts are created by different activities in different ecosystems. Preferably, they should also know which particular ecosystem components or functions are affected, and how impacts may vary with factors such as equipment used, time of year, prior skills, group size and group leadership.

Recent global reviews of recreation ecology research (Liddle, 1997; Buckley, 2004a, 2005b) found that, despite a generally upward trend in research effort, data are still sparse, crude and clumped. They are sparse in the sense that of all the various possible combinations of activity, ecosystem, impact type and management measures, only a very small proportion have so far been subject to scientific study. They are crude in the sense that by far the majority of studies have used very basic and unsophisticated approaches. They are clumped in the sense that some types of activity, some types of impact and some geographic areas have been studied in far more detail than others. Some of the more recent research is relatively sophisticated, but there does not seem to be any overall trend towards more subtle or scientifically detailed analysis.

Most of this research is in Europe and North America, and to a lesser extent in Australia, New Zealand and southern Africa (Buckley, 2005b). International comparisons are complicated by language differences. While there is an increasing recognition that ecosystems in different countries do not necessarily suffer the same impacts from the same activities, there is still a strong bias towards particular areas and particular types of impact. The two principal priorities for future research are thus: first, international comparisons of the impacts of similar activities in structurally similar but taxonomically distinct ecosystems in different countries and, second, a continuing attempt to identify and analyse the more subtle, complex and indirect impact mechanisms, which may often be the most significant ecologically.

Different impacts are more or less critical for different ecosystems, and there are too many types of impact to measure them all. Criteria are therefore needed to select particular suites of indicator parameters, which can reveal the extent, urgency and severity of ecotourism impacts, and the effectiveness of any management measures. Criteria for effective indicators, which could be used by parks agencies and other landholders in their management of tourism and recreation, were proposed by Buckley (1998c, 2003f) and Eagles and McCool (2002). Buckley (2003f), for example, proposed that indicators should be: discriminating, quantifiable, actionable, sensitive, ecologically significant, integrated and feasible in practice. Eagles and McCool (2002) independently put forward a similar set of criteria.

Progress towards adoption of such indicators, however, has been rather localized. Most protected area management agencies have limited resources for monitoring, and tourism and recreation may be less critical than weeds, fires, feral animals, poaching or pollution. Monitoring programmes are rarely planned with reference to predefined indicator criteria. Except in private conservation reserves, only a small number of private ecotourism enterprises monitor their own impacts in any reliable and repeatable manner.

Tools and technologies

Ecotourism enterprises themselves, and the managers of lands and waters where they operate, have access to a toolbox of techniques to minimize, mitigate or rehabilitate impacts. Where recreation impacts are significant, a variety of visitor management protocols have been put forward over recent decades (Eagles and McCool, 2002; Hendee and Dawson, 2002; Lockwood *et al.*, 2006). These visitor management protocols are conceptually straightforward and, to a large extent, simply formalize what parks agencies were doing in any event. There have indeed been some changes, e.g. to recreational activities permitted at different times and places, but these have been driven principally by increasing visitor numbers, conflicts between different users, and concerns over litigation and liability rather than through any efforts by the commercial ecotourism subsector.

A growing proportion of outdoor tourism and commercial recreation providers have adopted equipment and management practices to reduce environmental impacts, because of legal conditions in operating permits issued by landowners or land management agencies. A much smaller number of leading commercial ecotourism operators have designed new equipment, introduced new management practices, and developed codes and guidelines to reduce aggregate environmental impacts, beyond the requirements of permits and legislation (Buckley, 2003a, 2006).

Training and education

In addition to active steps by staff and guides, ecotourism operators and land managers can reduce aggregate impacts by educating commercial tour clients, and to a lesser extent independent recreational visitors, in minimal-impact practices. Such information is commonly only one component of environmental interpretation, so the widespread emphasis on interpretation as a component of ecotourism products and services does not necessarily imply broader adoption of minimal-impact training. People do not necessarily pay attention to such messages; if they do, they do not necessarily change their behaviour; and even if they do that, it does not necessarily reduce their impacts significantly. There have been very few successful attempts to test whether minimal-impact education actually does reduce the impacts of ecotour clients or other park visitors (Marion and Reid, 2007; Buckley and Littlefair, 2007). In fact, it seems that there have been only four. One relied solely on signs (Jacobi, 2003), and one on brochures reinforced by rangers (Oliver *et al.*, 1985). The other two relied on guides, one on a coral reef (Medio *et al.*, 1997) and one in a subtropical rainforest (Littlefair, 2004). It is thus by no means certain that educational approaches routinely reduce aggregate environmental impacts by either commercial ecotour clients or independent park visitors.

Post-trip footprints

Advocates of commercial tourism in protected areas have postulated repeatedly that ecotourism experiences may later lead clients to modify their lifestyles to reduce their overall ecological footprints. There is apparently no evidence for this assertion and no attempt to test it. It is arguable whether this is one of the goals of ecotourism, but if it is, there is no indication of progress. Indeed, insofar as many ecotourism clients travel internationally to take part in tours, their trips generate an increase in greenhouse gas emissions, which may well offset or outweigh any local benefits.

Generating positive impacts

Approaches

The key reason why ecotourism is of broad interest for development and policy, beyond its role as one of many different subsectors of the human economy, is its potential to make a positive contribution to conservation of biological diversity. This is perhaps the most disputed criterion in the various definitions of ecotourism, but without it, environmental management in tourism is not conceptually distinct from environmental management in any other industry sector, such as mining or forestry. Rather few of the many tourism operations marketed as ecotourism, however, actually make any deliberate positive contribution to conservation (Buckley, 2003a). Since even the best-managed ecotourism does produce environmental impacts, an ecotourism enterprise can only produce a positive environmental bottom line if it makes a contribution to conservation that outweighs those impacts.

Case studies examined by Buckley (2003a) and Kruger (2005) indicate that tourism only contributes to conservation if there is a strong legal and practical conservation management framework already in place before the tourism industry begins to grow. In that situation, with appropriate land tenure and economic instruments, tourism can contribute funding to support conservation management. If the conservation framework is not in place first, however, the evidence is that tourism grows without any internal self-regulation and with a net negative effect for conservation.

An effective conservation management framework may be either private or public. Ecotourism can provide funding either to operate private land as a conservation reserve, or to contribute to the management of public protected areas. The management issues, however, are somewhat different on public and private reserves, as outlined below.

There are also several less direct mechanisms by which ecotourism can potentially contribute to conservation. Operators or clients may provide support in cash or in kind to voluntary conservation groups and NGOs that lobby for conservation. They may provide employment and other economic support to local communities, which encourage those communities to conserve wildlife and habitats. Clients may themselves become political advocates and activists for conservation.

Private conservation reserves

On private land, the landowner has the right to determine what kind of tourism operations may be run, by whom, and under what commercial arrangements. The landowner also has the right to restrict and control access, which allows the tourism operation to provide an exclusive experience. Private reserves are generally smaller in area than public national parks, and all management costs, for land and wildlife as well as tourist facilities, must be met from private income, whether from tourism or otherwise.

In some parts of the world at least, there has been quite rapid recent growth in the number of private game reserves that offer tourism products, most commonly based on lodges but in some places only on day tours. The greatest growth seems to be in sub-Saharan Africa, particularly in southern Africa, but there are also examples from other countries and continents. Some representative cases are outlined below.

The private reserves of the Sabi Sands area adjacent to Kruger National Park operate long-established, internationally well-known and successful tourist lodges, some of them extremely upmarket, which effectively add 65,000 ha to the Kruger National Park conservation area, and support local populations of a number of endangered species. Phinda Private Reserve, adjacent to the Greater St Lucia World Heritage Area, plays a similar role. As with the Sabi Sands reserves, Phinda is a former cattle property, which has been purchased, fenced, rehabilitated and restocked specifically for tourism and conservation.

The 70,000-ha Madikwe Game Reserve in the northern part of South Africa, on the border with Botswana, also consists of former cattle properties restocked with game specifically for tourism. Unlike Phinda and some of the Sabi Sands properties, therefore, where private land-owners set out to create conservation reserves and then used tourism to fund operating costs, the Madikwe landowners deliberately adopted wildlife tourism as a more profitable land use than cattle grazing. They manage the Madikwe Reserve, and its vegetation and wildlife, specifically to present the most marketable wildlife tourism experience.

Private reserves have also expanded in number recently in the Eastern Cape Province of South Africa. Unlike Madikwe, however, these are not adjacent and co-managed properties, but smaller separate pieces of land where maintaining predator populations, in particular, is even more difficult. Some of these private reserves run their own tourist lodges; some allow visits during the day but do not offer accommodation; and some simply raise wildlife for sale to other reserves. One of the larger examples, which runs full-scale tourism operations, is Kwandwe Reserve (CC Africa, 2007). Kwandwe makes a significant contribution to conservation of the endangered blue crane.

In Central and Southern America, private conservation reserves funded at least partly by ecotourism include one at Tambopata in Peru (Rainforest Expeditions, 2008) and those operated by Rara Avis (2008), and Rios Tropicales (2008) in Costa Rica. In Asia, there are examples of private reserves at Ulu Ai in Malaysia (Borneo Adventures, 2008) and at El Nido in the Philippines (Ten Knots, 2008). In Australia, the Warrawong Reserve operated by Earth Sanctuaries (2008) is well known, and in New Zealand Arthur's Pass Wilderness Lodge (2008).

In East Africa, there is a similar though geographically more scattered set of conservation reserves funded by ecotourism, in areas around the major public national parks such as the Serengeti in Tanzania and Masai Mara in Kenya. The largest collection of these is probably the Northern Circuit operated by Conservation Corporation Africa (CC Africa) (Buckley, 2006). For reasons of historical land tenure, the operating areas are held as concessions from public land management agencies, essentially long-term leases, rather than freehold as in South Africa, but the outcomes are similar: these areas are used for conservation instead of farming or hunting. There is also a private marine reserve at Chumbe Island in Tanzania.

There are a number of instances around the world where private tour operators have established co-management arrangements between private and public conservation areas. The Sabi Sands reserves referred to earlier, for example, have removed the boundary fences separating them from Kruger National Park, so that wildlife can now move freely between public and private land. Dubai Desert Conservation Reserve, in the United Arab Emirates, consists of a privately owned core zone supported by the Al Maha Resort (2008), surrounded by a larger publicly owned reserve, which is also managed by Al Maha and was established at their request.

Conservation through communities and NGOs

Rather than buying freehold land for private conservation reserves, some ecotourism enterprises contribute to conservation through arrangements with local communities, support for voluntary conservation groups, or direct political lobbying. A number of privately owned wildlife tourism lodges in Africa, for example, operate on community-owned land under various lease and revenue-sharing arrangements. Examples include Kichwa Tembo Lodge immediately outside the western Masai Mara Nature Conservancy in southern Kenya, and a number of lodges in Botswana and Namibia (CC Africa, 2008; Wilderness Safaris, 2008). Additional examples are outlined in Buckley (2003a).

Such arrangements can contribute to conservation if local residents would otherwise use the area for farming or forestry, or hunt or collect particular species of high conservation value. If ecotourism can provide residents with sufficient financial incentive, either through employment or entrepreneurial opportunities, it may persuade them to convert to more conservation-orientated land management or reduce hunting. This applies as much to the more developed nations as to the developing world. Indeed, developed nations continue to log forests and dam rivers while simultaneously promoting forest and river tourism, and examples where ecotourism has successfully changed community land-use practices are even fewer in developed than developing nations.

Alternatively or additionally to community-based mechanisms as above, some ecotourism operators contribute to conservation through non-government organizations and trust funds. Some of these NGOs are large multinationals such as Conservation International or the WWF. Others are local single-purpose organizations such as Save the Rhino (2008) or Save the Cheetah (2008), which may be independent or may have been established by the ecotour operator itself. A distinction may be drawn between contributions by the tour operator itself, and contributions made directly by tour clients. In addition, the significance of any voluntary contributions depends on financial scale: trivial sums are more likely to be assessed as marketing ploys than as significant contributions to conservation. Most major international conservation NGOs have some past or ongoing involvement in using ecotourism as a conservation tool.

The WWF, for example, is a partner in: the Ngala Reserve in South Africa, operated by Conservation Corporation Africa; Spitzkoppe and Nyae-Nyae reserves in Namibia; a number of reserves in Nepal and India, and Prespa and Dadia-Lefkimi-Soufli reserves in Greece (Buckley, 2003a). Conservation International (CI) has established a suite of ecolodges and reserves in southern and central America, including Fazenda Rio Negro, Cristalina Jungle Lodge and Una Ecopark in Brazil, Chalalan Ecolodge in Bolivia and Wekso Ecolodge in Panama. It was also a partner in projects at Noslek Arbor in the Philippines, the Togian Islands in Indonesia, and Kakum in Ghana. The Nature Conservancy (TNC) played a major role in establishing Great Rivers National Park in Yunnan, China, and projects in Belize and Mexico. Birdlife International has successfully used ecotourism as a tool for conservation of rare birds on three islands in the Seychelles, and the Audubon Society has made major contributions to at least two wildlife sanctuaries in Belize.

Political advocacy for conservation by tour operators and associations

A third indirect mechanism for ecotourism operators to contribute to conservation is through political lobbying. This may include lobbying for the establishment of new protected areas, or for improved funding for protected area management agencies. It may also include lobbying for specific local actions or decisions, such as closing high-impact roads or refusing applications for high-impact developments or easements, e.g. for power lines across conservation areas. There are indeed examples of such approaches, but rather few relative to the scale of the tourism industry. World Expeditions, for example, lobbied to close a road across a World Heritage area in Tasmania, Australia (Buckley, 2003a, pp. 112–114) and several tourism industry associations recently lobbied for increased funding to Australian parks agencies (Australian Senate Standing Committee, 2007).

Post-trip conservation advocacy by ecotour clients

It has also been claimed on occasion, though with little or no basis, that ecotourism experiences may potentially convert clients to conservationists, i.e. if people have the opportunity to enjoy a beautiful natural environment while they are on holiday, this may later lead them to lobby for environmental protection more generally. This is a similar rationale to that which leads protected management agencies to promote recreational opportunities, in the hope of producing a political constituency to support conservation. For commercial ecotourism, the suggestion is that following their tour experience, clients might change their voting patterns, give money to conservation organizations or put their own time and effort into lobbying for conservation. There do not seem to be any reliable data to demonstrate whether such effects do in fact occur. A few people may indeed find a commercial ecotour to be a life-changing experience at a personal level, but unless those individuals go on to become major conservation lobbyists or donors, and their actions outweigh the impacts of other tourists whose behaviour remains unchanged, then the environmental bottom line will remain negative.

There would only be a net benefit for conservation under this mechanism if three conditions were all met. The first is a net increase in such conservation-supporting behaviours by ecotour clients, following their tours. It would not be enough to show, for example, that ecotour clients show more support for conservation, on average, than the population as a whole, because this could indicate only that people concerned about conservation are more likely to buy ecotourism products.

The second piece of evidence would be whether any such increase in conservation-related behaviour was actually effective, i.e. whether it yielded an actual increase in conservation. This could be measured by, for example, increases in areas protected or in populations of endangered species, which could be ascribed with reasonable confidence to an increase in conservation behaviour by former ecotour clients. The third criterion would be whether any such increase in actual conservation outcomes outweighed the negative ecological impacts of the ecotours concerned, as measured, for example, by effects on populations of endangered species or other relevant parameters.

To construct this overall argument with any degree of reliability, therefore, would require quite a complex and extensive set of data. In particular, since most conservation outcomes and indeed conservation-related policy decisions depend on a wide range of different factors, many of them political and hence difficult to deconstruct, this particular mechanism is likely to remain unproven. One can envisage a situation where, for example, a majority of ecotour operators in a particular geographic area might conceivably call upon all their past and current clients to mount a specific conservation campaign, which could produce a successful and identifiable outcome. To date, however, there do not yet seem to be any such instances reported. It is difficult or impossible, therefore, to assess whether there is any trend in the contributions of ecotourism to conservation through these potential indirect mechanisms.

Support for public protected areas

A large proportion of ecotourism enterprises make use of public protected areas, often in addition to other public and private lands (Buckley, 2004d). The majority operate under standardized permit systems set up by the management agencies. They may pay various fees and charges, but only as prescribed in permits. Some have obtained special privileges, often through historical or political means.

A few, however, provide support for the conservation agencies either in cash or in kind, either on a purely voluntary basis or as part of a negotiated arrangement for privileged access or activity rights. Examples of the former are summarized by Buckley (2003a, 2006), and of the latter by Buckley (2004j). One recent addition to this category is the construction of Mahua Kothi and Bhagvan Lodges at Bandhavgarh and Pench National Parks in India, both known for their tiger-watching opportunities (Taj Hotels, 2008).

There are also cases where particular commercial tour operators lent strong support and investment to the declaration of a particular conservation area, and were subsequently granted privileged access rights in recognition of their role. One such example is provided by Sunchaser Ecotours (2008) in Khutzeymateen Inlet, British Columbia, Canada.

As noted earlier, a high proportion of ecotourism operations make use of public protected areas such as national parks, Biosphere Reserves and World Heritage sites. An assessment of ecotourism's net costs and benefits for conservation in these areas is thus particularly critical in evaluating how well ecotourism may be achieving its goals.

The operations of protected area management agencies are largely determined by government legislation, budget processes and policy. For example, a requirement for social equity may be intended to ensure that whatever recreational opportunities are offered to any one person are offered equally to all. In practice, however, the interpretation of this ideal can be highly politicized. For example, there are intense debates about, for example: motorized versus non-motorized access; relative opportunities for different recreational activities in different places; different recreational preferences of different ethnic groups; opportunities for people with different levels of skill, fitness or disability; and many more.

Commercial tourism in public parks

The role and rights, if any, of private commercial tourism operations in public protected areas are particularly controversial. There is a history of commercial tourism in some public lands and some countries, but by no means all; there are major international differences in the types and scale of commercial activity permitted in different land tenures, and under what permit conditions and financial arrangements. Commercial tourism in protected areas, whether it is considered as ecotourism, is hence politically charged.

Where commercial operators simply want to take guided groups into a park under the same conditions as for private recreational groups, the level of controversy is relatively low. Examples include hiking, camping, canoeing and cross-country ski tours. Controversy may still arise, however, as to whether commercial clients and operators should pay the same fees as private individuals, or a higher or lower rate. All three of these options exist in practice (Buckley et al., 2003). Controversy can also arise where there are maximum group-size limits for private groups, and commercial operators want to exceed this limit.

A higher level of controversy arises where commercial tour operators ask for particular rights, which are not available to the general public. These may include, for example: exclusive or preferential access to a particular area of the park; the right to undertake an activity that is not available to private individuals in the park; the right to use equipment that is not permitted for the general public; or, for activities that are restricted in time or space, access to an earmarked quota that is not available to private groups. In Australia, for example, Odyssey Safaris has exclusive access to a particular area of Litchfield National Park in the Northern Territory, where it operates a private tourist camp during the dry season (Buckley, 2004j).

Permits to run the Grand Canyon of the Colorado River, USA, are the best-known example of a contentiously allocated quota. The majority of the quota is allocated to commercial tour operators, whereas private groups have to wait a decade and a half for an opportunity to run a non-commercial trip. Even where there are no restrictions on access, however, there may still be competition between commercial groups and independent recreation, if the same sites are popular with both. Heavily used rock-climbing sites and routes provide an example (Jakus and Shaw, 1997). Given the growing popularity of many such activities, such conflicts and controversies are likely to continue and indeed increase.

Many national parks and other protected areas worldwide allow various private tourism operations under permit or licence, but this does not necessarily provide any net gain for conservation. Indeed, in many cases, the permit fees barely cover the administration costs, and commercial tours and their clients simply add per capita to the impacts of private recreational visitors undertaking similar activities. In some cases, tour clients may create greater impacts than independent visitors, in other cases less; in some cases the per capita fees are higher, in others lower. In any of these cases, since protected area management agencies provide opportunities and infrastructure for recreation from the same overall publicly funded operating budget, which they use for conservation management, small-scale commercial tourism in public protected areas very rarely yields any immediate net financial resources for conservation. Any potential gains must thus necessarily be more indirect, through essentially political mechanisms.

Partnership proposals

One recent trend, in a number of developed nations including Australia, Canada and the USA, is for tourism interests to propose so-called partnerships with protected area management agencies under which private commercial tourism interests would gain exclusive or preferential rights to operate part of the park's facilities for some predefined return in cash or in kind. The most common proposal is to construct and operate hotels, lodges or other tourism accommodation inside a park, but there are also: proposals for exclusive access to particular areas of a park to run tours where clients will not see any other visitors; proposals to operate particular activities inside a park, which are not permissible for the general public; and even proposals to control access and charge and collect entry or activity fees.

Two key distinctions may be drawn. The first is between historical arrangements and future proposals. There are many instances where parks agencies have unavoidable legacies of past land tenure, infrastructure or political manoeuvres, and must establish strategies to address those legacies. In particular, there may be private enclaves, easements, buildings and roads that pre-date declaration of the park. Such prior enclaves and easements may carry private development and access rights, but this does not constitute a precedent for granting further such rights in future. Buildings may have heritage value, and infrastructure may be useful for public recreation; even if not, demolition may be impracticable and maintenance expensive. These may justify private partnerships to manage such past legacies. Indeed, there are numerous examples of tourist accommodation and facilities inside protected areas that either occupy enclaves or were established long since. There are numerous heritage buildings that have been handed over for private management and maintenance (Buckley, 2004j). None of these, however, provides justification for new private tourist buildings as other developments in public protected areas.

The second key distinction is between a concession, where a parks agency grants a limited contractual right under its own terms, and a commercial partnership, where arrangements may be much more complex and difficult for the parks agency to negotiate successfully. There is no clear dividing line, but both the scale and the financial model are critical. Concessions are commonplace. Campgrounds in a number of national parks in the USA, for example, are operated by private concessionaires who collect camping fees. Many of the private game lodges in sub-Saharan Africa are run on concessions from public parks and land management agencies.

The usual argument put forward in support of larger-scale and more complex financial proposals is that the private sector has more expertise in operating visitor facilities, and that this will free up parks staff for conservation work. On the other side of the coin, however, commercial operators are of course only interested in opportunities that provide a profit, so they will pick precisely those components of the park's activities that could help to fund conservation work. In addition, while commercial operators are indeed experienced at making a profit, they will not generally have any particular interest in providing the same opportunities equitably to all visitors. Equally, public-sector parks agencies are perfectly capable of operating their facilities at a commercial profit if they wish, but this is not generally their aim.

Private-sector tourist facilities in public protected areas, therefore, are unlikely to contribute to the aims of the protected area management agency, let alone to conservation, unless three criteria are met (Buckley, 2004j). First, such facilities need to fulfil a function that the parks agency itself does indeed want to provide. Second, the parks agency needs to have other mechanisms in place to provide for those visitors who do want to visit the park but don't want to purchase the particular tourism product on offer. Third, in addition to commercial profit for the entrepreneur, the financial arrangements need to provide a significant net benefit to the parks agency, outweighing both the environmental impacts of the commercial facility and the loss of a profit-making opportunity.

Such arrangements are indeed possible, and there are instances where all these criteria appear to be met, but they seem to be relatively rare. There are historical examples where, under social circumstances quite different from those currently applicable, parks agencies granted long-term development rights for remarkably little return. There does not appear to be any particular trend for more recent developments of this nature to have generated significant returns for conservation. There are, however, a number of relatively recent examples with good potential. These include, for example, leases granted for private lodges and exclusive access to surrounding areas in relatively remote sections of Kruger National Park in South Africa, and new developments currently underway by the Taj Hotel group and Conservation Corporation Africa in some of the tiger reserves of India (Taj Hotels, 2008). Equally, however, there are examples with negative outcomes such as at Seal Rocks in Australia (Buckley, 2004j).

Increasing effective scale

Approaches

Ecotourism can achieve little if it remains at micro scale. To reduce the overall impacts of the tourism industry, ecotourism principles and practices must spread throughout the sector. There are two main ways in which this could happen. If ecotourism remains strongly differentiated from the rest of the sector, then its influence could spread only by growth, so that the ecotourism subsector gradually makes up a larger and larger proportion of the industry as a whole.

Alternatively, the influence of ecotourism might spread in a more diffuse manner, if mainstream tourism gradually follows examples within the ecotourism subsector so that there is less and less differentiation between them. These options are not mutually exclusive; both could occur simultaneously. In assessing potential progress towards ecotourism goals, however, it is simpler to examine them separately.

Several different approaches have been employed in attempts to recognize and reward tourism operations that have adopted ecotourism practices. In particular, there are now numerous environmental awards, ecolabel and ecocertification programmes. Potentially, the extent of such programmes could provide a measure of expansion and/or mainstreaming as outlined above, but only if criteria they reflect are closely congruent with the avowed goals of ecotourism.

Growth

To quantify the degree to which ecotourism operations may have expanded in scale, would require time series information on the size distributions of ecotourism enterprises relative to the overall scale of the tourism sector as measured either in financial or human terms. Such data are not available for various reasons, notably the lack of a coherent definition of ecotourism for economic statistics purposes. Even for more broadly defined subsectors such as outdoor tourism as a whole, few reliable estimates are available.

The only reliable parameter available to assess growth in the ecotourism subsector is thus the number of individual companies that have grown to mainstream scale while maintaining their ecotourism credentials. Such operations do exist, but are relatively few in number. They fall into three main models. There are some that offer a single high-volume but well-managed product, essentially mass ecotourism. An example is Quicksilver Cruises (2008). There are some that offer a suite of similar products in different places, each of them low-volume and up-market, with a substantial turnover in aggregate. Examples include CC Africa (2008), Aurora Expeditions (2008) and Southern Sea Ventures (2008). There are some that offer a portfolio of different products, essentially as retail packagers or franchisers, but selecting only those local on-ground operations that comply with ecotourism criteria. Examples include World Expeditions (2008) and Natural Habitat Adventures (2008).

Mainstreaming

Despite early optimism that the ecotourism sector might serve as a test-bed for the introduction and trialling of new environmental technologies, in practice this does not seem to have occurred to any appreciable extent. A parallel suggestion, that environmental management techniques that are already in widespread use in other industry sectors could also be adopted within the tourism industry, has been followed to a certain degree. Only in rather limited instances, however, have there been real and significant reductions in environmental impact. By far the majority of effort has gone into measures that were in fact adopted simply to reduce costs, but that are promoted as if they were a reflection of corporate social responsibility.

The spread of improved environmental management practices across the tourism sector seems to be driven principally by factors such as environmental legislation and energy costs, which are not related specifically to tourism, and which apply particularly to the accommodation sector and to large-scale, fixed-site activities. Examples include changes to government codes and standards for buildings, infrastructure, impact assessment, engine emissions, noise control, energy efficiency, water prices, recycling and so on. Some of these changes in environmental legislation also apply to boats, aircraft and coaches.

The other possible factor is an increase in client expectations for at least a basic standard of environmental management across all components of the tourism industry. These expectations differ between tourists from different countries of origin, depending on the domestic environmental laws and policies in effect in those countries. The ecotourism sector may perhaps have contributed to these changing expectations, but this remains speculative.

Ecocertification

Considerable hopes were held out initially, that ecocertification could prove a key tool in the expansion of ecotourism principles, taking advantage of a presumed market demand for green business practices and products (Weaver, 2007a, b). In practice, these hopes have not yet been realized. Tourists have proved much more interested in programmes that purport to certify environmental quality of tourist destinations, than in those that purport to certify environmental performance of tour providers. Only international environmental award schemes seem to be accepted as independent accolades, and even those have shortcomings.

In addition, both membership-based and supply-chain ecocertification programmes focus almost entirely on easily achievable and easily verifiable criteria such as environmental interpretation and relatively minor and routine aspects of environmental management, which may be of little real significance in reducing the net environmental impacts of tourism. Many membership-based ecocertification schemes have been dogged by low take-up and consequently poor cash-flow, and have lowered their entry standards in response. As in other industry sectors, it seems that some at least of these schemes are simply political manoeuvres designed to stave off government control. One or two, notably that operated by Ecotourism Australia, have been adopted by protected area management agencies as a component of preferential permitting arrangements.

Ecocertification schemes based on supply-chain systems may overcome the cash-flow difficulty through links to product booking processes, but have yet to demonstrate their environmental credentials. Three slightly different models have been tried. The first, operated by a subsidiary of British Airways, endeavoured to establish an internal system under which third-party holiday providers would have to meet environmental management criteria set by BA. The system apparently did not survive and there seem to be no publicly available reports on the details of its operations. The second was used for a number of years by German tour retailer Touristik Union International. TUI also planned to use only suppliers with good environmental management performance, and established an electronic customer feedback system for its clients to comment on environmental aspects of their tours. This system is apparently also defunct and unreported.

The third is operated by a corporation known as World Hotel-Link (2008), spun off from a tourism development programme by the World Bank. WHL is an Internet-hosted booking system with a franchise-style and a web-based customer feedback system. In theory, the environmental component is a kind of moderated customer-to-customer information transfer system, with commercial implications for the individual companies involved if retail bookings reflect customer reports, and cash-flow for WHL provided through booking commissions. It remains to be seen how successful it may prove. The environmental component, though promoted initially, currently seems rather subdued.

Trends related to ecocertification would seem to be easy to track, but this applies only to their public presentation. There can be a considerable gap between claims made on corporate websites, and auditable changes on the ground. Most of the many tourism ecolabel and ecocertification programmes have some presence on the worldwide web, so it is not difficult to follow how many such schemes are in existence. Similarly, since the certifying schemes like to list their participants and the certified companies like to advertise their participation, one can track the nominal scale of each scheme.

To gain an accurate idea of trends in tourism ecocertification, however, several additional and more difficult steps are also required. First, companies that have gone to the effort of seeking certification under any one scheme often do so from several simultaneously, and also apply for awards using the same materials. There is thus a significant overlap in the membership of different ecocertification programmes. Second, when companies transfer from one programme to another, the scheme they have abandoned may not immediately remove them from listings. Third, many schemes now incorporate multiple tiers, where the lowest level effectively indicates only that a tourism operator or product has nominated itself for possible ecocertification at some future date. From an environmental management perspective, therefore, it actually means next to nothing. Where these bottom-tier participants make up the majority of a scheme's membership, the quoted size of the scheme concerned may be greatly inflated. In testing the take-up of ecocertification approaches in future years, all these factors must first be considered before any numerical data can be treated as reasonably reliable.

In addition, membership of an ecocertification programme does not in itself guarantee any improvement in environmental management. To assess this aspect requires: first, that the scheme concerned must publish both its certification criteria, and its entry, audit and expulsion procedures and practices; and second, that at least a sample of certified products or operators should be audited by an entirely independent auditor or researcher, in addition to any internal audit programme within the scheme itself, to verify whether claims on paper are matched by practices on the ground. Finally, to determine whether retail customers, regulators or any other stakeholders actually pay any attention to ecocertification programmes requires independent research on actual customer behaviour. Very little such research has been done to date.

Conclusions

Limited progress

Progress towards achieving the key goals of ecotourism through each of the mechanisms outlined above, is summarized in Table 15.1. The following conclusions may be drawn.

Overall, the evidence available indicates that as yet, ecotourism has had rather little effect on the aggregate environmental impacts of the tourism industry as a whole. For most of the evaluation parameters examined here, results could be summarized as 'some excellent examples, but not many of them'. This does not, however, necessarily imply that ecotourism has failed in its

Table 15.1. Progress towards ecotourism goals.

Goals and mechanisms	Parameters	Progress
Less negative impact		
Measurement	Indicators	Limited
Management	Adoption	Widespread
	Effectiveness	Little studied
Education	Adoption	Widespread
	Effectiveness	Scarcely tested
Lifestyle change	Footprints	Unknown
More positive effects		
Private reserves	Number, area	Small, growing
	Rare species	Significant for some
Help public parks	Donations	Few good examples
NGOs, community, lobby	Adoption	Limited examples
	Effectiveness	Unknown
Increase scale		
Expand enterprises	Large ecotours	Few, increasing
Mainstream principles	Environmental management	Some improvement, driven by laws?
Certify practices	Adoption	Limited
	Effectiveness	Minimal

goals. Large-scale social changes, particularly those involving public good rather than private gain, commonly take an extended period to spread.

Measures to reduce negative environmental impacts have indeed become widespread within the ecotourism subsector, and to a lesser degree across the industry as a whole. Ecotourism cannot necessarily claim credit for this, since it may be driven more by broader social concerns and regulatory changes, but it is in any event a step towards the goals of ecotourism. To date, however, most of the more widespread measures are rather minor. Enterprises with a major emphasis on minimizing impacts by all available means are rather rare.

Two of the mechanisms summarized in Table 15.1 hold particular promise for future achievement: expansion in individual ecotourism enterprises, and establishment of private conservation reserves funded by ecotourism. The main focus for the former is the growth of global nature tourism retailers, which specifically select local on-ground lodges and tours with good environmental credentials, and which in many cases have themselves won international independent environmental awards. The most recent development in this sphere is that retailers of this type have themselves formed marketing alliances and syndicates to capture a greater proportion of well-heeled, sophisticated but environmentally concerned clientele.

Support for private conservation reserves includes not only outright purchase, with rehabilitation and restocking if required, but also a variety of more complex arrangements involving community lands, leases and leasebacks, conservation organizations and trusts, and occasionally also public land management agencies. Ecotourism is not the only means of financial support for private conservation, though it is a significant one. Land trusts, taxation incentives for conservation, and possibly also carbon offsets may also play an increasing role in future.

Climate change

Consideration of carbon offsets raises the issue of climate change more broadly. Many of the most successful examples of private or community conservation funded by ecotourism rely on attracting rich nature tourists from rich nations to bring their money to poor communities in poor nations (Buckley, 2003a). This provides funds and incentives for local wildlife and habitat conservation in developing nations. In the process, however, the tour clients generate global environmental impacts through long-distance air travel (Simmons and Becken, 2004; Folke et al., 2006).

Where ecotourism enterprises and associations promote their products internationally as many do, the atmospheric impacts of the resulting long-distance air travel may far outweigh the effects of local environmental management measures on the actual tours. Many ecotourism companies do indeed attract most of their clients from developed nations, especially in Europe and North America, and offer many of their tours in developing regions of Africa, Asia and Latin America, or in relatively distant regions such as the Arctic and Antarctic, Pacific island nations, or outback Australia. It is precisely this pattern that has allowed ecotourism to contribute to the development of more impoverished communities (Buckley, 2003a).

The impacts of long-haul air travel must indeed be included in any accounting for the aggregate environmental outcomes of ecotourism, but it is difficult to assess them in direct conjunction with local impacts as outlined above, because different clients originate in different places. While on a tour, they each produce approximately the same net per capita impact, but in getting to the departure point, they may produce very different per capita impacts. To include air travel impacts in the net environmental accounting for any particular ecotourism product or enterprise, the origins of its clients must be known to calculate per capita air-travel emissions. This can only be approximate, since per capita emissions depend on aircraft load, as well as type and route, but it remains a significant direction for future research.

Research priorities

To assess the achievements of ecotourism more accurately, quantitative data will be needed to convert the report-card format of Table 15.1 to a numerical accounting. We are a long way from that goal at present. Indeed, one of the conclusions that may be drawn from this review is that far less academic effort has been devoted to evaluating ecotourism progress, than to defining ecotourism principles.

Meanwhile, however, the structure presented in Table 15.1 may provide some pointers for future research, which complement the current structure of the academic ecotourism literature presented by Weaver and Lawton (2007). In particular, that review identified a number of major clusters within the academic literature. An attempt to map those clusters against the evaluation themes used above is summarized in Table 15.1. As the results reported above indicate, data to evaluate progress towards the key goals of ecotourism are patchy at best. To track progress in a more comprehensive manner would require significant further research. Focusing on reduction of net environmental impacts for the reasons set out earlier, research priorities may be summarized as follows.

To track any reductions in negative impacts there are two key issues. The first is continuing research in recreation ecology, both to identify complex but ecologically significant impacts and to quantify the effectiveness of management tools. The second is detailed ecological footprint analysis, to incorporate the environmental effects of long-haul travel and any changes in individual post-trip lifestyles for ecotour clients.

The latter will also require social science research techniques, to track tourist behaviour patterns in detail over an extended period. The same applies to any attempted investigation of post-trip advocacy by ecotour clients. Perhaps the single key research priority, however, is to quantify the aggregate global positive contributions of ecotourism to conservation. A number of cases have been identified where ecotour operators do make such contributions either through private reserves or through support for NGOs, community groups or public protected areas, but the aggregate outcome remains unknown.

In addition to the practical difficulty in assembling a comprehensive global list of individual cases and quantifying their contributions, there are two significant theoretical barriers to be overcome. The first is that many of the effects concerned are essentially political, and the factors driving political decisions are notoriously hard to deconstruct reliably. The second is that ecotourism is effectively the commercial component of the outdoor recreation sector, as well as the outdoor recreation component of the commercial tourism industry. At a global scale, the contribution of commercial ecotourism may well be swamped by the changing dynamics of public protected area management and visitation. To quantify these issues worldwide will not be straightforward.

REVISION

Product patterns

- Particular growth in adventure tourism products
- Often including nature tourism elements
- For example, watching wildlife in remote areas
- Product growth: focus on luxury adventure
- Highly specialized, exclusive access
- Volume growth: short, unskilled tours close to gateways
- Especially combination products, adventure destinations
- Product pyramid provides continuing economic growth

Environmental management

- Practices and impacts vary greatly between companies and products
- Some have comprehensive and detailed programmes to minimize impacts
- Others boast about relatively trivial measures
- Very large-scale, high-impact tourist resorts are still commonplace
- Relatively few transport or accommodation providers go beyond legal compliance
- Only a small number have adopted best-practice designs and technologies
- There are certainly some lodges and tours with negligible impact
- But these are still very much the minority
- Greenwash and ecotourism lite are still commonplace
- Ecotourism principles have not yet been mainstreamed
- Sustainable tourism is much more rhetoric than reality
- Most ecocertification programmes have little effect
- Good guiding can reduce impacts of concerned clients
- But high-impact tourists often don't care
- So education and self-regulation don't substitute for standards and enforcement

Contributions to conservation

- Very few commercial ecotourism operations make a net contribution to conservation
- Barely 50 companies worldwide make direct conservation contributions
- Most contributions are small, outweighed by impacts

- A few companies do make significant net contributions
- Principally through tourism funding of private reserves
- Many more tour operators may make indirect contributions
- Mainly by maintaining political support for parks
- Political decisions are difficult to deconstruct
- So indirect contributions remain somewhat speculative and unquantified

Private reserves

- Conservation Corporation Africa, Phinda and others
- Various similar operators, East and South Africa
- Australian Wildlife Conservancies, Mornington and others
- The Nature Conservancy
- Conservation International
- BirdLife International

Amenity migration

- Increasing links between outdoor recreation opportunities, population migrations and property prices
- Economic scale of these effects far outweighs commercial tourism
- But many new migrants become tour clients or owners
- New migrants have different social, environmental and political attitudes than long-term residents
- Changes in land use and tenure
- Can sometimes convert farmland to conservation
- Alternatively, may mean more roads, fences and fires
- Latest trend is residential game reserves with strata titling

Business opportunities

- Outbound tourists from populous nations
- China, India, Brazil, Russia, etc.
- Different attitudes to environment than for North America or Europe
- Past experience with Japanese market indicates language skills will be critical
- Continuing global population growth and urbanization indicates outdoor tourism markets will remain buoyant
- Baby boomers currently main market for ecotourism products
- Wide age range for adventure tourism products

Policy implications

- Ecotourism can be an engine for local economic growth
- But need to put conservation framework in place first

- Whether public parks or private reserves
- Self-regulation of environmental management not effective
- Need regulations and standards for tourism as for other sectors
- Issues such as insurance law affect enterprise viability

Research priorities

- Need better knowledge of product patterns
- Both within and across activity subsectors
- Structure, price, duration, group size, etc.
- Also geographic patterns, regional signatures
- Need more crossover between tourism and recreation research
- Many conceptual approaches used in recreation work also relevant to outdoor tourism
- Need much more ecosystem-specific scientific research on environmental impacts
- Need new conceptual environmental and social accounting

REFLECTIONS

1. Do you think that ecotourism can best be described as: (i) a specialist subsector that is likely to continue as a niche market but unlikely to grow or to influence mainstream tourism to any great degree; (ii) a global trend in tourism that will gradually influence the entire mainstream tourism industry to become more sustainable; (iii) a short-lived fad that is already on the decline; (iv) an academic concept that has never really been reflected in the real world of practical tourism products; (v) a type of tourism that is continually evolving from, and recombining with, other specialist sectors so that it will survive and grow but not necessarily in its current form; (vi) all of the above, to various degrees; or (vii) none of the above but something different. Give detailed reasons for your choice.

2. Identify three different trends or predictions that tourism analysts have, at some point, made about the probable future of ecotourism, and when they were made. Based on subsequent evidence, how accurate did these predictions prove to be, or if it is still too early to tell, how accurate do you think they will be, and why?

3. The tourism sector can be affected by many large-scale economic and demographic factors outside the industry itself, e.g. population growth and urbanization; increasing fuel prices; terrorism; climate change; increasing wealth in large newly industrialized nations such as India, China and Brazil; and so on. How do you think that each of these factors, and any other large-scale factors you can identify, will affect the future of the ecotourism sector in particular, and why?

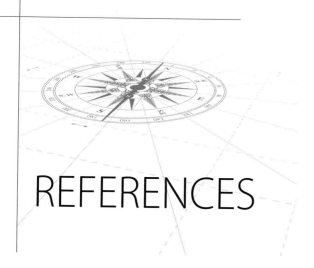

REFERENCES

Acott, T.G., Trobe H.L. and Howard, S. (1998) An evaluation of deep ecotourism and shallow ecotourism. *Journal of Sustainable Tourism* 6, 238–253.

Adventure Travel Society (2007) Making Vacation Dreams Come True for Over 30 Years. Accessed 2 April 2008. www.adventuretravel.com

Agardy, M.T. (1993) Accommodating ecotourism in multiple use planning of coastal and marine protected areas. *Ocean and Coastal Management* 20, 219–221.

Aguirre, A. and Dirzo, R. (2008) Effects of fragmentation on pollinator abundance and fruit set of an abundant understory palm in a Mexican tropical forest. *Biological Conservation* 141, 375–384.

Ahn, B.Y., Lee, B.K. and Shafer, C.S. (2002) Operationalizing sustainability in regional tourism planning: an application of the limits of acceptable change framework. *Tourism Management* 23, 1–15.

Aiello, R. (1998) Interpretation and the marine tourism industry, who needs it? A case study of Great Adventures, Australia. *Journal of Tourism Studies* 9, 51–61.

Akama, J.S. (1996) Western environmental values and nature-based tourism in Kenya. *Tourism Management* 17, 567–574.

Akama, J.S. and Kieti, D.M. (2003) Measuring tourist satisfaction with Kenya's wildlife safari: a case study of Tsavo West National Park. *Tourism Management* 24, 73–81.

Al Maha Resort (2008) A Member of the Leading Small Hotels of the World. Accessed 30 April 2008. http://www.al-maha.com/

Albuquerque, K. and McElroy, J. (1992) Caribbean small-island tourism styles and sustainable strategies. *Environmental Management* 16, 619–632.

Alderman, C.L. (1990) *A Study of the Role of Privately Owned Lands used for Nature Tourism, Education and Conservation*. Conservation International, Washington, DC.

Alderman, C.L. (1994) The economics and the role of privately-owned lands used for nature tourism, education and conservation. In: Munasinghe, M. and McNeely, J.A. (eds) *Protected Area Economics and Policy: Linking Conservation and Sustainable Development*. World Bank, Washington, DC, pp. 273–302.

Alessa, L., Kliskey, A. and Robards, M. (2004) Ecological impacts of ecotourism visitation on macroalgal beds in Pacific Rim National Park Reserve. In: Buckley, R.C. (ed.) *Environmental Impacts of Ecotourism*. CAB International, Wallingford, UK, pp. 349–360.

Alexander, S.E. (2000) Resident attitudes towards conservation and black howler monkeys in Belize: the community baboon sanctuary. *Environmental Conservation* 27, 341–350.

Allen, L.R., Long, P.T., Perdue, R.R. and Kieselbach, S. (1988) The impacts of tourism development on residents' perceptions of community life. *Journal of Travel Research* 27, 16–21.

Allen, L.R., Hafer, H.R., Long, P.T. and Perdue, R.R. (1993) Rural residents' attitudes toward recreation and tourism development. *Journal of Travel Research* 31, 27–33.

Allendorf, T. (2007) Residents' attitudes toward three protected areas in southwestern Nepal. *Biodiversity and Conservation* 16, 2087–2102.

Altman, J. (1989) Tourism dilemmas for Aboriginal Australians. *Annals of Tourism Research* 16, 456–476.

Amador, L.M.G. (1997) Ethnic, cultural and ecotourism. *American Behavioral Scientist* 40, 936–943.

Amante-Helweg, V. (1996) Ecotourists' beliefs and knowledge about dolphins and the development of cetacean ecotourism. *Aquatic Mammals* 22, 131–140.

Amo, L., Lopez, P. and Martin, J. (2006) Nature-based tourism as a form of predation risk affects body condition and health state of *Podarcis muralis* lizards. *Biological Conservation* 131, 402–409.

Anand, J. and Herath, G. (2002) Assessment of wilderness quality using the analytical hierarchy process. *Tourism Economics* 8, 165–182.

Anderson, G.R.V., Forbes, M.A. and Pirzl, R.M. (1996) A national overview of the development of whale watching in Australia. *Encounters with Whales 1995 Proceedings*. Australian Nature Conservation Agency, Canberra, pp. 5–16.

Andersson, J.E.C. (2007) The recreational cost of coral bleaching – a stated and revealed preference study of international tourists. *Ecological Economics* 62, 704–715.

Ap, J. (1992) Residents' perceptions of tourism impacts. *Annals of Tourism Research* 19, 665–690.

Ap, J. and Crompton, J. (1998) Developing and testing a tourism impact scale. *Journal of Travel Research* 37, 120–130.

Apps, C.D. and McLellan, B.N. (2006) Factors influencing the dispersion and fragmentation of endangered mountain caribou populations. *Biological Conservation* 130, 84–97.

Archabald, K. and Naughton-Treves, L. (2001) Tourism revenue-sharing around national parks in Western Uganda: early efforts to identify and reward local communities. *Environmental Conservation* 28, 135–149.

Archer, B. and Fletcher, J. (1996) The economic impact of tourism in the Seychelles. *Annals of Tourism Research* 23, 32–47.

Aresco, M.J. (2005) The effect of sex-specific terrestrial movements and roads on the sex ratio of freshwater turtles. *Biological Conservation* 123, 37–44.

Arlen, C. (1995) Ecotour, hold the eco: polluting rivers and bagging wildlife may be on the agenda. *US News and World Report* 118, 61–63.

Arrowsmith, C. (2003) Modelling potential for nature-based tourism. In: Buckley, R.C., Pickering, C. and Weaver, D. (eds) *Nature-Based Tourism, Environment and Land Management*. CAB International, Wallingford, UK, pp. 167–180.

Arthur's Pass Wilderness Lodge (2008) Wilderness Lodges of New Zealand. Accessed 30 April 2008. http://www.wildernesslodge.co.nz/arthurspass/

Ashley, C. and Row, D. (1998) *Enhancing Community Involvement in Wildlife Tourism: Issues and Challenges*. International Institute for Environmental Development, London.

Ashley, E.P., Kosloski, A. and Petrie, S.A. (2007) Incidence of intentional vehicle–reptile collisions. *Human Dimensions of Wildlife* 12, 137–143.

Ashworth, G. and Goodall, B. (eds) (1990) *Marketing Tourism Places*. Routledge, London.

Aurora Expeditions (2008) Cruising to the Heart of Nature. Accessed 9 September 2008. www.auroraexpeditions.com.au

Australian Dairy Adjustment Authority (2001) Dairy Legislation Introduced. Accessed 19 May 2008. http://www.daa.gov.au

Australian Department of Industry, Tourism and Resources (2002) *A Tourism Operator Perspective on Protected Areas*. Australian Department of Industry, Tourism and Resources, Canberra.

Australian Department of Industry, Tourism and Resources (2003a) *Pursuing Common Goals*. Australian Department of Industry, Tourism and Resources, Canberra.

Australian Department of Industry, Tourism and Resources (2003b) *Pursuing Common Goals – Opportunities for Tourism and Conservation*. Report ITR 2003/070. ADITR, Canberra.

Australia, National Tourism and Heritage Taskforce (2003) *Going Places: Developing Natural and Cultural Heritage Tourism in Australia* (2vv.). Environment Protection and Heritage Council, Canberra.

Australia Senate Standing Committee (2008) Accessed 30 April 2008. http://www.aph.gov.au/Senate/committee/legcon_ctte/

Ayala, H. (1998) Panama's ecotourism-plus initiative: the challenge of making history. *Cornell Hotel and Restaurant Administration Quarterly* 39, 68–75.

Aylward, B. (1992) Appropriating the value of wildlife and wildlands. In: Swanson, T.M. and Barbier, E.B. *Economics for the Wilds*. Earthscan Publications Limited, London, pp. 34–64.

Aylward, B., Allen, K., Echeverria, J. and Tosi, J. (1996) Sustainable ecotourism in Costa Rica: The Monteverde Cloud Forest Reserve. *Biodiversity and Conservation* 5, 315–343.

Azqueta, D. and Sotelsek, D. (2007) Valuing nature: from environmental impacts to natural capital. *Ecological Economics* 63, 22–30.

Baez, A. and Rovinski, Y. (1992) Ecotourism in Costa Rica: the tough road for remaining number one. *Adventure Travel Society Newsletter* 1, 6.

Bagri, A., Blockhus, J., Grey, F. and Vorhies, F. (1998) *Economic Values of Protected Areas. A Guide for Protected Area Managers*. International Unicom for Conservation of Nature, Gland, Switzerland.

Bahaire, T. and Elliott-White, M. (1999) The application of geographical information systems (GIS) in sustainable tourism planning: a review. *Journal of Sustainable Tourism* 7, 159–174.

Baker, A. St C. (2005) Recreation and tourism in areas of outstanding natural beauty: key influences on the policy making process. *Current Issues in Tourism* 8, 93–113.

Baker, C.P. and Holing, D. (1996) *World Travel: A Guide to International Ecojourneys*. Time-Life Books, New York.

Ballance, A., Ryan, P.G. and Turpie, J.K. (2000) How much is a clean beach worth? The impact of litter on beach users. *South African Journal of Science* 96, 210–213.

Ballantine, J.L. and Eagles, P.F.J. (1994) Defining Canadian ecotourists. *Journal of Sustainable Tourism* 2, 210–214.

Ballantyne, R. (1995) Interpreters' conceptions of Australian Aboriginal culture. *The Journal of Environmental Education* 26, 11–17.

Ballantyne, R. and Hughes, K. (2001) Interpretation in ecotourism settings: investigating tour guides' perceptions of their role, responsibilities and training needs. *The Journal of Tourism Studies* 12, 2–9.

Bandara, R. and Tisdell, C. (2004) The net benefit of saving the Asian elephant: A policy and contingent valuation study. *Ecological Economics* 48, 93–107.

Banks, S.C., Finlayson, G.R., Lawson, S.J., Lindenmayer, D.B., Paetkau, D., Ward, S.J. and Taylor, A.C. (2005) The effects of habitat fragmentation due to forestry plantation establishment on the demography and genetic variation of a marsupial carnivore, *Antechnius agilis*. *Biological Conservation* 122, 581–597.

Barke, M. (2004) Rural tourism in Spain. *International Journal of Tourism Research* 6, 137–149.

Barker, E. (1997) Forest management: recreationists taking a fee hike. *Lewiston* (ID) *Morning Tribune*, Outdoors, p. IC, 2 October.

Barkin, D. and Bouchez, C.P. (2002) NGO-community collaboration for ecotourism: a strategy for sustainable regional development. *Current Issues in Tourism* 5, 245–253.

Barkin, D. and Pailles, C. (1999) NGO-community collaboration for ecotourism: a strategy for sustainable regional development in Oaxaca. *Tourism Recreation Review* 24.

Barlow, B.A. (1994) Phytogeography of the Australian region. In: Groves, R.H. (ed.) *Australian Vegetation*, 2nd edn. Cambridge University Press, Cambridge, pp. 3–36.

Barnes, J., Burgess, J. and Pearce, D. (1992) Wildlife tourism. In: Swanson, T.M. and Barbier, E.B. (eds) *Economics for the Wilds: Wildlife, Wildlands, Diversity and Development*. Earthscan Publications, London, pp. 136–151.

Barnes, J.I. (1996) Economic characteristics of the demand for wildlife-viewing tourism in Botswana. *Development in Southern Africa* 13, 377–397.

Bartelme, J. (1994) Exploring ecotourism. *Environ* 14, 22.

Barve, N., Kiran, M.C., Vanaraj, G., Aravind, N.A., Rao, D., Shaanker, R.U., Ganeshaiah, K.N. and Poulsen, J.G. (2005) Measuring and mapping threats to a wildlife sanctuary in southern India. *Conservation Biology* 19, 122–130.

Baskin, J. (1996) The future of St. Lucia: key choices for decision makers. *Working Paper Land and Agriculture Policy Centre*. Land and Agriculture Policy Centre, Wits, South Africa.

Bauer, I. (1999a) The impact of tourism in developing countries on the health of the local host communities: the need for more research. *The Journal of Tourism Studies* 10, 2–17.

Bauer, T. (1999b) Towards a sustainable tourism future: lessons from Antarctica. In: Weir, B., McArthur, S. and Crabtree, A. (eds) *Developing Ecotourism into the Millennium: Proceedings of the Ecotourism Association of Australia*. Ecotourism Association of Australia, Brisbane.

Baumgartner, S., Becker, C., Faber, M. and Manstetten, R. (2006) Relative and absolute scarcity of nature. Assessing the roles of economics and ecology for biodiversity conservation. *Ecological Economics* 59, 487–498.

Beach, D.W. and Weinrich, M.T. (1989) Watching the whales. *Oceanus* 32, 84–88.

Beal, D.J. and Harrison, S.R. (1998) Modelling of demand, supply and efficient pricing of ecotourism in national parks. In: Tisdell, C.A. (ed.) *Tourism and Development: Economic, Social, Political and Environment*. Nova Science Publishers, Commack, NY, pp. 203–217.

Beale, C.M. and Monaghan, P. (2004) Human disturbance: people as predation-free predators? *Journal of Applied Ecology* 41, 335–343.

Beaumont, N. (1998) The conservation benefits of ecotourism: does it produce pro-environmental attitudes or are ecotourists already converted to the cause? In: Faulkner, B., Tideswell, C. and Weaver, D. (eds) *Progress in Tourism and Hospitality Research: Proceedings of the Eighth Australian Tourism and Hospitality Research Conference*. Bureau of Tourism Research, Canberra, pp. 273–275.

Beavers, J. (1997) *Community Based Ecotourism in the Maya Forest: A Case Study from Belize*. The Ecotourism Society, North Bennington, VT.

Bebbington, J., Brown, J. and Frame, B. (2007) Accounting technologies and sustainability assessment models. *Ecological Economics* 61, 224–236.

Becken, S. and Hay, J. (2007) *Tourism and Climate Change: Risks and Opportunities*. Channel View Publications, Clevedon.

Beeton, S. (1998) *Ecotourism: A Practical Guide for Rural Communities*. Landlinks Press, Collingwood, Victoria.

Beeton, S. and Benfield, R. (2002) Demand control: the case for demarketing as a visitor and environmental management tool. *Journal of Sustainable Tourism* 10, 497–513.

Bellemain, E., Swenson, J.E., Tallmon, D., Brunberg, S. and Taberlet, P. (2005) Estimating population size of elusive animals with DNA from hunter-collected faeces: four methods for brown bears. *Conservation Biology* 19, 150–161.

Belsky, J.M. (1999) Misrepresenting communities: the politics of community-based rural ecotourism in Gales Point Manatee, Belize. *Rural Sociology* 64, 641–666.

Bennett, A.F., Radford, J.Q. and Haslem, A. (2006) Properties of land mosaics: implications for nature conservation in agricultural environments. *Biological Conservation* 133, 250–264.

Bennett, M.A., Kriwoken, L.K. and Fallon, L.D. (2003) Managing bushwalker impacts in the Tasmanian wilderness World Heritage Areas, Australia. *International Journal of Wilderness* 9, 14–27.

Berg, H., Ohman, M.C., Troeng, S. and Linden, O. (1998) Environmental economics of coral reef destruction in Sri Lanka. *Ambio* 27, 627–635.

Berger, D.J. (1996) The challenge of integrating Maasai tradition with tourism. In: Price, M.F., Smith, V.L. and Price, M.F. (eds) *People and Tourism in Fragile Environments*. Wiley, Chichester, UK, pp. 175–198.

Berrow, S.D., Holmes, B. and Kiely, O.R. (1996) Distribution and abundance of bottle-nosed dolphins *Tursiops truncatus* (Montagu) in the Shannon Estuary. *Biological Environments* 96B, 1–10.

Berry, S. and Ladkin, A. (1997) Sustainable tourism: a regional perspective. *Tourism Management* 18, 433–440.

Beunen, R., Regnerus, H.D. and Jaarsma, C.F. (2008) Gateways as a means of visitor management in national parks and protected areas. *Tourism Management* 29, 138–145.

Billabong (2002) Accessed 20 May 2008. www.billabong.com

Binns, T. and Nel, E. (2002) Tourism as a local development strategy in South Africa. *Royal Geographical Society* 168, 235–248.

Bjerknes, A-L., Totland, O., Hegland, S.J. and Nielsen, A. (2007) Do alien plant invasions really affect pollination success in native plant species? *Biological Conservation* 138, 1–12.

Bjork, P. (1997) The marketing of Finnish eco-resorts. *Journal of Vacation Marketing* 4, 303–313.

Bjork, P. (2000) Ecotourism from a conceptual perspective, an extended definition of a unique tourism form. *International Journal of Tourism Research* 2, 189–202.

Black, R. and Crabtree, A. (eds) (2007) *Quality Assurance and Certification in Ecotourism*. CAB International, Wallingford, UK.

Black, R. and Ham, S. (2006) Improving the quality of tour guiding: towards a model for tour guide certification. *Journal of Ecotourism* 4, 178–195.

Black, R. and Weiler, B. (2005) Quality assurance and regulatory mechanisms in the tour guiding industry: a systematic review. *The Journal of Tourism Studies* 16, 24–37.

Blake, S. and Hedges, S. (2004) Sinking the flagship: the case of forest elephants in Asia and Africa. *Conservation Biology* 18, 1191–1202.

Blamey, R. and Hatch, D. (1998) Profiles and motivation of nature-based tourists visiting Australia. *Australian, Bureau of Tourism Research Occasional Paper 25*. BTR, Canberra.

Blamey, R.K. (1997) Ecotourism: the search for an operational definition. *Journal of Sustainable Tourism* 5, 109–130.

Blamey, R.K. (2001) Principles of ecotourism. In: Weaver, D.B. *The Encyclopedia of Ecotourism*. CAB International, Wallingford, UK, pp. 5–22.

Blamey, R.K. and Braithwaite, V.A. (1997) A social values segmentation of the potential ecotourism market. *Journal of Sustainable Tourism* 5, 29–45.

Blangy, S. and Nielsen, T. (1993) Ecotourism and minimum impact policy. *Annals of Tourism Research* 20, 357–360.

Blangy, S., Genot, J.C. and Criventchuk, M. (1996) Ecotourism in Berezinsky: opportunities and constraints. *Ecodecision* 20, 61–64.

Blom, A. (2000) The monetary impact of tourism on protected area management and the local economy in Dzanga-Sangha (Central African Republic). *Journal of Sustainable Tourism* 8, 175–189.

Blom, A. (2004) An estimate of the costs of an effective system of protected areas in the Niger Delta – Congo Basin forest region. *Biodiversity and Conservation* 13, 2661–2678.

Boarman, W.I. and Sazaki, M. (2006) A highway's road-effect zone for desert tortoises (*Gopherus agassizii*). *Journal of Arid Environments* 65, 94–101.

Bohringer, C. and Jochem, E.P. (2007) Measuring the immeasurable – a survey of sustainability indices. *Ecological Economics* 63, 1–8.

Boo, E. (1990) *Ecotourism: The Potentials and Pitfalls.* Worldwide Fund for Nature, Baltimore, MD, pp. 25–52.

Boo, E. (1992) Tourism and the environment: pitfalls and liabilities of ecotourism development. *WTO News* 9, 2–4.

Boo, E. and Lindberg, K. (1993) Ecotourism planning for protected areas. In: Hawkins, D.E. and Lindberg, K. (eds) *Ecotourism: A Guide for Planners and Managers.* The Ecotourism Society, North Bennington, VT, pp. 15–31.

Bookbinder, M.P., Dinerstein, E., Rijal, A., Cauley, H. and Rajouria, A. (1998) Ecotourism's support of biodiversity conservation. *Conservation Biology* 12, 1399–1404.

Boonzaier, E. (1996) Local responses to conservation in the Richtersveld National Park, South Africa. *Biodiversity and Conservation* 5, 307–314.

Borge, L., Nelson, W.C., Leitch, J.A. and Leistritz, F.L. (1991) Economic impact of wildlife-based tourism in Northern Botswana. North Dakota State University. *Agricultural Experiment Station.*

Bornemeier, J. (1997) Ecotourism for forest conservation and community development. In: Victor, M. and Durst, P.B. (eds). *Proceedings of an International Seminar held in Chiang Mai, Thailand.* Regional Community Forestry Training Center for Asia-Pacific, Bangkok.

Borneo Adventures (2008) The Borneo Specialist. Accessed 30 April 2008. http://www.borneoadventure.com/public/home/default.asp

Bosetti, V. and Pearce, D. (2003) A study of environmental conflict: the economic value of grey seals in southwest England. *Biodiversity and Conservation* 12, 2361–2392.

Bottrill, C.G. and Pearce, D.G. (1995) Ecotourism: towards a key elements approach to operationalising the concept. *Journal of Sustainable Tourism* 3, 45–54.

Boulton, R.L. and Clarke, M.F. (2003) Do yellow-faced honeyeater (*Lichenostomus chrysops*) nests experience higher predation at forest edges? *Wildlife Research* 30, 119–125.

Bowker, J.M., Cordell, H.K. and Johnson, C.Y. (1999) User fees for recreation services on public lands: a national assessment. *Journal of Park and Recreation Administration* 17, 1–14.

Boyd, J. (2007) Nonmarket benefits of nature: what should be counted in green GDP? *Ecological Economics* 61, 716–723.

Boyd, S.W. and Butler, R.W. (1996) Managing ecotourism: an opportunity spectrum approach. *Tourism Management* 17, 557–566.

Boyd, S.W. and Butler, R.W. (1999) Definitely not monkeys or parrots, probably deer and possibly moose: opportunities and realities of ecotourism in Northern Ontario. *Current Issues in Tourism* 2, 123–137.

Boyd, S.W., Butler, R.W., Haider, W. and Perera, A. (1994) Identifying areas for ecotourism in northern Ontario: application of a geographical information system methodology. *Journal of Applied Recreation Research* 19, 41–66.

Bramwell, B. (1999) Sustainable tourism. *Annals of Tourism Research* 26, 227–230.

Bramwell, B. and Lane, B. (2000) *Tourism Collaboration and Partnerships! Politics, Practice and Sustainability.* Channel View Publications, Clevedon, UK.

Bramwell, B. and Lane, B. (2007) Audiences and languages for sustainable tourism research. *Journal of Sustainable Tourism* 15, 1–4.

Bramwell, B. and Sharman, A. (1999) Collaboration in local tourism policy making. *Annals of Tourism Research* 26, 392–415.

Brander, L.M., Van Beukering, P. and Cesar, H.S.J. (2007) The recreational value of coral reefs: a meta-analysis. *Ecological Economics* 63, 209–218.

Brandon, K. (1996) *Ecotourism and Conservation: A Review of Key Issues.* The World Bank, Washington DC.

Briassoulis, H. (2002) Sustainable tourism and the question of the commons. *Annals of Tourism Research* 29, 1065–1085.

Briassoulis, H. (2003) Crete: endowed by nature, privileged by geography, threatened by tourism? *Journal of Sustainable Tourism* 11, 97–115.

Briassoulis, H. and van der Straaten, J. (2000) Tourism and the environment: an overview. In: Briassoulis, H. and van der Straaten, J. (eds) *Tourism and the Environment, Regional, Economic and Policy Issues.* Kluwer, Dordrecht, pp. 1–9.

Bridle, K.L. and Kirkpatrick, J.B. (2003) Impacts of nutrient additions and digging for human waste disposal in natural environments, Tasmania, Australia. *Journal of Environmental Management* 69, 299–306.

Bridle, K.L. and Kirkpatrick, J.B. (2005) An analysis of the breakdown of paper products (toilet paper, tissues and tampons) in natural environments, Tasmania, Australia. *Journal of Environmental Management* 74, 21–30.

Briereton, U.A. (1991) Tourism and the environment. *Contours Bangkok* 5, 18–19.

Broad, S. and Weiler, B. (1998) Captive animals and interpretation: a tale of two tiger exhibits. *Journal of Tourism Studies* 9, 14–27.

Broekhoven, G. (1996) *Non-timber forest products: ecological and economic aspects of exploitation in Colombia, Ecuador and Bolivia.* IUCN – The World Conservation Union, Cambridge.

Brown, G. and Essex, S. (1997) Sustainable tourism management: lessons from the edge of Australia. *Journal of Sustainable Tourism* 5, 294–305.

Brown, G.P., Phillips, B.L., Webb, J.K. and Shine, R. (2006) Toad on the road: use of roads as dispersal corridors by cane toads (*Bufo marinus*) at an invasion front in tropical Australia. *Biological Conservation* 133, 88–94.

Brown, I. (1989) Managing for adventure recreations. *Australian Parks and Recreation* 25, 37–40.

Brown, K., Turner, R.K., Hameed, H. and Bateman, I. (1997) Environmental carrying capacity and tourism development in the Maldives and Nepal. *Environmental Conservation* 24, 316–325.

Bruna, E.M., Vasconcelos, H.L. and Heredia, S. (2005) The effect of habitat fragmentation on communities of mutualists: Amazonian ants and their host plants. *Biological Conservation* 124, 209–216.

Bryan, B. (1991) Ecotourism on family farms and ranches in the American West. In: T. Whelan (ed.) *Nature Tourism: Managing for the Environment.* Island Press, Washington, DC, pp. 75–85.

Buckley, R.C. (1991a) Environmental planning and policy for green tourism. In: Buckley, R.C. (ed.) *Perspectives in Environmental Management.* Springer, Heidelberg, pp. 226–242.

Buckley, R.C. (1991b) Green taxes: legal and policy issues in the use of economic instruments for environmental management. *Revenue Law Journal* 2, 27–67.

Buckley, R.C. (1994a) A framework for ecotourism. *Annals of Tourism Research* 21, 661–669.

Buckley, R.C. (1994b) Ecotourism, national parks and fragile environments. *Tourism Ecodollars* 2, 1–22. EMIAA/ATIA, Brisbane.

Buckley, R.C. (1995) Pacific Rim: Seven Spirit Bay, Northern Territory. In: Hawkins, D.E., Epler Wood, M. and Bittman, S. (eds) *The Ecolodge Sourcebook for Planners and Developers.* The Ecotourism Society, North Bennington, VT, pp. 116–119.

Buckley, R.C. (1996) Sustainable tourism: technical issues and information needs. *Annals of Tourism Research* 23, 925–928.

Buckley, R.C. (1998a) International and Australian patterns in nature, eco and adventure tourism. *National Ecotourism Conference 1998*, Fraser Island, Queensland.

Buckley, R.C. (1998b) Ecotourism megatrends. *Australian International Business Review* December 98, 52–54.

Buckley, R.C. (1998c) Tourism in wilderness: M&M toolkit. In: Watson, A.E., Aplet, G.H. and Hendee, J.C. (eds) *Personal, Societal, and Ecological Values of Wilderness: Sixth World Wilderness Congress Proceedings on Research, Management, and Allocation* I. Rocky Mountain Research Station, Ogden, UT, pp. 115–116.

Buckley, R.C. (1999a) Tourism in the most fragile environments. *Tourism Recreation Research* 25, 31–40.

Buckley, R.C. (1999b) Tools and indicators for managing tourism in parks. *Annals of Tourism Research* 26, 207–210.

Buckley, R.C. (1999c) An ecological perspective on carrying capacity. *Annals of Tourism Research* 26, 705–708.

Buckley, R.C. (1999–2001) *Green Guide to White Water* (1999), *Green Guide to 4WD and Off-Road Tours* (2001). CRC Tourism, Gold Coast.

Buckley R.C. (2000a) NEAT trends: current issues in nature, eco and adventure tourism. *International Journal of Tourism Research* 2, 437–444.

Buckley, R.C. (2000b) Application of regulatory and voluntary instruments for sustainable tourism development in small islands. In: Varma, H. (ed.) *Island Tourism in Asia and the Pacific*. World Tourism Organization, Madrid, pp. 46–64.

Buckley, R.C. (2000c) Review of Hall, C.M. and Lew, A.A. Sustainable tourism: a geographical perspective. *Journal of Travel Research* 39, 238–241.

Buckley, R.C. (2001a) Major issues in tourism ecolabels. In: Font, X. and Buckley, R.C. (eds) *Tourism Ecolabelling*. CAB International, Wallingford, UK, pp. 19–26.

Buckley, R.C. (2001b) Environmental impacts. In Weaver, D. (ed.) *The Encyclopedia of Ecotourism*. CAB International, Wallingford, UK, pp. 374–394.

Buckley, R.C. (2002a) Public and private partnerships between tourism and protected areas. *Journal of Tourism Studies* 13, 26–38.

Buckley, R.C. (2002b) Tourism ecolabels. *Annals of Tourism Research* 29, 183–208.

Buckley, R.C. (2002c) Minimal-impact guidelines for mountain ecotours. *Tourism Recreation Research* 27, 35–40.

Buckley, R.C. (2002d) Review of Harrison, D. Tourism and the less developed world: issues and case studies. *Annals of Tourism Research* 29, 1192–1193.

Buckley, R.C. (2002e) Draft principles for tourism in parks. *Journal of Ecotourism* 1, 75–80.

Buckley, R.C. (2002f) Surf tourism and sustainable development in Indo-Pacific Islands. I. The industry and the islands. *Journal of Sustainable Tourism* 10, 405–424.

Buckley, R.C. (2003a) *Case Studies in Ecotourism*. CAB International, Wallingford, UK.

Buckley, R.C. (2003b) Environmental inputs and outputs in ecotourism: geotourism with a positive triple bottom line? *Journal of Ecotourism* 2, 76–82.

Buckley, R.C. (2003c) Adventure tourism and the clothing, fashion and entertainment industries. *Journal of Ecotourism* 2, 126–234.

Buckley, R.C. (2003d) Review of McCool, S.F. and Moisey, R.N. Tourism, recreation and sustainability: linking culture and the environment. *Annals of Tourism Research* 30, 271–273.

Buckley, R.C. (2003e) Pay to play in parks: an Australian policy perspective on visitor fees in public protected areas. *Journal of Sustainable Tourism* 11, 56–73.

Buckley, R.C. (2003f) The practice and politics of tourism and land management. In: Buckley, R.C., Pickering, C. and Weaver, D. (eds) *Nature-Based Tourism, Environment and Land Management*. CAB International, Wallingford, UK, pp. 1–6.

Buckley, R.C. (2003g) Ecological indicators of tourist impacts in parks. *Journal of Ecotourism* 2, 54–66.

Buckley, R.C. (ed.) (2004a) *Environmental Impacts of Ecotourism*. CAB International, Wallingford, UK.

Buckley, R.C. (2004b) Impacts of ecotourism on terrestrial wildlife. In: Buckley, R. (ed.) *Environmental Impacts of Ecotourism*. CAB International, Wallingford, UK, pp. 211–228.

Buckley, R.C. (2004c) Partnerships in ecotourism: Australian political frameworks. *International Journal of Tourism Research* 6, 75–83.

Buckley, R.C. (2004d) Ecotourism land tenure and enterprise ownership: Australian case study. *Journal of Ecotourism* 3, 208–213.

Buckley, R.C. (2004e) Impacts positive and negative: links between ecotourism and environment. In: Buckley, R.C. (ed.) *Environmental Impacts of Ecotourism*. CAB International, Wallingford, UK, pp. 5–14.

Buckley, R.C. (2004f) Environmental impacts of motorized off-highway vehicles. In: Buckley, R.C. (ed.) *Environmental Impacts of Ecotourism*. CAB International, Wallingford, UK, pp. 83–97.

Buckley, R.C. (2004g) Impacts of ecotourism on birds. In: Buckley, R. (ed.) *Environmental Impacts of Ecotourism*. CAB International, Wallingford, UK, pp. 187–209.

Buckley, R.C. (2004h) Using ecological impact measurements to design visitor management. In: Buckley, R. (ed.) *Environmental Impacts of Ecotourism*. CAB International, Wallingford, UK, pp. 287–296.

Buckley R.C. (2004i) Ecotourism and protected areas: context for environmental impacts. In: Buckley, R.C. (ed.) *Environmental Impacts of Ecotourism*. CAB International, Wallingford, UK.

Buckley, R.C. (2004j) *A Natural Partnership, Vol 2. Innovative Funding Mechanisms for Visitor Infrastructure in Protected Areas*. TTF Australia, Sydney.

Buckley, R.C. (2004k) Ecotourism planning and destination management in Vietnam. In: Diamantis, D. (ed) *Ecotourism: Management and Assessment*. Thomson Learning, London, pp. 313–322.

Buckley, R.C. (2005a) In search of the narwhal: ethical dilemmas in ecotourism. *Journal of Ecotourism* 4, 129–134.

Buckley, R (2005b) Recreation ecology research effort: an international comparison. *Tourism Recreation Research* 30, 99–101.

Buckley, R.C. (2006) *Adventure Tourism*. CAB International, Wallingford, UK.

Buckley, R.C. (2007) Adventure tourism products: price, duration, size, skill, remoteness. *Tourism Management* 28, 1428–1433.

Buckley, R. (2008) Testing take-up of academic concepts in an influential commercial tourism publication. *Tourism Management* 29, 721–729.

Buckley, R.C. and Araujo, G. (1997a) Green advertising by tourism operators on Australia's Gold Coast. *Ambio* 26, 190–191.

Buckley, R.C. and Araujo, G. (1997b) Environmental management performance in tourism accommodation. *Annals of Tourism Research* 24, 465–469.

Buckley, R.C. and Clough, E. (1997) World Ecotourism Congress. Who is selling what to whom? *Annals of Tourism Research* 24, 479–480.

Buckley R.C. and King H.J. (2003) Visitor-impact data in a land-management context. In: Buckley, R.C., Pickering, C.M. and Weaver, D. (eds) *Nature-based Tourism, Environment and Land Management*. CAB International, Wallingford, UK, pp. 89–99.

Buckley, R.C. and Littlefair, C. (2007) Minimal-impact education can reduce actual impacts of park visitors. *Journal of Sustainable Tourism* 15, 324–325.

Buckley, R.C. and Pannell, J. (1990) Environmental impacts of tourism and recreation in national parks and conservation reserves. *Journal of Tourism Studies* 1, 24–32.

Buckley, R.C. and Warnken, W. (2002) *Giardia* and *Cryptosporidium* in pristine Australian watercourses. *Ambio* 32, 84–86.

Buckley, R.C., Witting, N. and Guest, M. (2001) *Managing People in Australian Parks*. Griffith University, CRC Tourism, Gold Coast.

Buckley, R.C., Pickering, C.M. and Weaver, D. (eds) (2003a) *Nature-Based Tourism, Environment and Land Management*. CAB International, Wallingford, UK.

Buckley, R.C., Witting, N. and Guest, M. (2003b) Visitor fees, tour permits and asset and risk management by parks agencies: Australian case study. In: Buckley, R.C., Pickering, C.M. and Weaver, D. (eds) *Nature-based Tourism, Environment and Land Management*,. CAB International, Wallingford, UK, pp. 51–59.

Buckley, R.C., King, N. and Zubrinich, T. (2004) The role of tourism in spreading dieback disease in Australian vegetation. In: Buckley, R. (ed.) *Environmental Impacts of Ecotourism*. CAB International, Wallingford, UK, pp. 317–324.

Buckley, R.C., Pickering, C., Castley, G. and Growcock, A. (2006) Recent recreation ecology research in Australia. In: Siegrist, D., Clivaz, C., Hunziker, M. and Iten, S. (eds) *Exploring the Nature of Management*. University of Applied Sciences, Rapperswil, pp. 84–88.

Buckley, R., Ollenburg, C. and Zhong, L.S. (2008) Cultural landscape in Mongolian tourism. *Annals of Tourism Research* 35, 47–61.

Buglass, D. (1995) *Ecotourism as a Conservation Instrument? Making Conservation Projects More Attractive*. Weltforum Verlag, London.

Burger, J., Gochfeld, M. and Niles, L.J. (1995) Ecotourism and birds in coastal New Jersey: contrasting responses of birds, tourists and managers. *Environmental Conservation* 22, 56–65.

Burnett, G.W. and Aysal, M. (1991) Dominica – geographic isolation and tourism prospects. *Tourism Management* 12, 141–145.

Burnie, D. (1994) Ecotourists to paradise. *New Scientist* 142, 23–25.

Burns, D.L. (1997) Developing representations of user pays strategies in nature-based tourism settings. *Tourism Economics* 3, 241–248.

Burns, P.M., Burt, B. and Clerk, C. (1997) Ecotourism and national development. *Environment and Development in the Pacific Islands*. Australian National University, pp. 25, 201–215.

Burton, F. (1998) Can ecotourism objectives be achieved? *Annals of Tourism Research* 6, 755–758.

Burton Inc. (2005) *2005 Rider's Journal*. Burton, Burlington, VA.

Burton, R. (1998) Maintaining the quality of ecotourism: ecotour operators' responses to tourism growth. *Journal of Sustainable Tourism* 9, 117–142.

Busby, G. and Rendle, S. (2000) The transition from tourism on farms to farm tourism. *Tourism Management* 21, 635–642.

Bushell, R. (2003) Balancing conservation and visitation in protected areas. In: Buckley, R.C., Pickering, C. and Weaver, D. (eds) *Nature-based Tourism, Environment and Land Management*. CAB International, Wallingford, UK, pp. 197–208.

Butler, J.R., Hvenegaard, G.T. and Krystofiak, D.K. (1994) Economic values of bird-watching at Point Pelee National Park, Canada. In: Munashinghe, M and McNeely, J.A. (eds) *Protected Area Economics and Policy: Linking Conservation and Sustainable Development*. World Bank, Washington, DC, pp. 253–262.

Butler, R.W. and Boyd, S.W. (2000) *Tourism and National Parks: Issues and Implications*. Wiley, Chichester, UK.

Butler, R.W. and Waldbrook, L.A. (1991) A new planning tool: the tourism opportunity spectrum. *Journal of Tourism Studies* 2, 3–14.

Buultjens, J. and Davis, D. (2001) Managing for sustainable commercial whitewater rafting in northern New South Wales, Australia. *Journal of Tourism Studies* 12, 40–50.

Byrnes, T. and Warnken, J. (2004) Establishing best-practice environmental management: lessons from the Australian tour boat industry. In: Buckley, R., Pickering, C. and Weaver, D.B. (eds) *Nature-Based Tourism, Environment and Land Management*. CAB International, Wallingford, UK, pp. 111–122.

Caffyn, A. (2000) Is there a tourism partnership life cycle? In: Bramwell, B. and Lane, B. (eds) *Tourism Collaboration and Partnerships*. Channel View Publications, Clevedon, UK, pp. 200–229.

Campbell, L.M. (1999) Ecotourism in rural developing communities. *Annals of Tourism Research* 26, 534–553.

Canadian Pacific Hotels (1993) *Green Partnerships*. CPH, Montreal.

Carlsen, J. (1999) Tourism impacts on small islands: a longitudinal study of community attitudes towards tourism on the Cocos (Keeling) Islands. *Pacific Tourism Review* 3, 25–35.

Carlson, L.H. and Godfrey, P.J. (1989) Human impact management in a coastal recreation and natural area. *Biological Conservation* 49, 141–156.

Carson, R. (1993) The value of clean water: the public's willingness to pay for boatable, fishable and swimmable quality water. *Water Resources Research* 29, 2445–2454.

Casagrandi, R. and Rinaldi, S. (2002) A theoretical approach to tourism sustainability. *Conservation Ecology* 6, 13.

Cater, C. and Cater, E. (2007) *Marine Ecotourism: Between the Devil and the Deep Blue Sea*. CAB International, Wallingford, UK.

Cater, E. (1993) Ecotourism in the Third World: problems for sustainable tourism development. *Tourism Management* 14, 85–90.

Cater, E. and Lowman, G. (1994) *Ecotourism: A Sustainable Option*. Wiley, Chichester, UK.

Cater, E., Briguglio, L., Butler, R., Harrison, D., Filho, W.L. and Briguglio, L. (1996) *Ecotourism in the Caribbean: A Sustainable Option for Belize and Dominica?* Pinter, London.

Cavaco, C. (1995) Tourism in Portugal: diversity, diffusion, and regional and local development. *Tijdschrift Voor Economische en Sociale Geografie* 86, 64–71.

Ceballos-Lascurain, H. (1992) Tourism, ecotourism and protected areas. *Proceedings of IV Congress on National Parks and Protected Areas*. IV Congress of National Parks and Protected Areas, Caracas. IUCN, Gland, Switzerland.

Cessford, G.R. and Dingwall, P.R. (1994) Tourism on New-Zealand's Sub-Antarctic Islands. *Annals of Tourism Research* 21, 318–332.

Chambers, E. (1997) *Tourism and Culture: An Applied Perspective*. State University of New York Press, Albany, NY.

Chan, S.C. (1994) Whither Sarawak tourism? *Sarawak Gazette* 121, 23–25.

Charters, T. (Chair) (2002) Draft Cairns Charter on Partnerships for Ecotourism. Accessed 29 January 2003. www.ecotourism.org.au/charter.cfm

Charters, T. and Smith, E. (2004) Partnership for the future: tourism in Queensland's protected areas. In: Buckley R.C. (ed.) *Tourism in Parks: Australian Initiatives*. Griffith University, Gold Coast, pp. 150–169.

Chase, L.C. (1997) Ecotourism demand and differential pricing of national park entrance fees in Costa Rica. *Annual Meetings of the American Agricultural Economics Association*. Department of Agricultural, Resource, and Managerial Economics, Cornell University, Ithaca, NY, pp. 34–36.

Chase, L., Lee, D., Schulz, W. and Anderson, D. (1998) Ecotourism demand and differential pricing of national park access in Costa Rica. *Land Economics* 74, 466–482.

Chhetri, P., Arrowsmith, C. and Jackson, M. (2004) Determining hiking experiences in nature-based tourist destinations. *Tourism Management* 25, 31–43.

Child, B. (1996) The practice and principles of community-based wildlife management in Zimbabwe: the CAMPFIRE Programme. *Biodiversity and Conservation* 5, 369–398.

Chin, C., Moore, S., Wallington, T. and Dowling, R. (2000) Ecotourism in Bako National Park, Borneo: visitors' perspectives on environmental impacts and their management. *Journal of Sustainable Tourism* 8, 20–35.

Chirgwin, S. and Hughes, K. (1997) Ecotourism: the participants' perceptions. *Journal of Tourism Studies* 8, 2–7.

Chizhova, V.P. (2004) Impacts and management of hikers in Kavkazsky State Biosphere Reserve, Russia. In: Buckley, R.C. (ed.) *Environmental Impacts of Ecotourism*. CAB International, Wallingford, UK, pp. 377–381.

Christian, C.S., Potts, T.D., Burnett, G.W. and Lacher, T.E. (1996) Parrot conservation and ecotourism in the Windward Islands. *Journal of Biogeography* 23, 387–393.

Christian, S. (2007) Selling adventure tourism: a distribution channels perspective. *International Journal of Tourism Research* 9, 257.

Christie, P., White, A. and Deguit, E. (2002) Starting point or solution? Community-based marine protected areas in the Philippines. *Journal of Environmental Management* 66, 441–454.

Cigna, A.A. (1993) Environmental management of tourist caves. *Environmental Geology* 21, 173–180.

Clarke, J. (1997) A framework of approaches to sustainable tourism. *Journal of Sustainable Tourism* 5, 224–323.

Clawson, M. (1992) The demand for and value of outdoor recreation. In: Oates, W.E. (ed.) *The Economics of the Environment*. Edward Elgar, Aldershot, UK.

Clayton, C. and Mendelsohn, R. (1993) The value of watchable wildlife: a case study of McNeil River. *Journal of Environmental Management* 39, 101–106.

Clough, P. (1993) Economic Instruments and Visitor Services on the Public Estate. *New Zealand Institute of Economic Research, Ministry of Tourism* 1–10.

Coccossis, H. and Nijkamp, P. (1995) *Sustainable Tourism Development*. Avebury, Aldershot, UK.

Coghlan, A. and Prideaux, B. (2008) Encounters with wildlife in Cairns, Australia; where, what, who . . . ? *Journal of Ecotourism* 7, 68–76.

Cohen, J. and Richardson, J. (1995) Nature tourism vs. incompatible industries: megamarketing the ecological environment to ensure the economic future of nature tourism. *Journal of Travel and Tourism Marketing* 4, 107–116.

Cole, D. (1981) Managing ecological impacts at wilderness campsites. An evaluation of techniques. *Journal of Forestry* 79, 86–89.

Cole, D.N. (1995a) Experimental trampling of vegetation. Relationship between trampling intensity and vegetation response. *Journal of Applied Ecology* 32, 203–214.

Cole, D.N. (1995b) Experimental trampling of vegetation. Predictors of resistance and resilience. *Journal of Applied Ecology* 32, 215–224.

Cole, D.N. (2004) Impacts of hiking and camping on soils and vegetation. In: Buckley, R.C. (ed.) *Environmental Impacts of Ecotourism*. CAB International, Wallingford, UK, pp. 41–60.

Cole, D.N. and Hendee, J.C. (1990) Ecological impacts of wilderness recreation and their management. In: Hendee, J.C., Stankey, G.H. and Lucas, R.C. (eds) *Wilderness Management*. North American Press, Golden, CO, pp. 425–466.

Cole, D.N., Petersen, M.E. and Lucas, R.C. (1987) *Managing Wilderness Recreation Use: Common Problems and Potential Solutions*. USDA Forest Service, Ogden, UT.

Cole, S. (2007) Implementing and evaluating a code of conduct for visitors. *Tourism Management* 28, 443–451.

Colla, S.R., Otterstatter, M.C., Gegear, R.J. and Thomson, J.D. (2006) Plight of the bumble bee: pathogen spillover from commercial to wild populations. *Biological Conservation* 129, 461–467.

Colvin, J.G. and Dembner, S.A. (1996) Indigenous ecotourism: the Capirona programme in Napo Province, Ecuador. *Unasylva: Special Issue: Forest Conservation and Utilisation* 47, 32–33.

Conservation Corporation Africa (CC Africa) (2008) Reawaken your Soul. Accessed 19 May 2008. http://www.ccafrica.com/

Costanza, R., d'Arge, R., de Groot, R., Farber, S., Grasso, M., Hannon, B., Limburg, K., Naeem, S., O'Neill, R.V., Paruelo, J., Raskin, R.G., Sutton, P. and van den Belt, M. (1997) The value of the world's ecosystem services and natural capital. *Nature* 387, 253–260.

Cothran, D.A. and Cothran, C.C. (1998) Promise or political risk for Mexican tourism. *Annals of Tourism Research* 2, 477–497.

Cousins, J.A. (2007) The role of UK-based conservation tourism operators. *Tourism Management* 28, 1020–1030.

Crabtree, J.R., Leat, P.M.K., Santarossa, J. and Thomson, K.J. (1994) The economic impact of wildlife sites in Scotland. *Journal of Rural Studies* 10, 61–72.

Croft, D.B. (2000) Sustainable use of wildlife in Western New South Wales: Possibilities and problems. *Rangeland Journal* 22, 88–104.

Crosby, A. (1992) Ecotourism in Mexico: Yucatan Peninsula: the Mayan Route. *Natour* 10, 18–27.

Crosby, A. and Galan, M. (1992) Ecotourism development in Banc d'Arguin National Park, Mauritania. *Natour* 11, 18–27.

Crossley, J. and Lee, B. (1994) Characteristics of ecotourists and mass tourists. *Visions in Leisure and Business* 13, 4–12.

Cunningham, R.B., Lindenmayer, D.B. and Lindenmayer, B.D. (2004) Sound recording of bird vocalisations in forests. I. Relationships between bird vocalisations and point interval counts of bird numbers – a case study in statistical modeling. *Wildlife Research* 31, 195–207.

Curry, S. and Morvaridi, B. (1992) Sustainable tourism: illustrations from Kenya, Nepal and Jamaica. *Progress in Tourism Recreation and Hospitality Management* 4, 131–139.

D'Amore, L.J. (1993) A code of ethics and guidelines for socially and environmentally responsible tourism. *Journal of Travel Research* 31, 64–66.

Danielsen, F., Burgess, N.D. and Balmford, A. (2005a) Monitoring matters: examining the potential of locally-based approaches. *Biodiversity and Conservation* 14, 2507–2582.

Danielsen, F., Jensen, A.E., Alviola, P.A., Balete, D.S., Mendoza, M., Tagtag, A., Custodio, C. and Enghoff, M. (2005b) Does monitoring matter? A qualitative assessment of management decisions from locally-based monitoring of protected areas. *Biodiversity and Conservation* 14, 2633–2652.

Darrow, K. (1995) A partnership model for nature tourism in the Eastern Caribbean Islands. *Journal of Travel Research* 33, 48–51.

Davis, D., Banks, S., Birtles, A., Valentine, P. and Cuthill, M. (1997) Whale sharks in Ningaloo Marine Park; managing tourism in an Australian marine protected area. *Tourism Management* 18, 259–271.

Davis, D.C. and Tisdell, C.A. (1999) Tourist levies and willingness to pay for a whale shark experience. *Tourism Economics* 5, 161–174.

Davis, P.B. (1999) Beyond guidelines: a model for Antarctic tourism. *Annals of Tourism Research* 26, 516–533.

De Haas, H. (2000) A review of the sustainability of small scale ecotourism in Niue. In: Cukier, J. and Dixon, E. *Tourism Resources, Impacts and Planning.* Department of Geography, University of Waikato, Hamilton.

de los Monteros, R.L. (2002) Evaluating ecotourism in the natural protected areas of La Paz Bay, Baja California Sur, Mexico: ecotourism or nature-based tourism? *Biodiversity and Conservation* 11, 1539–1550.

de Oliveira, J.A.P. (2005) Tourism as a force for establishing protected areas: the case of Bahia, Brazil. *Journal of Sustainable Tourism* 13, 24–49.

de Roy, T. (1998) My treetop brush with a harpy. *International Wildlife* 28, 24–29.

Dearden, P. (1991) Tourism and sustainable development in northern Thailand. *Geographical Review* 81, 400–413.

Deng, J., King, B. and Bauer, T. (2002) Evaluating natural attractions for tourism. *Annals of Tourism Research* 29, 422–438.

Devkota, S.R. (2005) Is strong sustainability operational? An example from Nepal. *Sustainable Development* 13, 297–310.

Dewhurst, H. and Thomas, R. (2003) Encouraging sustainable business practices in a non-regulatory environment: a case study of small tourism firms in a UK national park. *Journal of Sustainable Tourism* 11, 383–403.

Dharmaratne, G.S., Yee, S. and Walling, L.J. (2000) Tourism potentials for financing protected areas. *Annals of Tourism Research* 27, 590–610.

Diamantis, D. (1998) Consumer behaviour and ecotourism products. *Annals of Tourism Research* 25, 515–518.

Diamantis, D. (1999) The concept of ecotourism: evolution and trends. *Current Issues in Tourism* 2, 515–518.

Diamantis, D. (2004) *Ecotourism Management and Assessment*. Thomson, London.

Din, K.H. (1988) Social and cultural impacts of tourism. *Annals of Tourism Research* 15, 563–566.

Dixon, J.A. and Sherman, B.P. (1991) Economics of protected areas. *Ambio* 20, 68–74.

Dixon, J.A. and van't Hof, T. (1997) Conservation pays big dividends in Caribbean. *Forum Applied Research Public Policy* 43–49.

Dixon, J.A., Scura, L.F. and van't Hof, T. (1993) Meeting ecological and economic goals: marine parks in the Caribbean. *Ambio* 22, 117–125.

Doan, T.M. (2000) The effects of ecotourism in developing nations: an analysis of case studies. *Journal of Sustainable Tourism* 8, 288–304.

Dogan, H. (1989) Forms of adjustment: sociocultural impacts of tourism. *Annals of Tourism Research* 16, 216–236.

Dombeck, J. (1998) Speech. Accessed 12 November 1998. www.fs.fed.au/intro/speech

Donohoe, H.M. and Needham, R.D. (2006) Ecotourism: the evolving contemporary definition. *Journal of Ecotourism* 5, 192–210.

Donohoe, H.M. and Needham, R.D. (2008) Internet-based ecotourism marketing: evaluating Canadian sensitivity to ecotourism tenets. *Journal of Ecotourism* 7, 15–43.

Douglas, A.J. and Johnson, R.L. (2004) The travel cost method and the economic value of leisure time. *International Journal of Tourism Research* 6, 365–374.

Douglas, A.J. and Taylor, J.G. (1998) Riverine based eco-tourism: Trinity River non-market benefits estimates. *International Journal of Sustainable Development and World Ecology* 5, 136–148.

Douglas, J.E. (1992) Ecotourism: the future for the Caribbean? *Industry and Environment* 15, 64–66.

Dowell-Hentall, P. (2001) Forest tourism in Tasmania. In: Buckley, R.C. (ed.) *Abstracts – Fenner Conference on Nature Tourism and the Environment*. Griffith University, CRC Tourism, Gold Coast, p. 18.

Dowling, R.K. (1993) Tourist and resident perceptions of the environment-tourism relationship in the Gascoyne Region, Western Australia. *Geo Journal* 29, 243–251.

Dowling, R.K. and Newsome, D. (2006) *Geotourism: Sustainability, Impacts and Management*. Butterworth-Heinemann, Oxford.

Dowling, R.K. and Sharp, J. (1997) Conservation–tourism partnerships in Western Australia. *Tourism Recreation Research* 22, 55–60.

DPIWE – Department of Primary Industries, Water and Environment (Tasmania State Government) (2005) Managing Phytophthora. Accessed 24 June 2008. http://www.dpiwe tas gov adinter nsf/

Driml, S.M. (1997) Bringing ecological economics out of the wilderness. *Ecological Economics* 23, 145–153.

Driml, S. (2002) Travel cost analysis of recreation value in the Wet Tropics World Heritage Area. *Economic Analysis and Policy* 32, 11–26.

Driml, S. and Common, M. (1995) Economic and financial benefits of tourism in major protected areas. *Australian Journal of Environmental Management* 2, 19–20.

Driml, S. and Common, M. (1996) Ecological economics criteria for sustainable tourism: application to the Great Barrier Reef and Wet Tropics World Heritage Areas, Australia. *Journal of Sustainable Tourism* 4, 3–16.

Driscoll, D.A. and Weir, T. (2005) Beetle responses to habitat fragmentation depend on ecological traits, habitat condition, and remnant size. *Conservation Biology* 19, 182–194.

Drost, A. (1996) Developing sustainable tourism for World Heritage sites. *Annals of Tourism Research* 23, 479–492.

Duffus, D. (1996) The recreational use of Grey Whales in the Southern Clayquot Sound, Canada. *Applied Geography* 16, 179–190.

Durst, P.B. and Ingram, C.D. (1998) Nature-orientated tourism promotion by developing countries. *Tourism Management* 9, 39–43.

Dwyer, L., Forsyth, P. and Spurr, R. (2004) Evaluating tourism's economic effects: new and old approaches. *Tourism Management* 25, 307–317.

Dyck, M.G. and Baydack, R.K. (2004) Vigilance behaviour of polar bears in the context of wildlife-viewing activities at Churchill, Manitoba, Canada. *Biological Conservation* 116, 343–350.

Dyer, P., Aberdeen, L. and Schuler, S. (2003) Tourism impacts on an Australian Indigenous community: a Djabugay case study. *Tourism Management* 24, 83–95.

Eagles, P.F.J. (1995) Tourism and Canadian parks: fiscal relationships. *Managing Leisure* 1, 16–27.

Eagles, P.F.J. (2002) Trends in park tourism: economics, finance and management. *Journal of Sustainable Tourism* 10, 132–153.

Eagles, P.F.J. and Cascagnette, J.W. (1995) Canadian ecotourists: who are they? *Tourism Recreation Research* 20, 22–28.

Eagles, P.F.J. and McCool, S.F. (2002) *Tourism in National Parks and Protected Areas: Planning and Management.* CAB International, Wallingford, UK.

Eagles, P.F.J. and Wind, E. (1994) Canadian ecotours in 1992: a content analysis of advertising. *Journal of Applied Recreation Research* 19, 67–87.

Earth Sanctuaries (2008) Warrawong Wildlife Sanctuary. Accessed 27 May 2008. http://www.warrawong.com/

Eber, S. (ed.) (1992) *Beyond the Green Horizon.* Worldwide Fund for Nature, Godalming.

Echeverria, J., Hanrahan, M. and Solorzano, R. (1995) Valuation of non-priced amenities provided by the biological resources within the Monteverde Cloud Forest Preserve, Costa Rica. *Ecological Economics* 13, 43–52.

Ecotourism Association of Australia (2002) Accessed 19 May 2008. www.ecotourism.org.au

Ecotourism Association of Australia (2007) Accessed 6 February 2008. www.ecotourism.org.au

Edington, J.M. and Edington, M.A. (1986) *Ecology, Recreation and Tourism.* Cambridge University Press, Cambridge, Melbourne, pp. 112–117.

Edington, J.M. and Edington, M.A. (1997) Tropical forest ecotourism: two promising projects in Belize. In: Stabler, M.J. (ed.) *Tourism and Sustainability Principles to Practice.* CAB International, Wallingford, UK, pp. 163–167.

Edwards, N., McLaughlin, W.J. and Ham, S. (1998) *Comparative study of ecotourism policy in the Americas – 1998.* University of Idaho, Moscow, ID, Volume 11.

Ellenberg, U., Mattern, T., Seddon, P.J. and Jorquera, G.L. (2006) Physiological and reproductive consequences of human disturbance in Humboldt penguins: the need for species-specific visitor management. *Biological Conservation* 133, 95–106.

Englin, J.E., McDonald, J.M. and Moeltner, K. (2006) Valuing ancient forest ecosystems; an analysis of backcountry hiking in Jasper National Park. *Ecological Economics* 4, 665–678.

Esprit, S. (1994) Dominica – managing the ecotourism option: a view of the planning and management tasks required by a national ecotourism policy. *Rural Extension Bulletin* 5, 31–36.

Estes, R.D., Atwood, J.L. and Estes, A.B. (2006) Downward trends in Ngorongoro Crater ungulate populations 1986–2005: conservation concerns and the need for ecological research. *Biological Conservation* 131, 106–120.

Ewert, A. and Shultis, J. (1997) Resource-based tourism: an emerging trend in tourism experiences. *Parks and Recreation* 32, 94–103.

Fagence, M. (1997) Ecotourism and Pacific Island countries: the first generation of strategies. *Journal of Tourism Studies* 8, 26–38.

Fairweather, J.R. and Maslin, C. (2005) Environmental values and response to ecolabels among international visitors to New Zealand. *Journal of Sustainable Tourism* 13, 82–98.

FAO (1989) *Trade Yearbook, 43.* FAO, Rome.

Farrell, B.H.G. and Runyan, D. (1991) Ecology and tourism. *Annals of Tourism Research* 18, 26–40.

Fennell, D. (2001) A content analysis of ecotourism definitions. *Current Issues in Tourism* 4, 403–421.

Fennell, D. (2002) *Ecotourism Programme Planning*. CAB International, Wallingford, UK.

Fennell, D. and Dowling, R. (2003) *Ecotourism Policy and Planning*. CAB International, Wallingford, UK.

Fennell, D.A. (1998) Ecotourism in Canada. *Annals of Tourism Research* 25, 231–235.

Fennell, D.A. (1999) *Ecotourism: An Introduction*. Routledge, London and New York.

Fennell, D.A. (2006) *Tourism Ethics*. Channel View Publications, Clevedon, UK.

Fennell, D.A. and Eagles, P.F.J. (1990) Ecotourism in Costa Rica: a conceptual framework. *Journal of Park and Recreation Administration* 8, 23–34.

Fennell, D.A. and Malloy, D.C. (1995) Ethics and ecotourism: a comprehensive ethical model. *Journal of Applied Recreation Research* 20, 163–168.

Fennell, D.A. and Malloy, D.C. (1999) Measuring the ethical nature of tourism operators. *Annals of Tourism Research* 26, 928–943.

Fennell, D.A. and Weaver, D.B. (1997) Vacation farms and ecotourism in Saskatchewan, Canada. *Journal of Rural Studies* 13, 467–475.

Figgiss, P. (1993) Ecotourism: special interest or major direction? *Habitat Australia* 8, 11.

Findlay, K.P. (1997) Attitudes and expenditures of whale watchers in Hermanus, South Africa. *South African Journal of Wildlife Research* 27, 57–62.

Finney, S.K., Pearce-Higgins, J.W. and Yalden, D.W. (2005) The effect of recreational disturbance on an upland breeding bird, the golden plover *Pluvialis apricaria*. *Biological Conservation* 121, 53–63.

Fischer, A. and van der Wal, R. (2007) Invasive plant suppresses charismatic seabird – the construction of attitudes towards biodiversity management options. *Biological Conservation* 135, 256–267.

Fischer, J., Lindenmayer, D.B., Barry, S. and Flowers, E. (2005) Lizard distribution patterns in the Tumut fragmentation 'natural experiment' in south-eastern Australia. *Biological Conservation* 123, 301–315.

Fisher, B. and Christopher, T. (2007) Poverty and biodiversity: measuring the overlap of human poverty and the biodiversity hotspots. *Ecological Economics* 62, 93–101.

Fix, P. and Loomis, J. (1997) The economic benefits of mountain biking at one of its meccas: an application of the travel cost method to mountain biking in Moab, Utah. *Journal of Leisure Research* 29, 342–352.

Floyd, M.R., Jang, H. and Noe, F.P. (1997) The relationship between environmental concern and acceptability of environmental impacts among visitors to two US national park settings. *Journal of Environmental Management* 51, 391–412.

Foggin, T. and Munster, D.O. (2000) Enhancing linkages between rural communities and protected areas in KwaZulu-Natal through tourism – abantu bayasizana (people helping people). *The Journal of Tourism Studies* 11, 2–10.

Folke, J., Østrup, J.F. and Gössling, S. (2006) Ecotourist choices of transport modes. In: Gössling, S. and Hultman, J. (eds) *Ecotourism in Scandinavia: Lessons in Theory and Practice*. CAB International, Wallingford, UK, pp. 157–165.

Font, A.R. (2000) Mass tourism and the demand for protected natural areas: a travel cost approach. *Journal of Environmental Economics and Management* 39, 97–116.

Font, X. (2002) Environmental certification in tourism and hospitality: progress, process and prospects. *Tourism Management* 23, 197–205.

Font, X. and Buckley, R.C. (eds) (2001) *Tourism Ecolabelling*. CAB International, Wallingford, UK.

Font, X. and Harris, C. (2004) Rethinking standards from green to sustainable. *Annals of Tourism Research* 31, 986–1007.

Font, X. and Tribe, J. (2000) *Forest Tourism and Recreation: Case Studies in Environmental Management*. CAB International, Wallingford, UK.

Font, X. and Tribe, J. (2001) Promoting green tourism: the future of environmental awards. *International Journal of Tourism Research* 3, 9–21.

Forbes, B.C., Monz, C.A. and Tolvanen, A. (2004) Ecological impacts of tourism in terrestrial polar ecosystems. In: Buckley, R.C. (ed.) *Environmental Impacts of Ecotourism.* CAB International, Wallingford, UK, pp. 155–170.

Forbes, W. (1998) Tourism in Curry County, Oregon. In: Hall, M. and Lew, A. (eds) *Sustainable Tourism: a Geographical Perspective.* Longman, London, pp. 119–131.

Forestell, P.H. (1993) If Leviathan has a face, does Gaia have a soul? Incorporating environmental education in marine eco-tourism programs. *Ocean and Coastal Management* 3, 267–283.

Forsyth, T. (1993) *Sustainable Tourism: Moving from Theory to Practice.* World Wide Fund for Nature, Godalming, UK.

Forsyth, T. (1997) Environmental responsibility and business regulation: the case of sustainable tourism. *Geographical Journal* 163, 270–280.

France, L.A. (1997) *The Earthscan Reader in Sustainable Tourism.* Earthscan, London.

Fraser, G.S. and Stutchbury, B.J.M. (2004) Area-sensitive forest birds move extensively among forest patches. *Biological Conservation* 118, 377–387.

Frechtling, D.C. (2006) An assessment of visitor expenditure methods and models. *Journal of Travel Research* 45, 26–36.

Freeman, A.N.D. (2004) Constraints to community groups monitoring plants and animals in rainforest revegetation sites on the Atherton Tablelands of far north Queensland. *Ecological Management and Restoration* 5, 199–204.

Garrod, B. and Fennell, D.A. (2004) An analysis of whalewatching codes of conduct. *Annals of Tourism Research* 31, 334–352.

Gartner, W.C. (2004) Rural tourism development in the USA. *International Journal of Tourism Research* 6, 151–164.

Gerber, L.R., Keller, A.C. and DeMaster, D.P. (2007) Ten thousand and increasing: is the western Arctic population of bowhead whale endangered? *Biological Conservation* 137, 577–583.

Gibbons, P. and Lindenmayer, D.B. (2007) Offsets for land clearing: no net loss or the tail wagging the dog? *Ecological Management and Restoration* 8, 26–31.

Giese, M. (1998) Guidelines for people approaching breeding groups of Adelie penguins. *Polar Record* 34, 287–292.

Giese, M., Handsworth, R. and Stephenson, R. (1999) Measuring resting heart rates in penguins using artificial eggs. *Journal of Field Ornithology* 70, 49–53.

Gilbert, D.C., Penda, J. and Friel, M. (1994) Issues in sustainability and the national parks of Kenya and Cameroon. In: Cooper, C. and Lockwood, A. (eds) *Progress in Tourism, Recreation and Hospitality Management*, Vol. 6. John Wiley, Chichester, UK, pp. 31–45.

Gillingham, S. and Lee, P.C. (1999) The impact of wildlife-related benefits on the conservation attitudes of local people around the Selous Game Reserve, Tanzania. *Environmental Conservation* 26, 218–228.

Gios, G., Goio, I., Notaro, S. and Raffaelli, R. (2006) The value of natural resources for tourism: a case study of the Italian Alps. *International Journal of Tourism Research* 8, 77–85.

Githiru, M. and Lens, L. (2005) Nest predation in a fragmented Afrotropical forest: evidence from natural and artificial nests. *Biological Conservation* 123, 189–196.

Gliddon, J. and Syvret, P. (2002) Riding high: the surfers who built an $8bn business. *The Bulletin* August 13, 20–24.

Goeft, U. and Alder, J, (2001) Sustainable mountain biking: a case study from the southwest of Western Australia. *Journal of Sustainable Tourism* 9, 193–211.

Goldberg, T.L., Gillespie, T.R., Rwego, I.B., Wheeler, E., Estoff, E.L. and Chapman, C.A. (2007) Patterns of gastrointestinal bacterial exchange between chimpanzees and humans involved in research and tourism in western Uganda. *Biological Conservation* 135, 527–533.

Goodman, R. (2002) Pastoral livelihoods in Tanzania: can the Maasai benefit from conservation. *Current Issues in Tourism* 5, 280–286.

Goodwin, H. (1996) In pursuit of ecotourism. *Biodiversity and Conservation* 5, 277–291.

Goosem, M. (2000) Effects of tropical rainforest roads on small mammals: edge effects in community composition. *Wildlife Research* 27, 151–163.

Gössling, S. (1999) Ecotourism: a means to safeguard biodiversity and ecosystem functions? *Ecological Economics* 29, 303–320.

Gössling, S. and Hultman, J. (eds) (2006) *Ecotourism in Scandinavia: Lessons in Theory and Practice*. CAB International, Wallingford, UK.

Gössling, S., Hansson, C.B., Horstmeier, O. and Saggel, S. (2002) Ecological footprint analysis as a tool to assess tourism sustainability. *Ecological Economics* 43, 199–211.

Gössling, S., Kunkel, T. and Schumacher, K. (2004) Use of molluscs, fish and other marine taxa by tourism in Zanzibar, Tanzania. *Biodiversity and Conservation* 13, 2623–2639.

Govers, R., Go, F.M. and Kumar, K. (2007) Promoting tourism destination image. *Journal of Travel Research* 46, 15–23.

Graham, K., Beckerman, A.P. and Thirgood, S. (2005) Human-predator-prey conflicts: ecological correlates, prey losses and patterns of management. *Biological Conservation* 122, 159–171.

Grainger, J. (2003) 'People are living in the park'. Linking biodiversity conservation to community development in the Middle East region: a case study from the Saint Katherine Protectorate, Southern Sinai. *Journal of Arid Environments* 54, 29–38.

Grand Canyon Private Boaters Association (2002) The Foundations of Inequity. Accessed 20 August 2002. http://www.gcpba.org/access/history.php3

Gray, M. and Kalpers, J. (2005) Ranger based monitoring in the Virunga-Bwindi Region of East-Central Africa: a simple data collection tool for park management. *Biodiversity and Conservation* 14, 2723–2741.

Green, E. and Donnelly, R. (2003) Recreational scuba diving in Caribbean marine protected areas: do the users pay? *Ambio* 32, 140–144.

Green, G. and Lal, P. (1991) *Charging Users of the Great Barrier Reef Marine Park*. Great Barrier Reef Marine Park Authority, Townsville, Australia, pp. 1–80.

Green, K. and Osborne, W. (1994) *Wildlife of the Australian Snowy Country*. Reed, Sydney.

Grekin, J. and Milne, S. (1996) Toward sustainable tourism development: the case of Pond Inlet NWT. In: Butler, R. and Hinch, T. (eds) *Tourism and Native People*. Thomson, London, pp. 76–106.

Griffin, S.C., Valois, T., Taper, M.L. and Scott, M.L. (2007) Effects of tourists on behaviour and demography of Olympic marmots. *Conservation Biology* 21, 1070–1081.

Grodsky, J. (1993) Certified green: the law and future of environmental labeling. *Yale Journal of Regulation* 10, 147–227.

Groom, J.D., McKinney, L.B., Ball, L.C. and Winchell, C.S. (2007) Quantifying off-highway vehicle impacts on density and survival of a threatened dune-endemic plant. *Biological Conservation* 35, 119–134.

Grotta, D. (1992) *The Green Travel Sourcebook*. Wiley, Chichester, UK.

Growcock, A.J.W. (2005) Impacts of camping and trampling on Australian alpine and subalpine vegetation. PhD thesis, Griffith University, Gold Coast, Australia.

Guclu, K. and Karahan, F. (2004) A review: the history of conservation programs and development of the national parks concept in Turkey. *Biodiversity and Conservation* 13, 1371–1390.

Guevara, J.R.Q. (1996) Learning through participatory action research for community ecotourism planning. *Convergence Toronto* 29, 24–40.

Gunatilleke, N. (1992) Tourist hotels in environmentally sensitive areas. *Loris* 19, 162–165.

Gunnarsdotter, Y. (2006) Hunting tourism as ecotourism: conflicts and opportunities. In: Gössling, S. and Hultman, J. (eds) *Ecotourism in Scandinavia: Lessons in Theory and Practice*. CAB International, Wallingford, UK, pp. 178–192.

Gunningham, N. and Grabosky, P. (1999) *Smart Regulation: Designing Environmental Policy*. Clarendon Press, Oxford.

Gurung, C.P. and De Coursey, M. (1994) The Annapurna Conservation Area Project: a pioneering example of sustainable tourism? In: Cater, E. and Lowman, G. (eds) *Ecotourism: A Sustainable Option?* Wiley, Chichester, UK, pp. 177–194.

Gurung, P.C. (1998) Ecotourism and conservation: hand in hand in the Annapurna region of Nepal. *Tigerpaper* 25, 19–23.

Haab, T.C. and McConnell, K.E. (2002) *Valuing Environmental and Natural Resources: The Econometrics of Non-Market Valuation*. Edward Elgar, Northampton, UK.

Haas, G. (2002) *Visitor Capacity on Public Lands and Waters: Making Better Decisions*. National Recreation and Park Associates, Ashburn, VA.

Hadwen, W.L. and Bunn, S.E. (2004) Tourists increase the contribution of autochthonous carbon to littoral zone food webs in oligotrophic dune lakes. *Marine and Freshwater Research* 55, 701–708.

Hadwen, W.L., Arthington, A.H. and Mosisch, T.D. (2003) The impact of tourism on dune lakes on Fraser Island, Australia. *Lakes and Reservoirs: Research and Management* 8, 15–26.

Hadwen, W.L., Bunn, S.E., Arthington, A.H. and Mosisch, T.D. (2005) Within-lake detection of the effects of tourist activities in the littoral zone of oligotrophic dune lakes. *Aquatic Ecosystem Health and Management* 8, 159–173.

Hadwen, W.L., Hill, W. and Pickering, C.M. (2007) Icons under threat: why monitoring visitors and their ecological impacts in protected areas matters. *Ecological Management and Restoration* 8, 177–181.

Hadwen, W.L., Hill, W. and Pickering, C.M. (2008) Linking visitor impact research to visitor impact monitoring in protected areas. *Journal of Ecotourism* 7, 87–93.

Haig, I. and McIntyre, N. (2002) Viewing nature: the role of the guide and the advantage of participating in commercial ecotourism. *Journal of Tourism Studies* 13, 39–48.

Hall, C.M. and Higham, J. (2005) *Tourism, Recreation and Climate Change*. Channel View Publications, Clevedon, UK.

Hall, C.M. and Page, S. (2006) *The Geography of Tourism and Recreation: Environment, Place, and Space*. Routledge, London.

Hall, C.M. and Piggin, R. (2002) The business knowledge of World Heritage sites: a New Zealand case study. *International Journal of Tourism Research* 4, 401–411.

Hall, D. (2004a) Rural tourism in southeastern Europe: transition and the search for sustainability. *International Journal of Tourism Research* 6, 165–176.

Hall, D. and Kinnaird, V. (1994) Ecotourism in Eastern Europe. In: Cater, E. and Lowman, G. (eds) *Ecotourism a Sustainable Option*. Wiley, Chichester, UK, pp. 111–136.

Hall, M. (2004b) Ecotourism policy. In: Diamantis, D. (ed.) *Ecotourism Management and Assessment*. Thomson, London, pp. 135–150.

Hall, M. and Lew, A. (eds) (1998) *Sustainable Tourism: a Geographical Perspective*. Longman, London.

Hall, M. and Wouters, M. (1994) Managing nature tourism in the Sub-Antarctic. *Annals of Tourism Research* 21, 355–374.

Hallwood, P. (2007) Contractual difficulties in environmental management: the case of wetland mitigation banking. *Ecological Economics* 63, 446–451.

Halpenny, E.A. (2001) *Marine Ecotourism: Guidelines and Best Practice Case Studies*. The Ecotourism Society, North Bennington, VT.

Hammit, W.E. and Cole, D.N. (1997) *Wildland Recreation: Ecology and Management*. Wiley, New York.

Hanneberg, P. (1994a) Ecotourism or ecoterrorism. *Environment* 17, 26.

Hanneberg, P. (1994b) Jukkasjarvi: ecotourism a local success. *Enviro* 17, 26–28.

Hardy, A., Beeton, R.J. and Pearson, L. (2002) Sustainable tourism: an overview of the concept and its position in relation to conceptualisations of tourism. *Journal of Sustainable Tourism* 10, 475–496.

Harper, P. (1997) The importance of community involvement in sustainable tourism development. In: Stabler, M.J. (ed.) *Tourism and Sustainability: Principles to Practice*. CAB International, Wallingford, UK, pp. 143–150.

Harris, C.C., Driver, B.L., Binkley, C.S. and Mendelsohn, R.O. (1987) Recreation user fees: pros and cons, an economic analysis. *Journal of Forestry* 85, 25–40.

Harris, C.M. (2005) Aircraft operations near concentrations of birds in Antarctica: the development of practical guidelines. *Biological Conservation* 125, 309–322.

Harris, G.M. and Pimm, S.L. (2004) Bird species' tolerance of secondary forest habitats and its effects on extinction. *Conservation Biology* 18, 1607–1616.

Harris, R. and Leiper, N. (1995) *Sustainable Tourism: an Australian Perspective*. Butterworth-Heinemann, Chatswood, Australia.

Harris, R., Griffin, A. and Williams, P. (2002) *Sustainable Tourism: a Global Perspective*. Butterworths, London, 311 pp.

Harrison, D. (2001) *Tourism and the Less Developed World: Issues and Case Studies*. CAB International, Wallingford, UK.

Harroun, L. and Boo, E. (1996) *Managing People in Parks: A Guide to Visitor Use in Natural Areas*. US World Wildlife Fund, Washington, DC.

Hawkins, D.E. (2004) A protected areas ecotourism competitive cluster approach to catalyse biodiversity conservation and economic growth in Bulgaria. *Journal of Sustainable Tourism* 12, 219–244.

Hawkins, D.E., Epler Wood, M. and Bittman, S. (1995) *The Ecolodge Sourcebook for Planners and Developers*. The Ecotourism Society, North Bennington, VT.

Healy, R.G. (1994) 'Tourist merchandise' as a means of generating local benefits from ecotourism. *Journal of Sustainable Tourism* 2, 137–151.

Hearne, R.R. and Salinas, Z.M. (2002) The use of choice experiments in the analysis of tourist preferences for ecotourism development in Costa Rica. *Journal of Environmental Management* 65, 153–163.

Heath, R.A. (1992) Wildlife-based tourism in Zimbabwe: an outline of its development and future policy options. *Geographical Journal of Zimbabwe* 23, 59–78.

Heberlein, T.A., Breymeyer, A. and Noble, R. (1996) Recreation and tourism management in protected areas. In: Breymeyer, A. and Nobel, R. (eds) *Biodiversity Conservation in Transboundary Protected Areas*. National Academy Press, Washington, DC, pp. 203–209.

Heinen, J.T. (1993) Park–people relations in Kosi Tappu Wildlife Reserve, Nepal: a socio-economic analysis. *Environmental Conservation* 20, 25–34.

Helsinga, J. (2003) Regulating ecotourism in Galapagos: a case study of domestic – international partnerships. *Journal of International Wildlife Law and Policy* 6, 57–77.

Hemmings, A.D. and Roura, R. (2003) Antarctic tourism. A square peg in a round hole: fitting impact assessment under Antarctic environmental protocol to Antarctic tourism. *Impact Assessment and Project Appraisal* 21, 13–24.

Hendee, J.C. and Dawson, C.P. (2002) *Wilderness Management*, 3rd edn. Fulcrum, Golden, CO.

Henle, K., Davies, K.F., Kleyer, M., Margules, C.R. and Settele, J. (2004a) Predictors of species sensitivity to fragmentation. *Biodiversity and Conservation* 13, 207–251.

Henle, K., Lindermayer, D.B., Margules, C.R., Saunders, D.A. and Wissel, C. (2004b) Species survival in fragmented landscapes: where are we now? *Biodiversity and Conservation* 13, 1–8.

Henning, D.H. (1993) Nature based tourism can help conserve tropical forests. *Tourism Recreation Research* 18, 45–50.

Herath, G. (1997) Ecotourism development in Australia. *Annals of Tourism Research* 24, 442–446.

Heslinga, J. (2003) Regulating ecotourism in Galapagos: a case study of domestic-international partnerships. *Journal of International Wildlife Law and Policy* 6, 57–77.

Higginbottom, K., Northrope, C. and Green, R. (2001) *Positive Effects of Wildlife Tourism on Wildlife*. CRC Tourism, Griffith University, Gold Coast.

Higgins, B.R. (2001) Tour operators. In: Weaver, D. (ed.) *Encyclopaedia of Ecotourism*. CAB International, Wallingford, UK, pp. 535–548.

Higham, J. and Lusseau, D. (2004) Ecological impacts and management of tourist engagements with cetaceans. In: Buckley, R. (ed.) *Environmental Impacts of Ecotourism*. CAB International, Wallingford, UK, pp. 171–186.

Higham, J.A. and Dickey, A. (2007) Benchmarking ecotourism in New Zealand: A c. 1999 analysis of activities offered and resources utilised by ecotourism businesses. *Journal of Ecotourism* 6, 67–74.

Higham, J.E.S. and Bejder, L. (2008) Managing wildlife-based tourism: edging slowly towards sustainability? *Current Issues in Tourism* 11, 75–83.

Higham, J.E.S. and Lusseau, D. (2007) Urgent need for empirical research into whaling and whale watching. *Conservation Biology* 21, 554–558.

Hill, C. (2004) Farmers' perspectives of conflict at the wildlife agriculture boundary: some lessons learned from African subsistence farmers. *Human Dimensions of Wildlife* 9, 279–286.

Hill, G., Rosier, J. and Dyer, P. (1995) Tourism development and environmental limitations at Heron Island, Great Barrier Reef: a response. *Journal of Environmental Management* 45, 91–100.

Hill, J., Woodland, W. and Gough, G. (2007) Can visitor satisfaction and knowledge about tropical rainforests be enhanced through biodiversity interpretation and does this promote a positive attitude towards ecosystem conservation? *Journal of Ecotourism* 6, 75–85.

Hill, W. and Pickering, C.M. (2006) Vegetation associated with different walking track types in the Kosciuszko alpine area, Australia. *Journal of Environmental Management* 78, 24–34.

Hillman, R. (2004) Principles for managing commercial tour operators in Australia's protected areas. In: Buckley, R.C. (ed.) *Tourism in Parks: Australian Initiatives*. Griffith University, Gold Coast, pp. 73–78.

Himachal Helicopter Skiing (2001) Welcome to the World's Top Heliskiing. Accessed 15 April 2008. http:// www.himachal.com

Hinch, T. (1998) Ecotourists and Indigenous hosts: diverging views on their relationship with nature. *Current Issues in Tourism* 1, 120–124.

Hinch, T.D. and Swinnerton, G.S. (1993) Tourism and Canada's North-West Territories: issues and prospects. *Tourism Recreation Research* 18, 23–31.

Hjalager, A. (1999) Consumerism and sustainable tourism. *Journal of Travel and Tourism Marketing* 8, 1–20.

Hodgson, A.J., Marsh, H. and Corkeron, P.J. (2004) Provisioning by tourists affects the behaviour but not the body condition of Mareeba rock-wallabies. *Wildlife Research* 31, 451–456.

Holden, A. and Kealy, H. (1996) A profile of UK outbound 'environmentally friendly' tour operators. *Tourism Management* 17, 60–64.

Holmern, T., Nyahongo, J. and Roskaft, E. (2007) Livestock loss caused by predators outside the Serengeti National Park, Tanzania. *Biological Conservation* 135, 534–542.

Holmes, N., Giese, M. and Kriwoken, L.K. (2005) Testing the minimum approach distance guidelines for incubating Royal penguins. *Biological Conservation* 126, 339–350.

Holmes, T., Alger, K., Zinkhan, C. and Mercer, E. (1998) The effect of response time on conjoint analysis estimates of rainforest protection values. *Journal of Forest Economics* 4, 7–28.

Holzapfel, R. (2000) Ethics in ecotourism – blueprint for a code of conduct and practice. In: Cukier, J. and Dixon, E. *Tourism Resources, Impacts and Planning*. University of Waikato, Hamilton, pp. 195–206.

Honey, M. (1999) *Ecotourism and Sustainable Development: Who Owns Paradise?* Island Press, Washington, DC.

Honey, M. (ed.) (2002) *Ecotourism and Certification: Setting Standards in Practice*. Island Press, Washington, DC.

Horn, C. and Simmons, D. (2002) Community adaptation to tourism: comparisons between Rotorua and Kaikoura, New Zealand. *Tourism Management* 23, 133–143.

Horwich, R.H. (1998) Effective solutions for howler conservation. *International Journal of Primatology* 19, 579–598.

Horwich, R.H., Murray, D. and Saqui, E. (1993) Ecotourism and community development: a view from Belize. In: Lyon, J., Godfrey, D., Lindberg, K., Hawkins, D.E. and Lindberg, K. (eds) *Ecotourism a Guide for Planners and Managers*. Ecotourism Society, North Bennington, VT, pp. 152–168.

Hoyt, E. (2000) *Whale-Watching 2000: Worldwide Tourism Numbers, Expenditures, and Expanding Socioeconomic Benefits*. International Fund for Animal Welfare, Crowborough, UK.

Hudson, S. (2002) *Sport and Adventure Tourism*. Haworth Hospitality Press, New York.

Hughes, R. (2001) Animals, values and tourism – structural shifts in United Kingdom dolphin tourism provision. *Tourism Management* 22, 321–330.

Hulme, D. and Murphree, M. (2001) *African Wildlife and Livelihoods: The Promise and Performance of Community Conservation*. Heinemann, Portsmouth, NH.

Hummel, J. (1994) Ecotourism development in protected areas of developing countries. *World Leisure and Recreation* 36, 17–23.

Hundloe, T. and Hamilton, C. (1997) *Koalas and Tourism: An Economic Evaluation*. The Australia Institute, Canberra.

Hunter, C. (1997) Sustainable tourism as an adaptive paradigm. *Annals of Tourism Research* 24, 850–867.

Hunter, C. and Shaw, J. (2007) The ecological footprint as a key indicator of sustainable tourism. *Tourism Management* 28, 46–57.

Husbands, W. (1994) Visitor expectations of tourism benefits in Zambia. In: Uysal, M. (ed.) *Global Tourist Behavior*. International Business Press, Binghamton, NY, pp. 21–38.

Hvenegaard, G.T. (1994) Ecotourism: a status report and conceptual framework. *The Journal of Tourism Studies* 5, 24–35.

Hvenegaard, G.T. and Dearden, P. (1998) Ecotourism versus tourism in a Thai National Park. *Annals of Tourism Research* 25, 700–720.

Hviding, E. and Bayliss-Smith, T. (2000) *Islands of Rainforest: Agroforestry, Logging and Ecotourism in Solomon Islands*. Ashgate, Aldershot, UK.

Inskeep, E. (1987) Environmental planning for tourism. *Annals of Tourism Research* 14, 118–135.

International Hotels Environment Initiative (IHEI) (1993) *Environmental Management for Hotels*. Butterworth-Heinemann, Oxford.

International Tourism Partnership (2008) Going Green. Accessed 26 May 2008. http://www.tourism-partnership.org/pages07/Publications.html

Ioannides, D. (1995) A flawed implementation of sustainable tourism: the experience of Akamas, Cyprus. *Tourism Management* 16, 583–592.

Isaacs, J.C. (2000) The limited potential of ecotourism to contribute to wildlife conservation. *Wildlife Society Bulletin* 28, 61–69.

Jaakson, R. (1997) Exploring the epistemology of ecotourism. *Journal of Applied Recreation Research* 22, 33–40.

Jackson, J. (2007) Attitudes towards the environment and ecotourism of stakeholders in the UK tourism industry with particular reference to ornithological tour operators. *Journal of Ecotourism* 6, 34–66.

Jackson, S.F., Kershaw, M. and Gaston, K.J. (2004) The buffer effect and the selection of protected areas for waterbirds in Britain. *Biological Conservation* 120, 137–143.

Jacobi, C. (2003) *An Experiment Using Signs to Reduce Visitor-Built Cairns in Acadia National Park. ANP Natural Resource Reports 2002–04*. USDI National Park Services, Bar Harbor, ME.

Jacobson, S.K. and Robles, R. (1992) Ecotourism, sustainable development, and conservation education: development of a tour guide training program in Tortuguero, Costa Rica. *Environmental Management* 10, 701–713.

Jakus, P. and Shaw, W.D. (1997) Congestion at recreation areas: empirical evidence on perception, mitigating behaviour and management preferences. *Journal of Environmental Management* 50, 389–401.

Jamrozy, U., Backman, S.J. and Backman, K.F. (1996) Involvement and opinion leadership in tourism. *Annals of Tourism Research* 23, 908–924.

Jansen-Verbeke, M. and Go, F. (1995) Tourism development in Vietnam. *Tourism Management* 16, 315–321.

Jenkins, O. (1993) Marketing and the ecotourism paradox. Honours thesis, University of Sydney, Sydney.

Jim, C.Y. (1989) Visitor management in recreation areas. *Environmental Conservation* 16, 19–32.

Johannesen, A.B. (2007) Protected areas, wildlife conservation, and local welfare. *Ecological Economics* 62, 126–135.

Johansson, J.T. (1998) King of the hill. *Ski*, January 98, 21–22.

Johnsen, N. (1998) Maasai in a tourists' paradise: a process of poverty and sedentarisation. *Indigenous Affairs* 2, 10–19.

Johnson, J. (2004) Impacts of tourism-related in-migration: the Greater Yellowstone region. In: Buckley, R.C. (ed.) *Environmental Impacts of Ecotourism*. CAB International, Wallingford, UK, pp. 25–40.

Johnson, J. and Borrie, M. (2003) Moving nearer to heaven: growth and change in the Greater Yellowstone Region, USA. In: Buckley, R.C. Pickering, C.M. and Weaver, D. (eds) *Nature Tourism and the Environment*. CAB International, Wallingford, UK.

Johnston, F.M. and Johnston, S. (2004) Impacts of road disturbance on soil properties and on exotic plant occurrence in subalpine areas of the Australian Alps. *Arctic, Antarctic and Alpine Research* 36, 201–207.

Johnston, F.M. and Pickering, C.M. (2001) Alien plants in the Australian Alps. *Mountain Research and Development* 21, 284–291.

Jolly, D.W. and Rasmussen, D.R. (1991) Use of islands for propagation of endangered species and ecotourism. *American Journal of Primatology* 24, 110.

Jones, M.E. (2000) Road upgrades, road mortality and remedial measures: impacts on a population of Eastern quolls and Tasmanian devils. *Wildlife Research* 27, 289–296.

Jorge, M.L.S.P. (2008) Effects of forest fragmentation on two sister genera of Amazonian rodents (*Myoprocta acouchy* and *Dasyprocta leporina*). *Biological Conservation* 141, 617–623.

Jukofsky, D. (1998) Guides in their own backyards. *Nature Conservation Magazine* 48, 18–24.

Jule, K.R., Leaver, L.A. and Lea, S.E.G. (2008) The effects of captive experience on reintroduction survival in carnivores: a review and analysis. *Biological Conservation* 141, 355–363.

Jurowski, C., Uysal, M. and Williams, D.R. (1997) A theoretical analysis of host community resident reactions to tourism. *Journal of Travel Research* 36, 3–11.

Kalafatis, S.P. and Pollard, M. (1999) Green marketing and Ajzen's theory of planned behaviour: a cross-market examination. *Journal of Consumer Marketing* 16, 441–460.

Kaltenborn, B.P., Haaland, H. and Sandell, K. (2001) The public right of access: some challenges to sustainable tourism development in Scandinavia. *Journal of Sustainable Tourism* 9, 417–433.

Kangas, P., Shave, M. and Shave, P. (1995) Economics of an ecotourism operation in Belize. *Environmental Management* 19, 669–673.

Kariel, H.G. (1989) Socio-cultural impacts of tourism in the Austrian Alps. *Mountain Research and Development* 9, 59–70.

Karlsson, J. and Sjostrom, M. (2007) Human attitudes towards wolves, a matter of distance. *Biological Conservation* 137, 610–616.

Karxzmarski, L, Cockcroft, V.G., McLachlan, A. and Winter, P.E.D. (1998) Recommendations for the conservation and management of humpback dolphins, *Sousa chinensis* in the Algoa Bay Region, South Africa. *Koedoe* 41, 121–130.

Kastenholz, E. (2004) 'Management of demand' as a tool in sustainable tourist destination development. *Journal of Sustainable Tourism* 12, 388–408.

Kelly, C., Pickering, C.M. and Buckley, R.C. (2003) Impacts of tourism on threatened plant taxa and communities in Australia. *Ecological Management and Restoration* 4, 37–44.

Kelly, J., Haider, W., Williams, P.W. and Englund, K. (2007) Stated preferences of tourists for eco-efficient destination planning options. *Tourism Management* 28, 377–390.

Kerkvliet, J. and Nowell, C. (2000) Tools for recreation management in parks: the case of the Greater Yellowstone's blue-ribbon fishery. *Ecological Economics* 34, 89–100.

Kerley, G. (1997) The winning game: an ecotourism success story that almost never happened. *African Wildlife* 51, 27–29.

Kerley, G.I.H., Knight, M.H., de Kock, M. and de Kock, M. (1995) Desertification of subtropical thicket in the Eastern Cape, South Africa: are there alternatives? *Environmental Monitoring and Assessment* 37, 211–230.

Khan, F. (1996) Living on the margins: ecotourism and Indigenous people in southern Africa. *African Wildlife* 50, 22–24.

Kimmel, J.R. (1999) Ecotourism as environmental learning. *Journal of Environmental Education* 30, 40–45.

King, B., Pizam, A. and Milman, A. (1993) Social impacts of tourism: host perceptions. *Annals of Tourism Research* 20, 650–665.

King, D.A. and Stewart, W.P. (1996) Ecotourism and commodification: protecting people and places. *Biodiversity and Conservation* 5, 293–305.

Kinnaird, M.F. and O'Brien, T.G. (1996) Ecotourism in the Tangkoko DuaSudara Nature Reserve: opening Pandora's Box? *Onyx* 30, 65–73.

Klaric, Z. (1991) Nautical tourism and island eco-tourism: the Yugoslav experience. In: Seminar on New Forms of Demand and New Products, Nicosia (Cyprus), 8–9 May 1991. World Tourism Organization, pp. 60–65.

Klenosky, D., Frauman, E., Norman, W. and Glenger, C. (1998) Nature-based tourists' use of interpretive services: a means-end investigation. *Journal of Tourism Studies* 9, 26–36.

Klocker, U., Croft, D.B. and Ramp, D. (2006) Frequency and causes of kangaroo-vehicle collisions on an Australian outback highway. *Wildlife Research* 3, 5–15.

Knapman, B. and Stoeckl, N. (1995) Recreation user fees: an Australian empirical investigation. *Tourism Economics* 1, 5–15.

Knapp, D. and Barrie, E. (1998) Ecology versus interpretation: the analysis of two different messages. *Journal of Interpretation Research* 3, 21–38.

Koch, E., Ghimire, K.B. and Pimbert, M.P. (1997) *Ecotourism and Rural Reconstruction in South Africa: Reality or Rhetoric?* Earthscan, London.

Kock, M.D. (1996) Zimbabwe: A model for the sustainable use of wildlife and the development of innovative wildlife management practices. In: Taylor, V.J. and Dunstone, N. (eds) *The Exploitation of Mammal Populations.* Chapman & Hall, London, pp. 229–249.

Kokkranikai, J., McLellan, R. and Baum, T. (2003) Island tourism and sustainability: a case study of the Lakshadweep Islands. *Journal of Sustainable Tourism* 11, 426–447.

Koku, J.E. and Gustafsson, J. (2003) Local institutions and natural resource management in the South Tongu District of Ghana: a case study. *Sustainable Development* 11, 17–35.

Korakandy, R. (1998) Towards the development of recreational fisheries in Kerala: an economic perspective. *Tourism Recreation Research* 23, 3–9.

Kousis, M. (2000) Tourism and the environment: a social movements perspective. *Annals of Tourism Research* 27, 468–489.

Kozak, M. and Nield, K. (2004) The role of quality and eco-labelling systems in destination benchmarking. *Journal of Sustainable Tourism* 12, 138–148.

Krannich, R.S., Eisenhauer, B.W., Field, D.R., Pratt, C. and Luloff, A.E. (1999) Implications of the National Park Service recreation fee demonstration program for park operators and management: perceptions of NPS managers. *Journal of Park and Recreation Administration* 17, 35–52.

Krausse, G.H. (1995) Sustainable tourism for remote atolls in the Pacific. *International Journal of Sustainable Development and World Ecology* 2, 166–181.

Kretchman, J.A. and Eagles, P. (1990) An analysis of the motives of ecotourists in comparison to the general Canadian population. *Loisir-et-Societe* 13, 499–508.

Kruger, O. (2005) The role of ecotourism in conservation: panacea or Pandora's box? *Biodiversity and Conservation* 14, 579–600.

Laarman, J. and Gregersen, H. (1996) *Making Nature-based Tourism Contribute to Sustainable Development: a Policy Framework, Policy Brief Environmental and Natural Resources Policy and Training Project.* EPATMUCIA, Madison, WI.

Lai, P.H. and Nepal, S.K. (2006) Local perspectives of ecotourism development in Tawushan Nature Reserve, Taiwan. *Tourism Management* 27, 1117–1129.

Laird, J. (1993) Laos pins tourism hopes on unspoiled nature and culture. *Our Planet* 5, 8–10.

Lang, C. and O'Leary, J.T. (1997) Motivation, participation, and preference: a multi-segmentation approach of the Australian nature travel market. *Journal of Travel and Tourism Marketing* 6, 159–177.

Langholz, J. (1999) Exploring the effects of alternative income opportunities on rainforest use: insights from Guatemala's Maya biosphere reserve. *Society and Natural Resources* 12, 139–149.

Langoya, C.D. and Long, C. (1997) Local communities and ecotourism development in Budongo Forest Reserve, Uganda. *Network Paper Rural Development Forestry Network* 22, 1–14.

Laurance, W.F., Alonso, A., Lee, M. and Campbell, P. (2006) Challenges for forest conservation in Gabon, Central Africa. *Futures of Bioregions* 38, 454–470.

Lawrence, T.B., Wickins, D. and Phillips, N. (1997) Managing legitimacy in ecotourism. *Tourism Management* 18, 307–316.

Lawton, L.J. (2001) Public protected areas. In: Weaver, D. (ed.) *Encyclopedia of Ecotourism.* CAB International, Wallingford, UK, pp. 287–302.

Lee, C.-K. (1997) Valuation of nature-based tourism resources using dichotomous choice valuation method. *Tourism Management* 18, 587–591.

Lee, C.-K. and Han, S.-Y. (2002) Estimating the use and preservation values of national parks' tourism resources using a contingent valuation method. *Tourism Management* 23, 531–540.

Lee, C.-K., Lee, J.-H. and Han, S.-Y. (1998) Measuring the economic value of ecotourism resources: the case of South Korea. *Journal of Travel Research* 36, 40–46.

Lee, D.N.B. and Snepenger, D.J. (1992) An ecotourism assessment of Tortuguero, Costa Rica. *Annals of Tourism Research* 19, 367–370.

Lee, W.H. and Moscardo, G. (2005) Understanding the impact of ecotourism resort experiences on tourists' environmental attitudes and behavioural intentions. *Journal of Sustainable Tourism* 13, 546–565.

Lees, A.C. and Peres, C.A. (2006) Rapid avifaunal collapse along the Amazonian deforestation frontier. *Biological Conservation* 133, 198–211.

Lemon, M., Lynch, T.P., Cato, D.H. and Harcourt, R.G. (2006) Response of travelling bottlenose dolphins (*Tursiops aduncus*) to experimental approaches by a powerboat in Jervis Bay, New South Wales, Australia. *Biological Conservation* 127, 363–372.

Leones, J., Colby, B. and Crandall, K. (1998) Tracking expenditures of the elusive nature tourists of southeastern Arizona. *Journal of Travel Research* 36, 56–64.

Leung, Y. and Marion, J. (1999) Spatial strategies for managing visitor impacts in national parks. *Journal of Park and Recreation Administration* 17, 2–38.

Leung, Y. and Marion, J.L. (2004) Managing impacts of camping. In: Buckley, R.C. (ed.) *Environmental Impacts of Ecotourism*. CAB International, Wallingford, UK, pp. 245–258.

Lew, A. (1998) Ecotourism trends. *Annals of Tourism Research* 25, 742–746.

Lewis, A. and Newsome, D. (2003) Planning for stingray tourism at Hamelin Bay, Western Australia: the importance of stakeholder perspectives. *International Journal of Tourism Research* 5, 331–346.

Li, W. (2004) Environmental management indicators for ecotourism in China's nature reserves: a case study in Tianmushan Nature Reserve. *Tourism Management* 25, 559–564.

Liddle, M. (1997) *Recreation Ecology: The Ecological Impact of Outdoor Recreation and Ecotourism*. Chapman and Hall, London.

Lindberg, K. (1991) *Policies for Maximising Nature Tourism's Ecological and Economic Benefit*. World Resources Institute, Washington, DC.

Lindberg, K. (2001a) *Natural Areas Revenue Generation Through User Fees: Overview*. The International Ecotourism Society, North Bennington, VT.

Lindberg, K. (2001b) Economic impacts of ecotourism. In: Weaver, D. (ed.) *The Encyclopedia of Ecotourism*. CAB International, Wallingford, UK, pp. 363–378.

Lindberg, K. and Aylward, B. (1999) Price responsiveness in the developing country nature tourism context: review and Costa Rican case study. *Journal of Leisure Research* 31, 281–299.

Lindberg, K. and Enriquez, J. (1994) *An Analysis of Ecotourism's Economic Contribution to Conservation and Development in Belize*. World Wildlife Fund, Washington, DC.

Lindberg, K. and Huber, R. (1993) Economic issues in ecotourism management. In: Huber, R.M., Lindberg, K. and Hawkins, D.E. (eds) *Ecotourism a Guide for Planners and Managers*. The Ecotourism Society, North Bennington, VT.

Lindberg, K., Enriquez, J. and Sproule, K. (1996) Ecotourism questioned: case studies from Belize. *Annals of Tourism Research* 23, 543–562.

Lindberg, K., McCool, S. and Stankey, G. (1997a) Rethinking carrying capacity. *Annals of Tourism Research*. 24, 461–464.

Lindberg, K., Goulding, C., Huang, Z., Mo, J., Wei, P. and Kong, G. (1997b) Ecotourism in China: selected issues and challenges. In: Oppermann, M. (ed.) *Pacific Rim Tourism*. CAB International, Wallingford, UK, pp. 128–143.

Lindberg, K., Epler Wood, M. and Engeldrum, D. (1998) *Ecotourism: A Guide for Planners and Managers*, Volume 2. The Ecotourism Society, North Bennington, VT.

Lindberg, K. and McKercher, R. (1997) Ecotourism: a critical overview. *Pacific Tourism Review* 1, 65–79.

Lindenmayer, D.B., Pope, M.L. and Cunningham, R.B. (2004) Patch use by the greater glider (*Petauroides volans*) in a fragmented forest ecosystem. II. Characteristics of den trees and preliminary data on den-use patterns. *Wildlife Research* 31, 569–577.

Lindgren, A., Lodin, L. and Schonfeldt, I. (1997) *Ecotourism in Western Samoa – For Better or For Worse*. Swedish University of Agricultural Sciences, Uppsala.

Lindsey, P.A., Alexander, R.R., du Toit, J.T. and Mills, M.G.L. (2005) The potential contribution of ecotourism to African Wild Dog *Lycaon pictus* conservation in South Africa. *Biological Conservation* 123, 339–348.

Lindsey, P.A., Roulet, P.A. and Romanach, S.S. (2007) Economic and conservation significance of the trophy hunting industry in sub-Saharan Africa. *Biological Conservation* 134, 455–469.

Lipke, D.J. (2001a) Good for whom? Forget playing up the environment, data increasingly shows that its better to stress a product's health benefits for humans. *American Demographics* 23, 36–38.

Lipke, D.J. (2001b) Green marketing: green homes. *American Demographics* 23, 50–56.

Littlefair, C.J. (2004) Reducing impacts through interpretation, Lamington National Park. In: Buckley, R.C. (ed.) *Environmental Impacts of Ecotourism*. CAB International, Wallingford, UK, pp. 297–307.

Littlefair, C. and Buckley, R.C. (2008) Interpretation reduces ecological impacts of visitors to World Heritage Areas. *Ambio* 32, 84–86.

Liu, J.C. and Var, T. (1986) Resident attitudes toward tourism impacts in Hawaii. *Annals of Tourism Research* 13, 193–214.

Liu, J.C., Sheldon, P.J. and Var, T. (1987) Resident perception of the environmental impacts of tourism. *Annals of Tourism Research* 14, 17–37.

Lober, J. (1992) Using forest guards to protect a biological reserve in Costa Rica: one step towards linking parks to people. *Journal of Environmental Planning and Management* 35, 17–41.

Lockwood, M., Worboys, G. and Kothari, A. (2006) *Managing Protected Areas: a Global Guide*. Earthscan, London.

Loker-Murphy, L. and Pearce, P.L. (1995) Young budget travelers: backpackers in Australia. *Annals of Tourism Research* 22, 819–843.

Long, V.H. (1992) Tourism development, conservation, and anthropology. *Practicing Anthropology* 14, 14–17.

Lonsdale, W.M. and Lane, A.M. (1994) Tourist vehicles as vectors of weed seeds in Kakadu National Park, northern Australia. *Biological Conservation* 69, 277–283.

Loomis, J. (2006) A comparison of the effect of multiple destination trips on recreation benefits as estimated by travel cost and contingent valuation methods. *Journal of Leisure Research* 38, 46–51.

Loot, G., Aldana, M. and Narvarrete, S.A. (2005) Effects of human exclusion on parasitism in intertidal food webs of central Chile. *Conservation Biology* 19, 203–212.

Lorimer, K. (2006) *Code Green*. Lonely Planet, Melbourne.

Lovelock, B. (2002) Why it's good to be bad: the role of conflict in contributing towards sustainable tourism in protected areas. *Journal of Sustainable Tourism* 10, 5–30.

Loveridge, A.J., Searle, A.W., Murindagomo, F and Macdonald, D.W. (2007) The impact of sport-hunting on the population dynamics of an African lion population in a protected area. *Biological Conservation* 134, 548–558.

Lubeck, L. (1991) East African safari tourism: the environmental role of tour operators, travel agents and tourists. In: Kusler, J. (ed.) *Ecotourism and Resource Conservation*. Omnipress, Madison, WI, pp. 115–133.

Lück, M. and Kirstges, T. (2003) *Global Ecotourism Policies and Case Studies: Perspectives and Constraints*. Channel View Publications, Clevedon, UK.

Lumsdon, L.M. and Swift, J.S. (1998) Ecotourism at a crossroads: the case of Costa Rica. *Journal of Sustainable Tourism* 6, 155–172.

Lusseau, D. and Higham, J. (2004) Managing the impacts of dolphin-based tourism through the definition of critical habitats: the case of bottlenose dolphins (*Tursiops* spp) in Doubtful Sound, New Zealand. *Tourism Management* 25, 657–667.

Luzar, E.J., Diagne, A., Gan, C. and Henning, B.R. (1995) Evaluating nature-based tourism using the new environmental paradigm. *Journal of Agricultural and Applied Economics* 27, 544–555.

Luzar, E.J., Diagne, A., Gan, C.E.C. and Henning, B.R. (1998) Profiling the nature-based tourist: a multinomial logit approach. *Journal of Travel Research* 37, 48–55.

McCain, C.M. (1997) Honduran ecotourism. *Women in Natural Resources* 18, 36–38.

McCarthy, T.M., Fuller, T.K. and Munkhtsog, B. (2005) Movements and activities of snow leopards in southwestern Mongolia. *Biological Conservation* 124, 527–537.

McClung, M.R., Seddon, P.J., Massaro, M. and Setiawan, A.N. (2004) Nature-based tourism impacts on yellow-eyed penguins *Megadyptes antipodes*: does unregulated visitor access affect fledging weight and juvenile survival? *Biological Conservation* 119, 279–285.

McCool, S.F. and Lime, D.W. (2001) Tourism carrying capacity: tempting fantasy or useful reality. *Journal of Sustainable Tourism* 9, 372–388.

McCool, S.F. and Moisey, R.N. (eds) (2001) *Tourism, Recreation and Sustainability.* CAB International, Wallingford, UK.

McCool, S.F. and Stankey, G.H. (2001) Managing access to wildlands for recreation in the USA: Background and issues relevant to sustaining tourism. *Journal of Sustainable Tourism* 9, 389–399.

McCulley, R.B. (1999) Wilderness Management Plan for Grand Canyon National Park and the Colorado River. MES thesis, University of Strathclyde, UK.

McDonald, J. (2001) The financial liability of park managers for visitor injuries. *Environment and Planning Law Journal* 18, 579–588.

McDougall, K.L. (2001) Colonization by alpine native plants of a stabilized road verge on the Bogong High Plains, Victoria. *Ecological Management and Restoration* 2, 47–52.

McDougall, K.L. and Wright, G.T. (2004) The impacts of trampling on feldmark vegetation in Kosciuszko National Park, Australia. *Australian Journal of Botany* 52, 15–320.

McDougall, R., Testoni, L., Hall, N., Murray, F. and Switzer, M. (2004) Opportunities for developing natural and cultural heritage tourism in Australia. In: Buckley, R.C. (ed.) *Tourism in Parks: Australian Initiatives.* Griffith University, Gold Coast, pp. 31–54.

McFarlane, B.L. and Boxall, P.C. (1996) Participation in wildlife conservation by birdwatchers. *Human Dimensions of Wildlife* 1, 1–14.

McGehee, N.G. (2007) An agritourism systems model: a weberian perspective. *Journal of Sustainable Tourism* 15, 111–124.

McIntosh, A.J. and Bonnemann, S.M. (2006) Willing Workers on Organic Farms (WWOOF): the alternative farm stay experience? *Journal of Sustainable Tourism* 14, 82–99.

McIntosh, R.W., Goeldner, C.R. and Ritchie, J.R.B. (1995) *Tourism and the Environment.* Wiley, New York.

McIntyre, G. (1993) *Sustainable Tourism Development: Guide for Local Planners.* World Tourism Organization, Madrid.

McIntyre, N., Jenkins, J. and Booth, K. (2001) Global influences on access: the changing face of access to public conservation lands in New Zealand. *Journal of Sustainable Tourism* 9, 434–450.

McIvor, C. (1997) Management of wildlife, tourism and local communities in Zimbabwe. In: Ghimire, K.B. and Pimbert, S.P. (eds) *Social Change and Conservation: Environmental Politics and Impacts of National Parks and Protected Areas.* Earthscan, London, pp. 214–238.

MacKay, K.J. Lamont, D.E. and Partridge, C. (1996) Northern ecotourists and general tourists: an intra-provincial comparison. *Journal of Applied Recreation Research* 21, 335–337.

McKercher, B. (1998) *The Business of Nature-Based Tourism.* Hospitality Press, Melbourne.

McKercher, B. (2001) The business of ecotourism. In: Weaver, D.B. (ed.) *The Encyclopedia of Ecotourism.* CAB International, Wallingford, UK, pp. 565–577.

McKercher, B. and Robbins, B. (1998) Business development issues affecting nature-based tourism operators in Australia. *Journal of Sustainable Tourism* 6, 173–188.

McKercher, R. (1993) Some fundamental truths about tourism: understanding tourism's social and environmental impacts. *Journal of Sustainable Tourism* 1, 6–16.

McLaren, D. (1998) *Rethinking Tourism and Travel.* Kumarian, Sterling, VA.

MacLellan, R. (1999) An examination of wildlife tourism as a sustainable form of tourism development in Scotland. *International Journal of Tourism Research* 5, 375–387.

McNeely, J.A. and Thorsell, J.W. (1989) Jungles, mountains, and islands: how tourism can help conserve the natural heritage. *World Leisure and Recreation* 31, 29–39.

McNeely, J.A., Miller, K.R., Reid, W.V., Mittermeier, R.A. and Werner, T.B. (1991) *Conserving the World's Biological Diversity.* WRI, WCU, World Bank, WWF and Conservation International, Washington and Gland.

Mader, R. (2002) Latin American ecotourism: What is it? *Current Issues in Tourism* 5, 272–279.

Magro, T. and de Barros, M (2004) Understanding use and users at Itatiaia National Park, Brazil. In: Buckley, R.C. (ed.) *Environmental Impacts of Ecotourism*. CAB International, Wallingford, UK, pp. 361–376.

Maharana, I., Rai, S.C. and Sharma, E. (2000) Valuing ecotourism in a sacred lake of the Sikkim Himalaya, India. *Environmental Conservation* 27, 269–277.

Maher, P., Steel, G. and McIntosh, A.R. (2003) Cutting edge: examining the experiences of tourists in Antarctica. *International Journal of Tourism Research* 5, 59–67.

Maille, P. and Mendelsohn, R. (1993) Valuing ecotourism in Madagascar. *Journal of Environmental Management* 38, 213–218.

Mak, J. and Moncur, J.E.T. (1998) Political economy of protecting unique recreational resources: Hanauma Bay, Hawaii. *Ambio* 27, 217–225.

Malek-Zadeh, E. (1998) Marketing Ecotourism to Travel Agents. Accessed 24 June 2008. www2. planeta.com/mader/planeta/0298/0298tourism.html

Mallett, J. (1998) Plenary address. *Seventh World Congress of Adventure Travel and Ecotourism*, Quito, Ecuador.

Mallick, S.A. and Driessen, M.M. (2003) Feeding of wildlife: how effective are the 'keep wildlife wild' signs in Tasmania's national parks? *Ecological Management and Restoration* 4, 199–237.

Mallord, J.W., Dolman, P.M., Brown, A.F. and Sutherland, W.J. (2007) Linking recreational disturbance to population size in a ground-nesting passerine. *Journal of Applied Ecology* 44, 185–195.

Malloy, D.C. and Fennell, D.A. (1998) Ecotourism and ethics: moral development and organisational cultures. *Journal of Travel Research* 26, 47–56.

Mangun, J.C. and Mangun, W.C. (2002) Wildlife watchers in the western United States: a structural approach for understanding policy change. *Human Dimensions of Wildlife* 7, 123–137.

Manning, E. (ed.) (1992) *Canada's Report on Government Initiatives in Support of Sustainable Tourism*. Tourism Canada, Ottawa.

Manning, R. (1999) *Studies in Outdoor Recreation*, 2nd edn. Oregon University Press, Corvallis, OR.

Manning, R.E. (2004) Managing impacts of ecotourism through use rationing and allocation. In: Buckley, R.C. (ed.) *Environmental Impacts of Ecotourism*. CAB International, Wallingford, UK, pp. 273–286.

Manning, R.E., Ballinger, N.L., Marion, J. and Roggenbuck, J. (1996) Recreation management in natural areas: problems and practices, status and trends. *Natural Areas Journal* 16, 142–146.

Manning, R.E., Lawson, S., Newman, P., Budruk, M., Valliere, W., Laven, D. and Bacon, J. (2004) Visitor perceptions of recreation-related resource impacts. In: Buckley, R.C. (ed.) *Environmental Impacts of Ecotourism*. CAB International, Wallingford, UK, pp. 259–272.

Manning, T. (1999) Indicators of tourism sustainability. *Tourism Management* 20, 179–181.

Mardini, N.K. (1995) Influence of ecotourism in the community development. *Role of Bamboo in Community Development*. 4th International Bamboo Congress, Bali, 19–22 June, pp. 18–25.

Marion, J.L. and Leung, Y. (2004) Environmentally sustainable trail management. In: Buckley, R.C. (ed.) *Environmental Impacts of Ecotourism*. CAB International, Wallingford, UK, pp. 229–244.

Marion, J.L. and Reid, S.E. (2007) Minimising visitor impacts to protected areas: The efficacy of low impact education programmes. *Journal of Sustainable Tourism* 15, 5–27.

Markwell, K.W. (1995) Ecotourist-attraction systems: examples from East Malaysia. *Tourism Recreation Research* 20, 43–50.

Markwell, K. and Weiler, B. (1998) Ecotourism and interpretation. In: Uzzell, D. and Ballantyne, R. (eds) *Contemporary Issues in Heritage and Environmental Interpretation*. The Stationery Office, London, pp. 98–111.

Marshall, A.J., Nardiyono, Engstrom, L.M., Pamungkas, B., Palapa, J., Meijaard, E. and Stanley, S.A. (2006) The blowgun is mightier than the chainsaw in determining population density of Bornean orangutans (*Pongo pygmaeus morio*) in the forests of East Kalimantan. *Biological Conservation* 129, 566–578.

Martin, S.R. (1999) A policy implementation analysis of the Recreation Fee Demonstration Program: convergence of public sentiment, agency programs, and policy principles? *Journal of Park and Recreation Administration* 17, 15–34.

Masberg, B.A. (1996) Using ecotourists to assist in determining the content for interpretation. *Journal of Park and Recreation Administration* 14, 37–45.

Mason, P. (1997) Tourism codes of conduct in the Arctic and Sub-Arctic region. *Journal of Sustainable Tourism* 5, 151–166.

Mason, P. and Cheyne, J. (2000) Residents' attitudes to proposed tourism development. *Annals of Tourism Research* 27, 391–411.

Mason, P., Johnston, M. and Twynam, D. (2000) The World Wide Fund for Nature Arctic Tourism Project. In: Bramwell, B. and Lane, B. (eds) *Tourism Collaboration and Partnership*. Channel View Publications, Clevedon, UK, pp. 98–116.

Mason, S.A. and Moore, S.A. (1998) Using the Sorensen Network to assess the potential effects of ecotourism on two Australian marine environments. *Journal of Sustainable Tourism* 6, 143–154.

Massinga, A. (1996) Between the devil and the deep blue sea: development dilemmas in Mozambique. *Ecologist* 26, 73–75.

Mbaiwa, J.E. (2005) The problems and prospects of sustainable tourism development in the Okavango Delta, Botswana. *Journal of Sustainable Tourism* 13, 203–227.

Medeiros, R., Ramos, J.A., Paiva, V.H., Almeida, A., Pedro, P. and Antunes, S. (2007) Signage reduces the impact of human disturbance on little tern nesting success in Portugal. *Biological Conservation* 135, 99–106.

Medina, L.K. (2005) Ecotourism and certification: confronting the principles and pragmatics of socially responsible tourism. *Journal of Sustainable Tourism* 13, 281–295.

Medio, D., Ormond, R.F.G. and Pearson, M. (1997) Effect of briefing on rates of damage to corals by SCUBA divers. *Biological Conservation* 79, 91–95.

Mehmetoglu, M. (2007) Nature-based tourists: the relationship between their trip expenditures and activities. *Journal of Sustainable Tourism* 15, 200–215.

Mehta, J.N. and Kellert, S.R. (1998) Local attitudes toward community-based conservation policy and programmes in Nepal: a case study in the Makalu-Barun Conservation Area. *Environmental Conservation* 25, 320–333.

Melbourne, B.A., Davies, K.F., Margules, C.R., Lindenmayer, D.B., Saunders, D.A., Wissel, C. and Henle, K. (2004) Species survival of fragmented landscapes: where to from here? *Biodiversity and Conservation* 13, 275–284.

Menkhaus, S. and Lober, D.J. (1996) International ecotourism and the valuation of tropical rainforests in Costa Rica. *Journal of Environmental Management* 47, 1–10.

Mercer, E., Kramer, R. and Sharma, N. (1995) Rain forest tourism – estimating the benefits of tourism development in a new national park in Madagascar. *Journal of Forest Economics* 1, 239–269.

Meric, J. and Hunt, J. (1998) Ecotourists' motivational and demographic characteristics: a case study of North Carolina travelers. *Journal of Travel Research* 36, 57–61.

Michael, G.S., Chi-Ok, O. and Ditton, R.B. (2007) Managing SCUBA divers to meet ecological goals for coral reef conservation. *Ambio* 36, 316–323.

Middleton, V.C. and Hawkins, R. (1998) *Sustainable Tourism: A Marketing Perspective*. Butterworth-Heinemann, Oxford.

Miller, K. and Tangley, L. (1991) *Trees of Life*. Beacon Press, Boston, MA.

Mitchell, R.E. and Reid, D.G. (2001) Community integration: island tourism in Peru. *Annals of Tourism Research* 28, 113–139.

Mmopelwa, G., Kgathi, D.L. and Molefhe, L. (2007) Tourists' perceptions and their willingness to pay for park fees: a case study of self-drive tourists and clients for mobile tour operators in Moremi Game Reserve. *Tourism Management* 28, 1044–1056.

Monz, C.A., Meier, G.A., Welker, J.M., Buckley, R.C., Cole, D.N. and Loya, W.M. (1996) Responses of moist and dry arctic tundra to trampling and warmer temperatures. *Bulletin of the Ecological Society of America* 77, 311.

Monz, C.A. and Twardock, P. (2004) Campsite impacts in Prince William Sound, Alaska, USA. In: Buckley, R. (ed.) *Environmental Impacts of Ecotourism*. CAB International, Wallingford, UK, pp. 309–316.

Moore, S.A., Smith, A.J. and Newsome, D.N. (2003) Environmental performance reporting for natural area tourism: contributions by visitor impact management frameworks and their indicators. *Journal of Sustainable Tourism* 11, 348–375.

Moran, D. (1994) Contingent valuation and biodiversity: measuring the user surplus of Kenyan protected areas. *Biodiversity and Conservation* 3, 663–684.

More, T. and Stevens, J. (2000) Do user fees exclude low-income people from resource-based recreation? *Journal of Leisure Research* 32, 341–357.

Moscardo, G. (1996) Mindful visitors: heritage and tourism. *Annals of Tourism Research* 23, 376–397.

Moscardo, G. (1998) Interpretation and sustainable tourism: functions, examples and principles. *Journal of Tourism Studies* 9, 2–13.

Moscardo, G. (1999) *Making Visitors Mindful*. Sagamore, Champaign, IL.

Moscardo, G. (2000) Understanding wildlife tourism market segments. An Australian marine study. *Human Dimensions of Wildlife* 5, 36–53.

Moscardo, G., Morrison, A.M. and Pearce, P.L. (1996) Specialist accommodation and ecologically-sustainable tourism. *Journal of Sustainable Tourism* 4, 29–52.

Mose, I. (1993) Hohe Tauern National Park: test case for 'soft tourism' in the Austrian Alps? Experiences with projects in the Upper Pinzgau Region. *Tourism Recreation Research* 18, 11–19.

Mosisch, T. and Arthington, A. (2004) Impacts of recreational powerboating on freshwater ecosystems. In: Buckley, R. (ed.) *Environmental Impacts of Ecotourism*. CAB International, Wallingford, UK, pp. 125–154.

Mowforth, M. and Munt, I. (2003) *Tourism and Sustainability*, 2nd edn. Routledge, London.

Muir, F. (1993) Managing tourism to a seabird nesting island. *Tourism Management* 14, 99–105.

Munasinghe, M. and McNeely, J.A. (eds) (1994) *Protected Area Economics and Policy: Linking Conservation and Sustainable Development*. World Bank, Washington, DC.

Munn, C.A. (1998) Adding value to nature through macaw-oriented ecotourism. *Journal of the American Veterinary Medical Association* 212, 1246–1249.

Munt, I. (1994) Eco-tourism or ego-tourism? *Race and Class* 36, 49–61.

National Outdoor Leadership School (NOLS) (2007) The Leaders in Wilderness Education. Accessed 10 March 2008. www.nols.edu

National Tourism and Heritage Taskforce (2003) *Going Places: Developing Natural and Cultural Heritage Tourism in Australia*. National Tourism and Heritage Taskforce, Environment Protection and Heritage Council, Canberra, May 2003.

Natural Habitat Adventures (2008) The Nature People. Accessed 27 May 2008. http://www.nathab.com/

Navrud, S. and Mungatana, E.D. (1994) Environmental valuation in developing countries: the recreational value of wildlife viewing. *Ecological Economics* 11, 135–151.

Nellemann, C., Stoen, O., Kindberg, J., Swenson, J.E., Vistnes, I., Ericsson, G., Katajisto, J., Kaltenborn, B.P., Martin, J. and Ordiz, A. (2007) Terrain use by an expanding brown bear population in relation to age, recreational resorts and human settlements. *Biological Conservation* 138, 157–165.

Nelson, J.G. (1994) The spread of ecotourism: some planning implications. *Environmental Conservation* 21, 248–255.

Nelson, J.G., Butler, R. and Wall, G. (1993) *Tourism and Sustainable Development: Monitoring, Planning, Managing*. Department of Geography, University of Waterloo, Toronto.

Nepal, S.K. (1997) Sustainable tourism, protected areas, and livelihood needs of local communities in developing countries. *International Journal of Sustainable Development and World Ecology* 4, 123–135.

Nepal, S.K. (2000) Tourism in protected areas: The Nepalese Himalaya. *Annals of Tourism Research* 27, 661–681.

Nepal, S.K. (2008) Tourism-induced rural energy consumption in the Annapurna region of Nepal. *Tourism Management* 29, 89–100.

Neves, F.M. and Bemvenuti, C.E. (2006) The ghost crab *Ocypode quadrata* (Fabricius, 1787) as a potential indicator of anthropic impact along the Rio Grande do Sul coast, Brazil. *Biological Conservation* 133, 431–435.

Nevin, O.T. and Gilbert, B.K. (2005) Perceived risk, displacement and refuging in brown bears: positive impacts of ecotourism? *Biological Conservation* 121, 611–622.

Newsome, D., Moore, S. and Dowling, R. (2002a) *Natural Areas Tourism: Ecology, Impacts and Management*. Channel View Publications, Clevedon, UK.

Newsome, D., Milewski, A., Phillips, N. and Annear, R. (2002b) Effects of horse riding on national parks and other natural areas in Australia: implications for management. *Journal of Ecotourism* 1, 52–74.

Newsome, D., Cole, D.N. and Marion, J.L. (2004a) Environmental impacts associated with recreational horse-riding. In: Buckley, R.C. (ed.) *Environmental Impacts of Ecotourism*. CAB International, Wallingford, UK. pp. 61–82.

Newsome, D., Lewis, A. and Moncrief, D. (2004b) Impacts and risks associated with developing, but unsupervised, stingray tourism at Hamelin Bay, Western Australia. *International Journal of Tourism Research* 6, 305–323.

Newsome, D., Dowling, R. and Moore, S. (2005) *Wildlife Tourism*. Channel View Publications, Clevedon, UK.

Newsome, D., Smith, A. and Moore, S.A. (2008) Horse riding in protected areas: a critical review and implications for research and management. *Currents Issues in Tourism* 11, 144–166.

Norris, R. (1992) Can ecotourism save natural areas? *National Parks* 66, 30–35.

Norris, R., Wilber, S., Oswaldo, L. and Marin, M. (1999) Global Journal of Practical Ecotourism, Community-based Ecotourism in the Maya Forest: Problems and Potentials. Accessed 10 December 2007. http://www.planeta.com/planeta/98/0598mayaforest.html

Northeast Natural Resource Centre (NNRC) (1997) *Wet, Wild, and Profitable*. A report on the economic value of water-based recreation in Vermont. NENRC, Montpelier, VT.

Notzke, C. (1999) Indigenous tourism development in the Arctic. *Annals of Tourism Research* 26, 55–76.

Nowacek, S.M., Wells, R.S., Owen, E.C.G., Speakman, T.R., Flamm, R.O. and Nowacek, D.P. (2004) Florida manatees, *Trichechus manatus latirostris*, respond to approaching vessels. *Biological Conservation* 119, 517–523.

Nyaupane, G.P., Morais, D.B. and Graefe, A.R. (2004) Nature tourism constraints: a cross-activity comparison. *Annals of Tourism Research* 31, 540–555.

Nyaupane, G.P. and Thapa, B. (2004) Evaluation of ecotourism: a comparative assessment in the Annapurna Conservation Area Project, Nepal. *Journal of Ecotourism* 3, 20–45.

Obua, J. and Harding, D.M. (1996) Visitor characteristics and attitudes towards Kibale National Park, Uganda. *Tourism Management* 17, 495–505.

Odum, H.T. (1988) Self-organisation, transformity, and information. *Science* 242, 1132–1139.

Olindo, P., Whelan, T. and Whelan, T. (1991) The old man of nature tourism: Kenya. Nature tourism: managing for the environment. Island Press, Washington, DC, pp. 23–38.

Oliver, S.S., Roggenbuck, J.W. and Watson, A.E. (1985) Education to reduce impacts in forest campgrounds. *Journal of Forestry* 83, 234–236.

Ollenburg, C. (2006) Farm tourism in Australia: a family business and rural studies perspective. PhD thesis, Griffith University, Gold Coast.

Ollenburg, C. (2008) Regional signatures and trends in the farm tourism sector. *Tourism Recreation Research* 33, 13–24.

Oost, M. (2007) Indirect effects of park visitors on bird population dynamics. PhD thesis, Griffith University, Gold Coast.

Orams, M.B. (1995) Towards a more desirable form of ecotourism. *Tourism Management* 16, 3–8.

Orams, M.B. and Hill, G.J. (1998) Controlling the ecotourist in a wild dolphin feeding program: is education the answer? *Journal of Environmental Education* 29, 33–39.

Ostergren, D., Solop, F.I. and Hagen, K.K. (2005) National park services fees: value for the money or a barrier to visitation? *Journal of Park and Recreation Administration* 23, 18–36.

Othman, J. and Othman, R. (1998) Economic benefits from wetland biodiversity: case of firefly recreation in Malaysia. *Tropical Biodiversity* 5, 65–74.

Outdoor Industry Association (2005) Outdoor Recreation Participation Study, 7th edn, for year 2004. Accessed 22 December 2005. http://www.outdoorindustry.org/pdf/2005ParticipationStudy.pdf

Outdoor Industry Association. (2007) Accessed 15 April 2008. http://www.outdoorindustry.org/gov.communications.php?sortyear=2007

Overton, J. and Purdie, N. (1997) Think local, act global? Reflections on sustainable development in the Pacific Islands. *Development Bulletin* 41, 37–39.

Paaby, P., Clark, D.B. and Gonzalez, H. (1991) Training rural residents as naturalist guides: evaluation of a pilot project in Costa Rica. *Conservation Biology* 5, 542–547.

Palacio, V. and McCool, S. (1997) Identifying ecotourists in Belize through benefit segmentation: a preliminary analysis. *Journal of Sustainable Tourism* 5, 234–243.

Pan, B., Maclaurin, T. and Crotts, J.C. (2007) Travel blogs and the implications for destination marketing. *Journal of Travel Research* 46, 35–45.

Parker, S. (1999) Collaboration on tourism policy making: environmental and commercial sustainability on Bonaire, N.A. *Journal of Sustainable Tourism* 7, 240–259.

Parker, S. and Khare, A. (2005) Understanding success factors for ensuring sustainability in ecotourism development in southern Africa. *Journal of Ecotourism* 4, 32–46.

Parsons, E.C.M. and Rawles, C. (2003) The resumption of whaling by Iceland and the potential negative impacts in Icelandic whale-watching market. *Current Issues in Tourism* 6, 444–448.

Parsons, E.C.M. and Woods-Ballard, A.J. (2003) Acceptance of voluntary whalewatching codes of conduct in West Scotland: the effectiveness of governmental versus industry-led guidelines. *Current Issues in Tourism* 6, 172–182.

Paryski, P. (1996) Can Haiti dream of ecotourism? *Ecodecision* 20, 55–60.

Paul, B.K. and Rimmawai, H.S. (1992) Tourism in Saudi Arabia Asir National Park. *Annals of Tourism Research* 19, 501–515.

Persoon, G., van Beek, H.H. and King, V.T. (1998) Uninvited guests: tourists and environment on Siberut. In: King, V.T. (ed.) *Environmental Changes in South East Asia*. Curzon Press Ltd, Richmond, UK, pp. 317–341.

Peter, A., Lindsey, R.A., Mills, M.G.L., Romanach, S. and Woodroffe, R. (2007) Wildlife viewing preferences of visitors to protected areas in South Africa: implications for the role of ecotourism in conservation. *Journal of Ecotourism* 6, 19–33.

Peters, C.M., Gentry, A. and Mendelsohn, R. (1989) Valuation of an Amazonian rainforest. *Nature* 339, 655–656.

Peters, K.A. and Otis, D.L. (2007) Shorebird roost-site selection at two temporal scales: is human disturbance a factor? *Journal of Applied Ecology* 44, 196–209.

Petram, W., Knauer, F. and Kaczensky, P. (2004) Human influence on the choice of winter dens by European brown bears in Slovenia. *Biological Conservation* 119, 129–136.

Phillips, N. and Newsome, D. (2002) Understanding the impacts of recreation in Australian protected areas: quantifying damage caused by horse riding in D'Entrecasteaux National Park, Western Australia. *Pacific Conservation Biology* 7, 256–273.

Pickering, C.M. and Hill, W. (2007) Impacts of recreation and tourism on plant biodiversity and vegetation in protected areas in Australia. *Journal of Environmental Management* 85, 791–800.

Pickering, C.M., Bear, R. and Hill, W. (2007) Indirect impacts of nature based tourism and recreation: the association between infrastructure and the diversity of exotic plants in Kosciuszko National Park, Australia. *Journal of Ecotourism* 6, 146–157.

Pigram, J. (1990) Sustainable tourism: policy considerations. *Journal of Tourism Studies* 1, 2–9.

Pigram, J.J. and Jenkins, J.M. (2006) *Outdoor Recreation Management,* 2nd edn. Routledge, London.

Pigram, J.J. and Sundell, R.C. (eds) (1997) *National Parks and Protected Areas: Selection, Delimitation and Management.* University of New England, Armidale.

Pitamahaket, P. (2002) The development of Kanchanaburi Ecotourism Cooperative: the first ecotourism cooperative of Thailand. In: Bornemeier, J., Victor, M. and Durst, P.B. *Proceedings of Ecotourism for Forest Conservation and Community Development.* Regional Community Forestry Training Centre, Bangkok, pp. 195–201.

Place, S.E. (1991) Nature tourism and rural development in Tortuguero. *Annals of Tourism Research* 18, 186–201.

Plathong, S., Inglis, G.J. and Huber, M.E. (2000) Effects of self-guided snorkelling trails on corals in a tropical marine park. *Conservation Biology* 14, 1821–1830.

Pleumarom, A. (1993) What's wrong with mass ecotourism. *Contours Bangkok* 6, 15–21.

Pleumarom, A. (1994) The political economy of tourism. *The Ecologist* 24, 142–147.

Pleumarom, A. (1995) Eco-tourism or eco-terrorism? *Environmental Justice Networker* 6.

Po-Hsi, L. and Scott, S. (2006) Marketing ecotourism through the internet: an evaluation of selected ecolodges in Latin America and the Caribbean. *Journal of Ecotourism* 3, 143–160.

Poirier, R. and Ostergren, D. (2002) Evicting people from nature: Indigenous land rights and national parks in Australia, Russia and the United States. *Natural Resources Journal* 42, 331–351.

Polonsky, M.J., Richins, H., Martin, F. and Davey, G. (1994) Are resorts utilising green marketing? An exploratory investigation of Australia's tourist facilities. *Greener Management International* 8, 58–72.

Porritt, J. (1996) Brilliant marketing scam: ecotourism is big business, and some operators are simply exploiting it. *African Wildlife* 50, 17.

Potts, F.C., Goodwin, H. and Walpole, M.J. (1996) People, wildlife and tourism around Hwange National Park, Zimbabwe. In: Price, M.F. (ed.) *People and Tourism in Fragile Environments.* Wiley, Chichester, UK, pp. 199–219.

Powell, M. (1996) Paradise and profit: strategies for sustainable development in the Umzimvubu District in Transkei. *African Wildlife* 50, 15–17.

Preisler, H.K., Ager, A.A. and Wisdom, M.J. (2006) Statistical methods for analysing responses of wildlife to human disturbance. *Journal of Applied Ecology* 43, 164–172

Preston-Whyte, R. (1996) Towards sustainable development in the Lake St. Lucia Area, South Africa. *International Journal of Environmental Studies* 49, 177–179.

Price, O.F. (2006) Movements of frugivorous birds among fragmented rainforests in the Northern Territory, Australia. *Wildlife Research* 33, 521–528.

Priestly, G.K., Edwards, J.A. and Coccossis, H. (1996) *Sustainable Tourism? European Experiences.* CAB International, Wallingford, UK.

Primack, R.B. (1998) *Timber, Tourists, and Temples: Conservation and Development in the Maya Forest of Belize, Guatemala, and Mexico.* Island Press, Washington, DC.

Primack, R.B. and Corlett, R. (2005) *Tropical Rain Forests: an Ecological and Biogeograpical Comparison.* Blackwell Publishing, Malden, Massachusetts.

Priskin, J. (2003) Physical impacts of four-wheel drive related tourism and recreation in a semi-arid, natural coastal environment. *Ocean and Coastal Management* 46, 127–155.

Priskin, J. (2004) Four-wheel drive vehicle impacts in the central coast region of Western Australia. In: Buckley, R. (ed.) *Environmental Impacts of Ecotourism.* CAB International, Wallingford, UK, pp. 339–348.

Pullin, A.S., Knight, T.M., Stone, D.A. and Charman, K. (2004) Do conservation managers use scientific evidence to support their decision-making? *Biological Conservation* 119, 245–252.

Queensland Travel and Tourism Corporation (1998) *Ecotrends, September 1998.* Queensland Travel and Tourism Corporation (now Tourism Queensland), Brisbane.

Quicksilver Cruises (2008) Quicksilver is the Barrier Reef. Accessed 27 May 2008. http://www.quick-silver-cruises.com/

Rai, S.C. and Sundriyal, R.C. (1997) Tourism and biodiversity conservation: the Sikkim Himalaya. *Ambio* 26, 235–242.

Rainforest Expeditions (2008) Accessed 30 April 2008. http://www.perunature.com/index.htm

Ramp, D., Wilson, V.K. and Croft, D.B. (2006) Assessing the impacts of roads in peri-urban reserves: road-based fatalities and road usage by wildlife in the Royal National Park, New South Wales, Australia. *Biological Conservation* 129, 348–359.

Rara Avis (2008) Rainforest Lodge and Reserve, Costa Rica. A New Way to Save the Rainforest. Accessed 30 April 2008. http://www.rara-avis.com/

Reed, M. (2000) Collaborative tourism planning as adaptive experiments in emergent tourism settings. In: Bramwell, B. and Lane, B. (eds) *Tourism Collaboration and Partnerships.* Channel View Publications, Clevedon, UK, pp. 247–271.

Rees, E.C., Bruce, J.H. and White, G.T. (2005) Factors affecting the behavioural responses of whooper swans (*Cygnus c. cygnus*) to various human activities. *Biological Conservation* 121, 369–382.

Reinius, S.W. and Fredman, P. (2007) Protected areas as attractions. *Annals of Tourism Research* 34, 839–854.

Richardson, J. (1993a) Australia takes sustainable tourism route. *The Ecotourism Society Newsletter* 3, 1–2,5.

Richardson, J. (1993b) Editorial. *Tread Lightly* 5, 3.

Richer, J.R. and Christensen, N.A. (1999) Appropriate fees for wilderness day use: pricing decisions for recreation on public land. *Journal of Leisure Research* 31, 269–280.

Rios Tropicales (2008) Best Outfitters on Earth. Accessed 30 April 2008. http://www.riostropicales.com/

Ritchie, J.R. (1998) Managing the human presence in ecologically sensitive tourism destinations: insights from the Banff-Bow Valley Study. *Journal of Sustainable Tourism* 6, 293–313.

Ritchie, J.R.B. (2000) Interest based formulation of tourism policy for environmentally sensitive destinations. In: Bramwell, B. and Lane, B. (eds) *Tourism Collaboration and Partnerships.* Channel View Publications, Clevedon, UK, pp. 44–77.

Rittenhouse, T.A.G. and Semlitsch, R.D. (2006) Grasslands as movement barriers for a forest-associated salamander: migration behaviour of adult and juvenile salamanders at a distinct habitat edge. *Biological Conservation* 131, 14–22.

Robinson, M. (1999) Collaboration and cultural consent: refocusing sustainable tourism. *Journal of Sustainable Tourism* 7, 379–397.

Rode, K.D., Farley, S.D. and Robbins, C.T. (2006) Behavioural responses of brown bears mediate nutritional effects of experimentally introduced tourism. *Biological Conservation* 133, 70–80.

Rodger, K., Moore, S.A. and Newsome, D. (2007) Wildlife tours in Australia: characteristics, the place of science and sustainable futures. *Journal of Sustainable Tourism* 15, 160–179.

Rodriguez, J.R.O., Parra-Lopez, E. and Yanes-Estevez, V. (2008) The sustainability of island destinations: tourism area life cycle and teleological perspectives. The case of Tenerife. *Tourism Management* 29, 53–65.

Rodriquez, S.L. (2008) Perceptions and attitudes of a Maasai community regarding wildlife-damage compensation, conservation, and the predators that prey on their livestock. *Human Dimensions of Wildlife* 13, 205–206.

Rolando, A., Captio, E., Rinaldi, E. and Ellena, I. (2007) The impact of high-altitude ski-runs on alpine grassland bird communities. *Journal of Applied Ecology* 44, 210–219.

Rosenthal, D.H., Loomis, J.B. and Peterson, G.L. (1984) Pricing for efficiency and revenue in public recreation areas. *Journal of Leisure Research* 16, 195–208.

Ross, S. and Wall, G. (1999a) Ecotourism: towards congruence between theory and practice. *Tourism Management* 20, 123–132.

Ross, S. and Wall, G. (1999b) Evaluating ecotourism: the case of North Sulawesi, Indonesia. *Tourism Management* 20, 673–682.

Rouphael, A.B. and Hanafy, M. (2007) An alternative management framework to limit the impact of SCUBA divers on coral assemblages. *Journal of Sustainable Tourism* 15, 91–103.

Rouphael, A.B. and Inglis, G.J. (1997) Impacts of recreational scuba diving at sites with different reef topographies. *Biological Conservation* 82, 329–336.

Rouphael, A.B. and Inglis, G.J. (2002) Increased spatial and temporal variability in coral damage caused by recreational SCUBA diving. *Ecological Applications* 12, 427–440.

Rudkin, B. (1996) Unable to see the forest for the trees: ecotourism development in the Solomon Islands. In: Hall, C.M., Hinch, T. and Butler, R. (eds) *Tourism and Indigenous Peoples*. Thomson, London, pp. 203–222.

Russell, C.L. and Ankenman, M.J. (1996) Orangutans as photographic collectibles: ecotourism and the commodification of nature. *Tourism Recreation Research* 21, 71–78.

Russell, S.V., Lafferty, G. and Loudoun, R. (2008) Examining tourism operators' responses to environmental regulation: the role of regulatory perceptions and relationships. *Current Issues in Tourism* 11, 126–143.

Ryan, C. (2002) Equity, management, power sharing and sustainability: issues of the 'new tourism'. *Tourism Management* 23, 17–26.

Ryan, C.A., Hughes, K. and Chirgwin, S. (2000) The gaze, spectacle and ecotourism. *Annals of Tourism Research* 27, 148–163.

Ryan, C. and Huyton, J. (2002) Tourists and Aboriginal people. *Annals of Tourism Research* 29, 631–647.

Ryel, R. and Grasse, T. (1991) *Marketing Ecotourism: Attracting the Elusive Ecotourist*. Island Press, Washington, DC.

Saarinen, J. (2006) Traditions of sustainability in tourism studies. *Annals of Tourism Research* 33, 1121–1140.

Saayman, M. and Saayman, A. (2006) Estimating the economic contribution of visitor spending in the Kruger National Park to the regional economy. *Journal of Sustainable Tourism* 14, 67–81.

Saleh, F. and Karwacki, J. (1996) Revisiting the ecotourist: the case of Grasslands National Park. *Journal of Sustainable Tourism* 2, 61–80.

Sanecki, G.M., Green, K., Wood, H. and Lindenmayer, D. (2006) The implications of snow-based recreation for small mammals in the subnivean space in south-east Australia. *Biological Conservation* 129, 511–518.

Sanson, L. and Smith, V.L. (1994) An ecotourism case study in Sub-Antarctic Islands. *Annals of Tourism Research* 21, 344–354.

Santiso, C. (1993) The Maya Biosphere Reserve: an alternative for the sustainable use of resources. *Nature and Resources* 29, 6–10.

Sasidharan, V., Kirakaya, E. and Kerstetter, D. (2002) Developing countries and tourism ecolabels. *Tourism Management* 23, 161–174.

Save the Cheetah (2008) Cheetah Conservation Fund. Accessed 30 April 2008. http://www.cheetah.org/

Save the Rhino (2008) Save the Rhino International. Accessed 30 April 2008. http://www.savetherhino.org/etargetsrinm/site/1/default.aspx

Scace, R.C., Grifone, E. and Usher, R. (1992) *Ecotourism in Canada*. Canadian Environmental Advisory Council, Ottawa.

Scarpa, R., Chilton, S.M., Hutchinson, W.G. and Buongiorno, J. (2000) Valuing the recreational benefits from the creation of nature reserves in Irish forests. *Ecological Economics* 33, 237–250.

Schaenzel, H. (1998) Wildlife viewing ecotourism on the Otago Peninsula: the experiences and benefits gained by penguin-watching visitors. Dissertation for Diploma in Tourism, University of Otago, Dunedin, New Zealand.

Schahinger, R., Rudman, T. and Wardlaw, T. (2003) Conservation of Tasmania plant species and communities threatened by *Phytophthora cinnamomi*: strategic regional plan for Tasmania. Technical Report 03/03, Nature Conservation Branch, Department of Primary Industries, Water and Environment, Hobart.

Schianetz, K., Kavanagh, L. and Lockington, D. (2007) Concepts and tools for comprehensive sustainability assessments for tourism destinations: a comparative review. *Journal of Sustainable Tourism* 15, 369–389.

Schneider, I.E. and Budruk, M. (1999) Displacement as a response to the federal recreation fee program. *Journal of Park and Recreation Administration* 17, 76–84.

Schroeder, H.W. and Louviere, J. (1999) Stated choice models for predicting the impact of user fees at public recreation sites. *Journal of Leisure Research* 31, 300–325.

Schulze, H. (1998) Nature conservation through ecotourism development – a case study of a village in the Lower Kinabatangan Area, Sabah. *Tigerpaper* 25, 12–17.

Selin, S. (2000) Developing a typology of sustainable tourism partnership. In: Bramwell, B. and Lane, B. (eds) *Tourism Collaboration and Partnerships*. Channel View Publications, Clevedon, UK, pp. 129–142.

Shackley, M. (1995a) The future of gorilla tourism in Rwanda. *Journal of Sustainable Tourism* 3, 61–72.

Shackley, M. (1995b) Just started and now finished – tourism development in Arunachal Pradesh. *Tourism Management* 16, 623–625.

Shackley, M. (1996) *Wildlife Tourism*. Thompson, London.

Shackley, M. (1998a) 'Stingray City' – managing the impact of underwater tourism in the Cayman Islands. *Journal of Sustainable Tourism* 6, 328–338.

Shackley, M. (1998b) Designating a protected area at Karanambu Ranch, Rupununi Savannah, Guyana: resource management and Indigenous communities. *Ambio* 27, 207–210.

Shackley, M. (1998c) *Visitor Management: Case Studies from World Heritage Sites*. Butterworth-Heinemann, Oxford.

Shackley, M. (1999) Tourism development and environmental protection in Southern Sinai. *Tourism Management* 20, 543–548.

Shafer, E.L., Carline, R., Guldin, R.W. and Cordell, H.K. (1993) Economic amenity values of wildlife: six case studies in Pennsylvania. *Environmental Management* 17, 669–682.

Sharma, P. (1998) *Environment, Culture, Economy, and Tourism: Dilemmas in the Hindu Kush Himalayas*. International Centre for Integrated Mountain Development (ICIMOD), Kathmandu, Nepal.

Shepherd, B. and Whittington, J. (2006) Response of wolves to corridor restoration and human use management. *Ecology and Society* 11, 2.

Sheppard, N. (2002) How ecotourism can go wrong: the cases of SeaCanoe and Siam Safari, Thailand. *Current Issues in Tourism* 5, 309–318.

Sherman, P.B. and Dixon, J.A. (1991) The economics of nature tourism: determining if it pays. In: Whelan, T. (ed.) *Nature Tourism: Managing for the Environment*. Island Press, Washington, DC, pp. 89–131.

Shrestha, R.K., Stein, T.V. and Clark, J. (2007) Valuing nature-based recreation in public natural areas of the Apalachicola River region, Florida. *Journal of Environmental Management* 85, 977–985.

Siderelis, C. and Moore, R.L. (2006) Examining the effects of hypothetical modifications in permitting procedures and river conditions on whitewater boating behavior. *Journal of Leisure Research* 38, 558–575.

Silva, G. and McDill, M.E. (2004) Barriers to ecotourism supplier success: a comparison of agency and business perspectives. *Journal of Sustainable Tourism* 12, 289–305.

Silverberg, K.E., Backman, S.J. and Backman, K.F. (1996) A preliminary investigation into the psychographics of nature-based travellers to the southeastern United States. *Journal of Travel Research* 35, 19–21.

Simmons, D.G. and Becken, S. (2004) The cost of getting there: impacts of travel to ecotourism destinations. In: Buckley, R. (ed.) *Environmental Impacts of Ecotourism*. CAB International, Wallingford, UK, pp. 15–23.

Simmons, G. (1998) Secret garden: Samoa says 'Talofa' to eco-tourism. *Pacific Wave* 114, 76–78.

Simpson, R. (1995) Towards sustainable tourism for Europe's protected areas – policies and practice. *Progress in Rural Policy and Planning* 5, 125–138.

Simpson, R. (1996) Recreation and tourism in Europe's protected areas: threat or opportunity? *Ecodecision* 20, 40–43.

Sindiga, I. (1995) Wildlife-based tourism in Kenya: land-use conflicts and government compensation policies over protected areas. *Journal of Tourism Studies* 6, 5–55.

Sindiga, I. (1999) Alternative tourism and sustainable development in Kenya. *Journal of Sustainable Tourism* 7, 108–127.

Singh, N. and Formica, S. (2007) Level of congruency in photographic representations of destination marketing organizations' websites and brochures. *Journal of Hospitality and Leisure Marketing* 15, 71–86.

Singh, S. and Singh, T.V. (1996) *Profiles in Indian Tourism*. APH, New Delhi.

Singh, S. and Singh, T.V. (1999) *Tourism Developments in Critical Environments*. Cognizant, New York.

Singh, T.V. (1991) The development of tourism in the mountain environment: the problem of sustainability. *Tourism Recreation Research* 16, 3–12.

Sirakaya, E. (1997a) Attitudinal compliance with ecotourism guidelines. *Annals of Tourism Research* 24, 919–950.

Sirakaya, E. (1997b) Assessment of factors affecting conformance behaviour of ecotour operators with industry guidelines. *Tourism Analysis* 2, 17–35.

Sirakaya, E. and McLellan, R.W. (1998) Modeling tour operators' voluntary compliance with ecotourism principles: a behavioural approach. *Journal of Travel Research* 36, 42–55.

Sirakaya, E. and Uysal, M. (1997) Can sanctions and rewards explain conformance behaviour of tour operators with ecotourism guidelines? *Journal of Sustainable Tourism* 5, 306–322.

Sisman, R. (1994) Tourism: environmental relevance. In: Cater, E. and Lowman, G. (eds) *Ecotourism: a Sustainable Option*. Wiley, Chichester, UK, pp. 57–67.

Sithole, E. (2005) Trans-boundary environmental actors: the Zambezi Society's campaign for sustainable tourism development in the Zambezi bioregion. *Journal of Sustainable Tourism* 13, 486–503.

Slinger, V. (2000) Ecotourism in the last Indigenous Caribbean community. *Annals of Tourism Research* 27, 520–523.

Smith, A. and Newsome, D. (2002) An integrated approach to assessing, managing and monitoring campsite impacts in Warren National Park, Western Australia. *Journal of Sustainable Tourism* 10, 343–359.

Smith, R.A. (1994) Planning and management for coastal eco-tourism in Indonesia: a regional perspective. *Indonesian Quarterly* 22, 148–157.

Smith, R.A. (1998) Sustainable tourism in Vietnam. *Annals of Tourism Research* 25, 765–767.

Smith, S.L.J. (2000) Measurement of tourism's economic impacts. *Annals of Tourism Research* 27, 530–531.

Smith, V.L. (1993) Safeguarding the Antarctic environment from tourism: suggestions and guidelines. *Tourism Recreation Research* 18, 51–54.

Sofield, T.B. (2002) Australian Aboriginal ecotourism in the Wet Tropics rainforest of Queensland Australia. *Mountain Research and Development* 22, 118–122.

Solomon, B.D., Corey-Luse, C.M. and Halvorsen, K.E. (2004) The Florida manatee and eco-tourism: toward a safe minimum standard. *Ecological Economics* 50, 101–115.

Somerville, H. (1992) *Airlines, Tourism and Environment.* GLOBE '92 Tourism Stream, Vancouver.

Southern Sea Ventures (2008) Tropical and Polar Sea Kayak Tours. Accessed 9 September 2008. www.southernseaventures.com

Spenceley, A. (2005) Nature-based tourism and environmental sustainability in South Africa. *Journal of Sustainable Tourism* 13, 136–170.

Sproule, K.W. (1996) Community-based ecotourism development: identifying partners in the process. In: Miller, J.D. and Malek-Zadeh, E. *The Ecotourism Equation: Measuring the Impacts.* Yale School of Forestry and Environmental Studies, Bulletin Series, New Haven, Connecticut, pp. 233–250.

Stabler, M.J. (ed.) (1997) *Tourism and Sustainability: Principles to Practice.* CAB International, Wallingford, UK.

Staiff, R., Bushell, R. and Kennedy, P. (2002) Interpretation in national parks: some critical questions. *Journal of Sustainable Tourism* 10, 97–113.

Steffan, C. (2004) Tourism in parks: pursuing common goals. In: Buckley RC (ed.) *Tourism in Parks: Australian Initiatives.* Griffith University, Gold Coast, pp. 55–72.

Stein, T.V., Denny, C.B. and Pennisi, L.A. (2003) Using visitors' motivations to provide learning opportunities at water-based recreation areas. *Journal of Sustainable Tourism* 11, 404–425.

Steinberg, M. (1993) Protecting wildlands through culturally compatible conservation. *Environmental Conservation* 20, 260–263.

Stern, C.J., Lassole, J.P., Lee, D.R. and Deshler, D.J. (2003) How 'eco' is ecotourism? A comparative case study of ecotourism in Costa Rica. *Journal of Sustainable Tourism* 11, 322–347.

Stevens, T.H. (2004) The contingent valuation of national parks: assessing the warmglow propensity factor. *Ecological Economics* 48, 488–489.

Stewart, W.P. and Sekartjakrarini, S. (1994) Disentangling ecotourism. *Annals of Tourism Research* 21, 840–842.

Stoeckl, N. (2003) A 'quick and dirty' travel cost model. *Tourism Economics* 9, 325–335.

Stoeckl, N., Smith, A., Newsome, D. and Lee, D. (2005) Regional economic dependence on iconic wildlife tourism: case studies of Monkey Mia and Hervey Bay. *Journal of Tourism Studies* 16, 69–81.

Stonehouse, B. (1990) A travellers code for Antarctic visitors. *Polar Record* 26, 56–58.

Stonehouse, B., Cater, E., Lowman, G. and Cater, C. (1994) Ecotourism in Antarctica. In: Cater, E. and Lowman, G. (eds) *Ecotourism: A Sustainable Option.* Wiley, Chichester, UK, pp. 195–212.

Stueve, A.M., Cock, S.D. and Drew, D. (2002) The Geotourism Study: Phase I Executive Summary. Accessed 19 May 2008. www.tia.org/pubs/geotourismphasefinal.pdf

Stynes, D.J. and White, E.M. (2006) Reflections on measuring recreation and travel spending. *Journal of Travel Research* 45, 8–17.

Sun, D. and Walsh, D. (1998) Review of studies on environmental impacts of recreation and tourism in Australia. *Journal of Environmental Management* 53, 323–338.

Sun, J.W.C. and Narins, P.M. (2005) Anthropogenic sounds differentially affect amphibian call rate. *Biological Conservation* 121, 419–427.

Sunchaser Ecotours (2008) Khutzeymateen Grizzly Bears. Accessed 30 April 2008. http:// www.citytel.net/sunchaser

Svoronou, E. and Holden, A. (2005) Ecotourism as a tool for nature conservation: the role of WWF Greece in the Dadia-Lefkimi-Soufli Reserve in Greece. *Journal of Sustainable Tourism* 13, 456–467.

Swanson, M.A. (1992) Ecotourism: embracing the new environmental paradigm, Caracas. *Proceedings, IV World Congress on National Parks and Protected Areas*, Caracas.

Swarbrooke, J. (1999) *Sustainable Tourism Management*. CAB International, Wallingford, UK.

Swarbrooke, J., Beard, C., Leckie, S. and Pomfret, G. (2003) *Adventure Tourism: the New Frontier*. Butterworth-Heinemann, London.

Symmonds, M.C., Hammitt, W.E. and Quisenberry, V.L. (2000) Managing recreational trail environments for mountain bike user preferences. *Environmental Management* 25, 549–564.

Taj Hotels (2008) Hotels Resorts and Palaces. Accessed 30 April 2008. http://www.tajhotels.com

Talbot, L.M., Turton, S.M. and Graharn, A.W. (2003) Trampling resistance of tropical rainforest soils and vegetation in the wet tropics of north east Australia. *Journal of Environmental Management* 69, 63–69.

Tarrant, M.A., Haas, G.E. and Manfredo, M. (1995) Factors affecting visitor evaluations of aircraft overflights of wilderness areas. *Society and Natural Resources* 8, 351–360.

Taylor, D.B. and Goldingay, R.L. (2004) Wildlife road-kills on three major roads in north-eastern New South Wales. *Wildlife Research* 31, 83–91.

Ten Knots (2008) El Nido Resorts. Accessed 30 April 2008. http://www.elnidoresorts.com/about-us.aspx

Tershy, B.R., Bourillon, L., Metzler, L. and Barnes, J. (1999) A survey of ecotourism on islands in north-western Mexico. *Environmental Conservation* 26, 212–217.

Teye, V., Sirakaya, E. and Sonmez, S. (2002) Residents' attitudes towards tourism development. *Annals of Tourism Research* 29, 668–688.

The International Ecotourism Society (2007) Uniting Conservation, and Sustainable Travel. Accessed 5 March 2008. http://www.ecotourism.org

Thomas, T. (1994) Ecotourism in Antarctica. The role of the naturalist-guide in presenting places of natural interest. *Journal of Sustainable Tourism* 2, 204–209.

Tisdell, C. (1997) Tourism development in India and Bangladesh: general issues, illustrated by ecotourism in the Sunderbans. *Tourism Recreation Research* 22, 26–33.

Tisdell, C.A. and Takahashi, S. (1992) Protected areas and nature conservation on and near Iriomote Island, Japan. *Tigerpaper* 19, 1–7.

Tisdell, C. and Wilson, C. (2002) Ecotourism for the survival of sea turtles and other wildlife. *Biodiversity and Conservation* 11, 1521–1538.

Tisdell, C. and Wilson, C. (2004) The public's knowledge of and support for conservation of Australia's tree-kangaroos and other animals. *Biodiversity and Conservation* 12, 2339–2359.

Tisdell, C. and Xiang, Z. (1996) Tourism development and nature conservation in Xishuangbanna, Yunnan: a case study. *Tigerpaper* 23, 20–28.

Tisdell, C. and Xiang, Z. (1998) Protected areas, agricultural pests and economic damage: conflicts with elephants and pests in Yunnan, China. *Environmentalist* 18, 109–118.

Tisdell, C., Wilson, C. and Nantha, H.S. (2005) Policies for saving a rare Australian glider: economics and ecology. *Biological Conservation* 123, 237–248.

Tobias, D. and Mendelsohn, R. (1991) Valuing ecotourism in a tropical rain-forest reserve. *Ambio* 20, 91–93.

Tour Operators Initiative for Sustainable Tourism Development (TOISTD) (2003) *Sustainable Tourism: The Tour Operators' Contribution*. United Nations Environment Program Division of Technology Industry & Economics, Paris.

Tourism Authority of Thailand (1996) *Policies and Guidelines: Development of Ecotourism*. Tourism Authority of Thailand, Bangkok.

Tourism Council Australia (2000) *Tourism Management in Protected Areas: Issues Papers*. TCA, Sydney.

Tourism Queensland (1999) *Ecotrends, March 1999*. Tourism Queensland, Brisbane.

Tourism Task Force Australia (2002) *Making National Parks a National Tourism Priority: Project Outline*. Tourism Task Force Australia, Sydney.

Trainor, S.F. and Norgaard, R.B. (1999) Recreation fees in the context of wilderness values. *Journal of Park and Recreation Administration* 17, 100–115.

Trauer, B.B. and McIntyre, N. (1998) World Heritage listing as an entrepreneurial event: an Australian case study. *Australian Parks and Recreation* 34, 44–47.

Turton, S.M. (2005) Managing environmental impacts of recreation and tourism in rainforests at the Wet Tropics of Queensland World Heritage Area. *Geographical Research* 43, 140–151.

Turton, S.M., Kluck, T. and Day, T.J. (2000) Ecological impacts of visitors at day-use and camping areas. In: Bentrupperbaumer, J.M. and Reser, J.P. (eds) *Impacts of Visitation and Use: Psychosocial and Biophysical Windows on Visitation and Use in the Wet Tropics World Heritage Area.* Cooperative Research Centre for Tropical Rainforest Ecology and Management, Cairns, pp. 123–134.

Twynam, D. and Johnston, M.E. (2002) The use of sustainable tourism practices. *Annals of Tourism Research* 29, 1165–1168.

Twynam, D., Johnston, M. Payne, B. and Kingston, S. (1998) *Ecotourism and Sustainable Tourism Guidelines: An Annotated Bibliography.* The Ecotourism Society, North Bennington, VT.

Twynam, G.D. and Robinson, D.W. (1997) *A Market Segmentation Analysis of Desired Ecotourism Opportunities.* Natural Resources Canada, Canadian Forest Service, Sault Ste Marie.

UN World Tourism Organization (2007) Committed to Tourism, Travel and the Millennium Development Goals. Accessed 19 May 2008. http://www.world-tourism.org/

UNEP and WTO (2002) Quebec Declaration on Ecotourism. Accessed 20 September 2002. mes/QuebecDeclareng.pdf

UNEP, UNESCO, WTO, Tour Operators Initiative for Sustainable Tourism Development (2003) Sustainable Tourism: The Tour Operator's Contribution. Accessed 27 November 2003. http://www.toinitiative.org/good_practices/case_studies

UNESCO (1998) *Resolution 1998/40.* UNESCO, Paris.

United Nations Environment Programme (1993) *Managing tourism in natural World Heritage sites.* United Nations Environment Programme/UNESCO, Paris.

United Nations Environment Program (1995) *Environmental Codes of Conduct for Tourism Industry.* Environmental Technical Report 29, UNEP, Paris.

Universal Studios (2002) Blue Crush. Accessed 19 May 2008. www.bluecrush.com

United States Department of Agriculture, Forest Service. (1999) Identification and Valuation of Wildland Resource Benefits. Accessed 16 July 2008. www.fed.us/rm/value

United States Department of Agriculture, Forest Service (2000) Forestry Service Strategic Plan (2000 Revision). Accessed 4 September 2002. http://www2.srs.fs.fed.us/strategicplan

United States Forestry Service (2002) US Department of Agriculture, Forest Service. America's Wildland Playground. Accessed 22 November 2002. www.fs.fed.us/news/agenda/wildland_ playground

United States Department of Interior and US Department of Agriculture (2001) *Recreation Fee Demonstration Program: Progress Report to Congress Fiscal Year 2000,* USDI and USDA, Washington, DC.

Vail, D. and Heldt, T. (2004) Governing snowmobilers in multiple-use landscapes: Swedish and Maine (USA) cases. *Ecological Economics* 48, 469–483.

van Beukering, P.J.H., Cesar, H.S.J. and Janssen, M.A. (2002) Economic valuation of the Lesuer National Park on Sumatra, Indonesia. *Ecological Economics* 44, 43–62.

van der Ree, R. (2006) Road upgrade in Victoria a filter to the movement of the endangered Squirrel Glider (*Petaurus norfolcensis*): results of a pilot study. *Ecological Management and Restoration* 7, 226–228.

van Lanh, L. and MacNeil, D.J. (1997) Ecotourism in Vietnam: prospects for conservation and local participation. *The Australian International Business Review 1997,* 45–52.

van Sickle, K. and Eagles, P.F.J. (1998) Budgets, pricing policies and user fees in Canadian parks' tourism. *Tourism Management* 19, 225–235.

Vieitas, C., Lopez, G. and Marcovaldi, M. (1999) Local community involvement in conservation – the use of mini-guides in a programme for sea turtles in Brazil. *Oryx* 33, 127–131.

Vogt, C.A. and Williams, D.R. (1999) Support for wilderness recreation fees: The influence of fee purpose and day versus overnight use. *Journal of Park and Recreation Administration* 17, 85–99.

Von Der Lippe, M. and Kowarik, I. (2007) Long-distance dispersal of plants by vehicles as a driver of plant invasions. *Conservation Biology* 21, 986–996.

Voodoo Dolls (2005) Voodoo Dolls. Accessed 19 May 2008. http://www.voodoodolls.com.au/

Vrslovic, D.U. (1996) The forests of Tierra del Fuego: the need to support sustainable ecotourism. *Industry and Environment* 3, 67–70.

Wahab, S. and Pigram, J.J. (1997) *Tourism, Development and Growth: the Challenge of Sustainability.* Routledge, London.

Wakefield, S. and Attum, O. (2006) The effects of human visits on the use of a waterhole by endangered ungulates. *Journal of Arid Environments* 65, 668–672.

Walker, T.A. (1991) Tourism development and environmental limitations at Heron Island, Great Barrier Reef. *Journal of Environmental Management* 33, 117–122.

Wall, G. (1997) Is ecotourism sustainable? *Environmental Management* 21, 483–491.

Wallace, G.N. and Pierce, S.M. (1996) An evaluation of ecotourism in Amazonas, Brazil. *Annals of Tourism Research* 23, 843–873.

Walpole, M.J. and Goodwin, H.J. (2000) Local economic impacts of dragon tourism in Indonesia. *Annals of Tourism Research* 27, 559–576.

Walpole, M.J., Goodwin, H.J. and Ward, K.G.R. (2001) Pricing policy for tourism in protected areas: lessons from Komodo National Park, Indonesia. *Conservation Biology* 15, 218–227.

Ward, C. (1997) Turtle power: community guides lead ecotourists on unique beach safaris. *African Wildlife* 51, 24–28.

Ward, J. (2000a) Relative economic benefits of logging and recreation in selected public forests of New South Wales, Australia. PhD thesis, Griffith University, Gold Coast, Australia.

Ward, J. (2000b) Measuring the economic value of recreation and tourism on Fraser Island. In: McArthur, S. and Dowling, R. (eds) *Australia – The World's Natural Theme Park; Proceedings of the Ecotourism Association of Australia National Conference.* Ecotourism Australia, Brisbane.

Ward, J. (2003) The net economic benefits of recreation and timber production in selected New South Wales native forests. In: Buckley, R., Pickering, C. and Weaver, D.B. *Nature-Based Tourism, Environment and Land Management.* CAB International, Wallingford, UK, pp. 61–76.

Warnken, J. and Buckley, R.C. (1997) Major 1987–93 tourism proposals in Australia. *Annals of Tourism Research* 24, 974–1019.

Warnken, J. and Byrnes, T. (2004) Impacts of tour boats in marine environments. In: Buckley, R.C. (ed.) *Environmental Impacts of Ecotourism.* CAB International, Wallingford, UK, pp. 99–124.

Warnken, W. and Buckley, R.C. (2004) Instream bacteria as a low-threshold management indicator of tourist impacts in conservation reserves. In: Buckley, R. (ed.) *Environmental Impacts of Ecotourism.* CAB International, Wallingford, UK, pp. 325–337.

Watson, A.E. (1999) Recreation fees and pricing issues in the public sector: Introduction to theme issue. *Journal of Park and Recreation Administration* 17, 9.

Watson, A. and Borrie, W.T. (2003) Applying public-purpose marketing in the USA to protect relationships with public land. In: Buckley, R.C., Pickering, C. and Weaver, D. (eds) *Nature-based Tourism, Environment and Land Management.* CAB International, Wallingford, UK, pp. 25–33.

Watson, A.E. and Herath, G. (1999) Research implications of the theme issues. *Journal of Leisure Research* 31, 325–334.

Watson, A. and Moss, R. (2004) Impacts of ski-development on ptarmigan (*Lagopus mutus*) at Cairn Gorm, Scotland. *Biological Conservation* 116, 267–275.

Watson, J.E.M., Whittaker, R.J. and Dawson, T.P. (2004) Habitat structure and proximity to forest edge affect the abundance and distribution of forest-dependent birds in tropical coastal forests of south-eastern Madagascar. *Biological Conservation* 120, 311–327.

Wearing, S. (1993) Ecotourism: The Santa Elena Rainforest Project. *Environmentalist* 13, 125–135.

Wearing, S. and Larsen, L. (1996) Assessing and managing the sociocultural impacts of ecotourism: revisiting the Santa Elena rainforest project. *Environmentalist* 16, 117–133.

Wearing, S. and Neil, J. (1999) *Ecotourism: Impacts, Potentials and Possibilities.* Butterworth-Heinemann, Oxford.

Weaver, D. (1998) *Ecotourism in the Less Developed World.* CAB International, Wallingford, UK.

Weaver, D. (2007a) Sustainable mass tourism: more smudge than nudge, the canard continues. *Tourism Recreation Research* 32, 73–75.

Weaver, D. (2007b) Towards sustainable mass tourism: paradigm shift or paradigm nudge? *Tourism Recreation Research* 32, 65–69.

Weaver, D. (2008) *Ecotourism*, 2nd edn. Wiley, Milton.

Weaver, D., Glenn, C. and Rounds, R. (1996) Private ecotourism operations in Manitoba, Canada. *Journal of Sustainable Tourism* 3, 135–146.

Weaver, D.A. (2005) Comprehensive and minimalist dimensions of ecotourism. *Annals of Tourism Research* 32, 439–455.

Weaver, D.B. (1991) Alternative to mass tourism in Dominica. *Annals of Tourism Research* 18, 414–432.

Weaver, D.B. (1993) Ecotourism in the small island Caribbean. *Geojournal* 31, 457–465.

Weaver, D.B. (1997) A regional framework for planning ecotourism in Saskatchewan. *Canadian Geographer* 3, 281–293.

Weaver, D.B. (2001) *The Encyclopedia of Ecotourism.* CAB International, Wallingford, UK.

Weaver, D.B. and Lawton, L.J. (2002) Overnight ecotourist market segmentation in the Gold Coast hinterland of Australia. *Journal of Travel Research* 40, 270–280.

Weaver, D.B. and Lawton, L.J. (2007) Twenty years on: the state of contemporary ecotourism research. *Tourism Management* 28, 1168–1179.

Weeks, B. (1996) Quality assurance and improvement in environmental training for tour operators and guides. PhD thesis, Griffith University, Gold Coast.

Weiler, B. (1993) Nature-based tour operators: are they environmentally friendly or are they faking it? *Tourism Recreation Research* 18, 55–60.

Weiler, B. and Davis, D. (1993) An exploratory investigation into the role of the nature-based tour leader. *Tourism Management* 14, 91–98.

Weiler, B. and Ham, S.H. (2001) Tour guides and interpretation. In: Weaver, D.B. (ed.) *The Encyclopedia of Ecotourism.* CAB International, Wallingford, UK, pp. 549–563.

Weiler, B. and Richins, H. (1995) Extreme, extravagant and elite: a profile of ecotourists on Earthwatch expeditions. *Tourism Recreation Research* 20, 29–36.

Welford, R. and Ytterhus, B. (1998) Conditions for the transformation of eco-tourism into sustainable tourism. *European Environment* 8, 193–201.

Wells, M.P. (1993) Neglect of biological riches: the economics of nature tourism in Nepal. *Biodiversity and Conservation* 2, 445–464.

Western, D. (1993) Defining ecotourism. Ecotourism-a-guide-for-planners-and-managers. *Report: Ecotourism Society.* North Bennington, VT.

Wheeller, B. (1994a) Ecotourism: a ruse by any other name. In: Cooper, C.P. and Lockwood, A. (eds) *Progress in Tourism Recreation and Hospitality Management.* Wiley, Chichester, UK, pp. 3–11.

Wheeller, B. (1994b) Egotourism, sustainable tourism and the environment – a symbiotic, symbolic, or shamolic relationship. In: Seaton, A.V. (ed.) *Tourism: the State of the Art.* Wiley, Chichester, UK, pp. 647–654.

Wheeller, B. (1997) Here we go, here we go, here we go eco. In: Stabler, M.J. (ed.) *Tourism and Sustainability: Principles to Practice.* CAB International, Wallingford, UK, pp. 39–50.

Wheeller, B. (2007) Sustainable mass tourism: more smudge than nudge – the canard continues. *Tourism Recreation Research* 32, 73–75.

Whelan, T. (1991) *Ecotourism and Its Role in Sustainable Development.* Island Press, Washington, DC.

Whinam, J. and Chilcott, N. (1999) Impacts of trampling on alpine environments in central Tasmania. *Journal of Environmental Management* 57, 205–220.

Whinam, J. and Chilcott, N. (2003) Impacts after four years of experimental trampling on alpine/sub-alpine environments in western Tasmania. *Journal of Environmental Management* 67, 339–351.

Whinam, J. and Comfort, M. (1996) The impact of commercial horse riding on sub-alpine environments at Cradle Mountain, Tasmania, Australia. *Journal of Environmental Management* 47, 61–70.

Whinam, J., Cannell, E.J., Kirkpatrick, J.B. and Comfort, M. (1994) Studies on the potential impact of recreational horseriding on some alpine environments of the Central Plateau, Tasmania. *Journal of Environmental Management* 40, 103–117.

Whinam, J., Chilcott, N., Ling, R. and Wyatt, P. (2003) A method to calculate environmental sensitivity to walker trampling in the Tasmanian Wilderness World Heritage Area. In: Buckley, R.C., Pickering, C. and Weaver, D. (eds) *Nature-based Tourism, Environment and Land Management.* CAB International, Wallingford, UK, pp. 151–165.

Whinam, J., Chilcott, N. and Bergstrom, D.M. (2005) Subantarctic hitchhikers: expeditioners as vectors for the introduction of alien organisms. *Biological Conservation* 2, 207–219.

Whitfield, D.P., Fielding, A.H., McLeod, D.R.A. and Haworth, P.F. (2004a) Modelling the effects of persecution on the population dynamics of golden eagles in Scotland. *Biological Conservation* 119, 319–333.

Whitfield, D.P., Fielding, A.H., McLeod, D.R.A. and Haworth, P.F. (2004b) The effects of persecution on age of breeding and territory occupation in golden eagles in Scotland. *Biological Conservation* 118, 249–259.

Wiegand, T., Revilla, E. and Moloney, K.A. (2005) Effects of habitat loss and fragmentation on population dynamics. *Conservation Biology* 19, 108–121.

Wight, P. (1996a) North American ecotourism markets: motivations, preferences, and destinations. *Journal of Travel Research* 35, 3–10.

Wight, P.A. (1996b) North American ecotourists: market profile and trip characteristics. *Journal of Travel Research* 34, 2–10.

Wight, P. (2002) Supporting the principles of sustainable development in tourism and ecotourism: government's potential role. *Current Issues in Tourism* 5, 222–244.

Wikelski, M., Foufopoulous, J., Vargas, H. and Snell, H. (2004) Galapagos birds and diseases: invasive pathogens as threats for island species. *Ecology and Society* 9, 5.

Wilderness Safaris (2008) Wilderness Safaris – Our Journeys Change People's Lives. Accessed 30 April 2008. http://www.wilderness-safaris.com/

Williams, D.R. (2001) Sustainability and public access to nature: contesting the right to roam. *Journal of Sustainable Tourism* 9, 361–371.

Williams, J., Read, C., Norton, A., Dovers, S., Burgam, M., Procter, W. and Anderson, H. (2001) Australia state of the environment report 2001. In: *Biodiversity Theme Report*, Canberra.

Williams, P.W. and Hunter, G. (2002) Assessing stakeholder perspectives on heli-skiing's socio-economic impacts in British Columbia's Rocky Mountains: applying a tourism impact scale. *Tourism Recreation Research* 27, 667–82.

Williams, R., Lusseau, D. and Hammond, P.S. (2006) Estimating relative energetic costs of human disturbance to killer whales (*Orcinus orca*). *Biological Conservation* 133, 01–311.

Wilson, K. (1997) Mozambique's Tchuma Tchato initiative of resource management on the Zambezi: a community perspective. *Society and Natural Resources* 4, 409–413.

Wilson, M.A. and Laarman, J.G. (1988) Nature tourism and enterprise development in Ecuador. *World Leisure and Recreation* 29, 22–27.

Wilson, R.F., Marsh, H. and Winter, J. (2007) Importance of canopy connectivity for home range and movements of the rainforest arboreal ringtail possum (*Hemibelideus lemuroides*). *Wildlife Research* 34, 177–184.

Wilson, S.M., Madel, M.J., Mattson, D.J., Graham, J.M., Burchfield, J.A. and Belsky, J.M. (2005) Natural landscape features, human-related attractants, and conflict hotspots: a spatial analysis of human–grizzly bear conflicts. *Ursus* 16, 117–129.

Wilton, J.J. and Nickerson, N.P. (2006) Collecting and using visitor spending data. *Journal of Travel Research* 45, 17–26.

Wolfe, K.J., Reid, D.G. and Reid, D.G. (1993) Tourism in the Eastern Arctic: coping with 'dangerous children'. *Journal of Applied Recreation Research* 18, 143–162.

Woods, B. and Moscardo, G. (1998) Understanding Australian, Japanese, and Taiwanese ecotourists in the Pacific rim region. *Pacific Tourism Review* 1, 329–339.

Woods-Ballard, A.J., Parsons, E.C.M., Hughes, A.J., Velander, K.A., Ladle, R.J. and Warburton, C.A. (2003) The sustainability of whale-watching in Scotland. *Journal of Sustainable Tourism* 11, 1–40.

World Commission on Protected Areas (2000) *Financing Protected Areas: Guidelines for Protected Area Managers*. IUCN, Gland.

World Commission on Protected Areas (2003) *Recommendations of the Vth World Parks Congress. Tourism as a Vehicle for Conservation and Support of Protected Areas*. Accessed 27 November 2003. http://iucn.org/ themes/wcpa/wpc2003/pdf/outputs/upc/ recommendations/pdf

World Ecotourism Summit (2002) Quebec. Accessed 2 April 2008. http://www.world-tourism.org/sustainable/IYE/quebec/anglais/index_a.html

World Expeditions (2008) Accessed 27 May 2008. http://www.worldexpeditions.com/au/index.php

World Hotel-Link (2008) Your Local Connection. Accessed 27 May 2008. http://www.whl.travel/

World Travel and Tourism Council (2007) Accessed 10 December 2007. http://www.wttc.org/

UN World Tourism Organization (2002) *Sustainable Development of Ecotourism: A Compilation of Good Practices*. WTO, Madrid.

UN World Tourism Organization (2007) Committed to Tourism, Travel and the Millennium Development Goals. Accessed 11 April 2008. http://www.world-tourism.org/

World Resources Institute, IUCN, UNEP. (1992) *Global Biodiversity Strategy*. World Resources Institute, Washington, DC.

Wysocki, L.E., Dittami, J.P. and Ladich, F. (2006) Ship noise and cortisol secretion in European freshwater fishes. *Biological Conservation* 128, 501–508.

Yamamoto, S., Shimomura, Y., Masuda, N. and Furukawa, S. (1998) Study on the current status and problems of green tourism in Japan. *Bulletin of the University of Osaka Prefecture Series B Agriculture and Life Sciences* 50, 39–47.

Yasue, M. (2006) Environmental factors and spatial scale influence shorebirds' responses to human disturbance. *Biological Conservation* 128, 47–54.

Yong, P. (1994) Challenges and opportunities in Sarawak's tourism industry. *Sarawak Gazette*, 121, 16–18.

Young, M. (1992) Ecotourism – profitable conservation? *Proceedings, Conference on Ecotourism Business in the Pacific*, University of Auckland, Auckland.

Young, M. (1999) Cognitive maps of nature-based tourists. *Annals of Tourism Research* 26, 817–839.

Young, M. and Wearing, S. (1993) *Ecotourism Discussion Paper*. Worldwide Fund for Nature Australia, Sydney.

Yu, D.W., Hendrickson, T. and Castillo, A. (1997) Ecotourism and conservation in Amazonian Peru: short-term and long-term challenges. *Environmental Conservation* 24, 130–138.

Yuan, M.S. and Christensen, N.A. (1994) Wildland-influenced economic impacts of nonresident travel on portal communities: the case of Missoula, Montana. *Journal of Travel Research* 32, 26–31.

Zeppel, H. (1998) Entertainers or entrepreneurs: Iban involvement in longhouse tourism (Sarawak, Borneo). *Tourism Recreation Research* 23, 39–45.

Zethoven, I.H. (1995) *Tourism and Ecologically Sustainable Development in Australia: A Discussion Paper.* Australian Conservation Foundation, Melbourne.

Ziffer, K.A. (1989) *Ecotourism: The Uneasy Alliance.* Conservation International, Arlington, VA.

Zografos, C. and Allcroft, D. (2007) The environmental values of potential ecotourists: a segmentation study. *Journal of Sustainable Tourism* 15, 44–66.

INDEX